THE RETURN OF THE SERPENTS OF WISDOM•

SPECIAL EDITION

Mark Amaru Pinkham

THE RETURN

OF THE

SERPENTS OF WISDOM

SPECIAL EDITION

BY MARK AMARU PINKHAM

ILLUSTRATIONS BY WILLIAM BROOKS, DON SWANSON & CHADWICK ST. JOHN

COVER PAINTING BY ALEX GREY

The Return of the Serpents of Wisdom - Special Edition

ISBN 978-1-64008-226-7

Published by
Fifth World Wisdom Press

Cover art by Alex Grey
© 1996

Illustrations by William Brooks,
Don Swanson & Chadwick St. John

Printed in the United States of America

TABLE OF CONTENTS

THE SERPENTS OF WISDOM AND THEIR WORLDWIDE ORGANIZATION

THE SERPENTS OF WISDOM IN ASIA

THE SERPENTS OF WISDOM IN THE AMERICAS

THE SERPENTS OF WISDOM IN ASIA MINOR AND AROUND THE MEDITERRANEAN

THE SERPENTS OF WISDOM IN NORTHERN EUROPE

PART II: ECLIPSE AND REVIVAL OF

THE WISDOM OF THE SERPENT

THE RETURN OF THE SERPENTS OF WISDOM

BECOMING A SERPENT OF WISDOM

APPENDIX I: THE TEACHINGS OF

THE SERPENTS OF WISDOM

treatise on how to attain the alchemical union of male and female.

The methods were hidden by symbolic keys to protect them from misuse. only those trained to recognize the hidden symbolism would have access to these powerful techniques. The goal was the same as in yoga though the symbolism was somewhat varied.

The common element in these systems was the use of the serpent. And I contend that this is not arbitrary, but rather the serpent is rooted in the deepest recesses of the human unconscious. which brings me back tot the client I mentioned earlier. She was a Freudian analyst referred to me by another therapist. She was concerned that recent serpent imagery proliferating through her mind was a sign of her impending psychosis or suppressed sexual desires. Whenever she closed her eyes, she saw snakes. At night while she slept, snakes and cobras writhed through her dreams as well. Finally, she was seeing snakes in broad daylight, real snakes coiled up on her doorstep or by her car, or crawling across her driveway. She was beside herself when she came to me frightened by the power of the imagery and not knowing what to do.

As we worked with the images of the serpents that had revealed themselves to her, a most fascinating thing happened. She reported that she could see and feel a serpent crawling up the inside of her spine. The serpent was moving towards her head when it stopped abruptly at her throat. She felt the physical sensation of burning and restriction. As I asked her to focus her awareness on the sensations, she realized that there were unspoken words, words that needed to be said to some important and significant people in her past. As I encouraged her to speak these words, she wept. Speaking her truth through a torrent of tears, she suddenly turned silent and still. A deep peace had come over her and the sensations in her throat turned from tension and restriction into a relaxed feeling of openness and bliss.

The rising of the serpent up her spine and into her throat literally freed her from some deeply held emotional material that had been restricting her creativity and power. The pathway was classic. It had been described by yogis thousands of years ago in ancient India.

I mention this anecdote because over the last few years I have seen a dramatic increase in numbers of people experiencing what are roughly grouped together as "transpersonal experiences." People from various walks of life, many of whom have no conscious knowledge of the serpent power, are having experiences similar to the client I just mentioned. There is a reason for this, and you will find it in the course of reading this wonderful manuscript.

From a mythological standpoint, we have entered a most remarkable time. The Return of the Serpents of Wisdom has been predicted by ancient civilizations. As the serpent of consciousness raises her head and rejoins with her beloved, we and the world will be changed.

Destiny and history are intertwined. By understanding the history of serpent mythology, its roots and lineages, we will be better prepared to deal with the return of this fundamental cosmic power. In this regard, Mark Amaru Pinkham is a wonderful and impeccable guide.

Tom Kenyon, M.A.

Introduction

For the past twenty years I have pursued a spiritual path which has taken me to distant countries around the globe, such as India, China and Peru. In these diverse countries I have studied the indigenous religious philosophies, cosmologies and sacred histories and adopted many spiritual disciplines as my own. One significant result of my planetary meanderings is that I have discovered a subtle thread linking most religious traditions together like tightly strung beads on a resplendent necklace.

The uniting thread I refer to is the ubiquitous symbol of the serpent and its affiliation to the masters and adepts of many of the world's spiritual traditions, Traditionally these diverse masters have been intimately connected with the snake, serpent or dragon and referred to by regional names denoting "serpent." They have been called Nagas ("snakes") in India, the Quetzlcoatls ("plumed serpents") in Mexico, the Djedhi ("snakes") in Egypt, the Adders ("snakes") in Britain, and the Lung ("dragons") in China, to name a few. Collectively they have been called the "Serpents of Wisdom" and associated with a worldwide network of spiritual adepts known as the Solar or Great White Brotherhood. Because of the immensely important role they have played in shaping many of the world's religious traditions, I have felt compelled to write this book about their history and teachings.

The story of the Serpents of Wisdom (and this book) begins with their appearance on Earth at the beginning of a long cycle which was destined to last 6 million years. They initially manifested upon dual "Motherlands," two large continents which once existed in the Atlantic and Pacific Oceans, where they began the dissemination of sacred teachings which would assist fledgling humankind in its quest to achieve spiritual enlightenment throughout the cycle. When their Motherlands eventually collapsed and began to sink to the bottom of their respective seas, the Serpents of Wisdom bundled up their ancient wisdom and migrated to various parts of the globe, where they were welcomed by the indigenous people as "Serpent" prophets. Under their guidance numerous "Dragon Cultures," which were comprised of colossal pyramids, multudinous serpent motifs, and ruled over by Dragon Kings, eventually came into existence. These Dragon Cultures continued to survive for many thousands of years.

Beginning approximately two thousand years ago, the Serpents of Wisdom and their Dragon Cultures encountered an inimical foe in the Christian Church. The patriarchs of the new Christian faith judged the old serpent wisdom to be heretical and began an initiative to completely stamp it out. Fortunately,

XIII

before these upstarts were successful in their iconoclastic campaign, many of the Serpents disappeared "underground" and were able to safely preserve their ancient knowledge. They later resurfaced as the Islamic Sufis and their eventual heirs, the Templars, Freemasons and Rosicrucians, who kept the flame of serpent wisdom alive while inspiring and organizing the revolutions which have slowly precipitated a democratic world.

The long story of the Serpents of Wisdom is about to come full circle as a New Age of Wisdom commences. This coming Golden Age, which is scheduled to begin at the start of the next millennium (coinciding with the completion of the 6 million year cycle), will herald a global "Return of the Serpents of Wisdom." Once again the planet will be inhabited by dynamic spiritual stalwarts aligned with the Will of Spirit and embodying the Wisdom and Power of the Serpent. The story of the Serpents will then have been officially completed and perhaps a new one will begin in its place.

I believe the re-telling of the history and teachings of the Serpents of Wisdom is very important for the era we live in. At a time when there is a movement to reconcile the world's religions, this book reveals their ancient, definitive links. It also gives a spiritual perspective to history when many of us feel lost in a technologically, mundane world. Finally, this book is especially relevant now because many people currently residing on Earth are the prophesied "returning Serpents" who will soon take a giant evolutionary leap and transform into spiritual adepts. They are the future leaders of our planet.

During the course of my travels I have aligned myself with the Worldwide Organization of the Serpents of Wisdom by gaining initiation into the Order of the Nagas of India, as well as the Order of the Amarus, the Inkan Serpents, and the Djedhi Serpents of Egypt. My current role within this ancient global organization is that of a synthesizer, historian and scribe. To perform this service I have tried to restrict my work to gathering accountable historical records, although I have also had to access the unwritten Akashic Records when irreconcilable gaps in authoritative information became manifold. You will find much synthesizing of diverse information throughout the book, but especially in the earlier chapters and in Appendix 1 where I have amalgamated the history and secret wisdom of many branches of the Serpents.

My hope is that the history and teachings of the Serpents of Wisdom as I have presented them in the following pages will reawaken memories in some, while providing a key to understanding the spiritual purpose of our Earth drama for others. Please read on with an open mind and heart.

Mark Amaru Pinkham

their identifyng symbol the "androgynous" golden asp. The Chinese Serpents of Wisdom, the Lung Dragons, chose as their definitive symbol the andr o genous azure or golden dragon. The Mesoamerica n Serpents of Wisdom, the Quetzlcoatls, adopted as the ir exclusive emblem the andr o gynous plumed or feathered serpent. The Serpents of Wisdom in India, the Nagas, adopted the royal hooded cobra as their distinctive motif (royalty is also symbolic of Spirit; the king is the hand of God on Earth).

THE FIRST SERPENT OF WISDOM

The primeval beginnings of the Serpents of Wisdom can be traced to the very dawn of time when all that existed was an unlimited ocean of consciousness. This infinite "ocean" of awareness was the androgynous, unmanifest Spirit or God, which☐ has also been referred to as Shiva or Brahman among the Hindus, the Tao among the Chinese, Ra among the Egyptians, and Yod He Vau He among the Hebrews. From out of this spiritual sea emerged the first form of Spirit, a resplendent dragon (see Appendix 1, 1.1), which was the first Serpent of Wisdom. Among the various branches of the Serpents of Wisdom around the globe this Primal Serpent has been called the Serpent Goddess, the Serpent on the Tree, the Plumed Serpent, the Azure Dragon, Shesha, Ammon Kematef, Kneph, Agathodeamon, Ea or Enki, Kon or Kan, and the Serpent Son.

As the first tangible form assumed by Spirit, the Primal Serpent was the vehicle of all God's powers, including the triune powers of creation, preservation and destruction. Through it, God created the entire universe (see Appendix 1, 1.4). The Primal Serpent was also the possessor of God's Divine Mind, the wellspring of all knowledge and all wisdom. For this reason, the Serpents of Wisdom worldwide have traditionally venerated the Primal Serpent as the premier and archetypal teacher. After attaining union with Spirit, they profess to become the mouthpieces for this archetypal teacher and the vehicles for its triune powers.

THE ANGELIC ORDERS OF SERPENTS

Following the Primal Serpent as Serpents of Wisdom were the various celestial Orders of Angels. At the head of this angelic hierarchy was the Sacred Seven, the seven Archangels or seven Sons of the Solar Spirit. These seven Archangels are the seven aspects of the Primal Serpent (see Appendix 1, 1.7-9). At the beginning of time they assisted in the creation of the cosmos and today they rule over the Serpent's seven principles as they manifest within the physical universe (i.e., the seven colors, seven sounds etc.). In the Australian tradition

3

these seven archangels are referred to as the seven colors of the Rainbow Serpent; in the Greek Gnostic tradition they are the seven Sons of the Serpent Goddess Sofia; in the Judea/Christian tradition they have been called the seven Archangels of YHVH and the Elohim.

Next in line after the archangels are an order of angelic luminaries known as the Seraphim. The Seraphim are flaming serpents, illuminated progeny of the Primal Fire Serpent. Since their creation, their function has been to rule over the dissemination and awakening of divine wisdom within evolving souls. Working in tandem with them are their cousins, the Cherubim. Cherubs (From Karabu or Kerubu, a name which means both Primal Serpent and "protecting

The Cherubim Dragons on the Ark of the Covenant

angel") sometimes manifest in the form of Zodiacal Dragons (Sphinxes) or as the two halves of the Primal Serpent, the Twins who protect and preserve the kingdom of their father/mother (see Appendix 1, 11.15-26). J.J. Hurtak, author of *The Keys of Enoch,* maintains that Cherubs are the guardians of the "passages of light which connect the physical worlds with the governments of the Mid-Heavens."[1] Through the protective assistance of the Cherubs embodied souls can safely pass into the terrestrial temples of wisdom and disembodied spirits can smoothly ascend into the upper heavenly realms of the universe.

Under the Seraphim and Cherubim in the celestial hierarchy are a multitude of angelic orders, seventy in number in seven dimensions (multiples of 7, number of the Primal Serpent). All these orders oversee different aspects of the creation while dwelling within the universal body of the Primal Serpent (its body eventually expands to become the entire universe see Appendix 1, Part 1).

THE EXTRATERRESTRIAL SERPENTS

Below the Angelic Serpents are the Orders of Extraterrestrial Serpents of Wisdom. These orders are composed of Serpents of Wisdom who inhabit planets, star systems and galaxies other than our own. As Intergalactic, Interstellar and Interplanetary Serpents they move freely between various planets and star groups via their immortal Dragon Bodies and/or sophisticated spacecraft. Sometimes they travel to new or evolving galaxies and solar systems in order to assist certain fledgling life forms through evolutionary stages of growth and development. Many who travel in spacecraft wear the emblem of the winged serpent upon their lapels as they hurdle through the cosmos to burgeoning locations in the universe. In this regard, there is at least one documented UFO encounter of the "third kind" in which the experiencer claimed to have seen the winged serpent emblem upon the uniforms of his alien contactors. [2]

For millions of years Extraterrestrial Serpents of Wisdom have been coming to our Solar System to assist in its evolution. During their periodic visitations they have established intergalactic and interstellar bases and built pyramidal structures on many planets, including Mars, Venus and the Earth (Within the last thirty years NASA has discovered pyramidal complexes similar to those of Giza, Egypt on Mars). With the help of these structures they have been□ able to monitor the phase of evolutionary development on a planet. When a planet and its inhabitants reach a pivotal transition period in evolution, the Extraterrestrial Serpents often travel there to help facilitate a paradigm shift.

CHAPTER 2
THE EARTH DRAGON & THE TWIN DRAGON LANDS

According to the legends of the Serpents of Wisdom, our part of the galaxy was created by the Serpent Goddess after she assumed the septenary form of the Celestial Serpent, the Pleiades. After the creation of Earth she sent her Serpent Son to give life and color to our planet, as well as to oversee the spiritual evolution of humanity. Upon his arrival, this Cosmic Serpent completely engulfed our planet in his dragon form while transmiting his own Spirit and consciousness inside the Earth. When his etheric dragon form crystallized it became all the colorful forms of nature, and his mind and will worked together as the Planetary Logos - the Planetary Mind and Will. From that moment onwards the will of the Son reigned supreme on Earth, and he would eventually become known by the earliest people as as the primal Dragon King of the World.

The mystical Serpents of Wisdom of Taoism continue to subscribe to this truth. For millennia they have maintained that the Earth is indeed the body of a dragon. It's rivers are the dragon's blood vessels, the mountains its back, and the clouds its breath. Similarly, the Yezidis of northern Iraq maintain that the Serpent Son anciently arrived in the form of a huge Peacock Angel of seven colors (the peacock and dragon are inter-related) and, after wrapping his etheric plumes around our planet became King of the World. His plumes still provide the backdrop and etheric support of all the Earth's vegetation.

Cycles of time begin when the Primal Serpent divides into its male/female polarity and end when they reunite. The division of the Earth Dragon into its male and female component parts, or "Twin Dragon Lands," began a six million year cycle of time. At that time our planet was suddenly covered over with grass and a tremendous increase in lush, colorful vegetation. This was the era of the first "Garden of Eden" (there have been many Edens, each of which has corresponded to the beginning of a different cycle of time.

The Twin Dragon Lands of the present cycle are known historically as Atlantis and Mu or Lemuria, the fabled Motherlands that manifested on opposite sides of the Earth The Pacific Continent of Lemuria was the first to manifest which is why of the two Motherlands it is more commonly known esoterically as Earth's Garden of Eden and the Cradle of Civilization. The full development of Atlantis came later and corresponded to the beginning of a 104,000 year cycle that we are ending now.

As the embodiment of the female polarity of the androgynous Earth Dragon, the Motherland of Lemuria brought forth a feminine, spiritual and artistic civilization characterized by certain divine qualities, such as love and acceptance, as well as living in harmony with the Earth. By contrast, the Motherland of Atlantis nurtured a male, aggressive and intellectual civilization dedicated to controlling and governing the world.

6

LEMURIA/MU/KUMARI NADU,

THE DRAGON LAND OF THE PACIFIC

Lemuria, the fabled Dragon Land of the Pacific, is recognized within the ancient records of many pan-Pacific cultures and alluded to them by a host of names. In recognition of its matriarchal status, for example, this legendary continent is referred to in Polynesian history as Hiva, a name synonymous with the Biblical Eve, the "mother of all living." Alternately, in reference to its dragon nature, Lemuria is also known as Mu (pronounced Moo), a name which closely approximates and appears to be related to the Polynesian name for dragon, "Mo,o." The Hindu records of India allude to the lost continent by the "dual" epithet of Kumari Nadu, a feminine name which suggests both "Motherland" and "Dragon Land of the Immortal Serpents."

The continent of Lemuria was first "discovered" by archaeologists who recognized a similarity between the animals and fauna on the chains of islands stretching between Africa and India which could have only been possible if the islands had once been joined together as a continuous peninsula or continent. The animal found most consistently on these islands was a monkey-like mammal called a lemur, so archaeologists pragmatically named this hypothetical continent "Lemuria."

Other studies conducted by anthropologists and mythologists around the same time suggested that the Indo-Madagascar continent did not stop at India, but had once continued across the Pacific. In view of their research, an ancient Africa-to-South America land mass was proposed & this larger continent usurped for itself the name of "Lemuria." Finally, when it was concluded that the western, Indo-Madagascar section of Lemuria had sunken to the bottom of the Indian Ocean well before its adjoining eastern part, it was this Pacific section that would commonly become known as Lemuria.

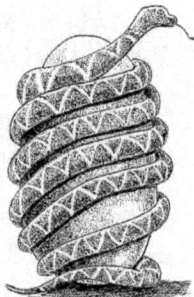

7

ANCIENT LEGENDS OF LEMURIA

Most of the research conducted by the Lemurian mythologists centered on the Polynesian tribes and other pan-Pacific peoples who possessed numerous legends of a sunken motherland. In almost every case the name accorded to this continent is female in gender, thus reflecting its female nature. According to the natives of Easter Island, for example, their island was once part of a much larger Pacific Continent known by the feminine name of Hiva, the gre ater portion of which sank to the bottom of the Pacific Ocean during a planetary cataclysm. The Polynesians of Hawaii echo this legend and assert tha t their island home was also once part of a great Pacific Motherland, which they maintain was known as "Havaii-ti-Hava ii," meaning "the land where life sprang into existence and developed growth." It is also referenced by them in their records as "Havai'i, " meaning "the steaming terra in over which moisture rained" (a reference to"Earth's fiery beginnings"),as well as "Rua," meaning "growth and development from fire." Rua is also the name of the Hawaiians' ancient mother goddess. The Land of Rua is said to be the "Garden of Eden," the first habitat of the human race.

In nearby India legends of an ancient sunken land were discovered among the Aryans and Tamils which seem consistent with those of the Polynesians. The French traveler and mythologist of the late 1800's, Louis Jacolliot, discovered nume rous references to a sunken continent called Rutas. In his book *Histoire des Vierges: Les Peuple et les Continents,* Jacolliot discusses this fabled land mass and concludes that Rutas was unquestionably the lost Lemuria and the original home of many of the first inhabitants of India. As possible corro boration for Jacolliot's thesis, certain Polynesian records assert that when Lemuria or Rua sank into the Pacific its inhabitants migrated with their records to India but later returned to the remaining Pacific islands as the Polynesians. So in India the name Rua may have evolved into Rutas. A definitive Hindu influence can be found today in the language of the Polynesians which is sprinkled with Sanskrit words

Another Indian scripture with apparent references to Lemuria is the Tamil text *Silappadikaram*. This scripture refers to a lost continent with the feminine name of Kumari Nadu or Kumara Kandam, which can be translated as "Land of Goddess Kumari," as we ll as "Land of the Kumara Immortals." Still ano ther Hindu refer ence to a lost continent in the Pacifc was discovered by James Churchward, a colonel of the British Army, during a visit to a Hindu temple/ monastery that is currently believed to be Shree Ekambaranatha Temple in Kanchipuram, India. Supposedly a monk in charge of the temple led the inquisitive Churc hward to a secret vault and showed him some anc ient tablets that were reputed to describe the destruction of an ancient motherland. After studying the tablets at length, Churchward concluded tha t the continent had once been in the Pacific and was known as MU.

Chinese legends which allude to the existence of Lemuria include that of an island-continent called Maurigosima. This fabled land mass supposedly sank to the bottom of the Pacific, but not before its king, Peiru-un, managed to escape to mainland China and help populate the country. An additional Chinese testimonial to Mu was discovered within the famous Buddhist cave of Dunhuang in Western China by a Taoist monk in 1900. This sacred cave had, for possibly thousands of years, been a gathering place for itinerant spiritual pilgrims traveling between China and the rest of Asia. When the dark, forbidding interior of the cave was explored, the monk found ancient Buddhist manuscripts in Tibetan and Sanskrit. One of the more conspicuous of these texts contained fragments of a map which revealed a very large continent in the Pacific, presumably a representation of Lemuria or a later vestige of the Pacific land mass.6

Another name and reference to Lemuria can be found in the western archeological community under the epithet of Sundaland, a sunken continent that includes the Sunda Shelf off the coast of Malaysia. In his book *Eden In The East*, Stephen Oppenheimer reveals the recently accepted belief that Sundaland was above the Pacific Ocean waves until it was consumed by the rising waters generated by the warming Earth ending the last Ice Age. Years of research reveal that Sundaland nutured a unique civilization that was taken west by missionaries and became the foundation of many Far Eastern cultures.

On the other side of the Pacific the existence of Mu can be ascertained within the oral tradition of the Andean and Inkan wisemen who claim that one their first ancestors, Aramu Muru, anciently arrived in the Andes from the lost continent with the spiritual teachings of Lemuria's Seven Ray Brotherhood. Their northern neighbors, the Hopis, also refer to Mu in their legends, but not as a solid landmass. They remember the continent as thousands of islands that once stretched across the Pacific Ocean, which were the remaining vestiges of Lemuria after a massive cataclysm. After "Island Hopping" across these island stepping stones the Hopis safely reached the west coast of the Americas. Glancing back, the Hopis witnessed a sudden Earth shift initiating the Fourth World that sunk many of their island steps to the bottom of the Pacific Ocean.

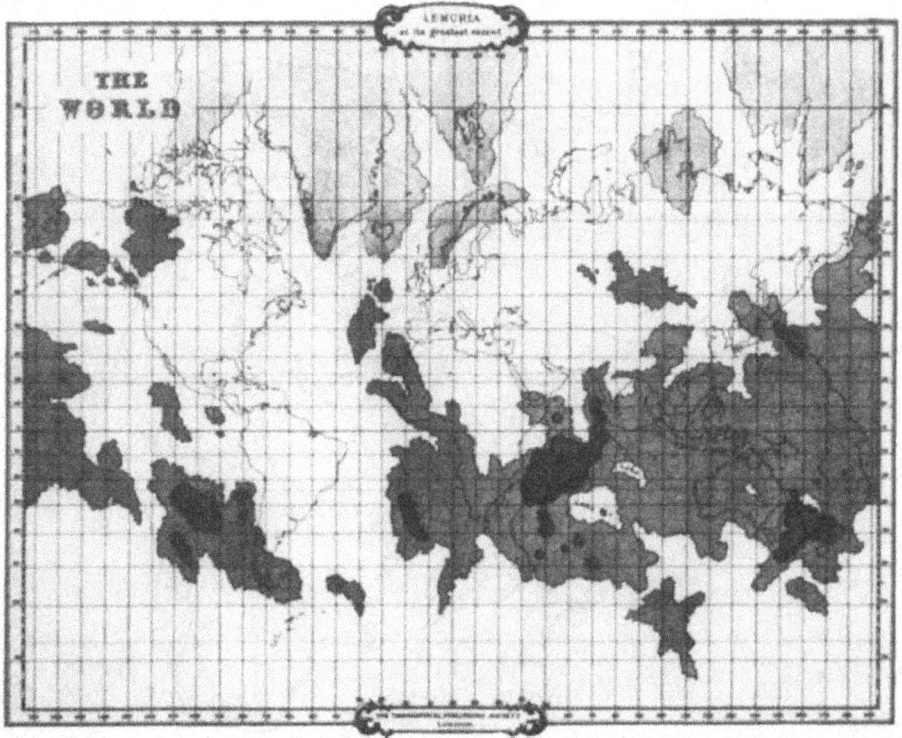

Lemuria at its greatest extent. From W. Scott-Elliot, Theosophist

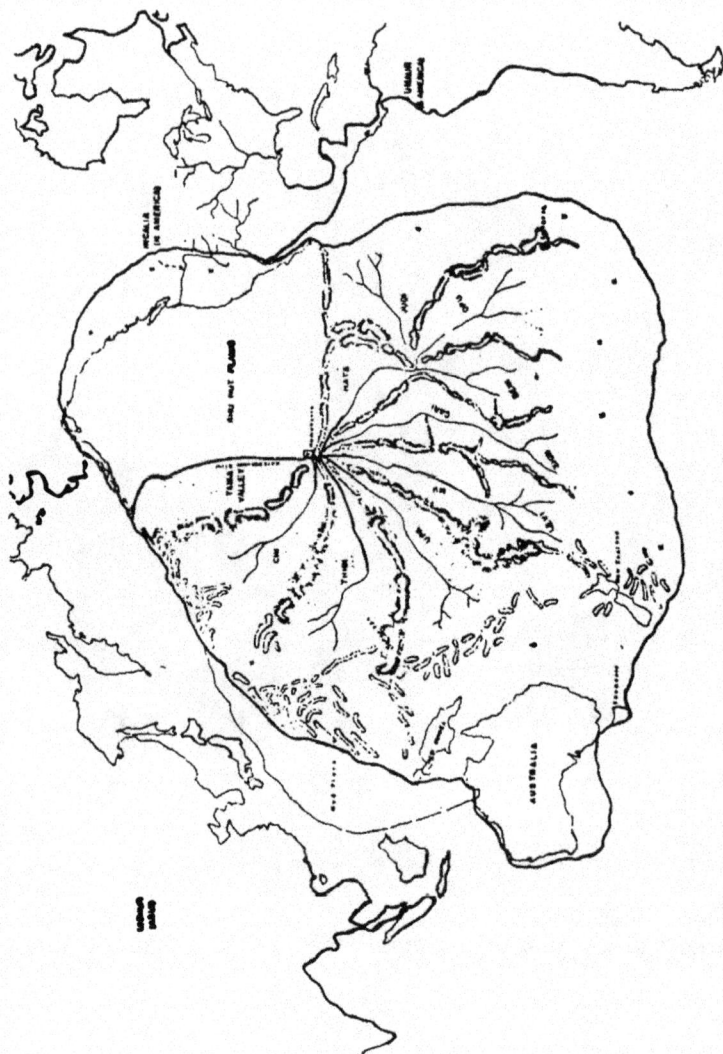

The Pacific Lemuria. From The Lemurian Fellowship

THE CIVILIZATION OF LEMURIA

THE EXTRATERRESTRIAL SERPENTS OF LEMURIA

Following the arrival of the Earth Dragon, Extraterrestrial Serpents of Wisdom began arriving on Lemuria from many corners of the cosmos to assist in the creation of what was destined to be a divine paradise. To produce this earthly paradise the alien emissaries used creative serpent powers to crystallize the shapes of the Lemurian landscape in accordance with the Divine Mind's predetermined plan. All solidified form inherited the spiraling imprint of the Primal Serpent along with one or more of the beast's seven principles (see Appendix 1, 1.19-22). Following the completion of this momentous work, some creator gods and goddesses elected to remain on Earth as protecting nature spirits and devas for the duration of the cycle.

When the work of the creator Serpents was completed some Extraterrestrial Serpents elected to serve fledgling humankind as teachers and/or priest kings. While acting as teachers of the practical and spiritual arts to their adopted people, these Serpents were a manifestation of the "Serpent on the Tree" in the Pacific "Garden of Eden." Collectively they are mentioned in creation myths worldwide as the two , four or seven immortal Twin Sons of the Serpent Goddess or Solar Spirit who arrived on as creators and culture bearers during the Creative Cycle of the Earth. Most of these early extraterrestrial culture bearers were andr ogynous. They identified with their inne r, androgynous spirits rather than their external male/female gender specific forms. Some. according to Plato, as well as the Babylonian Berossus and Edgar Cayce, reflected their inner and rogyny by being outwardly bisexual and possessing both male and female generative organs.9 According to author Alan MacGilvray in *Sipapuni,* certain Native American tribes currently remember these ET androgynies as the "Blue Stone He/She People." Since the arriving Serpents also wielded formidable Serpent Powers, states Plato, the "gods" felt threatened enough to divide them and their progeny into male and female forms and thereby weaken them. When that pivotal separation occurred, the souls of the androgynies were split into two halves and thus began a search through many lifetimes as each "half soul" sought to find and reunite with his or her "soul mate."

KUMARAS, ANDROGYNOUS SONS OF MU

An important delegation of androgynous Interplanetary Serpents on Mu were the Kumaras. These Extraterrestrial Serpents arrived from the Pleiades via Earth's neighboring planet, Venus. It is said that they came as a "brotherhood" of "Twin Boys" (they were actually androgynous immortal Sons of God tasked with the mission of assisting in the spiritual awake ning of their cousins on Earth. The Hindu Puranas or "Legends" remember the Kumaras as renunciate Avatars or Saviors who, as four eternally young, twin brothers served as the first teachers of the "Siddha Marg," the "Path of the Perfected Ones" that leads to the union of the inner polarity, activation of the alchemical Kundalini Serpent, and spiritual immortality. Their name, Kumara, reflects both their path to union as well as their inherent androgynous nature . The syllable Ma represents the female principle or matter; the syllable Ra is the identifying sound of the male principle or Spirit; and Ku is the sound of their union as the androgynous Serpent of Wisdom. The syllable Ku combines the letter K, an archetypal symbol and sound denoting both Serpent and wisdom, with Hu, the sound syllable of the Creator's breath or Serpent life force. It is the first syllable of Kundalini.

The Kumaras were led to Earth by the Pleiadian Adept Sanat Kumara, whose ET name is Karttikeya, meaning "Son of the Pleiades. Many souls who had incarnated on Earth had arrived in our galaxy through the portal of the Pleiades, which is a doorway to a higher dimensional universe known by the early Gnostics as the Pleroma, meaning the "Fullness of God." According to the seminal legend, the Gnostic Goddess Sophia inadvertently became lost in the Pleroma. When she as not able to find her way back her home in the higher universe she decided to create a denser universe that was a perfect reflection of the Pleroma. Our 3-D thus came into existence. the portal between dimensions was Sophia's seat in the new universe. This was the Pleiades, which the Gnostics referred to as the "Seven Pillars of Sophia." When humans were subsequently created on Earth Sophia sent her beloved son, Karttikeya, to Earth to enlighten them of their divine heritage. They deserved to know that God/Spirit dwelled within them as them.

Karttikeya's ET form that he had inherited fro m his mother Sophia was a six-headed body, with each head associated with one of the visible six stars of the Pleiades, but upon arriving on Earth he first assumed the form of the "Serpent on the Tree" in the Garden of Eden to teach early humanity - represented by Adam and Eve - the truth of their divinity. But the Eden allegory has levels of meaning. According to the Yogis, on one level the Serpent on the Tree symbolizes the serpent in the human body, the Kundalini Serpent, that dwells at the base of the inner "tree," the human spine. When a human is ready to know his or her divinity the Kundalini Serpent awakens and climbs the inner "tree" while awakening the chakras along its course, thereby revealing to such a person his or her divinity.

13

According to another creation legend, that of the Sumerians and Yezidis of Iraq, Sanat Kumara, whom they have known as Enki and the Peacock Angel, assisted in the creation of the human body. His contribution to the human form was a manifestation of himself as the Serpent Kundalini at the base of the spine, where it waits for its owner to know him or herself as the Infinite Spirit.

Sanat Kumara is another name of the ET that became the Earth Dragon & King of the World. He who is known in many ancient traditions and ascribed the forms of a snake, dragon, peacock and boy transmitted his consciousness into our planet and became the Spirit of our planet so he could direct the affairs of Earth while also overseeing the spiritual education and evolution of humanity. He thus became the Planetary Logos, humanity's first Savior, and the "King of the World" - inter-related roles he continues to assume today. On MU he would subsequently be recognized both as the first priest-king to sit upon the Dragon Throne of the ancient Dragon Land, as well as the founder of the Order of the Seven Rays. Named in reference to his birthplace, the Seven Sisters, as well as to himself and his mother Sophia, the Lord and Lady of the Seven Rays, the Order of the Seven Rays became the primary vehicle that Sanat Kumara and the Kumaras would use to inculcate humans with the Gnostic-Alchemical Path that leads to Kundalini arousal and enlightenment. Over thousands of years this order thrived while its teachers founded branches of it around the globe. Eventually it became known by its popular contemporary name, the Great White Brotherhood.

Sanat Kumara in his form of six-headed Karttikeya, "Son of the Pleiades."

14

Sanat Kumara on his Peacock-Dragon Throne
The Peacock, Dragon and Phoenix are interrelated forms.

Sanat Kumara in his form of Tawsi Melek, the "Peacock King," of the Yezidis

THE SPIRITUAL CULTURE ON LEMURIA

The culture which blossomed upon Lemuria became one of the most spiritually advanced cultures the world has ever seen. Its spiritual emphasis is reflected in one of the continent's names, Kumari Nadu, which can be translated Land of the Kumaras" or "Land of the Immortal Serpents."

In reference to the spiritual culture on Mu, *The Lemurian Fellowship,* an organization which is one of the authorities on Lemurian civilization, states: "The whole purpose of civilization on Mukulia (apparently a synthesis of Mu, Kumari, and Lemuria) was to create Masters or Saviors."12 In order to produce these Masters, the school of the Kumaras was divided into thirteen schools, each with progressively more advanced esoteric curriculums than its predecessor. Those who graduated through the ranks and became one of the immortals comprising the Thirteenth School (the number of the arisen phoenix dragon) received ordination as a Kumara and authorization to teach within the Order of Serpents. Then, as fully enlightened spiritual masters, these Lemurians completed their earthly incarnations as teachers, spiritual masters, and priest kings or priestess queens) upon their beloved Mu.

THE EMPIRE OF THE SUN

According to the records retrieved by James Churchward in India, the spiritual natives of Lemuria were Sun worshipers and one of the Pacific continent's epithets was "The Empire of the Sun."5 The definitive emblem of Mu was a version of the solar disc. Churchward's information is consistent with that received by Antón Ponce de León Paiva, a Peruvian man who studied directly with the Andean Elders, the modern spiritual descendants of Aramu Muru. Antón, the author of *The Wisdom of the Ancient ONE* and *In Search of the Wise ONE,* claims that a golden sun disc accompanied Aramu Muru to the Andes. The solar disc represented not the physical Sun but its essence, the transcendental Spirit, and was probably hung in one of the important Lemurian temples of the Sun worshipers before being transported to Peru. According to Antón, the upper echelon of these solar worshipers were members of the Intic Churincuna or Solar Brotherhood and Aramu Muru was a high ranking member of this elite organization (It was actually a "peoplehood" with both male and female members). When Aramu Muru landed in the Andes he wore the symbol of this brotherhood, the "mascaypacha," a miniature version of the solar disc, over his third eye. Many other adepts of the Solar Brotherhood had similarly worn the mascaypacha on Mu, some of whom, the Kapac Cuna (with Ka sound of the Serpents of Wisdom), the "bearers of the mascaypacha,"7 arrived at the same time or soon after Aramu Muru and then joined the ranks of his entourage. Once settled in Peru, Aramu Muru continued to wear the mascaypacha while serving as the first priest king of the Inkas, Manko Kapac.

The Solar Brotherhood was another name for the Kumara Brotherhood and its prized possession, the golden sun disc, apparently united the definitive symbols of both organizations. According to *Secret of the Andes* by Brother Philip, the pen name used by George Hunt Williamson, AramuMuru's solar disc was reputed to have inscribed within its center an ank, the timeless symbol of both Venus and the immortal Kumaras. While further elaborating upon the characteristics of the sun disc, Williamson states that it was a powerful tool used for healing as well as interdimensional communication and travel throughout the empire of Mu. It supposedly had the power to teleport the user to any location in the universe and was reputed to cause earthquakes and even change the rotation of the Earth when struck appropriately by a trained priest.

LEMURIAN HOMES AND GARDENS

The Lemurians were such spiritually evolved beings that many of them existed in high frequency physical forms or Dragon Bodies of pure life force. They were, therefore, acutely attuned to the subtle vibrations surrounding them. For this reason it was imperative for them to construct buildings and landscapes which generated vibratory fields which were soothing and spiritually uplifting to their own. Their public parks, for example, were paradisiacal gardens full of exotic plants, waterfalls and minerals, such as amethyst, lapis lazuli, rose and clear quartz. While taking meditative strolls through these peaceful gardens, the auric fields of the Lemurians would interface and sympathetically resonate with their exotic surroundings, thereby allowing them to achieve high states of spiritual consciousness and ecstatic communion with Spirit. In such refined states of awareness they were also able to easily communicate with and receive guidance from the Lemurian devas and nature spirits who protected the gardens while existing in dimensional realms higher than their own.[13]

In order to make their private and public enclosures spiritually uplifting, the Lemurians constructed them in the energy conductive shapes of pyramids, domes and spheres. Then, to further harmonize with the Earth and the serpentine energy patterns of the life force, the golden proportion and measurements based upon the radius of the Earth were incorporated into the dimensions of these structures.

SEDONA, ARIZONA, ANCIENT PORT CITY
OF THE LEMURIANS

Because of their auric sensiti vities, many Lemurians were fully aware of the Earth's etheric energy grid. They knew that the planet's dragon lairs had the property of amplifying and purifying whatever was placed within their parameters; so they consistently constructed their parks and temples directly over these power spots. Some of the more powerful vortexes thus ch osen became the sites of entire Lemurian holy cities. One holy "mecca," for example, was built over a huge dragon's lair in the area of what is now Sedona, Arizona.

Upon the vortex of Seona, which eventually became a colony of the Lemurians built numerous energy conductive temples and pyramids. Within these sacred structures they could readily manipulate their own and each others auric fields in ways which promoted spiritual growth and evolutionary development. Many of these temples were not "temples" in the ordinary sense of the word, but solid iron and quartz crystal- imbued sandstone structures that acted as EEM, Earth Energy Modulators, that finely tuned Earth's vortexual energies to specific frequencies as it moved through them. Some EEM temples stretched across much of what today is known as Boynton Canyon and marked the center of the massive Sedona vortex. These temples comprised one of the principal planetary thrones and courts of Sanat Kumara. Here in Sedona, the Planetary Root Chakra, the King of the World existed as the pure Serpent Kundalini power.

A VISIT TO SEDONA'S "CANYON OF THE TEMPLES"

In February 1987 I personally "saw" Sedona as it must have appeared during its Lemurian occupation. This psychic vision occurred after arriving in Sedona during a belief crisis (and the biggest snow storm in twenty yearsl), and being directed by one of the local shopkeepers to Boynton Canyon, perhaps the most powerful of the four major vortexes in the area.

Following the shopkeeper's instructions, I left my hotel early the next morning, traveled to the entrance of Boynton Canyon and then trudged through its foot high new snow for at least two miles. The n, over come by a sudden wave of inspired guidance, I felt compelled to examine one of the canyon walls. Scanning the upper portion of the w a ll, I spotted a ledge jutting out from it that I intuitively knew I needed to climb up to. Even though I could see the ascent was going to be a difficult one and I would be forced to trail-blaze most of the way, something told me it was imperative I reach that ledge. After reaching my destination I brushed off the ledge's covering of new fal len snow and sat down to enjoy the picturesque canyon which sprawled out below me. I quickly decided I knew why I had been guided there. The spot was special.

It provided an ideal vantage point for surveying most of the canyon. Feeling spiritually inspired, I proceeded to surround myself with photographs and illustrations of some well known spiritual teachers whose guidanc e had assisted me during times of confusion in the past. Then, after making eye contact with each master, I closed my eyes and began to repeat a penitent prayer of "God give me something to believe in again." Within thre e minutes a still voice within me loudly commanded "Look in front of you." I slowly opened my eyes and my gaze instantly fell upon two ornate columns carved into the canyon wall directly in front of me. Stunned at the colossal dimensions of the columns but questioning my own ability to discern reality from fantasy, I quickly scanned the vista below me and, to my amazement, found the entire canyon decidedly different than how it had been just moments before. Instead of viewing a landscape comprised solely of bare red rock, snow covered bushes and peeled madrone trees, almost everywhere I looked I could make out the shapes of perfectly formed temples, most of which were rock hewn and apparently constructed out of stone similar to the red rock of the canyon. Some were so completely in harmony with the ir surroundings that I had to look very closely to make out their definiti ve shapes. In the center of all these temples I noticed a radiant silver pyra mid, perhaps made of metal, with golden discs attached to all four sides. If there was a door into the pyramid I could not spot it. In hopes of getting a closer look at the temples, I took out the binoculars I had had the apparent good foresight to bring with me that day and noticed that many of them were embellished with orna te carvings similar to tho se I had seen covering the sacred temples of India. Interspersed among these temples I could distinguish numerous statues of men and women who appeared to be dancing. Some of the female dancers held baskets on the ir heads, possibly containing some kind of fruit. With my binoculars I could also ascertain what appeared to be the image of one human head straddling another which was attached to one of the canyon's walls. Again the voice spoke resolutely within and advised me that this was the symbol of an anc ient colony of Mu. At that point the entire experience became crystal clear to me. My prayer had apparently opened my psychic vision and I as seeing fourth dimensional structures which had been placed there by the colonists of Mu sometime in the very distant past.

Only days later after leaving Boynton Canyon did I become aware of the esoteric legends of Sedona and its Mu or Lemurian affiliations. One interesting legend suggested that a Lemurian crystal city was built under Boynton Canyon and this subterrane an complex now contributes to the canyon's tremendous vortexual power. Another legend maintained that records of Mu were anciently inscribed upon "Telonium Tablets"14 and secreted away in the vicinity of Sedona.

Still another myth asserted that the "Arc of Mu,"[14] a structure built to commemorate the visitation of a delegation of Venusians, possibly the Kumaras, lies buried near Sedona under tons of wind-blown, desert sand. Apparently some of these esoteric mysteries were passed down within the indigenous tribes of the Sedona area, the Hopis and Yavapai, whose members all recognize the immense sanctity of both Sedona and Boynton Canyon.

A KUMARA REMEMBRANCE

Soon after my visit to Sedona's Canyon of Temples I had an experience which revealed my ancient connection to Lemuria and perhaps why I had been drawn to a former colony of Mu. This event occurred one day as I was hiking through the thick forests near my home in Washington State.

For many days leading up to my hike I had been feeling a growing urgency to known who I was at a soul level and what my true purpose on Earth was. I had been experiencing a period of underlying dissatisfaction with life and wondered what my true calling and "next step" was going to be. Almost as soon as I set off on my fateful hike these feelings seemed to burst within me.

While walking along an idyllic river flanked on both sides by dark green ferns and wild flowers, my peaceful mood unexpectedly turned into one of desperation and I soon found myself crying out to my guides and teachers to reveal to me that which my soul burned to know. "Awaken me, open me up-NOW!" was my adamant prayer. When assistance finally arrived, it spoke to me in that firm, familiar voice I recognized from the canyon at Sedona. This time the voice instructed me to hike to the top of a nearby hill and there I would find my answer.

After excitedly scurrying up to the hill's summit, I was greeted by a circle of tall fir trees surrounding a thick bed of ferns which together adorned the small hill like a huge crown. Again the voice spoke and advised me to lie down within the ferns. I quickly obeyed and as I nestled into my soft earthen bed a supernatural process began to occur around and within me. I felt the crown of my head suddenly opened up, almost as if someone had removed a part of my skull, and a river of white light began to pour into it while simultaneously engulfing my entire body. I could perceptively feel the scintillating radiations of this cool life force as it moved throughout all the cells of my brain and see its shimmering glow as it covered my body like a long, white gown. It felt both incredibly soothing and empowering.

As it satiated me, the nurturing effulgence initiated a profound inner awakening. A part of myself which had been slumbering for countless ages spontaneously awoke and slowly emerged into my consciousness. As it arose,

19

it smoothly meshed with and empowered my norma l "self." My personality was simultaneously transformed and I realized that I was now in the possession of a thick English accent.

Then the memories started to come. They were apparently the recollections of this old part of myself which, by now, had now taken full control of my consciousness. I or it, I could not distinguish between us anymore, suddenly remembered having been on Earth many tho usands of years previously. Memories of residing as a priest king on a Pacific island paradise which was once part of ancient Lemuria filled my head. Apparently at that time the pan-Pacific continent had broken up into many smaller island s and these linke d together to form a gigantic chain across the great ocean. ln my small sector of Mu, which was close to what is now the coast of China, I had administered to my subjects as an enlightened monarch and, appare ntly, as an illumine d Kumara. I had been a vassal of the great Pleiadean-Venusian Master Sanat Kumara who was, at the time, the grand emperor over all the islands of Mu. While attending to my royal duties I remembered traveling extensively throughout Mu and had even visited the area of Washington I was now living in.

When my revelatory trance subsided a bit, my mind turned to the present state of my physical body. Although I could not see it as clearl y anymore, the white light still coursed through me and the feeling of being electrically charged by it remained tangible. As I sat up upon my bed of ferns I recognized that this "new" cosmic empowerment was very familiar. It had been my natural state as an "androgynous" L emurian priest king of the Kumara lineage. While on Mu his power had enabled me to telepathically communicate with Sanat Kumara and the other Masters of Earth's hierarchy, as well as with beings on other planets and dimensions. lt had also allowed me the freedom to travel to any destination in an instant, eithe r by air shuttle or teleportation.

When the transmutation into my former Lemurian self was fully complete, I aro se to my feet, victorious. Picking up a stick as my royal staff, I joyfully descended the small hill and set off into the dense forest while continually proclaiming in my English accent "I'm back, I'm back." It was truly an exhilarating feeling to realize that I had returned to a place which I had once inhabited thousand s of years before. I felt so full of life after having been asleep for so long.

As I bound ed along und er the rows of towering evergreen trees another part of my prayer began to be answered. I was told that I had returned to Earth at this time because the planet is completing a great cycle of time which had begun with Lemuria and those of us who had been Kumaras or worked in tandem with those enlightened sages were now returning in fresh bodies to assist the transition into a new age. This coming golden era, I was inform e d, was to be the World of Venus, the World of Love, and the World of the Kumaras. I had been reborn in an area which had previously been a part of Mu in order to reclaim some of the soul force I had possessed as a Lemurian priest king - my one incarnation in which I had achieved full mastery. I could then better assist the planet during its transition phase.

After hours of blissfully flying through the forest in my supernaturally charged body, my exhilaration began to turn bitter sweet. What had been exuberance began to turn into confusion and despair. It was getting dark and I thought I should return to my home, but any attraction for my "previous" life as a husband and acupuncturist had now vanished. I was a king and so I should rule a kingdom. But, of course, that was a ridiculous notion. Praying once again for assistance from my guides I was informed that my dilemma had been expected. And that was precisely why they would not have revealed my past and future to me unless I had asked so fervently. So, with great compassion for an intrepid, but often times headstrong, human being, they began a process of contracting my consciousness. Within a couple days my personality and life was back to normal, but this blessed experience had permanently transformed my life for the better.

ATLANTIS/PAN/ITZAMANA
THE DRAGON LAND OF THE ATLANTIC

Similar to its "twin" in the Pacific, Atlantis, the Dragon Land of the Atlantic, is remembered in ancient legends around the globe as a Motherland, a land of immortals, and a "Garden of Eden." Greek legends refer to this motherland as Hespera and portray it as a paradisiaca! "Garden of Eden" at the western end of the world where the Dragon Ladon, the "Serpent on the Tree," once guarded the golden apples of wisdom. Hespera was a title for Venus, the planet of immortality, thus designating Atlantis to have been a "Land of Immortals." In other references to it the Greeks alluded to the Atlantic motherland as the land of "Poseid" or "Poseidon," a name for Neptune. In *The Secret Doctrine* the occultist H.P. Blavatsky maintains that Neptune was both a manifestation of the Primal Dragon as well as "the symbol of Atlantean magic"[15] (in most cultures the serpent or dragon has been the perennial symbol of magic). Neptune, like the Primal Dragon, was born out of the cosmic sea and possessed the triune powers of Spirit which were symbolized by his three pronged trident (see Appendix 1: Creation). Moreover, his progeny were five pair of "preserving" Twins, each twin pair being a representation of one of the five elements comprising the body of the Primal Dragon. Neptune's land, Atlantis, was, therefore, a true "Dragon Land."

Echoing the testimony of Greek mythology, the archives of the Native Americans also remember Atlantis as an ancient Dragon Land. Their records refer to it as Itzamana, meaning the "Dragon Land," or as the Old Red Land, home of the red colored fire god or fire serpent.[11] Some tribal records, such as those of the Algonquins, alternately refer to Atlantis as Pan, the name anciently adopted by the Greeks for their famous goat god. According to certain esoteric records of the early Egyptians and Greeks, goat god Pan was originally a black dragon/goat venerated on Atlantis and later brought to the Mediterranean via missionaries of the Motherland.

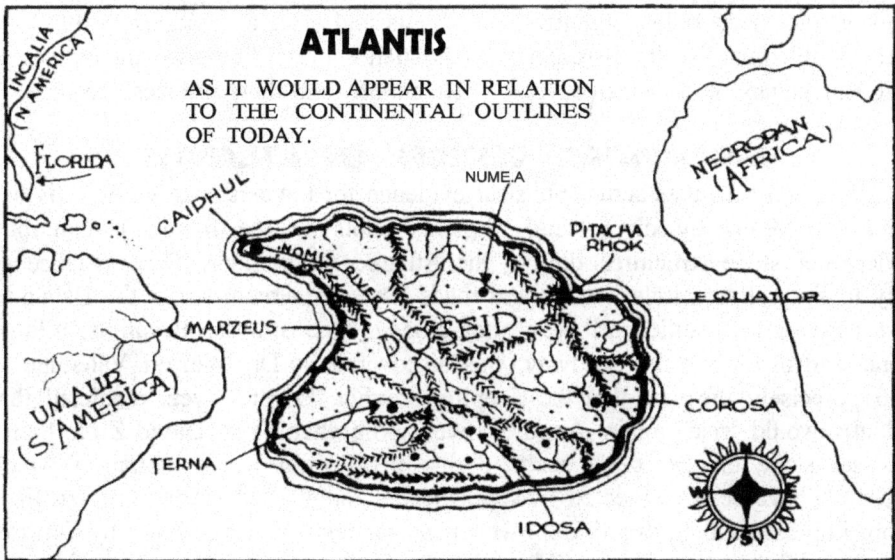

Atlantis at some point in its evolution. From: The Lemurian Fellowship

SURVIVING PROOF OF ATLANTIS

Unfortunately, other than Plato's famous history of Atlantis found in the *Timaeus* and *Critias,* conclusive records of the continent's existence are not in great abundance today. Lost are the numerous references to it which were once inscribed upon the ancient walls and pillars of Egyptian temples or stored within the countries libraries. Most of these records were destroyed by vandals, iconoclastic dictators and conquerors. One such historical text, claims the late astronomer Carl Sagan, was called "The True History of Mankind Over the Last

100,000 Years."₁₆ It was destroyed along with thousands of similar texts during the burning of the library of Alexandria.

Some Atlantean records which escaped the ravages of time are reputed to still exist within underground caverns and secret temple vaults in such places as Tibet and the Sahara Desert. Others are rumored to have been preserved down to the time of the Renaissance among the natives of the Canary Islands and then destroyed. When European explorers first set foot upon the Canaries they were welcomed by fair skinned natives, the self-proclaimed descendants of the Atlanteans, who were shocked to encounter humans other than themselves who had survived the planetary deluge and the destruction of their ancient motherland. The Europeans found the Canary Island natives conducting their lives just as the people of Plato's Atlantis supposedly had. They mummified their leaders, sacrificed bulls, organized bull fights and elected 10 kings to rule over them. Unfortunately, the disrespectful Christian explorers branded the natives as heretical pagans and destroyed both their culture and their priceless records. [17]

UNDERWATER VESTIGES OF ATLANTIS

In recent times actual physical evidence for the existence of Atlantis has been discovered by divers and airplane pilots in the form of numerous underwater stone structures dotting the Atlantic ocean floor. The existence of fifty to sixty stone circles, walls and roads have been recorded in the Bahamas and the eastern Atlantic/Caribbean area alone.₁₈ One of these megaliths, a large stone wall or ceremonial roadway, was discovered by Dr. Manson Valentine in 1967, precisely the year that the sleeping prophet, Edgar Cayce, predicted that Atlantis would "rise" again. Another diver and archeologist, David Zink, found colossal stone blocks while scuba diving off Bimini Island, some of which appear to have been connected by sophisticated tongue and groove construction. More impressive than this find, however, was a huge pyramid found by Dr. Ray Brown while scuba diving within the Bermuda triangle. After locating the immense edifice and swimming around it a few times, Dr. Brown found a door and went through it. Here is his personal account of what he found inside: "The opening was like a shaft debouching into an inner room. I saw something shining. It was a crystal, held by two metallic hands. I had on my gloves and I tried to loosen it. It became loose. As soon as I grabbed it I felt this was the time to get out and not come back"₁₈ Later, after extensive examination, the crystal was determined to be round in shape and contained four pyramidal inclusions within its matrix. Those who have examined it since have theorized that it was once either an "interdimensional communication device" and/or part of a "worldwide system of pyramid-crystal energy generators"? which anciently

23

helped balance the Earth's electromagnetic field. Currently Dr. Brown travels around the world conducting seminars and lectures while displaying his "Atlantean" crystal.

THE CIVILIZATION OF ATLANTIS

THE EXTRATERRESTRIAL SERPENTS OF ATLANTIS

Many Extraterrestrial Serpents came to Atlantis and served this motherland as spiritual teachers and priest kings. Some of these Serpents are especially noted for assisting the Atlanteans in developing the "individuated minds" and sharp intellects for which the progeny of Neptune became famous.

MESSENGERS FROM THE CELESTIAL SERPENT

Some of the Interstellar Serpents on Atlantis came from the Celestial Serpent, the Pleiades. According to the records of the Cherokees or Tslagis (their ancient name) these androgenous Serpents are known as the "Sacred Seven," and said to have once traveled from the universal "seat of the Divine Mind," the Pleiades, in order to instill within developing humankind the "spark of individuated mind" (the intellect and sense of separate self). Once on Earth the Pleiadian missionaries mated with the human population and their progeny spread throughout Atlantis."

The ancient Pleiadian-Atlantean union alluded to by the Cherokees was also mentioned by the ancient Greek historians Apollodorius and Diodorus. Apollodorius claimed that two of the seven Pleiadian sisters, Celoene and Alcyone, had intercourse with the king of Atlantis, Poseidon, and the offspring of their union eventually populated Atlantis. Diodorus claimed that the Pleiadean sisters "laid with the most renowned heroes and gods and thus became the first ancestors of the larger portion of the race of human beings."[17] Echoing the Greeks and Cherokees, the Mayans also refer to an ancient visitation by the Pleiadeans. They, however, record in the *Popul Vuh* that a skirmish broke out between the extraterrestrial missionaries and some of the earthmen after which 400 male youths regretfully returned to their homeland within the Seven Sisters.

THE SIRIANS, MASTERS OF THE SERPENT FIRE

Some Interstellar Serpents also arrived in the Atlantic motherland from the Sun's sister star, Sirius, and brought to the Atlanteans the wisdom of awakening the serpent power through alchemy. Leading up to their arrival, the Sirians had become galactic guardians of the secrets of uniting the polarity. They were adept alchemists who sought to seed their alchemical wisdom to humanoids evolving in other parts of the galaxy. Their definitive symbol, which was a cosmic reflection of their spiritual accomplishments and alchemical knowledge, was comprised of three straight lines which together formed a triangle-sometimes with an all-seeing eye in the center. The triangle symbolized that the polarity (the two corners at the base) emanates from, and eventually reunites into, the androgynous Spirit (the apex at the top). The Sirian symbol was alternately that of three circles, called the "Chintamani," which represented the three stars of the trinary Sirian group.

According to legend, when the Sirians arrived on Earth they oversaw the creation and expansion of the Atlantean arm of the Great White Brotherhood. They taught the secrets of alchemy to their spiritual brethren and gifted them with a timeless symbol of polarity union, a stone brought from Sirius cut in the shape of a heart. This "Chintamani Stone" was originally given to the Emperor Tazlavoo of Atlantis and later became the possession of the Dalai Lama of Tibet. At one point it was borrowed by the newly formed League of Nations and later returned east by the famous Russian painter Nicholas Roerich.

Sirius, known as the Great White Lodge of our galaxy, established secret schools or lodges on Atlantis for the dissemination of alchemy. When Atlantis was later destroyed, their secrets and triangular emblem traveled to Egypt where they served as the foundation for new lodges in North Africa. The Sirian symbol was later passed down within the European lodges of Freemasonry, such as the Illuminati, and later incorporated into the Seal of the United States of America.

The Sirian missionaries are currently remembered among the Dogon people of Africa as serpent-featured missionaries who once visited their tribe and taught them both astronomical and mystical wisdom. The Freemasons remember their alchemical forefathers as the precursors of the Biblical Sons of Lamech, anti-diluvian workers of fire. A Hebrew reference to Sirians and/ or Pleiadians is contained in *The Book of Enoch* which refers to a group of "fallen angels" (fallen to Earth?) headed by Azzazel (a.k.a. Lucifer) who came to Earth during an early period of Earth's development and imparted the wisdom of alchemy to the "Daughters of Men." This Hebrew legend refers to the alien visitors as the Nephilim and as the "People of the Shem," the "People of the Rocketships."[21] Sumerian texts mention the periodic visitations of wise Serpents called Anunnakni some of whom may have come from Sirius-a deduction convincingly reached by Robert Temple in *The Sirius Mystery* (St. Martin's Press, NY). Temple reveals that the Sumerian Anunnaki were often referred to as the "Sons of Anu" and contends that Anu may be the star Sirius. The symbol of Anu, the king of heaven in the Sumerian pantheon of gods, was the jackal, an esteemed animal image worshipped in Egypt as Anu-bis, symbol of the Dog Star Sirius.

THE CULTURE OF ATLANTIS

The culture on Atlantis went through two primary stages of growth. Initially the Dragon Land harbored a spiritually based civiliz ation governed by extraterrestrial teachers and immortal Serpents of Wisdom, a group which Edgar Cayce refers to as the "Sons of the Law of One."9 During a later stage, states the sleeping prophet, the Atlantean culture deteriorated into "self-aggrandizement," military control, and a materialistic exaltation of the intellect and ego. The chief progenitors of this later culture were a materialistic group which Cayce refers to as the "Sons of Belial." During their reign many of the pure Atlantean Serpents were forced to immigrate to other parts of the world, such as Mu, or become clandestine.

THE FROZEN SNAKES OF ATLANTIS

To assist their spiritual transformations and later, to fuel their advanced technology and deadly weaponry, the Atlanteans harnessed the power of the life force which arrived as celestial rays from the cosmos and moved within the Earth as the explosive fire serpent, Volcan.11 In order to collect, store and amplify the life force once it arrived at certain dragons' lairs upon the Earth's surface, the Atlanteans placed both pyramids, replicas of Volcan's volcanic homes, as well as huge generator crystals over strategic vortexes. Referred to in the Cayce readings as "fire stones,"9 such massive quartz crystals were "frozen snakes"-actual physical representations of the fiery, serpentine life force. On the molecular level they were comprised of innumerable tetrahedrons, the geometric forms which correspond to the element of fire, which united to form double helix spirals, the archetypal shapes of the serpent. The spiraling matrices of these "fire stones" naturally collected and magnified the explosive energy of the Earth's fire serpent along with the power of the serpentine solar rays which emanated from the Sun. The greatest of the fire stones are reputed to have generated enough power to either fuel huge cities or decimate entire armies. When used as weapons they could, with laz er-like accuracy and intensity, project their formidable power out through their precision faceted apexes.

THE CHERUB DRAGONS AND
KABEROI BROTHERHOOD OF ATLANTIS

Besides seeking to acquire the power of the serpent, the Serpents of Wisdom on Atlantis also sought to gain the wisdom of the Primal Serpent by communing with the celestial Order of Serpents known as the Kerubs or

Cherubim. According to information derived from secret sources, the esoteric historian Lewis Spence stated in his book *The Occult Sciences in Atlantis* that "The Cherubim were those who were most commonly consulted by the Atlantean sages of the highest rank."[22] Each Atlantean Master aligned with one Cherub, which he recognized to be his Higher Self and angelic guardian, and strove to fully integrate that dragon's wisdom and power through a regimen of purifying yogic disciplines. According to Spence's information, many Atlantean masters who completed the spiritual alchemy and fully united with their Cherubim became members of a fraternity of spiritual adepts known as the Brotherhood of the Kerub or Kaberoi (Kaberoi is another name for Cherubim), a title which begins with the K or Ka sound and denotes a Serpent of Wisdom and Son/Daughter of God. The name Kaberoi also means "powerful through fire,"[15] and designates the members of this organization to be adepts purified by the transformative, serpent fire and wielders of its immense power. The Kaberoi were also known as the Sons of Neptune, which was simply another name for Sanat Kumara, the first Cherubim. These Kaberoi Adepts arrived on Atlantis directly from Lemuria, as well as the Pleiades, Sirius and other Star Nations of the cosmos. Kaberoi is also another name for Kumara.

With the demise of Atlantis, some missionaries of the Kaberoi Brotherhood traveled to Egypt and Phoenicia and, as the Kaberoi or "Seven Sons of Sydyk" (Sydyk or Zedek is Melchizedek, and King Melchizedek is another name for the leader of the Kumaras and King of the World, Sanat Kumara), they were instrumental in establishing mystery school traditions in those countries. Their Egyptian and Phoenician descendants later made commemorative images of the Kaberoi & worshipped them in the form of two, three, four, or seven eternally young, twin boys. In Egypt, the Kaberoi were also known as the Sons of Ptah, who was a manifestation of Neptune/Poseidon and ancestor to the Roman fire god Vulcan.

THE DRAGON KINGS OF ATLANTIS

The Grandmaster of the Order of the Kaberoi was the dominant priest king of Atlantis (there were ten reigning kings) descended directly from Neptune or Sanat Kumara. This emperor inherited the wisdom and power of his distinguished predecessors and wore their ancient Venusian Crown (Sanat Kumara arrived from the Pleiades via Venus). One symbol of the emperor's lineage and authority was Neptune's three pronged trident, a sacred power object which had been passed down a long line of monarchs beginning with Neptune/Sanat Kumara and served as the ruler's scepter and principal ceremonial instrument. Made of the finest metals and precious gems, the trident assisted the priest king in manifesting his royal decrees.

Reconstructions of Atlantis's royal palace.
The palace of the kings was in the center of the concentric circles.

Nicholas Roerich and the Sirian Chintamani Stone.

Atlantean Priest King Wearing The Venusian Crown.
Drawing by Chadwick St. John www.inkshadows.com

As a wielder of the serpent fire and descendant of Neptune, the Atlantean priest king was also recognized to be an incarnation of Neptune. As such, he was closely aligned with the underground fire serpent, which was Neptune in his manifestation of Volcan. As the Primal Serpent, Neptune was the power that exists within both the sea and the land. Volcan was Neptune's manifestation under the surface of the Earth and within volcan-oes. It was his power that triggered both earthquakes and volcanic eruptions. To designate themselves representatives of Volcan, the Atlantean kings ceremoniously wore a tuft of white feathers at the apex of their cone-shaped Venusian Crown to represent volcanic smoke. At one point there was a lineage of Atlantean priest kings named Votan with very strong affiliations with Volcan. According to the esoteric traditions of certai n Native Ame rican tribes, the dynasty of Votan, known as the House of Votan, were very powerful and served as the ruling dynasty during the legendary continent's final hours.

One of the priestly duties of the Atlantean priest kings was to lead a ceremonial danc e around a sacred fire for the purpose of summo ning and appropriately worshiping Volcan, the invisible god dwelling within the fire's flames. The resulting occult power produced from this efficacious rite could be used for individual empowerme nt as well as for the protection and material growth of the entire motherland. When Atlantean missionaries left the motherland, this important rite was taken to other countries where, as the Crown Dance, it was led by a dancer wearing a replica of the Votans' royal volcano crown followed by other dancers wearing flaming, trident-shaped headdresses symbollic of the motherland.11

THE SISTERHOOD OF SERPENTS

Alongside of the Kaberoi Brotherhood there existed upon Atlantis a Sisterhood of female Serpents of Wisdom similarly comprised of a hierarchy of adepts striving to unify with their Cherubim or Higher Selves through intensive yogic disciples. They served alone or alongside their brothers as priestesses within many of the Atlantean temples, especially those dedicated exclusively to the Serpent Goddess. When they left Atlantis they traveled both east and west to North Africa, Mexico, the Mediterranean, Asia Minor, and South America where, as the historical Amazons, they founded numerous important mystery school traditions in honor the Serpent Goddess. Wherever they settled, these Amazons became famous for wearing snake skins into battle and religiously worshipping prolific images of the Serpent Goddess, such as the Greek Medusa.

CHAPTER 3

THE DISPERSION OF THE SERPENTS OF WISDOM

During the time of Lemuria and Atlantis, and especially just before and during their respective destructions, the early Serpents of Wisdom led migrations of culture-bearing colonists from the twin Motherlands to predetermined locations upon the Earth's surface. In these virgin areas they established colonies and founded new Dragon Empires based upon the civilizations they had left behind.

Many of the Lemurian colonists migrated to the area surrounding the Pacific Ocean, i.e. the Pacific rim. Then for the following thousands of years the settlements they established reflected the ancient Lemurian spirituality, its artistic sensitivity and its predilection for harmonizing with the universal will. By contrast, many of the Atlantean colonists migrated to the continental land masses surrounding the Atlantic and spawned empires based upon the exaltation of the intellect as well as the spiritual principles espoused by the Kaberoi Serpents of Wisdom. Some of the post-Atlantean cerebral cultures they engendered produced sophisticated technology which could effectively control the Earth and all her inhabitants.

DISPERSION OF THE ATLANTEAN SERPENTS

THEIR IDENTIFYING TRADEMARKS

According to legend, before permanently departing from their motherland the Atlantean Serpents of Wisdom were instructed by their Grandmaster, King Votan III, the last reigning monarch of the House of Votan, to take with them the distinguishing trademarks of their ancient organization and utilize them in their new lands. These exclusive markings included the Serpents' sacred esoteric name, their ceremonial dress, and their traditional serpentine symbology. King Votan also advised his people to wear a version of the royal Venus Crown with a tuft of feathers at the top simulating vocanic smoke during their sacred ceremonies and include within their new tribal names the sounds of Ka or Ko, as well as the letter K, the timeless denominations of both wisdom and serpent (they are synonymous the serpent *is* the archetypal symbol for wisdom.)

29

For ages Ka or K had been an ancient seed sound of the Primal Serpent's various names, Kon, Kan and Kerub and had been incorporated into the name of the Serpents' Atlantean organization, the Kaberoi. Finally, as one last parting request, Votan advised the migrating Serpents of Wisdom to gather together at the end of each 104 year cycle to share wisdom they had acquired during the cycle.[11] The 104 year cycle constitutes a microcosm of the large 104,000 year grand cycle, which also ends in a universal Serpent gathering .

SERPENT COLONISTS OF NORTH AFRICA AND THE MEDITERRANEAN

Leading up to their final audience with King Votan, many Serpents of Wisdom had traveled to North Africa and the Mediterranean where, as seafaring traders called Atlantides, they had established trading posts and colonies. Following their final farewells to their beloved king, many Atlantean Serpents permanently resettled within these eastern colonies.

In obediance to Votan, once the transplanted Atlantide Serpents were established in their new colonial lands, they quickly adopted the serpentine names they desired to be henceforth known by. One branch of Serpents took for themselves the serpentine name of Carian, pronounced K-rion. The "ar" in Carian was a secret sound syllable which denoted the Atlantean fire god and ion was a name for the sea. Altogether, the three parts of the name denoted the "Serpent sea people of the Atlantean fire god." Another branch of Serpents became known as the Eus-Cara. With the "C" pronounced as a "K," Eus-Cara carries a similar meaning to that of Carian. A third branch of Serpents referred to themselves as the Tuaraks, a name which translates into the "Serpent people of the all glorious fire god."[11] Historically the Carion, Eus-Cara and Taurak people are known as the Phoenicians, Basques and Tuaregs respectively.

After adopting a serpent name of their choice, many of the transplanted Serpents further revealed their serpentine affiliations by tattooing snakes or dragons upon their bodies, or emblazoning them along the shafts and handles of their swords and daggers. They also sailed in dragon-shaped vessels and covered themselves in snake skin armour before going into battle.

THE SERPENT TUAREGS

The Tauraks were an important branch of mercantile Atlantides who successfully made the permanent transition from Atlantis to their established colonies in North Africa. According to the records of their contemporary descendants, the nomadic Taureg people of the Sahara Desert, these seafaring

30

Atlantides first arrived in North Africa during the pre-deluge era when the large territory contained within its borders a large ocean, the Triton Sea. Referred to in *The Histories* of Herodutus, this great sea was boarded on its western end by the Atlas Mountains and populated throughout by a multitude of islands. Once the Tauraks had established lucrative trade relations with the indigenous people inhabiting the Triton Sea's rim and some of its islands, they founded permanent colonies for themselves within these areas. One large island of the sea was specially chosen by the Tauraks' to serve as an important base because its three centrally located mountains formed the shape of a trident, the classic symbol of their Atlantic motherland. The Tauraks hollowed out these mountains, constructed underground galleries and temples within their cavernous interiors, and then used them as libraries for their sacred records and halls for the enactment of their sacred rites. A second major headquarters of the Tauraks' was built in their rim territories within the Atlas Mountains under the guidance of a hero known as "Hercules." Referred to in Egyptian texts as "Shu," this Taurak leader existed 17,000 years before the Egyptian King Amasis and possessed as his definitive symbol the serpent.

During the last major Earth shift which sunk Atlantis, the Triton Sea was drained and the Tauraks' island settlements became towering mountain ranges. After bidding a final fairwell to their beloved motherland, the Tauraks permanently relocated to their trident-shaped island headquarters, which became part of the Ahaggar Mountain range of southern Algeria, as well as to their other colonies in the Atlas Mountains. They also subsequently founded additional settlements in the North African lowlands.

When the terrain of North Africa finally became arid desert, the Tauraks or Tuaregs, their modem name, became nomadic desert traders. They continued to wield the serpent-engraved swords of their ancestors, however, as well as their predecessors triangular-shaped shields with red crosses ornamenting the center, ancient symbols of the Atlantean fire serpent. In order to protect themselves and their interests, the Tuaregs also acquired marauding tendencies, and for this reason they have garnered the nickname of the "blue vengeance."

In recent times visitors have been allowed to journey within the Tuaregs' ancient caverns of the Ahaggar Mountains and experience for themselves the vestiges of an Atlant.ean civilization which still remains intact. The experiences of a few of these intrepid visitors were disclosed to L. Taylor Hansen and recorded in her book *The Ancient Atlantic*. Apparently such explorers return home with astonishing tales of underground tunnels covered with murals of the Tuaregs' ancestors, the Serpent Tauraks, who are depicted wielding swords with snakes inscribed upon their blades and/or daggers embossed with tridents. Some

31

Ancient North Africa

A Crown Dancer

visitors are taken through the Tuareg's prodigious library, the shelves of which are packed with thousands of ancient texts, many of which chronologue the history of the Tuaregs as far back as their existence on Atlantis. Guests to the underground temples of the Tuareg also report encountering live Ourans, monstrous green reptiles which are venerated as physical representations of the Tuareg's serpent ancestress or "Grandmother." Many visitors are also blessed with the opportunity of spending the night within the Tuareg's underworld and being in attendance during a performance of their spectacular "Crown Dance," a sacred ritual which was anciently performed on Atlantis in honor of Volcan, the fire serpent.

CANAAN, LAND OF THE FIRE GOD OR FIRE SERPENT

During the time the Tuaregs settled their North African territories, other branches of the Serpent Atlantides simultaneously established colonies around the group of land-locked lakes and inland seas which existed in the area of what is now the Mediterranean Sea. One branch of these Atlantides were the Tyrrhenians, the people after whom the present Tyrrhenian Sea is named. The Tyrrhenians eventually split in half to become the Etruscans and the Carians or Phoenicians, a tribe which eventually migrated to Canaan (pronounced Kā-nan, with K sound of the Serpents), a territory on the Asia Minor coast which can be translated as the "Land of the Fire Serpent."

The final migration of the early Phoenicians to Asia Minor is referred to in the Holy Bible as the colonization of Noah's grandson Canaan. According to the Book of Genesis, following the great deluge, Canaan, the son of Ham, led a group of colonists to the Asia Minor coast and founded a colony named Canaan. Since Can is the universal name of the fire serpent, the name Canaan implies "he of the fire serpent," thus suggesting that the patriarch's country was the "Land of the Fire Serpent."

Once settled in Canaan the Carians or Phoenicians set up altars to the Kaberoi Twins, symbolic representations of their Atlantean forefathers of Atlantis, for daily worship. They also sailed throughout the Mediterranean in ships with "Pataci," images of Volcan as the fire god Ptah, attached to their prows, thus designating themselves to be "Serpent sea people of the Fire God."

THE SERPENT COLONISTS OF EGYPT

Other branches of Atlantides who sailed down the Mediterranean Valley or across the Triton Sea to found colonies along the Nile River are known in history as the Egyptians. Remains of their discarded vessels may be the Ibex (a kind of mountain goat) heads found buried in the Egyptian desert.11 Apparently once attached to the prows of their ships, these carved goat heads are presumably representations of Pan, the goat god of the Atlanteans, which was a version of Neptune-Volcan, the mighty fire god.

THE LINEAGE OF THOTH-HERMES, THE SERPENT MASTERS

Leading the first Egyptians to their new North African homeland were a lineage of Atlantean Serpents of Wisdom. Historically they are known as the Thoth-Hermes Serpent Masters and referred to in old Egyptian texts as the god Thoth or Djehuty and as the Djedhi, titles which contain the prefix "Dj," meaning Serpent. [23] The androgynous serpentine nature of these adepts was reflected in the Egyptian glyph of Thoth's symbolic animal, the Ibis, which was a "dual" bird with both black and white coloring.

In the later Greek texts of Hellenic Egypt the Thoth-Hermes Masters were known simply as Hermes, a name which "signifies a Serpent."[24] They were also referred to as Tresmegistus and Chiram or its variations of Khirm, Khurm and Khur-om (all begin with the K sound of the Serpent). Tresmegistus and Chiram both denote "One in essence, but three in aspect" or "Thrice Great." Chiram, an archetypal name for the fire serpent and the name which Hermes is believed to have evolved from, is inclusive of the three consonants of Cheth, Resh and Mem, seed syllables of the three elements of air, water and fire which unite as the androgenous Serpent Fire.[24] These three seed syllables comprising Chiram also denoted the androgyny of the Thoth-Hermes Masters as well as the three powers of the serpent wielded by them. The definitive emblems of Hermes Tresmegistus consisted of the Primal Serpent, Agathodeamon, as well as the caduceus, an archetypal symbol of both the cosmic tree and the human spine, paths of the spiralling fire serpent.

While in Atlantis the Thoth-Hermes Masters had been high ranking members of the Kaberoi Brotherhood and served their people as both hierophants of the mysteries as well as divine priest kings. When the Motherland was destroyed, these Thoth-Hermes Masters traveled as culture bearers to new lands where they reprised their former Atlantean roles. One renowned Thoth-Hermes became a priest king and teacher of Egypt, while another Thoth-Hermes, Tautus (a Phoenician rendering of the name Thoth), apparently traveled with the Carians to their new land and reigned as the first priest king of the Phoenicians. Because of the dispersal to these two Thoth-Hermes to disparate locations, the Carthaginian historian (circa 1400 B.C.) Sanconiathon could later assert that Tautus had been a priest king of both Egypt and Phoenicia.

35

Another member of the Thoth-Hermes Masters apparently became a leader of the migrating Atlantide Tuaregs. This dynamic leader and culture bearer is known as Shu in Egyptian texts and among the Tuaregs as Hercules, a name which the famous Greek historian Pausinius contended was originally a name for Thoth-Hermes.25 If Pausanius's assertion is indeed true, then the leaders of the Tuaregs, Phoenicians and Egyptians may have all been initiates of the same Atlantean lineage of Thoth-Hermes.

THOTH-HERMES IN EGYPT

The very first members of the Thoth-Hermes lineage who poured into Egypt did so during the later days of Atlantis. Legend has it that the arrival of one of them coincided to a time immediately preceding the great deluge which decimated the Motherland. This incipient Thoth-Hermes, referred to by the Egyptian historian Iamblichus as "the first to teach the path to god" (i.e., to the Egyptians) landed in Egypt with a group of sacred scientists and builders which Sanconiathon refers to as the "Serpent Tribe." Also referred to by him as the "Seven Sons of Sydyk" and alluded to to in the Edfu "Building Texts" (of Edfu, Egypt) as the "Seven Sages" who arrived from the "Homeland of the Primeval Ones,"26 these Kaberoi scientists built a giant pyramid which was to serve as a beacon and monitor for Extraterrestrial Serpents, as well as a guide for later colonists in North Africa. It was also to function as a storehouse for the sacred Atlantean records and built watertight to resist the flood waters of the encroaching deluge. According to Iamblichus, the Atlantean records were also inscribed upon two columns and then secreted within an impenetrable cave near Thebes.

After the flood waters had sufficiently receded another wave of colonists arrived in Egypt. Led by either the same Thoth-Hermes who built the pyramid or another Master of the same lineage, the hidden tablets and columns were promptly recovered from their sealed tombs and then transcribed into a series of manuscripts which later served as the definitive texts of the Egyptian priesthood. This second Thoth-Hermes is also believed to have brought with him from Atlantis a tablet made of solid emerald. This Tabula Smaragdina or "Emerald Tablet" was covered with esoteric precepts which had been authored and signed by Thoth-Hermes under his name of Chiram. It was supposedly one of four tablets which had been specially created on Atlantis to serve as permanent scrolls for the secrets of alchemy, the process by which base metals could be transmuted into gold and humans could transform into gods and goddesses. When the Atlantean Serpents dispersed from the Motherland, these four tablets were taken to the four corners of the Earth.27 One of them found its way to the

Mayan civilization in the Yucatan Peninsula and another, the fabled Egyptian tablet, became a prized possession of the Egyptian priesthood. The contents of this Egyptian tablet was later transcribed into a scriptural format and taken into the heartland of Euro pe where it became the definitive text of the Renaissance alchemists.

KHEM, THE LAND OF THE FIRE SERPENT

After constructing numerous temples and pyramids, the Kaberoi sacred scientists and adepts of the Thoth-Hermes lineage, which history asserts were the "first to teach the worship of the Serpent," chiseled images of their fire serpent god for daily veneration. In Egypt the Atlantean fire serpent Neptune-Volcan evolved into Ptah, the fire god, which historian Manetho calls the most ancient of Egyptian gods. At his city of Memphis, Ptah/Volcan/Neptune was venerated in conjunction with the twin effigies of his two sons, the Kaberoi Twins, who had been the founders of the Kaberoi Brotherhood on Atlantis. Neptune-Volcan's other manifestation on Atlantis. Pan, the goat-dragon with a black color, a color of the Fire Serpent, evolved in Egypt into a deity called Khem (with the Serpent K sound), one of the first eight gods worshiped by the Egyptians according to Herodutus. As Khem, Pan was venerated in the city of Mendes as a fiery dark goat god, and in southern Egypt he took the form of Min, an anthropomorphic version of the fertilizing and nurturing Serpent Power or life force.28

Just as Volcan/Neptune had been on Atlantis both Ptah and Kh em were eventually elevated to the status of Egypt's patron deities and the land was duly named after them. The later name of "Egypt" was derived from Ptah, and the country's early name of Khem, Khemmit or Khemi, which meant the "Land of Khem," the "Land of the Fire Serpent," or simply "the Black One,"23 was derived from Khem. Ptah's city was Memphis, the first capital city of a united Egypt, and another important city of the empire was Chemmo or Chemmi, a city in the center of the country dedicated to Khem's goat form. The Greeks eventually renamed the city Panopolis, the "City of Pan," after the name of their version of the Atlantean goat god. The name Khem later provided the root for the Arabic word Al-chemy, the process of transmutation via the influence of the serpent fire.

According to Sir J. Gardener Wilkenson, a British archeologist who spent years traveling throughout Egypt and studying its hieroglyph writings during the 1800's, the name Khem was written by the Egyptians as Khm, Khem or Kham, the rendering or Kham, the rendering and pronunciation of which approximates that of Ham, the name of one of Noah's son who colonized much of Africa and Asia after the flood. Stemming from his research, Sir Gardener theorized that the land of Khem was the land of Ham.28 This would make Ham synonymous with Volcan/Pan and his entourage of colonists (as well as those of his colonizing sons) would, therefore, have been colonists from Atlantis.

EGYPTIAN COLONIZATION ACCORDING TO THE CAYCE RECORDS

According to the testimony of the famous "sleeping prophet," Edgar Cayce, Atlantean colonists began pouring into Egypt between 28,000-10,000 B.C. Cayce claimed to have had an incarnation during this period as the high priest Ra-T a who supposedly helped organize the incoming waves of colonists fro m the Motherland. Ra-T a also assisted Thoth-Hermes in the construction of the Great Pyramid and Sphinx, an event which, according to the clairvoyant, occurred around 10,000 B. C. Cayce contends that the original function of the Great Pyramid was that of a temple of initiation as well as a storage vault for Atlantean records. He claims that there was an adjoining chamber, referred to as the "Hall of Records," which was specially constructed between the Sphinx and the Great Pyramid to serve as a hidden library for the ancient records.[9]

HISTORICAL RECORDS OF EGYPT'S EXTREME ANTIQUITY

In support of the Akashic Records accessed by Cayce, there are numerous authentic Egyptian records which similarly allude to a pre-diluvian civilization in Egypt. The Royal Papyrus of Turin, for example, refers to a lineage of priest kings which began ruling at least 36,620 years ago in Egypt. During 13,420 of those years the country was ruled by the Shemsu Hor, an apparent title given to the descendants of the "Seven Sages" who arrived with Thoth- Hermes. [26] Manetho, a priest and historian of Heliopolis whose name means "Truth of Thoth," claimed to have inherited the records of Tho th-Hermes and found within them references to dynasties which had ruled Egypt 24,000 years before his time. T he Greek historian Diodorus was told by Egyptian priests that "divine" dynasties of gods governed their country for 18,000 years and mortal dynasties ruled for another 5,000 years . Herodutus claimed to have seen 341 wooden statues of high priests who had supposedly succeeded each other at the great temple of Thebes since the creation of the edifice, 11,000 years before his arrival.

There are also enduring records in stone which point to Egypt's possible pre -diluvian existence. Foremost of these records are the imposing Great

Pyramid and Sphinx. John Anthony West and Dr. Robert Schoch recently astonished the world by conclusively proving that the weather damage on the Sphinx could only have occurred by water and the last time there was enough water in Egypt to produce such significant damage was over ten thousand years ago. Their earth-shaking discovery could possibly carry the beginnings of Egyptian culture back to at least 8 -10,000 B. C. The Great Pyramid also appears to have been affected by and perhaps submerged in water at one time as indicated by salt deposits found coating the walls of the the Queen's Chamber and sea shells seen scattered around the base of the pyramid by Herodotus and other ancient travelers to Egypt.

THE SERPENT COLONISTS OF GREECE

While Egypt was becoming a great Dragon Empire, another branch of dispersing Atlanteans traveled down inland rivers and seas within the Mediterranean area to what is now Greece and the islands of the Aegean Sea. Like their brothers and sisters who had reached North Africa, these explorers were initially mercantile Atlantides who established colonies in the Mediterranean area both before and after the great deluge which destroyed the last vestiges of the Motherland.

COLONISTS OF THE SERPENT GOD DESS NEITH/ATHENE

According to Plato's dialogues, the story of the Atlanteans' arrival in Greece was recounted in detail to the Athenian statesman Solon by the temple priests of Khem. These priests, whom the archaeologist L. Taylor Hansen asserts were the ministers of Volcan/Ptah, maintained that a pre-diluvian Atlantean migration of worshipers of the Serpent Goddess Neith/Athene had anciently founded a colony in the vicinity of Athens, Greece, which they dedicated to Athene. One thousand years later they founded a sister colony to it in Sais, Egypt, which they dedicated to Athene's Egyptian counterpart, Neith. To complete their startling story, the priests of Khem stated that the colonists of ancient Athens subsequently developed into a mighty military power and distinguished themselves by defeating a fleet of power obsessed Atlanteans who attempted to conquer them. In commemoration of their victory, the citizens of later Greece annually celebrated the feast of Panathenaea, the name of which unites Pan, a name of Atlantis, with Athens.

According to the Greek historians Jane Harrison and Robert Graves, following their early colonization efforts in the Mediterranean, the worshipers of the Serpent Goddess Neith/Athene continued to pay homage to their deity in the form of a serpent, a sphinx, or a female goddess covered with snakes.[25,29]

later Greece and Egypt Neith/Athene became fully humanized and her serpentine nature was thereafter reflected in the slithering snakes which adorned her shield and swords as well as the image of a serpent at her feet which the Greek Pausanius claims to have seen next to her during a visit to the Parthenon of Athens. Her ancient serpentine aspect was also absorbed by her serpent Son who became the crocodile god Sobek in Sais, and Erechthonius, the snake coiled on the sacred olive tree, in Athens. The humanized Athene fully retained her association to Serpent Wisdom, however, and as the "Goddess of Wisdom" she was said to have been born from the head of Zeus (in each culture the Serpent Goddess is a synonymous with the wisdom of the highest deity).

THE PELASGIANS, THE SEAFARING SERPENTS

Following the great flood, the pre-diluvian worshippers of Athene/Neith were joined in Greece by a fresh wave of colonists arriving directly from Pan or indirectly from the Motherland via Libya and Egypt. One of the best known of these later settlers was Deucalion, the Greek Noah, who is reputed to have survived the flood in order to help repopulate Greece. Deucalion began a wave of post-diluvian settlers to Greece called Pelasgians, "Peoples of the Sea." The name Pelasgian is actually an inclusive denomination applied to all early Greek seafaring colonists and their descendants by the later Aryan invaders. The title is inclusive of the Danaans, Amazons and others who left Atlantis and arrived in Greece via Egypt and Libya. Uniting all these sub-groups of Pelasgians was the worship of the Primal Serpent and/or goat god as Dana, Athene Nieth, Ophion and Pan.

THE ARKADIANS AND THEIR DRAGON/GOAT GOD PAN

According to the ancient Greek records preserved by Pausanius, following the deluge the first Pelasgian colonists on mainland Greece settled in Arcadia. Their leader, Pelasgos, became king of Arkadia and his son, Lykaon, founded the region's first city, Lykosoura. Like other branches of seafaring Atlanteans it is possible that these early Arkadians may have arrived at their new homeland aboard goat-fish or dragon vessels which had heads of the goat god Pan affixed to their prows. The Arkadians' connection to the goat god is undeniable and historical. Once established in Greece they made Pan their principal deity and their country became known as the "Land of Pan."

THE DANAANS, THE PEOPLE OF SERPENT WISDOM

The Danaans made their entrance into history during pre-diluvian times as tribe of mercantile Atlantides who sailed routes between the Atlantean Motherland their colonies on the shores of the ancient Triton Sea in North Africa. They were seafaring magicians and sages who referred to themselves as the People of the Serpent/Moon Goddess Dana. The root of Dana, Dan, meaning "wisdom" or "knowledge," implys that these followers of Dana were the "People of Serpent Wisdom." The name Dana was also intimately associated with magic. As Diana, Dana was venerated during the later Middle Ages of Europe as patroness of the female mysteries, witchcraft and magic.

Just before and during the destruction of Atlantis, many seafaring Danaans sailed directly to the eastern end of the Mediterranean and established colonies in the areas which are now Greece, the Aegean islands and Asia Minor. Other Danaan colonists traveled first to Egypt before reaching Greece and helped to found Panopolis, the city of the Atlantean goat god, Pan. Their eventual voyage from Khem to mainland Greece is remembered in Greek mythology as the migration of Danaus, the son of Belus, King of Panopolis, who sailed to Greece with his fifty daughters. Upon reaching the Peloponnese, asserts the legend, Danaus became monarch of a kingdom whose capital was Argos. Here his people built a famous temple in honor of Dana and placed within it an image of Dana's "mother," the cow goddess Io, who was also known as Ia-Hu, the winged cow or dragon sphinx.[29]

By the beginning of the first millennium B.C. various branches of Danaans had established settlements in much of Greece and the Aegean Sea. They established serpent worshipping colonies on many islands including the Island of Rhodes (the name of which was derived from a Syrian word for serpent and related to the English rodent) and the Island of Cyprus, which was anciently known as Ia-Dan, the Isle of Dan. Rhodes subsequently became the headquarters of a Danaan brotherhood of magicians called Telchines who, according to Diodorus, had the power to heal, change the weather at will and "shape-shift" into any desired physical form. Other well known Danaan settlements were founded in the Baleric Islands, the Taurus Mountains, and in Syria. One Danaan clan of colonists was assimilated into the Hebrew tribal system as the Tribe of Dan while another group traveled north to the British Isles and there became known as the Tuatha de Danaan, the "People of the Goddess Dana."[29]

THE AMAZONS, THE FEMALE SERPENTS

Like their cousins the Danaans and Tauraks, the Amazons, another group of mercantile Atlantides, also established pre-diluvian trade routes throughout the Triton Sea and the Mediterranean area. Greeks legends state that

41

they came from Hespera or the Hesperides, a paradise region at the western end of the Earth where the mythological Serpent Ladon guarded the golden apples of wisdom. The name Hespera is a title for Atlantis when the motherland stretched across the Atlantic as one continuous land mass, and the Hesperides denotes the continent when, after a cyclical devastation, it was divided up into numerous islands. [11]

The patroness of the Amazons was the androgynous Serpent Goddess Athene/Neith of Atlantis who was worshipped in the forms of a serpent, a serpent bearing human matriarch, and the double headed battle axe. These fierce women aspired to emulate their androgynous deity by becoming courageous warriors and by incarnating a male, aggressive spirit into their female bodies. While fighting in the name of their serpentine heroine Nieth/Athene, the Amazons covered their bodies in snake skins and brandished her symbol, the "androgynous" battle axe.

When they succeeded in establishing permanent trading colonies within Libya's ancient Lake Triconis, a name for the great Triton Sea, the Amazons settled upon an island replica of their motherland which they similarly referred to as Hespera. Here the Amazons established shrines to the Serpent Goddess and elected three queens to rule over them. These three queens represented the three pronged trident, ancient symbol of Atlantis, as well as the triune powers of the Goddess and the three phases of the Moon.

Eventually the Amazons migrated to Greece and the Aegean Sea where they established island shrines to the Goddess on Lemnos, Lesbos and Samothrace. On both Lemnos and Lesbos they dedicated cities to their three queens and observed secretive rites to the Goddess which men were strictly forbidden from attending. On Samothrace they built a sanctuary to Hecate, a manifestation of the Serpent Goddess in her dark, destructive aspect. Hecate represented the third phase of the Moon, the phase associated with death, transformation and resurrection. The most sacred of Amazonian initiations in the Aegean occurred in Hecate's Zerynthian cave/temple on Samothrace.

After establishing shrines and colonies along the Asia Minor coast, such as at Ephesus, the Amazons moved inland and founded their principal Asian headquarters on the shores of the Black Sea. From this seaside citadel of Colchis, the Amazons made periodic incursions into Asia for conquest and for sexual liaisons with nomadic tribes of Scythian males. Colchis subsequently became one of the primary centers for the dissemination of the female mysteries and the worship of Hecate. In her patronage over the mysteries, Hecate was assisted at Colchis by Medusa, one of the mythological Gorgon sisters and an aspect of Athene/Neith. With her hair of snakes, Medusa was, like Hecate, the fountainhead of Serpent wisdom, a personification of the dark phase of the moon, and the wielder of the destructive/transformative power of the Goddess. Those women who administered the rites at Colchis wore Gorgon or Medusa masks thereby designating themselves to be manifestations of the wisdom of the Serpent Goddess.

THE KABEROI SERPENTS OF WISDOM IN THE AEGEAN

Since they had been intimately involved with administering the sacerdotal rites on Atlantis, many members of the Kaberoi Brotherhood arrived in Greece and the Islands of the Aegean as priests of the migrating Pelasgians. In their new lands they and their descendants became known as the Dactyloi, Kouretes, and Korybantes, three titles which incorporate the hard K sound of the Serpents. While displaying the abilites of extraordinarily powerful wizards (according to Strabo), these colonial adepts established branches of their brotherhood and gave initiations into their ancient order. On Samothrace they bestowed initiation into the Kaberoi Brotherhood in the presence of two images, statues of the forever-young, Kaberoi Twin Boys, which were venerated as representations of the ancient founders of their tradition On Crete, where accepted legend maintained that "the first one hundred men (on the island) were Dactyloi and their sons were the Kouretes," they dressed themselves in white robes and sandals and gave initiations within caves high in the Cretan mountains. Other Kaberoi Serpents of Wisdom, the Korybantes, are reputed to have reached Asia Minor, perhaps as part of the Carian migration, where they administered the secret rites and taught the sacred wisdom.

THE SERPENT COLONISTS OF MESOPOTAMIA

THE DRAGON ENKI AND THE ANUNNAKI

Middle Eastern legends suggest that Mesopotamia may have also been a burgeoning port-of-call for seafaring Serpents of Wisdom from Atlantis. According to ancient historians, the land was visited repeatedly by culture bearers whose emblem was the goat-fish. The goat-fish, an ancient symbol of Neptune/Pan, represented the form of the Atlantean dragon god as well as the distinctive vessels his devotees sailed throughout much of the world in: ships with goat heads attached to their prows.

According to certain Sumerian texts, as well as Greek translations of the Middle Eastern history anciently recorded by the Babylonian initiate Berosus, Enki or "Oannes," whose symbol was the goat-fish, arrived in Mesopotamia with his entourage, the Anunnaki (also called the "repulsive" or "dragon-faced Annedoti" by the Greek translators), at four different times, and each time taught the native people many of the mundane and spiritual arts. Their visits were 30,000 years apart, an interval which is conspicuously close to 26,000 years, the duration of one Precession of the Equinoxes, thus⬜ implying that the purpose of each arrival by Enki and his Serpent follower⬜ was to initiate a new cycle of time by infusing the ancient Mesopotamian population with a fresh outpouring of culture and wisdom.

While some waves of Anunnaki probably came from Sirius, some Sumerian texts seem to imply that at least one delegation came from Atlantis. According to one well known translator of Middle Eastern texts, George Michanowsky, Atlantis is remembered in the early Sumerian scriptures as NI-DUK-KI, a sacred paradise surrounded by water which once existed in an epoch preceding a planetary deluge.16 It is also referred to as Dilmun in the texts, the home of Enki, the goat-fish. Such references suggest that Enki was indeed a Mesopotamian name for Pan/Neptune, the dragon-goat of the Motherland.

One of the early visits of Enki's Serpent People in Mesopotamia, state the Sumerian texts, coincided with a period when many Atlantean missionaries and traders were seeking new territories of the world for colonization. Their visit preceded a devastating flood which occurred during the Age of Leo, or close to 11,000 B.C., the traditional date for the sinking of Atlantis.21 Following their arrival, Enki's Serpent People constructed a great empire with Eridu, the City of Enki, as its premier city and capital. With its strategic positioning near the entrance to the Euphrates river, Eridu, meaning "home built far away" (far from Atlantis?), apparently afforded the ancient Serpent mariners an ideal location from which they could easily sail to and from Atlantis. Within their capital city the Anunnaki (referred to in Sumerian texts as "the fifty Anunnaki of the city of Eridu"21) built a great temple in honor of Enki, the E-Apsu or Temple of Wisdom, and embellished it inside and out with shimmering silver and lapis lazuli. Following its construction, the Anunnaki proceeded further inland and built four more anti-diluvian cities in Mesopotamia, the most important of which was Sippar, city of the Sun god Shamash.

After consolidating their colonies, Enki's Anunnaki chose a lineage of priest kings to rule over their new Mesopotamian kingdom. In Sumerian texts these kings are collectively referred to as a lineage of 10 pre-flood priest kings known as the AB-GAL, the "Masters of Knowledge,"16 and⬜ "the Seven Elders." They are depicted with fish-like bodies, thus indicating that they were wise Serpents (Enki had a fish tail) who dwelt in the Apsu, the sea of wisdom, and implying that they came from across the ocean. Perhaps they were missionaries from Atlantis and members of the Kaberoi Brotherhood. Their myth exactly parallels that of Egypt's "Seven Sages" or Kaberoi who arrived in ocean vessels from the devastated island of "the Primeval Ones" and worshipped a black goat god. Interestingly, certain texts seem to imply that one of the Seven Elders, King Enmenduranki, the seventh pre-flood monarch of Sumeria, may have been one of the Thoth-Hermes masters. Enmenduranki's name on the Sumerian pre-flood king list corresponds to that of Enoch, the seventh patriarch on the Hebrew pre-flood list-and Enoch is a Hebrew name for Thoth-Hermes (the Hebrew list is believed by some to be a spurious copy of the earlier Sumerian).

Leading up to the great deluge, Enki, acting in his compassionate role as preserver and savior of humanity, instructed the tenth antediluvian priest king, Ziusandra, to build an ark in order to save himself, his family and vestiges of the pre-flood civilization. In order to preserve the wisdom of the Anunnaki, Enki also advised Ziusandra to inscribe the secret knowledge of the Seven Elders upon stone tablets and then deposit them in Sippar.

Following the flood, Ziusandra and his ark came to rest upon a hill. When he and his cargo finally disembarked from the vessel, a new cycle of time had begun, a cycle Ziusandra was not destined to a be a part of. As a reward for his obedience, the savior Enki blessed the Sumerian Noah with the gift of enlightenment and made clear his passage into the paradise realms of the immortals. Before he began his ascent into the heavens, however, Ziusandra mobilized the remaining survivors of the flood and led them to the hidden tablets in Sippar. The information on these tablets was then transcribed into scriptural format and the resulting texts became the possession of the Anunnaki of the post-diluvian Mesopotamia. One of these texts, a "Book of Wisdom," was authored by Ziusandra himself and gave instructions on spiritual practice, magic and ritual. [31] Another of these texts is reputed to have found its way into the famous library of the Assyrian king Assurbanipal.

THE SERPENT COLONISTS OF BRITAIN

THE PHERYLLT

Great Britain may have been another destination of migrating Atlanteans. According to certain occult myths, the first colonists in some parts of the British Isles were the Priests of Pharon or the Pheryllt, an order of powerful magicians and spiritual masters which some esoteric historians contend migrated directly from Atlantis. The Pheryllt were worshippers of the Serpent Goddess Keridwen (with K sound of the Primal Serpent) which they depicted as a human goddess covered with serpents and holding the reigns of a chariot drawn by fierce dragons. From their patroness they learned the secrets of summoning, directing, and awakening the spiritual fire within themselves and others. Their adeptship in the alchemical arts is reflected in their name, Pheryllt, meaning "Alchemists."

For their spiritual headquarters the Pheryllt built Emrys, the "ambrosial city," on a cliff overlooking the Irish Sea. Also called Dinas Affaraon, the place of the "higher powers," and later referred to as the "City of the Dragons of Beli," Emrys was the seat of the mysteries of the Serpent Goddess Keridwen and the location of initiation rites into her sacred cult.[32] Here the Pheryllts practiced alchemy and yoga and imbibed mind-expanding, hallucinogenic herbs mixed within the "Cauldron of Keridwen."

The Pheryllt are famous for having established orders of both male and female Druids. These Druids, also called Adders or Serpents, became the judges, ministers and magicians of the later Celts. One of the outstanding orders of female Druidesses, referred to in legend as the Nine Guardians of the Cauldron of Keridwen, are believed to have been stationed on the Ile de Sein near the coast of France. According to the Roman historian Pomponius Mela, these Druidesses were "endowed with singular powers" and could "raise the winds and seas, turn themselves into animals, cure wounds and diseases, and predict the future."[32]

DISPERSION OF THE LEMURIAN SERPENTS

THE SERPENT COLONISTS OF INDIA

Being in close proximity to Lemuria and having been a part of the pan-Pacific land mass during its earliest period of existence, India or Bharata Varsha, its ancient name which means Land of Bharat," was an obvious destination for migrating Serpents of Wisdom from Mu. The sub-continent eventually engendered a prolific culture of Nagas or Serpents from the Motherland.

THE KUMARA AGASTYA

One of the Indian colonies founded by the Lemurians is referred to in the *Ramayana* and other semi-mythical texts as the Pandyan Kingdom. The Pandyan Kingdom existed upon a land mass which was contiguous to the southern most tip of Bharata Varsha and had once been part of Kumari Nadu or Mu. As an empire it flourished for thousands of years until, according to Tamil records, the greater part of it was swallowed up by a series of devastating floods.

The greatest Serpent of Wisdom of the Pandyan Kingdom was Agastya,

The ancient Pandyan Kingdom uniting India with Mu

Sage Agastya carries the trident of Shiva

Shree Ekambaranatha Temple, Kanchipuram, India

James Churchward and the Continent of Mu

an immortal Master of Yoga and diminutive sage who stood less than five feet tall. Agastyar was a direct disciple of Sanat Kumara and taught the Serpent path that leads to immortality. During his tenure as hierophant of the Pandyan Kingdom the Sage Agastya founded Sangams or "literary academies" for the preservation of the ageless wisdom of the Kumaras. He also established the first Tamil grammar which, according to an annotation by the Sage Eraynar in the Tamil Text, *Kalaviyal Iholkappiyam,* was washed away in a major flood which partially devastated the Pandyan civilization.4

When most of the Pandyan isthmus finally descended to the bottom of the Indian Ocean, Agastyar took the ancient teachings of immortality and traveled to the northern most part of the Pandyan Kingdom, an area known historically as the Pandya Kingdom of South India with its capital city of Madurai. Agastya set up an ashram for the dissemination of the teachings of the Kumaras within South India's majestic Pothigai Hills and from there the timeless wisdom was eventually transported by his students into the heartland of India. According to another legend of his travels, at some point Agastyar journeyed north to Mount Kailas in the Himalayas where he is reputed to have received the secrets of Yoga directly from Shiva, the Lord of the Nagas (Naga means "Serpent").

THE NAACALS OR NAGA MAYAS

Following, and apparently preceeding the destruction of Lemuria, one wave of colonists arrived from Mu known as Naacals (pronounced Naa-kals with K sound of the Serpents) or Naga Mayas. During the 19th century the legends of their migration were revealed to Colonel James Churchward, an officer of the Royal English Anny, and later incorporated into a series of books on Mu published by Churchward.

According to his own testimony, during the late 1800s Colonel Churchward visited a temple in India (now believed to be Shree Ekambaranatha Temple in Kanchipuram) and was informed by the presiding priest that some very ancient tablets were concealed within a secret vault of the temple. He told the colonel that the tablets told the story of a people called Naacals; Naga Mayas or "Serpents" who had anciently migrated from a continent in the Pacific called Mu and later established a colony in India Churchward persuaded the monk to break open the vault and allow him to examine the tablets.

Finding the stone tablets in a badly deteriorated condition, Churchward was, after much tedious effort, able to piece together a series of pictographs from their crumbled remains. He then spent the next two years learning to decipher the symbols until he was able to formulate a coherent story from them. The resulting story then became the foundation for a series of books in which Churchward claimed that the pictographic text not only confirmed the voyage of the Nagas to India but also gave a vivid accounting of the destruction of their motherland, Mu.

In order to gain further proof of the tablets, Churchward claims to have traveled to a Buddhist temple in Burma. There he was told by the high priest that the Naacal tablets and their priceless information once resided within Burma but they were irreverently stolen and carted off to India. The angry priest then rudely spit at Churchward's feet before quickly turning his back on the startled colonel.

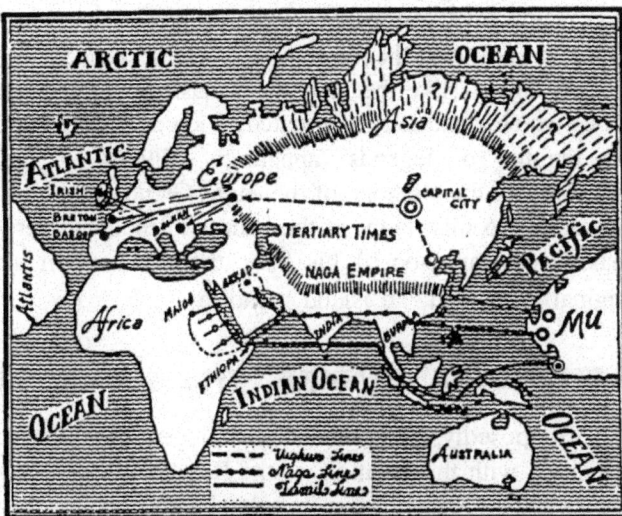

Churchward's map of the Naga Empire

Churchward's corroborative research also included indepth studies of many Hindu legends, such as those in the *Ramayana*. In the famous version of the text authored by the sage Valmiki Churchward located a passage which referred specifically to the Naacals. The text maintained that the early Naga Maya had anciently sailed to Burma and then to India "from the land of their birth in the east." Then, states the text, the Nacaals proceeded to Babylonia and Egypt and were instrumental in establishing mystery schools in those countries.

THE MIGRATION OF SERPENT NAGAS IN THE HINDU SCRIPTURES

The migration of Naga Serpents to Bharata Varsha from Mu might also be alluded to in other authoritative scriptures of India, but under a different name. For example, some texts allude to Rutas, a lost continent from which, asserts the French translater Louis Jacolliot, many of the original inhabitants of India migrated. Rutas appears to be the Hindu term for Rua, a Polynesian name for the lost Pacific continent of Mu.

According to Vedic sources of historical information researched by David Frawley, an American who is also an acclaimed Vedic scholar, one of the earliest lineages of priest kings in India are listed in some scriptures as having been descended from the Bhrigus, an order of spiritual adepts which the texts imply arrived in the sub-continent from someplace across a great sea, perhaps Mu. In *Gods, Sages, and Kings,* Frawley delineates a lineage of monarchs which began with the migrating Bhrigus, passed through the "Serpent King," King Nahusha (like the Hebrew Nahash or Serpent), and then divided into five tribes which eventually populated much of India.33 One additional Vedic source, the Puranas or legends, apparently alludes to the Nagas and their island homeland in the allegory of the eagle Garuda and his brothers, the Naga snakes. According to this myth, at the behest of their mother Garuda allowed the Naga snakes to climb aboard his back then flew them across a great sea to their original homeland, an island paradise.

THE RAMA EMPIRE, THE SOLAR/SERPENT DYNASTY

Supposedly, states one esoteric legend, the arrival of the Nagas fromMu coincided with the creation of the Rama Empire. King Rama was the monarch of this empire which, from its capital cities of Ayodhya and Nagpur, the City of Nagas, covered much of the Indian sub-continent. An enlightened priest king, an Avatar or pure incarnation of Spirit, Rama was part of the Solar Race or Lineage which was descended directly from the Solar Spirit. The Solar Race appears to be the Vedic denomination for the Solar Brotherhood or Kumara lineage which had its early manifestation on Mu. Like Rama, the early Lemurian Kumaras were Avatars descended directly from the Solar Spirit. Both the Kumaras and Rama were manifestations of the polarity united, a truth revealed by their names Ku-Ma-Ra and Ra-Ma (Ra-male, Ma-female).

Rama's Empire was a Solar/Serpent Dynasty. As C.F.Oldham rightly contends in his classic, *The Sun and the Serpent,* all ancient Solar Dynasties were also Serpent Dynasties because the Primal Serpent always accompanies and protects its Lord, the Solar Spirit.[34] Within Rama's Solar/Serpent Dynasty there were seven Rishi Cities or sacred centers of learning (seven, the ancient number of the Serpent) which were governed by adept Rishis or Nagas, the Indian Serpents of Wisdom. Many of these Rishi Cities survived into historical times and are today identified with some of the ancient cities of Northern India and the Indus Valley, an area which some archaeologists are now claiming was settled more than 12,000 years ago. Supposedly the seven cities of Rama's Empire were once attacked by the imperialistic Atlanteans with their sophisticated weaponry and the result can be found today as rocks within certain Indus Valley cities which have been found completely fused together, a phenomenon which could have only occurred under extremely high heat, such as a nuclear blast. In proximity to these rocks have also been found skeletons with as high a concentration of radioactivity as those which survived the nuclear bombings of Hiroshima and Nagasaki. [35]

THE SERPENT COLONISTS
OF CHINA AND TIBET

THE NAGA SERPENTS IN CHINA: THE UIGHER EMPIRE

In his book *The Children of Mu* James Churchward claims that according to the Naacal tablets the Nagas of Mu also colonized China and Tibet and created a kingdom in the eastern extremity of Asia known as the Uigher Empire. The leaders of this colony were great conquerors who eventually pushed the boundaries of their empire all the way into Europe. Supposedly many of their descendants became the fair skinned Aryans of history.

Churchward's Empire has apparently been known about within traditions other than that of the Naacals. The great Master Gurdjieff, for example, claims to have been part of an expedition which once searched for one of the Uigher's lost cities, but unfortunately found it buried under tons of desert sand. The map they followed to the city may have had its origin within the very ancient

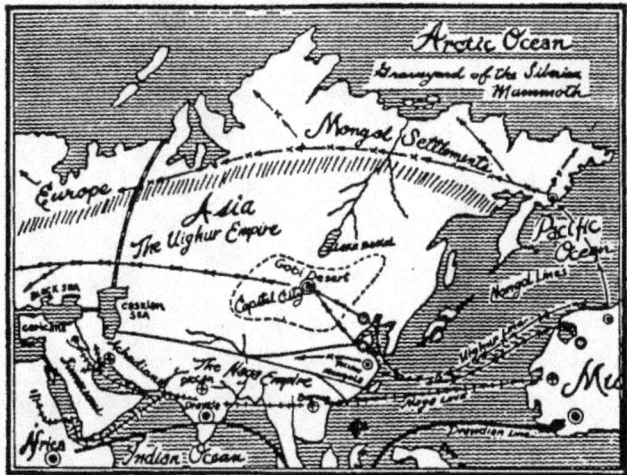

Churward's map of the Uigher Empire

Sun/Moon Brotherhood of Central Asia which Gurdjieff was secretely initiated into. Supposedly the patriarchs of this brotherhood had arrived from Mars during an early epoch of Earth's history.

Years after Gurdjieff's futile expedition, Professor Kosloff, a Russian archaeologist, traveled to approximately the same area in the Gobi Desert the team had been led to. In hopes of uncovering the remains of what he believed would be the Uigher Empire's capital city of Karakota, Kosloff dug down 50 feet until his shovel uncovered a tomb full of unique relics. Among the artifacts was a painting depicting a young ruler and his queen, perhaps the king□ and queen of Churchward's empire. Using advanced dating techniques Kosloff roughly estimated the age of this painting to be at least 18,000 years old. In association with the royal couple was an emblem consisting of a circle divided into four sections in the center of which was a symbol very similar to the Greek letter Mu, perhaps referring to the Pacific continent of that name. Within the tomb was also a small statue of two figures, perhaps a male and a female, which were joined together in one body - possibly a representation of a Lemurian androgyny. Working quickly, Kosloff was able to photograph the symbols□ and statue before the Chinese authorities instructed him to reseal the tomb and□ rebury its contents.

Kosloff's Androgyny

THE RE-LOCATION OF THE LEMURIAN KUMARAS

Perhaps playing a pivotal role in the formation and administration of the Uigher Empire were the immortal Kumara Serpents who also arrived in China at a time preceding Mu's final destruction. The Kumaras, masters of Mu's Thirteenth School, chose China, and specifically Tibet, as a new eastern headquarters for their order of Serpents because of the safety afforded by its high mountains (they knew a planetary deluge was imminent) and because of the elevated land's inherent purity. Once in the precipitous land of snow and ice the Kumaras stored their ancient records and artifacts in the cavernous tunnels which ran under the present city of Lhasa and then proceeded to establish communities in other parts of China. The records of their relocation are still preserved within the legends of some Tibetan monks today.[35]

After the Kumaras had ensconced themselves in Tibet, adepts from all over the globe began to travel there either physically or within their Dragon Bodies of light . Within what was to become the eastern headquarters of the Seven Ray Order or Great White Brotherhood. Here aspiring and confirmed initiates attended special convocations and/or underwent pivotal initiations.

Synchronous with the transference of the Thirteenth School, Sanat Kumara occupied a shimmering golden palace in what is now the Gobi Desert of China and Mongolia. Surrounding his magical fortress in the City of the Seven Gates or "City of the Serpents", was a ring of etheric serpents which served Sanat Kumara as his loyal, protective sentinels. Once settled in his splendid castle, the great Lemurian monarch continued to rule as King of the World from an unseen dimension. According to M.P. Hall, a Rosicrucian adept who personally befriended a Hindu Master and visitor to the City of Seven Gates, throughout the years Sanat Kumara has consistently convened a special assemblyof Serpent adepts at his palace at the end of each Serpent Cycle of seven years.[36]

CITIES OF THE IMMORTAL SERPENTS OF WISDOM: HSI WANG MU/SHAMBALLA/OLMOLUNGRING

What may have been sacred cities of the Uigher Empire have been located in the lofty mountains of Tibet, China and Central Asia. Asian cultures have consistently ascribed to these magical mountains the location of bases and communities of the Serpents of Wisdom. The Kirghiz people of Central Asia, for example, claim that on one of the mountains of the Kun Lun range exists the city of Janaidar, the headquarters of an order of spiritual adepts who cover themselves with long white robes. [37] The Chinese Taoists similarly allude to a community of adepts in the Kun Luns, called Hsi Wang Mu (the Teachers of Mu?), which they describe as a shimmering city of palaces made of priceless gems, such as diamonds and jade, which has for ages been the destination of countless Dragons or Serpent of Wisdom who have achieved immortality. Supposedly it was Lao Tzu's destination when a border guard stopped him and asked him to write down his wisdom for future generations. The Tibetan Buddhists locate a similar abode of mystical adepts in northern Asia which they call Shamballa. Visited by numerous Serpents of Wisdom, including the lineage of Panchen Lamas whose city of Shigatse in Tibet is said to be linked to it by tunnels, this paradise is similarly populated with temples covered with emeralds and diamonds, which stand among numerous "golden roof pagodas. "[37] The people of the land wear "turbans and white robes,"[37] speak Sanskrit and continuously devote themselves to the study of the Kala Chakra, a form of esoteric Buddhism. Shambhalla, the Heart Chakra of Earth, is laid out in the form of an eight petal heart lotus. It is one of the planetary courts of Sanat Kumara, the Spirit of Earth, who sits upon a throne in the center of Shamballa just as each person's inner Spirit sits upon the throne within their heart. Finally, an additional paradise region in the mountains of Tibet which is alluded to in the records of the ancient Bon religion is Olmolungring. The Bon shamans claim that Olmolungring was founded 18,000 years ago and ruled by Shenrab, their first king. Olmolungring and Shambhalla both have a special relationship with the Himalayan Mt. Kailash, the Crown Chakra of Earth, which is another important court of the King of the World.

THE LAKE OF THE SERPENTS

Another mythical mountain community of legend in the Pamir Mountain range is commonly referred to in many Asian texts as the "Lake of the Nagas," the "Lake of the Dragons," or the "Lake of the Serpents." Surrounded by majestic snowcapped peaks, the Lake of the Serpents is often referred to in the texts as a Garden of Eden and one of the original homes of the Asian Serpents of Wisdom. Throughout the present cycle immortal sages have periodically descended down the precipitous mountain slopes contiguous to this azure lake in the clouds in order to disseminate their yogic wisdom among developing humankind. Some of their timeless wisdom, for example, became the foundation of Agni Yoga or "Fire Yoga" which, according to its famous Russian proponent, Nicholas Roerich, was originally disseminated by the Serpents in the "Valley of the Brahmaputra" located directly below the jewel-like Lake of the Nagas.[39]

AGHARTHA, SUBTERANNEAN KINGDOM OF THE SERPENTS

Besides their lofty mountaintop retreats, the Serpents of Wisdom from Mu also founded colonies within the network of tunnels and caverns which run underneath China and Tibet. One such subterranean colony, known as Aghartha, was founded thousands of years ago by the Lemurian Serpents seeking to avert certain destruction from an impending deluge. Their underground kingdom has supposedly been populated by themselves and their descendants ever since.

Legends maintain that the civilization of Aghartha is connected to the outside world through a series of tunnels, some of which terminate inside certain Tibetan monasteries and the cave temples of Tunhung in western China and Ellora and Ajanta in India. Periodically a representative of Aghartha will travel to the surface of the Earth through these tunnels in order to share with humanity an important teaching or prophecy. According to one account, in 1890 the King of Aghartha followed one of the tunnels to the Sakkai Monastery in Mongolia. He was given a royal seat in the abbey and then proceeded to tell a gathering of monks about dramatic changes which would befall the planet during the ensuing hundred years.[40]

Aghartha may be a subterranean branch of Shamballa. The monarch ruling both places is a representative of Sanat Kumara and channels his immense power and wisdom. Or he could be Sanat Kumara himself. According to one Mongolian description of him, the King of Aghartha is an immortal young man who anciently arrived from the planet Venus and whose name is OM. This exactly fits the description of Sanat Kumara from Tamil, Hindu, and other sources.

THE ISLANDS OF THE BLESSED, VESTIGES OF MU?

Other vestigial settlements of the Serpents from Mu may be located on a chain of islands in the Gulf of Chihli off the coast of China. Referred to in the Taoist texts as the Islands of the Blessed, this chain may be the remains of one of Mu's sunken mountain ranges and the domicile of some of the ancient continent's remaining immortals.

The Islands of the Blessed were often alluded to by many of the early Taoist writers and adepts, some of whom claimed to have actually seen the

THE KINGDOM OF SHAMBHALLA

Shambhalla is a kingdom deep with the mountains of Central Asia. It is built in the form of a lotus, with its territories surrounding the inner capital city of Kalapa like petals on a flower. Shambhalla is the Heart Chakra of the world and mirrors the human eight petal Hridaya Heart Chakra. On the central throne of the lotus of Shambhalla sits Sanat Kumara, or an incarnation of him, just as the inner Spirit sits within the human Heart Chakra. Tibet Buddhist legends about Shambhalla maintain that its monarch is an incarnation of the peacock-riding Amitabha. Amitabha is the Tibetan Buddhist form and name for the Hindu Sanat Kumara.

The King of Aghartha, monarch of the world. This image was published in Amazing Stories, May 1946. The accompanying article states:

"He came here ages ago from the planet Venus to be the instructor and guide of our then just dawning humanity. Though he is thousands of years old, his appearance is that of an exceptionally well developed and handsome youth of about sixteen. When mankind is ready for the benefits he can bring, he will emerge and establish a new civilization of peace and plenty."

islands when the weather conditions were accommodating. According to the testimony of the ancient Taoist sage Lieh Tzu there are five prominent Islands of the Blessed including Fang Chang, Ying Chou, and P 'eng-lai the largest of the isles. Lieh Tzu claimed that all the islands are inhabited by god-intoxicated immortals dwelling in transparent, light bodies (Dragon Bodies). They live within structures made of jade and gold and walk among radiant animals which are also etheric. For sustenance the immortals consume the mushrooms of immortality which grow profusely on the islands or drink from the elixir of immortality which continually flows from the islands' jade fountains.

During the Chin Dynasty the emperor Shih Huang Ti sent the sage Hsu Fu on an expedition to the Islands of the Blessed with instructions to return with some of the precious mushrooms of immortality. Hsu Fu found the islands and consumed some of the mushrooms himself but was prevented from taking any with him. For a second expedition the persistent emperor gave Hsu Fu 3000 young boys and girls to exchange for the precious mushrooms, but the sage and his cargo were never heard of again.

THE SERPENT COLONISTS OF THE AMERICAS

AMARAKA: LAND OF THE SERPENTS

Being situated between both Atlantis and Lemuria made the Americas both a stepping stone and permanent destination for Serpent colonists traveling from both Motherlands. It was also a favorite destination for Extraterrestrial Serpents arriving from the Pleiades & other parts of the cosmos. According to the descendants of the early Lemurian record keepers, the Andean Elders, the entire American land mass was anciently known as Amaraka, the "Land of the Immortals"[7] or the "Land of the Wise Serpents." The title Amaraka is derived from the Quechuan-Lemurian word Amaru, meaning snake or serpent (Quechua the language of the Inkas, is derived from Runa Sima, the primal tongue spoken on Lemuria), and ends in the syllable "ka" which denotes both land and life. Apparently echoing the recollections of the Andean Elders, writer H.P. Blavatsky maintains in *The Secret Doctrine* that America is referred to in the Hindu Puranas (legends) as Potala, the Kingdom of the Nagas (Serpents).[15]

THE SERPENT COLONISTS
OF SOUTH AMERICA

ARAMU MURU, THE SERPENT MURU

One of the earliest immortal Serpents from Mu to colonize Amara ka was Aramu Muru or Amaru Muru, the Serpent Muru. According to legend, moments before Mu's final demise the Serpent Muru along with his consort Arama Mara boarded an airship and headed to South America with a cargo of sacred records and artifacts, including a huge golden Sun Disc. The mountains of South America, the Andes, resonated to the same yin vibration as their beloved Mu and were thus considered suitable for the preservation of Lemurian culture. They were also home to the city of Paititi, one of the planetary headquarters of the Seven Ray or Solar Brotherhood, an organization Aramu Muru had been a high ranking member of on Mu.

Upon setting his craft down near the sacred Andean lake of Titicaca, Aramu Muru proceeded to build a monastery for the preservation and dissemination of the Lemurian teachings. This abbey, known as the Monastery of the Seven Rays, became the headquarters of a brotherhood founded by Aramu Muru, the Brotherhood of the Seven Rays. Throughout the secret vaults and caverns situated within and underneath this secluded monastery the Serpent Muru stored an assortment of precious Lemurian records and artifacts, including the sacred Sun Disc. After completing his monastery, Aramu Muru traveled with his entourage of Serpents, the Kapac Cuna, to the banks of Lake Titicaca and built the City of Serpent Wisdom, Tiahuanako, before finally venturing into the heartland of Peru to found the empire of the Inkas. When he eventually ascended the throne of the Inkas as their first priest king, Amam Muru assumed the "serpent" name of Manco Kapac. The title "Ka-pac" carries the meaning of Serpent, wisdom and "spiritually wealthy."

For thousands of years the monastery which had been built by Aramu Muru served as a refuge and secret mystery school for all serious spiritual seekers within the Andes as well as throughout the entire world. However, only recently with the publication of *The Weaver and the Abbey* and *Secret of the Andes* has its existence become public knowledge. The *Secret of the Andes* by George Hunt Williamson was based both on channeled sessions in which the spirit of Brother Philip, an actual resident of the monastery, spoke to the author through a medium, as well as testimonials acquired from a group of pilgrims who made a journey to the abbey in the late 1950's and early '60s. According to the information thus compiled by Williamson, the monastery is situated in the

"Valley of the Blue Moon" deep within the A n d e s Mountains. This semi-tropical valley is fed by "hundreds of beautiful waterfalls (which) dash down great rocks to bring clear pure water from the Andean glaciers into the

According to one legend, Aramu Muru's Monastery of the Seven Rays is close to this magical mountain that resembles a man with his arms outstretched in welcoming.

valley."10 Supposedly a race of little people, perhaps the ancient Lemurians, are the indigenous population of this magical valley.

One member of the party of pilgrims interviewed by Williamson, the late Sister Thedra, remained five years at the abbey after completing the arduous journey to it. She claimed that many ancient records existed there and that there were both highly evolved and very unusual looking people living within the monastery (possibly descendants of Mu and the Extraterrestrial Serpents). When she left the monastery, Sister Thedra returned to her native North America and founded a branch of the Lemurian/Seven Rays Brotherhood called *The Association of Sananda and Sanat Kumara.* Since its inception, *ASSK* has been dedicated to spreading the inspirational teachings of the Solar or Great White Brotherhood and its leader, Sananda Kumara or Jesus Christ, while preparing humankind for an inevitable paradigm shift at the end of current cycle. When Sister Thedra passed on in 1992 her ashes were divided into two portions, one of which was scattered over Lake Titicaca while the other was buried in a small plot at Samana Wasi near Cuzco, the outer retreat of the Solar Brotherhood.

PAITITI, ANCIENT SEAT OF THE ANDEAN SERPENTS

According to the secret knowledge revealed to Antón Ponce de León Paiva by the Andean Elders, Aramu Muru's Monastery was built on the road to Paititi, the most ancient seat of the Andean Serpents. Paititi exists deep within the Andes and Aramu Muru's monastery lies between it and Lake Titicaka.

Long before Aramu Muru arrived from Lemuria Paititi was a Golden City of spiritual wisdom. The name of the city, Paititi, is possibly derived from the Quechuan Pay Quiquin, meaning "The Second Sun," thus revealing the citadel's solar affiliations. Paititi existed during such an early epoch of time that some believe it may have originally been situated on the banks of an ancient sea which once stradled much of northern South America. Legends reveal that close by it was another city of light, Akakor, constructed by colonizing ET Serpents from the planet Shwerta, as well as the ET & Lemurian constructed Tiahuanako.

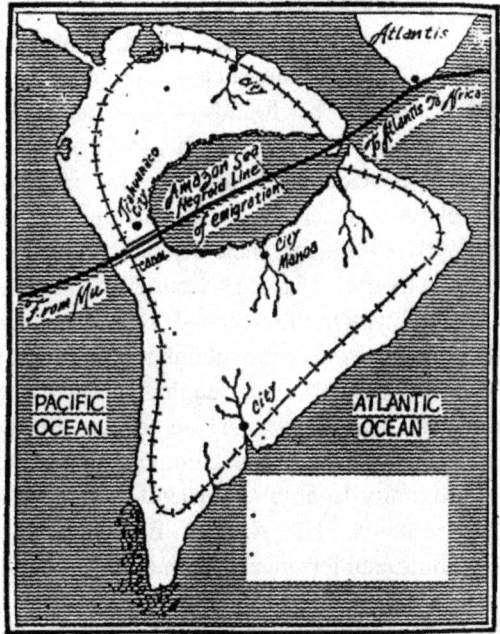

The ancient South American Sea according to Churchward

Legends assert that Paititi is a shimmering city of golden temples. It is entered through a huge, golden gate, on either side of which crouch solid-gold pumas with eyes made of glistening emeralds. At one time many of the residents of this golden city had, like Aramu Muru, achieved the highest spiritual state, union with Inti, the Solar Spirit. Some were physically immutable and lived for hundreds of years. Occasionally groups of immortal Serpents of Wisdom from Atlantis, Lemuria, and certain star systems, such as Sirius, would congregate at Paititi in order to share their spiritual wisdom in an environment of peace and love. Even today, claim the Andean Elders, spiritual adepts from around the world and the outer cosmos will occasionally gather for secret conclaves deep within the Andes Mountains.

During the last major Earth cataclysm Paititi was pushed up to its present elevation on top of Apu Katini in the Andes. Much later in time Paititi would become the last refuge of Incas fleeing from the Spanish Conquistadors. The Incas' long association with the golden city became evident during the reign of the Inka Tupac Amaru, a member of the Paititi Secret Society, who wore the medallion of that elite organization over his royal breast.

CCUSILLUCHAYOC, PERUVIAN MONUMENT TO THE COLONIZING LEMURIANS

Proof of the ancient colonization of Peru by the Serpents from Lemuria can currently be found on the physical plane near an outcropping of rock overlooking Cuzco. Here a group of monkeys carved in relief upon a block of granite provide the setting for the monument of Ccusilluchayoc, "The Place of Monkeys," which, according to the Andean Elders, marks the location where a huge flying saucer anciently landed in the Andes from a land across the "Great River" to the west, i.e., Lemuria.7 The saucer brought explorers and colonists, some of which intermarried with the indigenous population thereby investing the people of the mountains with their spiritual Lemurian seed. These culture bearers from Mu also taught the Andean people many sacred andmundane arts they had learned within the schools of the Kumaras on Mu. When they finally died their coffins were ceremoniously interred under the soil of Ccusilluchayoc in proximity to an underground initiation chamber that is perpetually guarded by two serpents. The Andean Elders believe that their tombs, artifacts, and the adjoining subterranean chamber will be discovered in the very near future.

The Place of the Monkeys is currently regarded to be an interdimensional portal which can be used for interdimensional journeys and communication. Unfortunately it is sometimes patronized by many Andean Shamans practicing black magic and therefore not always safe forspiritual work.

THE ANCIENT INKAS

Proof of the great antiquity of Andean civilization can also be found in certain authentic Spanish histories of the Inkas. For example, according tothe Inkan records gathered by one of the first Spanish chroniclers in Peru, Fernando Montesinos, there were actually two Inkan empires, the historical one and a much more ancient one. Montesinos contended that the capital of the first empire, Cuzco, was founded by the first Manko Kapac (a.k.a. Aramu Muru). When a catastrophic earthquake decimated this early capital, Cuzco was abandoned and the Inkas fled to a mountain top retreat. While inhabiting this mountain colony (believed by some historians to be Machu Picchu), a second Manko Kapac was born. He subsequently led the Inkas back to Cuzco and founded the historical Inkan capital upon the foundations of the old one.41

Confirmation for the antiquity of Andean civilization has also come thro ugh the work of certain astro nomers wh o cl aim to have discovered very anc ient celestial alignments in some of the Inkan ruins. Studies conducted at Machu Picchu and Tiahuanako by Arthur Posnansky, an archaeologist who spent thirty years studying the sites, and Rolf Müller, professor of astronomy at the University of Potsdam in Germany, have revealed that certain astronomical indicators, such as the Intiwatana (the "Hitching Post of the Sun") at Machu Picchu, were in perfect alignment with fixe d star positions of the fifth and middle of the third millenniums B.C., thereby suggesting a possible Inkan occupation at these times. Posnansky further determined that Tiahuanako was astronomically aligned with celestial positions during the much e arlier date of 10,050 B.C. and may, therefore, have even been colonized by Lemurian settlers as legends maintain.

ATLANTEAN MIGRATIONS NORTH VIA PERU

After Aramu Muru led an infiltration of Lemurian colonists into the And es, legends suggest that many settlers from Atlantis also colonized the mountains and assisted in the construction of the hilltop megaliths of the "Inkas." The Andean Elders maintain that the influence of Atlantean builders can be seen as the small blocks which form the walls of certai n Inkan enclosures in contrast to the massive polygonal shaped blocks (those gigantic stones commonly associated with the Andean megaliths) which were set into place by the Lemurians. According to north Ame rican legends, after completing their sojourn in the Andes some Atlanteans tra veled north to become the ancestors of certain Native American tribes.

THE SERPENT APACHES

One North American tribe which claims to be descended from the early Atlantean colonists of Peru are the Mescalero Apaches of Arizona. Their fascinating history was recorded by Lucille Taylor Hansen in her book *The Ancient Atlantic* following a visit to the tribe in the early 1960s.

According to secret informa tion retained by Asa Delugio, the Mescalero Apache chief who confided in Hansen, the Apache ancestors were originally "Serpents" who fled in boats from a sinking island homeland in the Atlantic called Pan or the Old Red Land . Following a series of adventures these refugees arrived in the And es where, as the "Men of the Mountains" they assisted in the construction of many megalithic stone cities (Tiahuanako, Machu Picchu) as well as a network of "Serpent Tunnels" which they burrowed into the mountains. Eventually they were conquered by marauding And ean bands of savage warriors and forced to travel north, which they did through a Pan-Amcerican, pre-existing tunnel system (perhaps created by the first Serpents of Amaraka) and by various sea routes. Their misfortune followed them, however, and when the tribe finally arrived in southwestern North America they were once again besieged by hostile forces in the form of Athapascan speaking Indians. The male members of the migrant Mountain Men were then slaughtered and the remaining women were forced to mate with their conquerors. The descendants of this union between the Athapascans and Atlantean Serpents became the Mescalero Apaches.

When L. Taylor Hansen first heard this astounding legend of the Apaches' ancient origins, she realized that she had stumbled upon a gold mine. Having been an inveterate enthusiast of Atlantean lore for many years, Hansen believed that the Mescalero Apaches might somehow serve as a missing link in a plausible reconstruction of the Atlanteans' dispersion. This belief and the Apaches' amazing story were confirmed soon afterwards when she attended the Mescalero Apache Crown Dance, a ritual dance which had once been performed on the Motherland in honor of the ancient Atlantean fire god. During one memorable summer's day, Hansen watched spellbound as a troupe of Apache men with bodies painted from head to toe with serpents entered a ceremonial arena from the east, direction of the ancient Atlantean homeland of their forefathers. Led by the Apache Chief wearing the ancient Atlantean volcanic crown with thirteen points surmounted by a tuft of feathers and followed by four other dancers wearing trident shaped headdresses, symbol of the ancient motherland, the troupe circled a large fire while making symbolic gestures to its flames and the unseen fire god dwelling within. After respectfully worshipping their god, the performers completed the dance and left the arena from the direction they had come. Hansen recorded all she had observed and later discovered that an identical dance was performed by the North African Tuaregs, a people who also claimed to be descended from Atlantean Serpents.

Following the dance, Hansen received some surprising information regarding the headdress worn by the lead dancer. Apparently the unique crown of thirteen points had anciently been worn by the monarchs of the House of Votan, the kings who ruled over Atlantis during the motherland's later days, before being passed down a line of rulers to become the traditional headdress of the Mescalero Apache Chief. Those Apache Chieftains who honorably wore it, including the great Geronimo, became renowned for their supernatural powers as had the priest kings of Atlantis.

When Ms. Hansen returned to the Mescaleros a few days after the Crown Dance she brought with her the lid to a jar which had recently been discovered within a temple of the 1st Dynasty of Egypt. The lid had an image painted upon it which she suspected was that of a d a n c e r participating in the Crown Dance. Her suspicions were later confirmed by Chief Asa Delugio who, after seeing it, commanded his people to collect all the possessions of the tribe and offer them as exchange for the lid. According to the ruler, the lid accurately depicted the dance as it had been preformed on the motherland of Atlantis. When Hansen commented that the lid had been attached to a

The Venus Crown of the Apaches once worn by the Atlantean Kings The 13 triangles up and down the sides and the 8 at bottom represent the Venus Cycle of 8 years, when it rotates around the Sun 13 times.

jar full of red clay which, unfortunately, had been broken and lost, the Mescalero chief sadly announced that he was sure that the red clay had been taken from the land of red soil, the Old Red Land.

THE LAKOTA-SIOUX SNAKES

"This (Peru) is the land of our beginning, where we went from the Old Red Land even before it sank, because this land is as old as the Dragon Land of the Fire God (Atlantis)."[11]

These words were spoken by Shooting Star, chief of the Sioux tribe, during a visit to Peru. The chief's belief that he had returned to an old "stomping ground" of his ancestors was confirmed by the special handshake a group of native Peruvian shamans greeted him with. It was the traditional handshake exchanged by his forefathers, the Atlantean Serpents.

Shooting Star's ancestors were the "Turtles," a branch of the fire worshipping Atlantean Serpents. According to their ancient records, following the destruction of the Old Red Land the Turtles traveled on ships to the Caribbean Islands (originally settled by the Ka-rib, Serpents from Atlantis) and thc continent of South America before finally arriving at the Mississippi Delta region. Here they were met by their ancient brothers, the Iroquois Serpents (the name Iroquois means Serpents), who followed them up the river in snake skin covered boats to a territory in the far north. After settling in their new homeland, the Turtles became known as the Lakota (with the K sound of the Serpents) and the Sioux, meaning "Snakes." According to the late Deecod ah of the extinct Elk tribe of the Algonquins, the long journey of the two tribes is commemorated at Serpent Mound in Ohio, which depicts a turtle leading a snake.

The Sioux's early South American connections are apparently corroborated by the word Waka or Wakan, a term found in the dialects of both the Lakota and certain Peruvian tribes. The natives of coastal and highland Peru called the spirits of the unseen world and anything unusual or mysterious as Waka. Similarly, for ages the Sioux have referred to the spirits of the unseen world as Wakan. Their name for the all pervasive, unseen Great Spirit is Wakan Tonka, which means "the Great Mysterious."

THE SERPENT COLONISTS
OF NORTH AMERICA

Along with the Apaches and Sioux numerous other North American tribes also claim to have originated as Serpents on Atlantis or Pan before migrating to America. Most of these tribes, however, reached the North American continent d irectly from the Old Red Land rather than first passing through Central or South America. One such tribe is the Algonquins, perhaps the first natives in North America. The Algonquins claim to have originated in Pan and anciently referred to themselves as Pauns, a name which may have carried the meaning of "colonists from Pan." Another early North American tribe, the Annishnabeg, may have also come d irectly from Atlantis. The name Annishnabeg means "the people from before where the Sun rises," a reference to the Atlantic Ocean. The name of another North American tribe with possible Atlantean roots is Oklahoma, a name meaning "Sun people of the Redland (Atlantis?)." According to Hansen many other North American tribes apparently d esignated themselves as Atlantean Serpents by incorporating the distinguishing K sound within their names. The tribes of this group include the Oklahoma, Muskogian, Choctaw, Cherokee, Mohawk, Comanche and Chickasaw.

Other Native America legends gathered by L. Taylor Hansen maintain that the ancestors of some the tribes were led from Atlantis to the eastern coast of the Americas by a grand son of Votan III, the last reigning priest king of the House of Votan. Upon his arrival in the new land Prince Votan became famous for authoring a book in which he described the identifying marks of a Serpent. Entitled "Proof that I Am a Serpent,"[11] this book supposedly circulated among many of the North American tribes down to the time of the European invasion when it was either destroyed or hidden. The momentous arrival of young Votan and his colonizing party from Pan was for many years commemorated annually by the native North Americans in a feast of Thanksgiving. Later, this Thanksgiving feast was adopted by the English pilgrims to honor their own arrival.

THE KUMARAS OF MOUNT SHASTA

While much of the east coast of North Ame rica was being colonized by the Serpents of Wisdom from Atlantis, some of the continent's western extremity was being settled by the migrating Serpents from Lemuria. One notable base of Mu's colonial expansion was Mt. shasta, a mountain located in the the northern part of California. According to a legend held by the Rosicrucians and other esoteric gro ups, just before some of the last remaining island vestiges of Lemuria sank beneath the waves of the Pacific Ocean, many of the Kumara immo rtals decided to relocate to Mt. Shasta, a mountain which had once been attac hed to Mu and retained the continent's spiritual, yin vibration The mountain also generated the loving vibrations of the heart chakra and was, therefore, compatible to those produced by the migrating Kumara s. Supposedly the immortals from Mu created a civilization on, within, and even under Shasta, and they continue to still exist there today. The City of Telos under Shasta connects with subterranean Aghartha.

Over the years many people have claimed to have tuned into the Kumaras, their etheric civilization and their loving vibrations which continually encircle Mt. Shasta. One of the more famous sensitives of this group is the late Sister Thedra. Sister Thedra was instructed by Sananda Kumara (Jesus Christ) to settle on Mt. Shasta because the sacred mountain provided the ideal environment for channeling the wisdom of the Kumaras, and Sananda had specially chosen her to be his prophetess for the coming Earth changes. On the road leading up Mt. Shasta Sister Thedra established the vehicle for Sananda's planetary clarion call, *The Association of Sananda and Sanat Kumara.* Another less known sensitive, Andrea Mikana-Pinkham, first received transmissions from the Kumaras while in a meditativ e trance at the 10,000 foot level of Shasta. According to her own account of the event never before had Andrea experienced such pure love and wisdom. With tears of ecstasy streaming down her face, she communed with the androgynous essence of all Sons and Daughters of God. Andrea currently resides in Sedona, Arizona where she channels the wisdom of the Kumaras in the shadow of a planetary court & throne of Sanat Kumara.

THE SERPENT COLONISTS OF MEXICO

Since it was situated in the center of the Western Hemisphere and the destination of numerous oceanic currents, Mesoamerica was, like other parts of the Americas, a popular port-of-call for many missionary Serpents of Wisdom arriving from both Motherlands. Some of these colonizing Serpents, such as Pacal Votan, Itzamna, and Quetzlcoatl, eventually became teachers and priest kings of their adopted peoples.

TAMOANCHAN: "THE PLACE WHERE THE
PEOPLE OF THE SERPENT LANDED"

Perhaps the earliest written record of the arrival of Serpent missionaries to Mesoamerica was composed by Bernardo de Sahagun, a Franciscan monk, who arrived in Mexico following the Spanish conquest and became the official historian for his people. Through numerous conversations with the Nahuatl "old people" he learned that the forefathers of the Mesoamericans were Serpents who "came (east) from the direction of Florida, (they) came sailing along the coast, and disembarked in the port of Panuco ... "42 In their colonizing party were "wise men" who had all "the writings, the books, and the paintings" from their homeland (Atlantis?). These Serpents built a city called Tamoanchan.

Two hundred years after Sahagun's history was published, Edward Thompson, a United States consul and archaeologist who was sent to Mexico, was able to elaborate on the arrival of the early Mesoamerican Serpent colonists. The source of much of his information came from certain Mayan brotherhoods, such as the secret Brotherhood of Sh'Tol, which Thompson was fortunate enough to gain initiation into. Through his spiritual mentors Thompson learned that the meaning of Tamoanchan was "the Place where the People of the Serpent landed." And, as Sahagun had rightfully claimed many years earlier, the ancient city had been built along the banks of the Panuco river, the entrance to which was near Tuxpan on the Veracruz coast. The founders of the port city, Thompson discovered, were the "Chanes" or "People of Serpent" who arrived in vessels possessing sides which "shone like the scales of serpents' skins and to the simple natives who saw them approaching they appeared to be great serpents coming swiftly toward them." Upon disembarking these Serpents appeared to be "clad in strange garments and (they) wore about their foreheads emblems like entwined serpents. The wondering natives who met them at the shore saw the manner of their coming with the symbol of the Sacred Serpent, which they worshiped, on their brows... "43

PACAL VOTAN, HE OF THE SERPENT LINEAGE

Another Mexican port-of-call of the ancient Serpents of Wisdom was Valum Votan. According to the Spanish chroniclers, this was where Pacal Votan, "he of the Serpent lineage" and possibly a descendant of the Atlantean Votans, disembark edwith his crew of "petticoated" (robed) missionaries after sailing down the Usumacinta River of the Yucatan Peninsula. Apparently Pacal's arrival occurred at such an early period in the history of Mexico that later historical texts remembered him as one of the first patriarchs in the Americas. In one reference to him, for example, he was called the "first man on the Yucatan whom God hath sent to parcel out the land which is now known as America."[44]

After coming ashore at Valum Votan, Pacal and his robed Serpent entourage traveled inland to a specially selected site and constructed the holy city of Palenque. After installing himself as the priest k ingof a new empire, Pacal Votan served his Mexican subjects for many years as both a teacher and monarch. When he died he was honorably interred in a pyramid which is known today as the Temple of Inscriptions.

Before leaving the Earth Pacal took the time to author an autobiography within which he included a detailed description of his obscure origins. The text survived for hundreds or perhaps thousands of years, but was finally destroyed in a fire in 1691 A.D. by the fanatic Christian Bishop of Chiapas, Nunez de la Vega. Fortunately, salient points of the manuscript were preserved by a certain Brother Ordonez before it was completely consumed in flames. Based upon this salvaged information, Brother Ordonez would later record in his diary that Pacal Votan had come from the land of Valum Chivim and arrived in Mexico via the "Dwelling of the Thirteen Serpents."

Jose Arguelles in his book *The Mayan Factor* speculates that Valum Chavin may refer to a base of the Extraterrestrial Serpents of Wisdom on the Pleiades and its star Maia. Perhaps Pacal Votan came to Earth as an ET Intergalactic Serpent missionary and arrived in Mesoamerica via Atlantis, a continent which L. Taylor Hansen's records allude to as "the Dwelling of the Thirteen Gods."[11]

ITZAMNA, IGUANA HOUSE

Another famous Serpent colonist of the Yucatan remembered in the historical records of Mesoamerica is Itzamna, a name which means dragon and "Iguana House." Also known as "the Serpent of the East," Itzamna was the ancient patriarch of the Itza Mayas and the Son of Hunab Ku, the Great Spirit. His symbol was the Tau cross, symbol of the breath of life and Serpent Son of God.

According to the Mayan *Books of Chilam Balam* and the *History of Zodzil* by Juan Darreygosa, a work which is based upon a text entitled *The Unedited Documents Relating to the Discovery and Conquest of New Spain* (Mesoamerica), Itzamna and his people, the Ah-Canule, the "People of the Serpent," were "the first to populate Yucatan after the flood (of Atlantis?)." Itzamna and the Ah-Canule first settled on the island of Cozumel before migrating to the Yucatan mainland and constructing the cities of Chichen Itza, Izamal, Ake, and Uxmal.

Itzamna's possible Atlantean origins can be deduced by his name and references to him in certain Mayan scriptures. The name Itzamna is a close approximation to Itzamana, one of the Native American appellations for the Dragon Land of Atlantis. In a famous frieze which had been taken from the Mayan settlement of Tikal and stored in the Berlin Museum before its destruction during World War II, Itzamna was depicted as a dragon faced refugee hurriedly rowing away from what appears to be an island besieged by fire and cataclysmic destruction. A Mayan glyph informs us this island is in the east, the direction of Atlantis.

Today many of the indigenous peoples of the Yucatan remember the Serpent Itzamna as their first culture bearer and teacher. It was Itzamna ... "who gave names to all the rivers and divisions of the land; he was the first priest and taught them the proper rites wherewith to please the gods and appease their ill will; he was the patron of the healers and diviners and had disclosed to them the mysterious virtues of plants... it was Itzamna who first invented the characters or letters in which the Mayas wrote their numerous books... "[45]

QUETZLCOATL, THE PLUMED SERPENT
Perhaps the most famous Mesoamerican Serpent of Wisdom to come from the east is Quetzlcoatl or Kukulcan (both names pronounced with the K sound of the Serpents), a culture bearer whose name means "Plumed Serpent" and whose symbol, like Itzamna's, is the Tau cross, symbol of polarity union. According to legend, Quetzlcoatl initially appeared to the indigenous people of Mexico clothed in a long white robe embroidered with red or black crosses, the symbol and colors of the Atlantean fire serpent. Accompanying him was an entourage of builders and masters of both the practical and spiritual arts. While carrying a large staff, Quetzlcoatl led this band of missionaries throughout Mexico and left a trail of megalithic cities and pyramids in his wake. Supposedly one of these pyramids, the pyramid of Cholua, was constructed in part to help the Mexican natives survive the high waters of an encroaching flood (the flood

of Atlantis?). When his work was accomplished, Quetzlcoatl is reputed to have boarded a dragon-shaped vessel covered with snake skins and left Mexico in the direction from which he had come.

Similar to the many Thoth-Hermes of the Egyptian tradition, the Quetzlcoatl of legend was only one of a series of Plumed Serpents who colonized and ruled in Mesoamerica. Perhaps the first Quetzlcoals arrived as part of the culture of Tamoanchan, a name which in the Mayan vernacular translates into "The land of the Plumed Serpent."[46] The lineages of Plumed Serpents these early Tamoanchan Quetzlcoatls helped establish ruled as the priest kings and spiritual masters of the later Olmec, Toltec, Mayan, and Aztec civilizations.

THE ANCIENT CAN OR SERPENT DYNASTY

Evidence of a Serpent dynasty perhaps even more ancient than Tamoanchan was discovered in Mexico by a Frenchman, Augustus Le Plongeon, the first western archaeologist to study the Mayan culture and ruins of Mesoamerica. Le Plongeon claims to have been led by Mayan natives through the thick jungles of Mexico to a mausoleum near Chichen Itza within which were the remains of King Coh, an ancient king of the Can or "Serpent" dynasty. Covering the mausoleum walls were serpentine motifs chronicling the long history of this archaic Can dynasty. One such motif depicted King Cob engulfed within the protective coils of a twelve headed serpent, Nonoca Can, the totem animal of the Can dynasty. Next to this illustration was a legend which stated that the 12 heads on Nonoca Can represented the 12 Can dynasties which had collectively reigned over Mexico for 18,000 years prior to King Cob. In order to date the existence of Coh, Le Plongeon followed clues in the Troano Manuscript, a Mayan scripture, and estimated that the king reigned 16,000 years ago. By adding 18,000 and 16,000 together Le Plongeon estimated that the first Serpent dynasties in Mexico were in existence at least 34,000 years ago.[44]

Soon after Le Plongeon's discovery, a good friend of the French archaeologist, James Churchward, theorized that the Can Dynasty had been a colony of the ancient Naga Maya from Mu. This made sense to Le Plongeon since he had heard legends of the Naga Maya from his guides in Mexico. Churchward's theory was indirectly corroborated soon afterwards by a discovery made by another archaeologist, William Niven. While sifting through an excavation in an area between Texcoco and Haluepantla, Niven found over 20,000 stone tablets which were covered with unusual symbols, some of which were identical to the ones Churchward had seen covering the Naacal Tablets in India. Since the Mexican tablets were found in conjunction with the remains of three buried rooms, the first of which was estimated by Niven to have belonged to a civilization which had existed at least 50,000 years ago, they were apparently synchronous with, and perhaps relics of, the ancient Can Dynasty. Given the tablets' similarity to the Naacal Tablets, their creators, i.e., the artisans of the Can Dynasty, could definitely have been a branch of the Naga Maya from Mu.

CHAPTER 4

THE WORLDWIDE DRAGON CULTURE

Once the Serpents of Wisdom of Lemuria and Atlantis had succeeded in founding colonies and kingdoms throughout the Earth, the "Dragon Culture" they had brought with them from the Motherlands quickly established itself as a worldwide phenomenon. For millennia thereafter, or until the modern Christian era, the elements of this Dragon Culture could be found as an integral part of most major empires and countries around the globe.

THE ELEMENTS OF THE DRAGON CULTURE

There were seven (number of the Dragon) principal elements of the Worldwide Dragon Culture. They included:

1. Construction of megalithic temples, pyramids and Dragon Communities over dragons' lairs.
2. Observance of universal burial customs to preserve the Dragon Body.
3. The observance of dragon calendars determined by the movements of the Celestial Dragons: the Pleiades, Venus, the Moon etc.
4. Rule by a priest king who was an embodiment of the Primeval Dragon and referred to as a "Dragon," the "Twins" and/or the Solar Spirit enveloped in matter.
5. Veneration of a Dragon Creator of the Universe.
6. The adoption of a "Dragon" name to invoke the power of Spirit and as a title for the Serpents of Wisdom.
7. The practice of yogic disciplines by which a spiritual seeker could unite the polarity, raise the inner fire serpent and transform into a Serpent of Wisdom.

These seven elements and their manifestations in the civilizations around the world will be covered in the following chapter.

I. CONSTRUCTION OF MEGALITHIC TEMPLES, PYRAMIDS, AND DRAGON COMMUNITIES OVER DRAGONS' LAIRS

DRAGONS' LAIRS AND GARDENS OF EDEN

When the Serpents of Wisdom left the Motherlands they traveled along the Earth's etheric highway of dragon lines to vortexual intersections or "dragons' lairs" (see Appendix). These high powered vortexes were naturally occurring "Gardens of Edens," places of creation on the Earth's surface where the male/female principles united to produce an abundance of life force. Such places were recognized by the Serpents as ideal locations for civilizations to prosper.

Upon reaching their respective dragons' lairs, the colonizing Serpents made use of the three powers of the Primal Dragon to build their new empires. The creative and preserving powers of the serpent life force were harnessed for the purposes of fertilization, the erection of towering buildings and material abundance. The destructive/transformative power of the serpent was utilized for the purposes of spiritual growth and evolution.

HOMES OF THE SERPENT

The colonizing Serpents knew that the dragon living within each dragon's lair took the form of a serpentine spiral of energy. Some adepts could even psychically "see" its spiralling, etheric body. In order to capture, amplify and fully utilize this cone shaped spiral, the Serpents placed special energy conductive structures, such as pyramids, ziggurats, mounds, stone circles and obelisks, over the vortexes. When placed in the center of a dragon's lair these megalithic forms became the physical home of the etheric serpent and its spiralling body continually moved up, down and around both the inside and outside of such structures. In order to make them more conductive, Phi or the Golden Proportion, the numerical constant which determines the serpent spiral, was incorporated into the dimensions of these structures. Using Phi as a base measurement insured that the megaliths would fully harmonize with the movement of the life force.

DRAGON COMMUNITIES

When the serpent life force spiralled down one of its megalithic homes and met the ground, some of its life producing essence was transferred into a network of dragon lines which branched off from the conductive structure. This essence then traveled within the Earth's etheric corridors for many miles in all

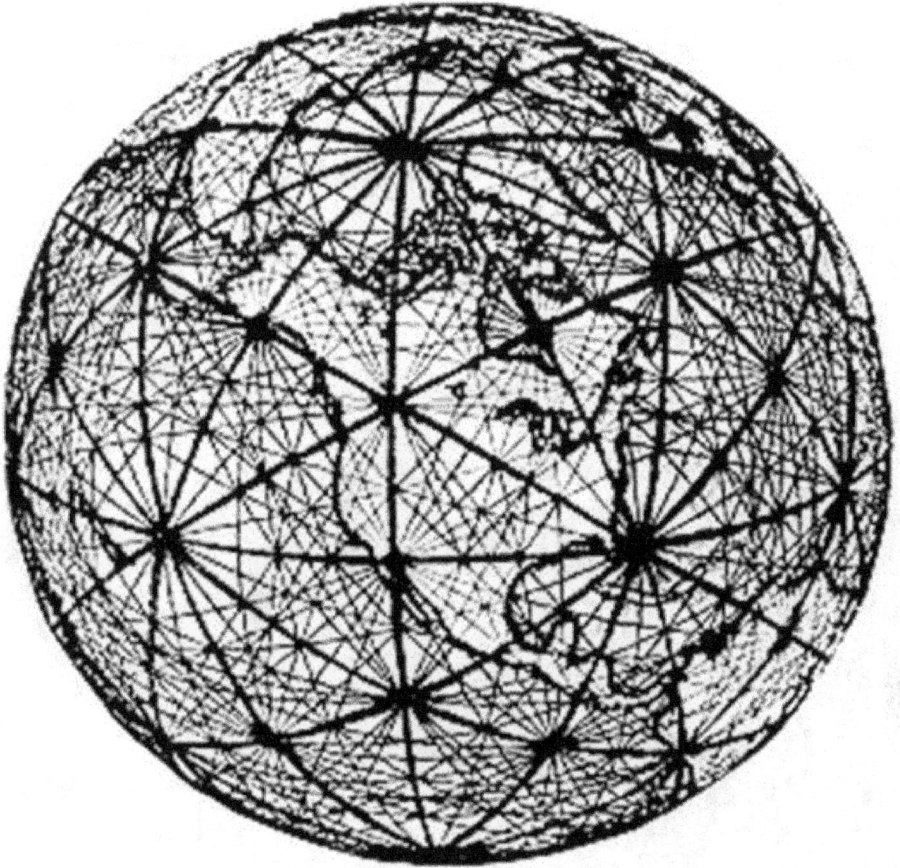

*Earth's "Dragon Body" of Dragon Lines
and Dragon Lairs*

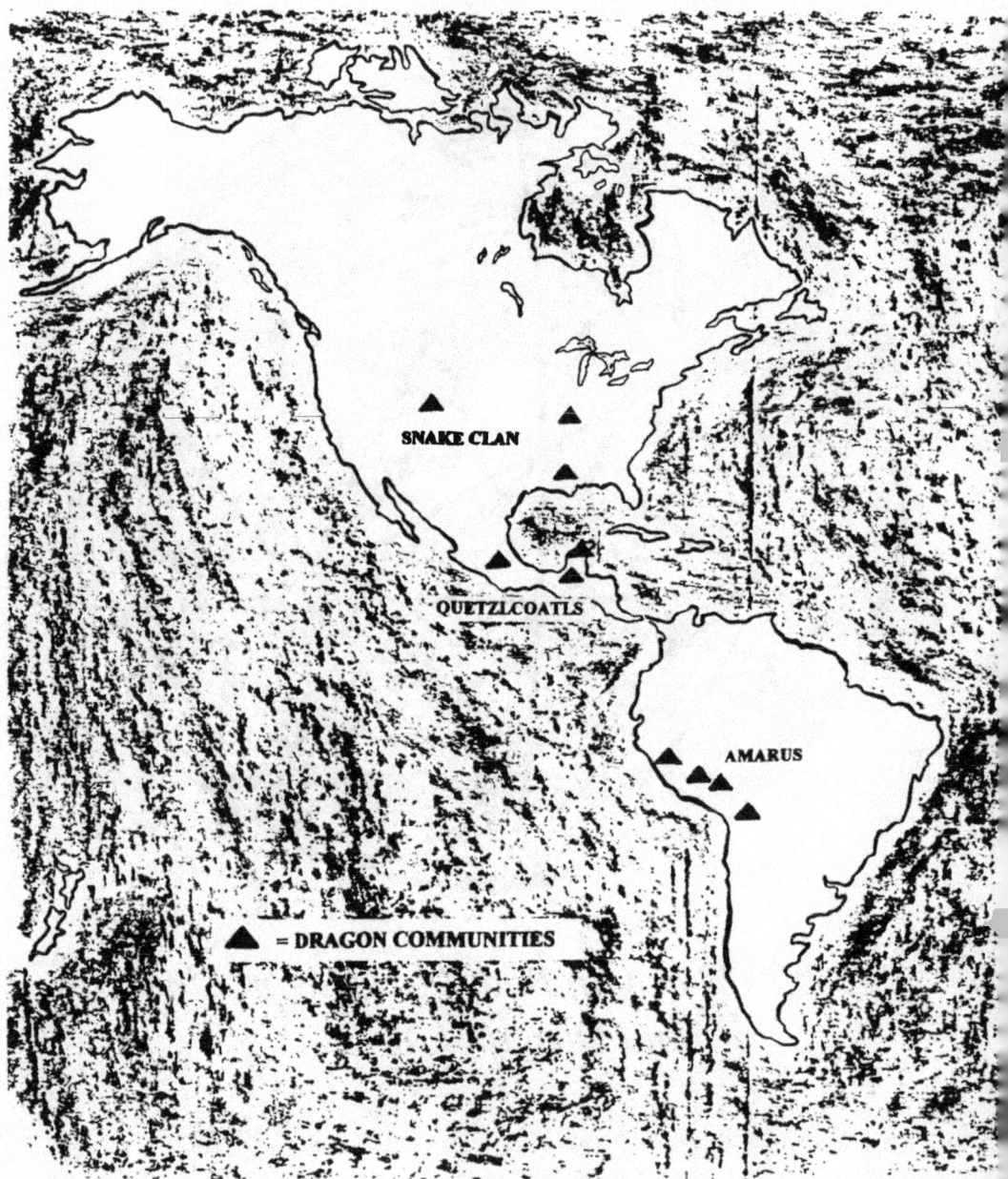

SNAKE CLAN

QUETZLCOATLS

AMARUS

▲ = DRAGON COMMUNITIES

The Worldwide

RUID ADDERS

DACTYLOI

ASHIPU

LEVITES

DJEDHI

NAGAS

LUNG DRAGONS

TUAREGS

Dragon Culture

directions. In order to harness this dispersing life force and not let it dissipate, the colonizing Serpents strategically set dwellings and buildings along its pathways and then tied them together in geometrical grid formations. In the form of crosses, triangles, six pointed stars and spirals, these geometric al circuits were able to retain the emanations of the central megalith while circulating its nourishing life force to all the structures within the grid. Collectively, all the structures comprising such grids produced self sufficient "Dragon Communities."

THE WORLDWIDE DRAGON COMMUNITY

Since they were set over vortexes, all the individual Dragon Communities were naturally connected to one another via the Earth's network of dragon lines. In this way they created a planetary or Worldwide Dragon Community. While circulating throughout this larger planetary community the life force would sequentially pass from one Dragon Community to another until it had completely encircled the Earth's Grid. Messages relayed between the individual Dragon Communities could also be broadcast along the dragon lines. Their transmission and reception was facilitated by the cone or pyramidal shape of the central megaliths which thereby functioned as antennae.

Some special Dragon Communities were strategically built upon very powerful dragons' lairs and could monitor the communications and amount of life force circulating within a large portion of the planetary grid. These significant Dragon Communities were chosen as "Control Centrals" for their part of the planetary grid and as planetary headquarters for the Serpents of Wisdom.

THE GALACTIC DRAGON COMMUNITY

The Earth' s Grid naturally tied into the larger Extraterrestrial Grid of interstellar and interplanetary dragon lines, thus making the Worldwide Dragon Community a member of a Galactic Dragon Community. These celestial or "axiatonal lines"[1] emanate out of planets and star systems before eventually arriving on Earth to connect with the planetary grid. Ultimately they unite with the human etheric grid of subtle energy vessels (see Appendix 1, 11.10), thereby uniting each Earth human with the larger Galactic Community.

In order to be fully connected to the Extraterrestrial Grid, Serpents of Wisdom around the Earth strategically oriented their pyramids, mounds and temples to significant star positions such as Sirius, Arcturus, the Pleiades, and Orion. In doing so they aligned with the axiatonal lines streaming to Earth from these stars while simultaneously establishing a link for the reception of communication coming from their space brothers and sisters, the Extraterrestrial Serpents of Wisdom.

THE WORLDWIDE DRAGON COMMUNITY

THE GRIDS AND MEGALITHS OF EGYPT

THE GREAT PYRAMID: COLOSSAL HOME OF THE SERPENT

One of the most powerful Dragon Communities upon the Earth's grid and a principal destination of both the early Extraterrestrial and planetary Serpents of Wisdom was built by migrating Atlantean Serpents on the Giza Plateau in Egypt. This Dragon Community and the huge vortex it sat upon was powerful not only because of its significant position upon the world grid, but also by virtue of its location in the exact geographical center of the land mass it sat upon. Such positioning made the Giza vortex a perfect balance of north and south and a unify ing point of the polarity.

To design and supervise the construction of the most powerful megalith of the Giza Dragon Community, the Great Pyramid, one of the Serpent Masters of the lineage of Thoth-Hermes was dispatched to Egypt by the Kaberoi Brotherhood of Atlantis. He was assisted in this task by the "Seven Sages," who were other Kaberoi adepts, as well as Extraterrestrial Serpents that had been in intimate contact with the Motherland and had chosen the structure to be one of their principal receiving and monitoring stations on Earth. Using the inherent creative power of the vortex along with sophisticated anti-gravity technology, the Great Pyramid's building crew easily maneuvered into place 2.3 million blocks weighing approximately 2.5 tons apiece. While using phi as a base measurement for the pyramid's dimensions, finely cut limestone blocks were set into place at an angle of approximately 52 degrees (5+2=7), the "angle of the Serpent," along with quartz crystal infused granite to fully magnify the pyramid's indwelling Serpent life force, and to intensify signals being transmitted to a from the pyramid to ET and Earth-based Serpents of Wisdom.

ON OR HELIOPOLIS, TEMPLE OF THE PHOENIX DRAGON

Following the completion of the Great Pyramid, the colonizing Serpents of Atlantis, and their later descendants, marked many of the other dragons' lairs on the Egyptian grid with energy conductive markers called obelisks. Obelisks are "frozen snakes" which support the Serpent life force as it spirals between Heaven and Earth. Their shape was presumably inspired by huge generator crystals, such as the Atlantean "Fire Stones," the life force accumulators and amplifiers which had been placed over powerful vortexes on the Motherland.

The first obelisk in Egypt was built over a dragon's lair at a site called Anu, Heliopolis, or On, the sacred "City of the Solar Spirit," which was situated across the Nile River from the Gre at Pyramid. This first obelisk consisted of an oblong stone monolith upon which rested a pyram idal or conical shaped stone called a Ben Ben stone. The Ben Ben stone was named after the Benu or Phoenix, a form of the Dragon which lived in the vortex but was also continually arriving as life force from the Sun. The energy of the Phoenix was considered to be especially potent at the beginning of a new cycle of time just as the power of the Dragon or Serpent was in other cultures. To illustrate this event an allegory arose at Anu which maintained that the Phoenix would come to perch upon the obelisk at the beginning of each new Phoenix/Dragon Cycle.

Eventually the priest scientists of On constructed a temple around their primary obelisk and called it the Het Benben, the "Temple of the Phoenix." Soon after its construction another obelisk was built at Letopolis and tied to the Anu "frozen snake" by dragon lines. These two obelisks were in turn united by dragon lines to the Great Pyramid and thereby created a powerful triangulation of energy and an expanded Dragon Community.47

KARNAK-THEBES, PILLARED TEMPLE OF THE SERPENT

Besides their utilization of obelisks, the sacred scientists of Khem also placed pillared temples over their dra gons' lairs. Similar to a pyramid or obelisk a pillared temple amplifies and fac ilitates the movement of the serpent life force in or out of a vortex. Each pillar of such a temple is a cosmic tree upon which the serpent is continually moving between Heaven (the roof of the temple) and Earth (floor of the temple).

The greatest of Egyptian pillared temples, the Temple of Ammon Ra, was built over a powerful vortex at Karnak, Thebes (with its K sound, Karnak was designated an official dwelling place of the serpent). Entered between two large obelisks flanking its entrance, the temple of Ammon Ra consisted of a long hallway lined with two rows of colossal pillars. This grand hallway led to the center of the temple within which was located the naos or home of the god Ammon. During the summer solstice, the rays of the Sun activated each tree/pillar as it traveled down the corridor before fully illuminating the indwelling statue of Ammon Ra. Each pillar was approximately 60 feet tall and 60 was the nwnber of years comprising an important Egyptian cycle of time; a cycle which was reputedly based upon the number of teeth in the mouth of a crocodile, a manifestation of the serpent in Khem. Therefore, "serpentine dimensions" were apparently incorporated into the tree/pillars of Karnak.

EGYPTIAN SERPENT TUNNELS

Connecting the Egyptian pyramids and temples was a network of large caverns and tunnels within which the Serpents of Wisdom of Khem traveled and conducted many of their secret rituals. Traditionally these tunnels followed the course of energy lines and led to underground caverns and important dragon lairs. While commenting on this network H.P. Blavatsky wrote in *The Secret Doctrine*: "There were numerous catacombs in Egypt, some of them of a very vast extent. The most renowned of them were the subterranean crypts of Thebes and Memphis. The former, beginning on the western side of the Nile, extended towards the Bian desert, and were known as the Serpent's catacombs, or passages."

GRIDS, MEGALITHS AND DRAGON COMMUNITIES OF THE MEDITERRANEAN

During and after they were constructing megaliths over the dragons' lairs of Egypt, the Serpents from Khem joined with their ancient Atlantean brothers and sisters, the Pelasgians, Libyans, Amazons and colonists from Asia Minor, in order to transport the universal Dragon Culture to many other vortex centers throughout the Mediterranean. At these places they created awesome Dragon Communities around powerfully charged megalithic circles and temples.

MALTA, THE SERPENT SPIRALS

One of the first places in the Mediterranean chosen by the dispersing Serpents of Wisdom as a location for a Dragon Community was Malta. Before the deluge that sunk Atlantis and created the Mediterranean Sea, Malta had been colonized by the Atlantean Serpents & "Fat Lady" temples were built in honor of their Serpent Goddess. Many serpent images and elongated skulls of these early Serpents have been found on Malta. After the Great Flood Malta provided the Serpents with a base from which they could regulate the flow of mariner traffic and information throughout the entire Mediterranean basin.

On Malta the Serpents designed a megalithic temple compound which served as both an astronomical observatory and a Mediterranean mystery school. Its natural megalithic cave temples and hand-carved Hypogeum were used for sacred purposes and its dark tunnels simulated the path of the deceased soul through the dark, forbidding underworld. The entire island was once swarming with a network of secret tunnels and caverns used to unite with the Earth Mother and for initiations. And judging by the mushroom-shaped altars of Malta, it appears as though hallucinogenic mushrooms may have once played a pivotal role in these subterranean rites.[48]

To symbolically designate Malta as a dragon's lair, the builders of the island's many temples inscribed recurring spirals upon their blocks. The spirals were drawn singularly, representing the Serpent Goddess, and in pairs or as trinities representing her double or triple powers of creation, preservation, and destruction. The island was also originally known as Ma Lato, the place of Mother Lato, the Serpent Goddess. Worship of the Serpent Goddess in the form of a nine foot tall human goddess with alternating heads was performed within the main temple of Hal Tarxien by the priests and priestesses of Malta.

CRETE, THE SERPENT LABYRINTH

Another important Dragon Community of the Mediterranean Grid was built upon Crete, an island kingdom from which priest kings ruled over the entire eastern end of the Mediterranean.

Crete was comprised of numerous dragons' lairs. Some of these vortexes manifested as the island's lofty, "cosmic mountains" which were natural unifiers of Heaven and Earth. Within their upper caves the Dactyloi priests, descendants of the Kaberoi Serpents of Atlantis, gave secret initiations into their ancient order. Another Cretan power spot located within the lower elevations of the island became the site of the famous Cretan Labyrinth, a ritual testing ground for candidates seeking initiation into the mysteries of the Serpent Goddess and her divine Bull Son. The meandering form of the Labyrinth evolved out of the spiralling shape of the dragon's lair over which it was built. Another labyrinth, the palace/temple of the Cretan priest kings in Knossos, was similarly designed in the form of the serpent spiral it rested upon.[49] In his palace/temple the priest king Minos gave initiation into the island's Serpent/Bull cult.

GRIDS, MEGALITHS AND DRAGON COMMUNITIES OF ITALY, GREECE AND ASIA MINOR

During and after the construction of the megaliths of Malta and Crete many Serpent missionaries of the Worldwide Dragon Culture also traveled to other grid points in the rim territories surrounding the Mediterranean. In Italy, Greece, Spain and Asia Minor they supervised the construction of giant megalithic monuments and prolific Dragon Communities.

While colonizing Italy and Greece, the early Serpents of Wisdom of the Etruscan and Pelasgian cultures supervised the erection of megalithic monuments over powerful dragons' lairs and then united them by roads placed directly over etheric dragon lines. Many of these Etruscans' "dragon" roads were later improved upon by the empire minded Romans whose sorcerers were known to travel to their intersections and use the serpent power emanating from the underlying vortexes to empower their magic. The Greeks marked their vortexual road crossings with Hermes, phallic counterparts of the obelisks of Egypt which similarly united Heaven and Earth. The Greek dragon roads terminated at the largest of the Hermes which were often placed at the center of Greek cities or villages, thus revealing that the early Greek cities were also Dragon Communities built around vortexes.

Some of the more powerful vortexes in Greece, such as Eleusis, Athens, Delphi, and Thebes were chosen specifically as locations for sacred cities and Dragon Communities. Within the vortex of Eleusis was constructed a huge pillared temple 2717 square meters in size, as well as an underground initiation labyrinth. Over the dragon's lair in Athens was built the Acropolis and its pillared Parthenon which was oriented towards the Pleiades. As a home of the serpent, the Parthenon incorporated into its dimensions Phi, the serpent spiral (the ratio of its height to its base was 5:8, the Phi proportion). At Delphi the vortex, which was recognized to be an omphalos or "navel of the world," took the shape of a deep chasm over which a "Pythion Priestess" sat in a trance while speaking the oracles of the indwelling serpent power. The original temple at Delphi was painted red and black, the colors of its resident fire serpent. Over the vortex of Thebes, the famous "City of Seven Gates" or "City of the Dragon," the legendary Mycenaean king, Kadmus, built a palace/temple complex within which initiations into the Aegean mysteries, such as those of the Kaberoi, could be administered. The palaces of other Mycenaean kings were also built upon the foundations of ancient Pelasgian temples and thereby similarly set upon dragons' lairs.

One of the most astonishing megaliths assembled by the Mediterranean Serpents is today located at Ba'albek, Lebanon along the Asia Minor coast. Consisting of blocks weighing nearly one million pounds, this megalith was originally built in the form of a huge platform and later, during Roman times, became the foundation for the famous Temple of Jupiter. Arab legends maintain that the blocks were set into place by a "tribe of giants" soon after the deluge. These giants may have come directly from Atlantis or indirectly from Egypt as a similar legend in Britain maintains that giants from Africa were the original builders of Stonehenge. It is also possible that the Ba'albek platform was set into place by giant Extraterrestrial Serpents. Two proponents of this theory, a Soviet scientist named Dr. Agrest and the Mesopotamian archaeologist Zecharia Sitchin, have expressed a common belief that the platform was erected by aliens to serve as a landing pad for their visiting spacecraft.

GRIDS, MEGALITHS AND DRAGON COMMUNITIES OF THE EUROPEAN COAST

Many missionaries of the Dragon Culture eventually sailed from their colonies in the Mediterranean and Northern Africa and, as the Iberian peoples, created Dragon Communities along the Atlantic and northern coasts of Europe. Because of their extensive coloniz ingefforts Sibylle von Cles-Reden, the author of *The Realm of the Great Goddess,* could later declare: "Towards the end of the first half of the second millennium Atlantic Europe presented the appearance of an organic whole, united by trade, religion and megalithic buildings"50 (i.e., the WW Dragon Culture).

As a sign of their solidarity, the migrating Serpents of Wisdom constructed megaliths with identical serpent motifs throughout Spain, France, Greece, Italy, Ireland and the Mediterranean. The duel spirals at the passage grave of New Grange, Ireland, are, for example, identical to those inscribed upon the blocks comprising the temples of Malta. Similarly, many of the same symbols found within the Mycenaean excavations of Greece have been found decorating the megaliths of Northern Europe.

Perhaps the most impressive serpent temple constructed by the Dragon Culture missionaries along the Atlantic coast of Europe was in France at Carnac or Caim-hac, the "Serpent Hill." This open air temple originally consisted of 11 rows of standing stones, 10,000 in all, which were arranged in the shape of a seven mile long undulating serpent. The cousin of this temple is the pillared temple in the Egyptian serpent city of the same name, Karnac.

GRIDS, MEGALITHS AND DRAGON COMMUNITIES OF BRITAIN

The Dragon Culture arrived in the British Isles via sea and land routes taken by the Iberians, the Egyptians, the Tuatha de Danaan and the Pheryllt. Together these migrant Serpents of Wisdom covered the British dragons' lairs with stone circles, mounds, menhirs and tors (earthen mounds). The tors were manifestations of the mound form of the Primal Serpent and the stone circles were conceived of as being "Temples of Keridwen" or homes of the Serpent Goddess.32

The British megaliths were all united by Ley Lines (the English term for dragon lines) into Dragon Communities. These Dragon Communities were in turn eventually amalgamated into one national British Dragon Community which included the communities of Stonehenge, Avebury, Glastonbury, Bath, and those on the sacred Druidic Islands of Man, Wight, Iona, and Anglesey. Either Stonehenge, Avebury, and/or one of the sacred isles of the magical Druids,could have served as Control Centrals of this northern grid. Perhaps the pivotal vortex was Iona, the "Druid's Isle", or perhaps the Isle of Wight, anciently called "The Dragon's Isle"5 1and recognized to be a natural fount of serpent power.

STONEHENGE, BUILT BY AFRICAN SERPENTS OF WISDOM

The most spectacular of the British stone circles built by the colonizing Serpents is now known as Stonehenge. According to the legend referred to in the *Histories of the Kings of Britain,* by the twelfth century historian and Welsh scholar, Geoffrey of Monmouth, the original builders of Stonehenge were "giants" who traveled from North Africa (Egyptian Serpents of Wisdom?!) and first erected the megalith in Ireland. Then, at the behest of King Ambrosius, the Druid Merlin used his magical powers to transport the stones of Stonehenge to their present location in England.

Within the last hundred years a growing body of evidence has accumulated in support of Geoffrey's tale. It has, for example, been satisfactorily proven that North African architects from Egypt could have built Stonehenge. Along with the Megalithic Yard, the builders of the megaltih used the Royal Cubit, the same unit of measurement incorporated into the design of the Great Pyramid of Giza and other Egyptian temples (see: *The Sphinx and the Megaltihs* by John lvimy, Harper and Row). It has also been convincingly proven that the stones used in Stonehenge's construction were transported from Ireland, Wales or perhaps both countries. The "blue stones" of Stonehenge apparently came originally from Preselly Mountain in southern Wales, 250 miles away. Considering this formidable distance and the ponderous weight of the stones, a logical explanation for their transport was some form of magic. Each stone weighs approximately five tons and would have required 16 men per ton to drag over land if they had been moved manually.

AVEBURY, BUILT IN THE SHAPE OF A GREAT SERPENT

Some stone circles built by the Serpent colonists in Britain assumed the shape of the winged-disc/ureus serpent motif which was a traditional symbol of the Serpents of Wisdom in Egypt. One of the more exceptional circles of this design was set over the dragon's lair of Avebury around 2600 B.C., thereby placing its construction at nearly the same time as Stonehenge and raising the distinct possibility of common architects.

In their original farm the standing stones of A vebury were arranged in the shape of a huge slithering serpent with a circle or disc attached to its back. Within this large circle were two smaller circles which, according to William Stuckely, one of the first researchers in recent times to investigate the British

The Avebury Serpent Temple

megaliths, represented the dual aspects of the androgynous Serpent, i.e., the Sun and Moon or the "Twins." Stuckely claimed that an almost identical arrangement of stones to that of Avebury once existed in nearby Stanton Drew in Somerset, [52] thereby further fueling a theory for the existence of an ancient organization of roving Serpent architects.

GLASTONBURY TOR, THE SPIRALING SERPENT MOUND

Of all tor mounds set into place by the colonizing Serpents in Britain the most significant and strategic appears to be the one erected at Glastonbury. Tor mounds are Heaven/Earth mediators that unite the polarity and give birth to the Serpent. Like the tree in the fabled Garden of Eden, they serve as axis mundis that the serpent moves up and down upon. The Serpent of Glastonbury Tor is easily recognized. It is marked physically by a serpentine trail that winds around the tor seven times, the number of the Serpent. The focus of power is at the apex of the tor, where Heaven and Earth unite and the dragon force is at its most potent. Here both cosmic and terrestrial currents of energy enter or exit the Earth's grid and religious ceremony and initiations are greatly enhanced. Today St. Michael's Tower stands tall and proud at the summit of Glastonbury Tor in commemoration of the archangel who tamed the dragon and held his power in one spot with his sword.

In ancient times Glastonbury was a special destination for alchemists. It was renowned as a place where the polar opposite Red and White Springs united together in the tor to produce the Serpent Power. Water from the springs were gathered up by alchemists to produce their alchemical elixirs. The Serpent Power of the Tor was also known to be generated by two special Dragon Lines, St. Michael's Line and St. Mary's Line, that also united inside the huge mound.

As a place of alchemy, Glastonbury also became a reliquary for the Holy Grail and anciently colonized by Joseph of Arimathea bearing the original Cup of Christ. Legends state that soon after the crucifixion of Jesus Christ, the Apostle Philip instructed Joseph to take the Holy Grail, the sacred cup which had caught the blood of the crucified Messiah, and travel with it to Britain. When Joseph arrived at the Glastonbury vortex he planted his staff into its alchemically charged soil and flowers immediately blossomed from it. Recognizing this as a sign from God that he had found his destination, Joseph proceeded to construct a small geometrically designed Dragon Community in the center of which was built the first Christian Church of Europe. The Grail is reputed to have eventually ended up hidden within Chalice Well or Chalice Hill next to Glastonbury Tor.

THE SERPENT TUNNELS OF BRITAIN

There are many legends of underground caverns and tunnels connecting the British megaliths and used by the northern Serpents of Wisdom. Some legends maintain that the Druids commonly traveled an underground tunnel system between their mystery schools and the various megalithic sites around Britain. Lewis Spence believes a portion of this system still exists under Luogh Derg in Ireland.[53] Supposedly the Druids conducted many of their most esoteric ceremonies and spine chilling initiations within these fabled subterranean passageways and their cavernous outcroppings. Other myths maintain that an entire underground community of elves and magicians called the Tuatha de Danaan, the legendary guiding spirits of the Druids, still thrives in a network of tunnels which pass underneath Ireland.

GRIDS, MEGALITHS AND DRAGON COMMUNITIES OF NORTH AMERICA

The Dragon Culture reached North America via missionaries from Atlantis, Lemuria, Africa and Europe. By the time of the European invasion the Algonquin (or Paun), Iroquois, Lakota, Cherokee, Chippewa, and others of Atlantean and Lemurian heritage had erected 40,000 burial mounds, stone circles and pyramids throughout the North American Grid and surrounded many with flourishing Dragon Communities. Much of their productivity centered in and around the Mississippi Valley area where, as the historical Adena (which existed as early as 2000 B.C.), Hopewell and Temple Mound cultures, they erected thousands of pyramidal mounds, stone circles and serpent mound effigies.

THE TEMPLE MOUND COMMUNITIES

The early North American Dragon Communities are referred to historically as "Temple Mound Communities." They were prodigious in number and it is believed that hundreds of these communities once existed within the Mississippi River Valley alone. In designing such communities the North American Serpents surrounded centrally located pyramids and mounds with dwellings strategically placed in a variety of geometric grid patterns, such as octagons or pentagons. These megalithic communities often swelled to accommodate as many as 25,000 inhabitants.

The central mound or pyramid of a Temple Mound Community was the focus of the community's worship and decision making. On the apex of the mound was often a continuously burning flame, symbol of the Great Spirit and the Serpent Fire, which flourished on the summit. In some cases the worship of this "sacred fire" was overseen by a special class of fire priests, who were descendants of the Serpent Atlanteans that had brought the worship of the Fire Serpent from the Motherland. Surrounding the sacred flame were important temples, governmental buildings and astronomical observatories used for calculating the cycles of certain celestial indicators such as the Sun, Moon, Venus and the Pleiades.

According to the late Dee- coo- dah, a native of the extinct Elk Nation of the Algonquins, at the end of a 52 or 104 year Serpent Cycle a Temple Mound Community would often cease to exist. The eternal flame on top of the pyramid would then be extinguished and the histories of the community and its tribe would be permanently sealed up inside of the mound.

THE SERPENT MOUND OF ST. LOUIS

The Control Central of the eastern North American network of Dragon Communities was located at St. Louis, Missouri. Here, at what is now Chohokia Mound, the Pauns or Algonquins, and later the Lakota and Iroquo is, built a pyra midal complex over a vortex adjacent to the Mississippi River. The strategic position of this dragon lair, midway up the Mississippi, promoted trade and allowed the North American Serpents of Wisdom to monitor the other Dragon Communities throughout the Mississippi Valley.

At its height the politico/religious capital of St. Louis contained numerous pyramids and mounds scattered across a seven mile radius. In the center of the vortex was the largest pyramid, now referred to as "Monks' Mound" and "Serpent Mound." This immense structure, which was created fro m earth and covered with multi-colored painted logs, is reputed to have covered 14 acres, risen 100 feet in the air and thereby rivaled even the Great Pyramid in size and grand eur. Projecting from its base, like the spokes on a wheel, was a network of dragon lines marked physically by streets and avenues. These stre ets united the central Serpent Mound with the other mounds and dwellings within the Dragon Community.

CHACO CANYON, THE DRAGONS LAIR OR SIPAPU

The principal Control Central of the southwestern grid of North America was Chaco Canyon, New Mexico, a Dragon Community built over one of the Anasazis' (the "Ancient Ones") principal dragons' lairs or "sipapus." The sipapus, meaning "navels," were believed by the Anasazis to unite Heaven and Earth to the underworld as well as to connect the current Fourth World with the previous three worlds. Because of its special importance as a major sipapu, a large percentage of Anasazi roads, most of which were built over pre-existing dragon lines, led to the Chaco Canyon metropolis.

In its heyday the Dragon Community of Chaco Canyon was comprised of innumerable subterranean temples known as Kivas interspersed among 12 huge pueblos which provided accommodations for over 7000 people. The kivas, meaning "worlds below," were apparently built over the minor vortexes of Chaco. They were large circular holes in the ground which supplied each clan (snake, bear, antelope etc.) with a meeting place and ceremonial theater. Their different diameters were believed to have possibly generated a variety of frequencies, perhaps corresponding to the seven chakra centers.

GRIDS, MEGALITHS AND DRAGON COMMUNITIES OF MESOAMERICA

The missionaries of the Dragon Culture in Mesoamerica were the founders of Tamoanchan who united with other pioneering Serpents arriving from around the globe, such as the famous culture bearers Pacal Votan, Quetzlcoatl, Itzamna. Together these Serpents covered the Middle American grid with mounds, pyramids, temples and Dragon Communities. By the time of the European invasion, at least 20,000 megaliths were securely in place.

PALENQUE, SERPENT CITY OF THE TREE/CROSS

Like the Great Pyramid of Giza, the dragon's lair of Palenque was placed in the geographic center of the huge land mass it sat upon- the Western Hemisphere- thus making it a perfect balance of male and female energies. Because of its location at the center of the hemisphere, Palenque became the western seat of the world tree/cross and an important Garden of Eden. Representations of the city's distinctive symbol, the tree/cross, were placed within two of its temples, the Temple of the Cross and the Temple of the Foliated Cross. Legends assert that the "Eden" of Palenque was the headquarters of Pacal Votan, the first man and culture bearer on the Yucatan whom God "hath sent to parcel out the land which is now known as America."

Palenque was built in the center of a triangular grid which covered much of the Yucatan Peninsula, the three corners of which were the Mayan sacred sites of Chicheo Itza, Tres Zapotes, and Kaminaljuyu.[1] From this strategic position Palenque served as the Control Central of the Yucatan Dragon Community. The megalithic design adopted for the holy city was reminiscent of Egyptian and/or Atlantean models and points to a worldwide organization of architects. Egyptian influence is clearly evident in both the 52 foot high pyramid surmounted by a temple, and the Tower of the Four Winds. Similar to the pyramid tombs of the pharaohs, the Temple of Inscriptions incorporated the number 52 and was built for the interment of a king's (Votan's) embalmed body

86

and sarcophagus. Such interment procedures were commonly observed in Egypt and possibly Atlantis, but not in Mesoamerica. The four tiers or levels of the Tower of the Four Winds also have their Egyptian counterparts. They closely resemble the four levels of the "coffer" or roof which covers the Kings Chamber in the Great Pyramid of Giza.54

TEOTHIUACAN, CITY OF THE PLUMED SERPENT

Another Dragon Community which may also have been built according to Atlantean and/or Egyptian models was Teotihuacan, Control Central of the western Mexican grid. The main temple or pyramid at Teotihuacan, the Pyramid of the Sun, has approximately the same base dimension as the Great Pyramid of Giza, 754 feet, and incorporates within it the same unit of measurement as the famous Egyptian edifice, the Royal Cubit. Furthermore, the outer angle used in the construction of this Mexican megalith, 43 1/2 degrees, is identical to the slope of two Egyptian pyramids, the Bent Pyramid and the pyramid of Djoser.41 Finally, certain numbers incorporated into the Pyramid of the Sun and other structures within the Teotihuacan compound, 108, 216, 432, 864, and 1296, are standard measurements utilized in the construction of other megaliths throughout the globe and point to a common, worldwide organization of builders. 44

The settlement of Teotihuacan, which can be translated as the "City of the God Wahcan"55 or the "City of the Plumed Serpent," was laid out in the form of a huge cross. Near the site's center was constructed the Pyramid of the Sun, the principal home of the Teotihuacan Serpent and the complex's main ceremonial temple. Under the Pyramid of the Sun was dug seven caves in the form of a seven petaled flower representing the Serpent's seven principles. It was within these caves that the Quetzlcoatls or Plumed Serpents conducted magical rituals, stored important implements and manuscripts and conducted sacred initiations.

TENOCHTITLAN, CITY OF THE SERPENT HILL

Another Mesoamerican "Eden" and Dragon Community built over a vortex was Tenochtitlan, capital of the Aztec empire. The Aztecs were originally led to this vortex by their god, Huitzilopochtli, and found itmarkedby a tree/cross motif: an eagle perched upon the branches of a prickly pear tree or cactus. The cactus was removed and the principal pyramid temple of Tenochtitlan, Coatlicue or the "Serpent Hill," arose in its place. The other buildings and dwellings of Tenochtitlan were subsequently arranged around Coatlicue in geometrical formations.

The Serpent Hill or Templo Mayor, as the Spanish called it, was divided at its summit to become two separate temples, symbolic of the Serpent Twins. The twin temple on the right was dedicated to the Solar Male Twin, Huitzilopochtli, and was painted red, like the fiery Sun. The one on the left was dedicated to the watery Female Twin, Tlaloc, and was painted blue like the ocean. These "Twin" temples were perfectly aligned with the annual cycle of the Sun. During the eq uinoxes the solar rays would pierce the exact center of the common area between the twin temples and strike the opposing Temple of the Plumed Serpent, thus symbolizing that the Twins were unified as the Primal Dragon when the days and nights were of equal length.

GRIDS, MEGALITHS AND DRAGON COMMUNITIES OF SOUTH AMERICA

The Dragon Culture missionaries in South America came directly from the Motherlands or they arrived via Egypt, Phoenicia, and the northern and central parts of the Americas. Under the direction of the Amarus or Serpents massive blocks, some weighing hundreds of tons, were easily transported great distances and set over vortexes high in the Andes Mountains.

TIAHUANAKO, THE CITY OF SERPENT WISDOM

The first megalithic Dragon Community in the Andes was constructed by a team of Amarus consisting of Aramu Muru or Manko Kapac and the Kapac Cuna, Lemurian missionaries of the Seven Ray Order & Solar Brotherhood. They were assisted by Extraterrestrial Serpents from Venus and the Pleiades. Their premier city, now known as Tiahuanako, the "City of Wisdom" and "City of the Serpents," was built over a powerful vortex situated at the confluence of a multitude of dragon lines. Two of the major lines of this vortex created a huge etheric cross which stretched throughout South America and thus provided the Amarus with a communications network capable of monitoring the entire South American Grid. As Control Central for its part of the grid, Tiahuanako was anciently referred to as Taypikala, "the stone in the middle."

In the center of the Tiahuanako vortex the ancient Amarus constructed the Akapana, a huge 150 foot high pyramid. Built in seven tiers and in the shape of a colossal tau cross, the Akapana served as the center of the Tiahuanako Dragon Community and became one of the principal South American homes of the androgynous, septenary serpent. Around it was placed the number of the serpent as 49 huge, monolithic stones (7x7), many of which went into the construction of the adjacent solar temple of Kalasasaya, a name which can be translated in Sanskrit, Quechuan's sister language, as "the place of time" or "place where time began," thus apparently referring to Tiahuanako's function as

The Gate of the Sun and its 225 day Venusian Calendar. Proof of Venusian ET influence?

A model of Tiahuanko and its Akapana step pyramid.

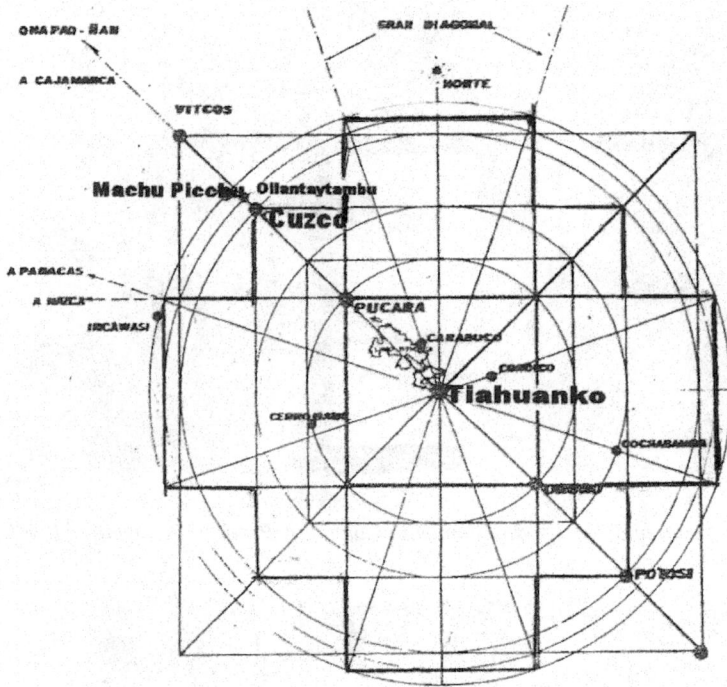

The Andean Chacana or Cross/Stairstep Grid with Tiahuanako in the very center.

the Garden of Eden of South America. The other monoliths provided the boundary walls for the nearby sunken "Serpent Temple" within which was placed prototypal human heads of the races which had been created by Viracocha (Viracocha is the anthropomorphic Spirit) at the beginning of the present cycle of time. When these temples were completed the culture bearing Amarus from Lemuria fully activated the entire megalithic complex with baptismal mantras and then proceeded to establish the customs, traditions, symbols and rites etc. which would characterize most of the Andean civilizations during the current cycle.

After completing their work at Tiahuanako the Amarus traveled throughout the Andes while constructing megaliths aligned with the Tiahuanako vortex. In the process they created a huge Andean Chakana pattern with Tiahuanako at its center. The Chakana was a symbol carved upon many of the blocks of Tiahuanako and other megalithic sites. It unites the form of the Greek Cross with the lightning or "stair step" image of the serpent, thus making it an Andean version of the "Serpent on the Tree/Cross."

Andean Chakana

OLLANTAYTAMBO, HEART TEMPLE OF THE ANDEAN SERPENTS

One of the first Drag on Communities constructed upon the Andean stairstep Grid by the dispersing Amarus was Ollantaytambo, a vortexual mountain upon which was built a huge megalithic temple. In the construction of this glorious temple of light, the function of which appears to have been that of an initiation temple for the opening of the Heart Chakra, the Amarus are believed to have been assisted by Sanat Kumara and some of the other Venusian immortals who journeyed from Mu and left their sig nature at the site as a stairstep motif of five "steps" (most stairstep designs were composed of three steps) which can still be seen engraved upon the only surviving wall of the ancient temple. This same wall is composed of contiguous megalithic stone panels, six in number, the number of the corners of a six pointed star, the symbol of polarity union. In conjunction with the number five, the ancient number of Venus, the planet of love, the six panels point to the temple's function as an initiation temple which was designed for both polarity union and the awakening of the androgynous consciousness existing within the human Heart Chakra. Across from tmple is a huge carving of the head of Tunupa. Tunupa is a name for Sanat Kumara, who in Peru was received as Viracocha incarnate.

CUZCO, THE PUMA/DRAGON'S NAVEL

An other importan t Dragon Commun ity built by the Amarus on the Andean grid soon after Tiahuanako was Cuzco, the capital of the ancient Inkan empire. Cuzco, mean in g "navel," was the confluent point of most major dragon lines which ran throughout the Inkan empire.

The place in Cuzco where most of the South American en ergy lines (and the roads constructed over them) converged became the site of a temple called the Intiwasi, the "Place of the Sun " (it was later renamed the Coricancha or "Temple of Gold" by the Spanish conquerors). Within this temple the most important ceremon ies for creating material prosperity and protection within the Inkan empire were con ducted The creative energy gen erated from these rituals would travel along the South American dragon lines and nourish all parts of the kingdom.

The buildings comprisin g the Dragon Commun ity of Cuzco were connected by dragon lines and arranged in the shape of a gigantic puma. **Along with the Condor and Serpent, the Puma is one of the three sacred animals of Andean cosmology. As the 3 parts of the Cosmic Dragon they correspond to the 3 worlds of Heaven, Earth and the underworld that the Cosmic Dragon became.**

The head of the Cuzco Puma is Sacahuma, "Speckled Head." Its better known name of Sacsayhuaman, meaning "satisfied falcon," is in reference to a massacre inflicted there by the Spanish against the Incas and the feeding frenzy of falcons that came afterwards.

Sacsayhuaman is a hill temple comprised of three rows of gigantic blocks placed in a zig-zag pattern. These massive boulders, some weighing as much as 200 ton s, represen t the puma's teeth an d the path of taken by the dragon curren t as it travels across the Sacahuma vortex. The primary point of power at Sacahuma is at the top of the hill, which is the top of the puma's head. Sometimes referred to as the puma's "eye," this sub-vortex is now delineated by a stone circle surrounded by water channels that further conduct and amplify the vortex's power. It is believed that a stone tower was anciently built upon the ston e circle and here the Inkan high priests would meditate to experience elevated states of spiritual awareness and 3rd eye activation.

MACHU PICCHU, TEMPLE OF THE CONDOR/DRAGON

The vortex of Machu Picchu was, like Tiahuanako and Ollantaytambo, another Andean Dragon Community built by the culture bearing Amarus with the assistan ce of Extraterrestrial Serpents an d the immortal Kumaras from Mu. The calling card of the Kumaras, the Venusian number of five, shows up repeatedly here as it does at Ollantaytambo. Within the main Temple Plaza, for the assistance of Extraterrestrial Serpents and the immortal Kumaras from Mu. The calling card of the Kumaras, the Venusian number of five, shows up repeatedly here as it does at Ollantaytambo. Within the main Temple Plaza, for example, was built a temple of five windows, two of which were later filled in. This temple is now known as the Temple of the Three Windows. Adjacent to this structure was a temple constructed with five windows and the dimensions of 5x7 meters.

Situated high atop the summit of a steep precipice and surrounded by a ring of snow-capped mountains, Machu Picchu was built in the shape of a condor, which is one of the three sacred animals the Cosmic Dragon divided into when creating the universe. This "Temple of the Condor" was once a natural astronomical observatory, as well as impregnable fortress against invaders. It was also a suitable landing pad for crafts arriving from Mu and the outer cosmos, and because of its high elevation, as well as the concentration of quartz crystal within its blocks, Machu Picchu was a natural antennae transmitting and receiving station. From Machu Picchu, the South American Serpents could easily communicate with Dragon Communities around the globe as well as with the celestial star bases of the Extraterrestrial Serpents of Wisdom.

Machu Picchu was also chosen because it is such a powerful vortex of energy. It is continually activated and amplified by the Urubamba River below and by the triangular grid of very "alive" mountains which surround it. The three mountains which mark the corners of this grid are currently named Machu Picchu, Putucusi, and Huayna Picchu. Their triangulation of energy effectively ties into and energizes Machu Picchu's own intrinsic grid of seven sub-vortexes united into the shape of two geometric triangles. The corners of these triangles are marked by temples and sacred and specially carved boulders

The Machu Picchu complex of temples was continually enlivened by serpent power arriving directly from the cosmos. This dynamic life force enters the compound through a carved stone block at the apex of a centrally located pyramid. This elaborately carved block, called the Inti Watana, the "Hitching post of the Sun," currently has a serpent spiraling around it and reaching towards the sky, thereby marking the place where the serpent life force arrives from the heavens and enters the temple compound. The path taken by the serpent life force once it descends the pyramid and then disperses throughout the complex is traced by the serpentine stairway, called the "Serpent's Body," which slithers down the side of the central edifice.

The Condor of Machu Picchu   *The Puma of Cuzco*

Machu Picchu: Temple of the Condor

ANDEAN SERPENT TUNNELS

Tiahuanako, Cuzco and many of the other major Andean sites were connected by an intricate tunnel system. Legends maintain that in the distant past the ancient colonizing Amarus and Atlantean "Men of the Mountains" built an intricate tunnel system within the Andes Mountains and used it both as an underground roadway as well as a locus for their most secret rituals. When the Spanish invaded Cuzco in the sixteenth century A.D. the Inkas followed these tunnels to safe havens in Peru and Bolivia. They also hid many of their most sacred treasures in the cavernous crypts adjoining the tunnels.

Legends also contend that the Andean tunnel system was part of a Panamerican tunnel system which once completely united all the Americas. According to her own testimony, during a visit to Peru in the late 1800s Helena Blavatsky learned of this tunnel system and its many branches. Some of the Inkas who confided in Blavatsky had apparently studied the course of the tunnel system from a map which once decorated a wall within the Coricancha and traveled portions of it themselves. From them she learned that one branch of the network extended from Tiahuanako to the coastal pyramids before taking a sharp turn and traveling 900 miles south. A second branch of the tunnel system extended from Tiahuanako to certain sites within the Amazon jungle. A third branch moved north from Tiahuanako, possibly connecting with Teotihuacan and other Mexican power spots, before terminating in the Arizona desert. [56]

GRIDS, MEGALITHS AND DRAGON COMMUNITIES OF MESOPOTAMIA

The Dragon Culture arrived in Mesopotamia via the missionary Anunnaki. They arrived in ships via the Persian Gulf before traveling up the Euphrates River and creating Dragon Communities around truncated pyramids called ziggurats. Each ziggurat was placed over the center of a dragon's lair and served as a Heaven/Earth mediator, a cosmic mountain, and a home to the spiraling Serpent. They were built with seven tiers and painted seven colors, representing the seven principles of the Serpent, as well as the seven planets and seven levels of the universe. As the acknowledged seat of the fire serpent, the Sumerians referred to these towering megaliths as ESH, meaning "heat source." [21]

The Control Central of the Mesopotamian grid was the Dragon Community of Babylon, a city which the Jewish historian Eupolemus claims was built by giants who survived the Deluge. Apparently these giants were the Anunnaki, the first Serpent missionaries of the Mesopotamian Dragon Culture and a branch of the Kumaras. One Babylonian text claims that the city was built by the Anunnaki at the behest of Marduck.

In the center of Babylon the Anunnaki builders erected the famous Tower of Babel, a truncated ziggurat raised to a staggering height of 300 feet. This colossal pyramid was known by the citizens of Babylonia as Etenanaki, the "Temple foundation of H eaven and Earth." Another important ziggurat was erected by the Serpents of Wisdom in the sacred city of Nippur and called DUR.AN.KI, meaning "The place where the bond between Heaven and Earth arose."[58] Nippur was situated on a vortex exactly between the Tigris and Euphrates Rivers, thus making it a perfect balance of the male and female principles and cradle of the Serpent

GRIDS, MEGALITHS AND DRAGON COMMUNITIES OF ASIA

The Dragon Culture arrived in Asia by missionaries from the direction of both oceans and both Motherlands. The vestiges of these Serpents can still be seen today as the hundreds and thousands of stone circles, pyramids, menhirs megalith temples and mounds which dot Asia from the Mediterannean Sea to the Pacific Ocean.

An important Dragon Community of the middle Asian Grid apparently once existed as a huge pyramidal complex in Siberia, Russia. These colossal

The largest pyramid on Earth.. Near Xian, China

94

pyramids were, according to several eye witness accounts, destroyed by a fleet of Soviet fighter planes in 1970.

A Dragon Community and Control Central of the east Asian grid was constructed 40 miles southwest of modern Xian in the province of Shensi, China. This ancient community of fifteen medium sized pyramids was arranged in a geometrical formation around a central earthen pyramid which rose approximately 1000 feet in the air, making it more than twice the size of the Great Pyramid of Giza (the Great Pyramid rises to a height of about 450 feet). Interestingly, the sum of all the pyramids together, 16, can be reduced to 7 (1+6=7) the archetypal number of the serpent.

Apparently the ruins of the ancient Chinese complex still exist and have been photographed by western pilots flying over the area. Unfortunately, when westerners have attempted to gain entrance to this pyramid compound from the ground the Chinese government has denied its existence. Those who have made an academic study of the complex claim to have found references to it in 5000 year old Chinese texts. Supposedly even in these antiquated texts the compound is referred to as ancient.

An important Dragon Community and Control Central of the Indian sub-continental grid was Kashi (now called Varanasi). Ka-shi, the "City of Light" or "City of the Serpent" was the most holy city in India. At one time in the center of Kashi was an awesome pyramidal complex called Bindh Madhu which was comprised of one large pyramid surrounded by four smaller pyramids. The pyramids of Bindh Madhu sat peacefully overlooking the Ganges for hundreds and thousands of years before the fanatical Muslim Emperor Aurangzeb turned them to dust.

Sister to Bindh Madhu was a pyramidal complex built by Indian Serpents of Wisdom in Cambodia, now known as Angor Wat. Possibly an ancient "Eden" for Southeast Asia, the ruins of Angor Wat reveal a temple with a version of the tree/cross motif similar to that of Palenque and a serpent temple completely covered with snake effigies.

THE SERPENT TUNNELS OF ASIA

Legend has it that all the Dragon Communities in Asia were once connected by a tunnel network which runs under the entire continent. Chinese/Tibetan esoteric legends maintain that this tunnel network connected the underground civilization of Aghartha with vortex points and Dragon Communities throughout Asia and even the Americas. Mentioned as probable entrance and exit points into this Asian tunnel grid are the Potala Palace in Lhasa; certain Tibetan monasteries, such as the Tashi Lhumpo Monastery in Shigatse; the Buddhist cave temple of Tunhung, and the Hindu cave temples of Elephanta and Ellora.

2. BURIAL PRACTICES OF THE WORLDWIDE DRAGON CULTURE

Intrinsic to most Dragon Communities worldwide were a standardized set of burial beliefs and practices. Inspiring these mortuary practices of the Dragon Culture was the universal belief that each person possessed two souls or two aspects to one soul. When a person died their lower or animalistic soul, the part of the soul attracted to worldly pleasures, lived on within a Dragon Body of low frequency life force which thereafter made as its eternal resting place a grave or tomb. This lower aspect of the soul was called the Ka in Egypt and Kwei in China (Ka is a universal name for the life force and both names include K, thus making them true Dragon Bodies). By contrast, the higher aspect of the soul, that which is primarily attracted to heavenly delights and communion with Spirit, left the grave and ascended within a Dragon Body of very high frequency life force (that which manifests as pure thought and light) to the upper paradise realms of the universe. This higher, Spiritual Soul was identified as the Ba in Egypt and the Shen in China.

To preserve and insure the wellbeing of the lingering animalistic soul certain measures were taken by the survivors of the dead. Mummification, embalming, the rite of placing jade in the mouth of the dead, and entombment within a mound or pyramid was practiced in Egypt, China, Europe and throughout the Americas to preserve the corpse and provide an eternal abode for the animalistic soul. In order to continually nourish the animal soul, partitioned rooms were constructed within pyramids or adjoining the tombs of the dead and offerings of food were daily made within them to the deceased Ka or Kwei. In the case of earthen mound tombs, such offerings were placed directly on or beside the mounds. Supposedly the Ka or Kwei (the etheric body of the deceased) would leave its pyramid or mound sanctuary and partake of the food offerings directly.

To assist the Ba or Shen in its ascension to the heavens, windows, holes or hollow tubes were inserted into the pyramid or mound, thereby providing unobstructed passage to the spiritual soul. Pyramids and obelisks placed over a dragon's lair assisted the upward ascent by literally catapulting the higher soul out of the grave and into the upper regions of the universe.

During its upward ascent, the spiritual soul was expected to travel through many intermediate realms before finally reaching its destination in the highest heavens. Part of the spiritual training required for initiates in Tibet,

Egypt and Mesoamerica prepared an aspirant for this important afterlife journey. Some of these initiates became members of an order of priests specially trained to assist the newly disembodied soul on its interdimensional travels. While seated next to the body of the deceased, such priests would read passages from a "Book of the Dead" which would describe in detail the signs and roadways to follow in the next world, there by assisting the passage of the ascending soul through the in-between realms and nether worlds.

To further assist the spiritual soul in its passage, the Egyptians, Greeks, Norse, Celts, Chinese and Americans included horses, shoes, carriages, and boats in the tombs of the deceased in order to help them cross the lakes, rivers and mountains they would likely encounter in the etheric realms. In Mesoamerica dogs were also buried with the dead to provide companionship on this journey. In Egypt actual maps of the next world were placed alongside the body of the deceased. And in Mexico, Tibet, Greece, and Egypt weaponry, armor and protective mantras were placed within the tombs of the departed in order to help them fend off demons who obstructed the spiritual soul's passage to the upper worlds.

When the spiritual soul finally reached its destination, it was often presumed that it would reprise in Heaven the role its owner had played on Earth. For this reason, the tools used by a person during his or her life were also buried in their tombs. To assist kings and emperors in reprising their royal roles in the next world, the Egyptians, Chinese, Mesopotamians and Inkas often slaughtered and buried their entire court staffs along with them.

3. THE DRAGON CALENDARS

Throughout the myriad Dragon Communities various calendars based upon the Cycles of the Serpent were calculated and faithfully observed. The most universally observed of these calendars was one based upon the annual movement of the Celestial Serpent, the Pleiades. Some cultures, such as the Harvey Islanders of the Pacific, divided the year into two halves, corresponding to the Pleiades spring and fall appearances on the horizon. Other Dragon Cultures, such as those of the Celts and Native Americans, began and finished their year with the sunset appearance of the Celestial Serpent and its ascension to the zenith of the midnight sky. Still other Dragon Communities of the Mesoameric ans, Hindus, Peruvians, and Chinese began and/or ended their calendars during the Pleiad month of October/November. Such cultures often had a Festival of Lights celebration at this time in honor of the Seven Sisters and those who had departed during the course of the previous year. Such celebrations assisted the liberated souls in making their final ascent back home to the Pleiades.

Other dragon calendars which were observed by Dragon Communities worldwide included: the lunar calendar which plotted the cycle of the Moon, a manifestation of Dana, the Serpent Goddess, as she traveled through the 28 divisions of the sky called the Nakshatras (India) or "Lunar Mansions" (China, Mesopotamia); the calendar of Venus, the Serpent Goddess of the Americas, with its 52 and 104 year cycles; the calendar of the Celestial Dragon, the Big Dipper, by which the Greeks and Chinese determined the cycle of the seasons; and the 26,000 year Precession of the Equinoxes, recognized by the Mesoameric ans, Egyptians, Greeks and Mesopotamians, which predicted the duration of the solar system's journey through the Zodiacal Body of the Primal Dragon.

4. THE DRAGON KINGS

The ruler of each Dragon Kingdom was a Dragon King. These priest kings were acknowledged by their subjects to be manifestations of the Primal Dragon and therefore physical vehicles for the Divine Mind and triune powers of Spirit. Such monarchs were Sons of the God/Goddess and androgynous embodiments of the "Twins." They united Spirit and matter, Heaven and Earth, or the male and female principles in one body. The royal emblems of these Dragon Kings traditionally took the shape of an androgynous dragon, snake, sphinx, peacock, plumed serpent, or an ank or tree/cross.

Many of the Dragon Kings were enlightened spiritual masters who had come directly from the Motherlands or had reached their kingdom after leaving an advanced civilization in another part of the globe (or another star system). Many were representatives of the Kumara, Kaberoi or Solar Brotherhoods or they were descended from ancient adepts who had been members of these organizations. Other Dragon Kings were considered to be lineal descendants of a mythical serpent or regarded as actual physical progeny of an etheric dragon.

The divine serpent powers of the Dragon Kings needed to be conscientiously safeguarded and replenished. In order to keep their powers strong, the Dragon Kings were required to live righteously and rule their kingdoms in accordance with the mandates of the Divine Will. A king who deterred from the will of Spirit would eventually see his powers wane and his empire crumble around him.

THE DRAGON PHARAOHS OF EGYPT

In Egypt the Dragon Kings were called Pharaohs. The word Pharaoh comes from Per âa meaning "royal house," thus designating the Egyptian Dragon King to be the house (the material shell or Dragon Body) within which the great Ra (the Spirit) resided.

As the union of Spirit and matter, each Pharaoh was an incarnation of Horus, the divine Spirit, living in a physical form contributed by Seth, the material principle. Thus, they were recognized to be androgynous embodiments of the two Twins and respectfully referred to as the "Two Twins," the "Two Falcons" or "Seth and Horus" united. Many Pharaohs attached to their crowns representations of their twin aspects in the form of a snake and bird (the serpent Uadjet and the vulture Nekhebit) and carried an ankh scepter, a version of the androgynous cross, as their official emblem and ceremonial power object. Their court titles also reflected their androgyny. Composed of at least four names, these official titles designated the Pharaoh as a descendant of Horus and Seth, the Lord of the shrines of Uadjet and Nekhebit, and the King of the North and South (north-Spirit and south-matter). In recognition of his divine status, the Pharaoh was the honorary Grandmaster of the Djedhi, the order of Serpents of Wisdom in Egypt founded by Thoth-Hermes and the Kaberoi Masters. The Dj of Djedhi denoted "Serpent" and many of the Dragon Pharaohs included this root syllable within their titular names. The first historical Pharaoh to do so was King Djer, the "Serpent King" of the First Dynasty. Following his lead were such monarchs as King Djoser, the serpent king of the Third Dynasty, and King Djederfra of the Fifth Dynasty.

The divine Pharaoh was venerated by his subjects as one who had completed human evolution and fully incarnated the power and wisdom of Ra. With immense serpent power and wisdom at his disposal, symbolized by the radiant golden asp he wore upon his diadem, the Pharaoh could perform any miracle, as well as make his beloved Egypt into a safe and prosperous nation. With but a wave of his scepter the great Dragon King Nectanebo, for example, is reputed to have vanquished entire invading armies or made the Nile River overflow its banks. If he or any other Pharaoh lived contrary to the will of Ra, however, their supernatural power would begin to wane and ruin would soon beset Egypt. In such cases, the Pharaoh's function as the hand and power of Ra on Earth would be temporarily or permanently relinquished.

After reigning for thirty years, some Pharaohs chose to renew their serpent power through the observance of the ritual of Sed. Performed in Memphis, this ritual required the Pharaoh to re-enact the union of upper and lower Egypt by sitting alternately on two thrones, thereby re-uniting Spirit and matter and rebirthing the life force.

THE DRAGON KINGS OF MESOPOTAMIA

Dragon Kings ruled all throughout the land of Mesopotamia. Some were lineal descendants of the Dragon Kings who ruled before the flood, "The Seven Elders," one of whom, King Enmenduranki, may have been a member of the lineage of Thoth-Hermes.

The Dragon Kings of the Sumerian/Babylonian Dragon Culture were recognized to be incarnations of the nature god Dammuzi or Tammuz who, along with his mother Inanna, was referred to as "the Serpent who emanated from the heaven god Anu."[31] As Tammuz, each monarch was the androgynous Son of the Goddess Inanna or Ishtar (the female principle) and the God Anu (the male principle). Since they were incarnations of Spirit, the Sumerian monarchs were often simply addressed to as "Lord" or "God."

As dragons and incarnations of Tammuz, the Dragon Kings acquired immense amounts of creative serpent power once they assumed office. Some of this power was passed on from one king to the next and some of it continually flowed to each monarch from the celestial bull gods Marduck and Enlil, the heavenly patrons of the throne. Once a year during the New Year's ceremony the Babylonian king's power was given a fresh infusion as the ruler touched the hand of the national statue of Marduck. As long as the Dragon King lived according to the will of Marduck during the ensuing year his Serpent power was guaranteed to remain abundant and his country prosperous.

The Dragon Kings of Elam were similarly regarded to be incarnations of the Primal Serpent. The greatest historical Dragon King of the country was Uatash Naprisha, a monarch who was honored in iconography with the upper body of a man and the lower body of a serpent. Because of the formidable serpent power wielded by this ruler, Elam experienced one of its greatest periods of prosperity during his reign.

The Dragon Kings of Assyria or upper Mesopotamia were proclaimed to be divine incarnations of the god Asshur. Asshur's manifestations included the Zodiacal Dragon or Sphinx, the symbol of which is believed to have hung over the throne of the incumbent priest king. As the union of the polarity, the Assyrian kings wore upon their ceremonial regalia an embroidered symbol of the foliated tree/cross which was flanked by two winged Twins.

THE DRAGON KINGS OF INDIA

The Dragon Kings of the Hindu Dragon Culture were prolific. The *Mahauyutpatti,* a Buddhist historical text, lists 80 ancient Naga or "Serpent" Kings. These Dragon Kings claimed lineal descent from the Lunar or Solar Race (such as King Rama), from the colonizing Naga Mayas or Nacaals from

100

Lemuria, or from a mythological serpent. Most adopted a serpent and/or a cosmic tree/cross motif as their royal insignias.

Those famous Naga Kings of India who were offspring or incarnations of mythical serpents included Balarama, prince of the Yadavas of Mathura, who was venerated as an incarnation of the Primal Serpent Shesha, as well as the legendary Dragon King Salivahana of P ratishthana who was believed to have been the actual son of the mythological Serpent Ananta. Another distinguished lineage of Dragon Kings, the Shishunagas of northeast India, traced their ancestry back to the mythical Serpent Shishunaga, while the Naga Kings of Chota Nagpur in Central India asserted that their lineage had begun with the mythological Naga Pundarika. In Kashmir the ancient Dragon Kings ascribed the founding of their royal lineage to the Naga Karkotaka.

The Dragon Kings of India were recognized to be wielders of abundant Shakti or life force. As long as they were physically and morally strong, Shiva, the Spirit, showered them with divine favor and their countries flourished. When they weakened from old age or the inhuman treatment of their subjects, so did their empires.

THE DRAGON EMPERORS OF CHINA

The ancient Dragon Kings of China were known by their subjects as Lung or "Dragons" and as the "first born Sons of Heaven and Earth." Their emblems, the five clawed, Azure or Golden Dragon, along with the seven stars of Ursa Major, the heavenly home of the Celestial Dragon, could often be found stitched upon their royal gowns.

Like their counterparts in India, many of the Chinese Dragon Emperors were lineal descendants of colonists from Mu (via Kun Lun, P 'eng lai, Aghartha Uigher etc.) or direct progeny of mythical dragons. Many of the earliest Dragon Emperors are depicted historically as having had the actual physical features of a dragon, such as an abnormal shaped head, multi-jointed arms, two pupils in each eye (characteristic of the all-seeing Dragon), leather-like skin, and whiskers (even at birth!). One such Dragon Emperor, the Emperor Yao, was reputed to have been the son of a great Red Dragon and possessed two pupils in each eye. Huang-ti, the "Yellow Emperor" of China's "Golden Age" was "immaculately conceived" by the Celestial Dragon which came to Earth as a beam of golden light from the Big Dipper and entered the womb of his mother. After a 24 month gestation period, Huang-ti was given birth to with both the appearance and wisdom of a dragon. Another Son of the Celestial Dragon, Emperor Yu, is reputed to have been born with the seven-starred figure of the Big Dipper etched upon his skin. His predecessor, the Emperor Shun, so resembled a living dragon that his family became repulsed by his appearance and even attempted to have him murdered.

As the Son of Heaven and Earth (Spirit and matter) it was the Dragon Emperor's function to establish the will of Heaven (the Tao) on Earth. To perform this function, the Chinese Dragon Kings were endowed with abundant Ling or life force. As long as the Dragon Kings remained righteous and lived in harmony with the Tao, their Ling remained strong. If they erred from the path of righteousness, however, their Ling would weaken and their empire was likely to crumble around them. Such was the fate of the evil emperor Shih Huang-ti, Dragon King of the Chin Dynasty.

THE PERUVIAN DRAGON KINGS

In Peru the Dragon Kings were the priest kings of the Inkas and the many Dragon Cultures that formed along or near the Pacific coast. The symbol of the Peruvian Dragon Kings was the Amaru, the snake, which was worn as part of their ceremonial regalia and carved in relief around the doorways of their palaces. Such serpent reliefs can still be found ornamenting the entrances of the palaces of the ancient Inkas in Cuzco and the Chimus of the coastal city of Chan Chan. To denote their unique association with the snake, the Dragon Kings of Chimu adorned their headdresses with one or more snakes which usually slithered horizontally across their fronts. The Inkan Dragon Kings similarly revealed their affiliation to the serpent by ceremonially wearing golden bracelets and anklets made in the form of snakes. Some Inkas, such as Tupac Amaru and Huayna Kapac, further designated themselves as serpents by adopting the titles of Amaru (serpent) or Kapac (serpent wisdom) as part of their royal names. The Inkas' association with the serpent continued well into Spanish times when the emblem of the colonial puppet Inka was that of a big snake.

The serpent emblem of the Inka during Spanish Colonial times

102

Like other Dragon Kings worldwide, the Inka Dragon Kings were the androgynous union of Spirit and matter. In order to designate themselves as incarnations and "Sons" of Inti, the Solar Spirit, they wore symbols of the Sun over their breasts and foreheads. Their androgyny was also revealed by their title, Inka, a name which could be interpreted to mean Spirit in a Dragon Body (In-Ka)or In-ka-rnation of Spirit into matter.

The serpent power wielded by the Dragon Kings of the Inkas was transferred to them from their predecessors as well as from the spiritual adepts of the Intic Churincuna (Solar Brotherhood) or Seven Ray Order from Mu. Such power was so immense that the incumbent Inka was forced to observe certain taboos, such as never wearing the same article of clothing twice.

THE MESOAMERICAN DRAGON KINGS

The Dragon Kings of Mesoamerica were the "Plumed Serpents." They were called Quetzlcoatls (Nahuatl for Plumed Serpent) among the Toltecs and Kukulcans (Mayan for Plumed Serpent) among the Maya. Their plumed serpent motif is the synthesis of the snake (symbol of matter) and plumes or feathers (symbol of Spirit), thus designating a Mesoamerican Dragon King to be the androgynous union of Spirit and matter.

Some of the earliest Dragon Kings in Mesoamerica were descended directly from the ancient Serpent Sons, Itzamna and Quetzlcoatl, who came from across the great sea and whose symbol was the cross, the symbol of polarity union. Perhaps beginning with them, the tree/cross became a definitive symbol of the Plumed Serpent monarchs and today depictions of the Middle American Dragon Kings in the form of tree/crossesor as foliated humans can still befound etched upon "tree stones" in many Central American megalithic settlements.

Throughout their long history, the androgynous Mesoamerican Plumed Serpent Kings were, like the Egyptian Pharaohs, recognized to be embodiments of the Twins, known in Mesoamerica as Hunapu or Quetzlcoatl (embodiment of Spirit), and Xbalenque or Tezcatilopoca (embodiment of matter), the "small, swift jaguar." In order to designate themselves as the union of this polarity, the Plumed Serpent Kings wore a tiara of quetzal plumes (symbolic of Spirit/Quetzlcoatl) upon their heads while covering their hands with gloves made out of jaguar fir (symbolic of the Jaguar Twin and Serpent Power). The jaguar, like the serpent, represented the raw power of Spirit. The two animals were used interchangeably in Mesoamerica and often united in the form of a serpent-jaguar. The Plumed Serpent Kings' jaguar power and "material" support was further represented by their royal thrones which were made in the shape of a jaguar's elongated body.

As both vessels of the serpent/jaguar's explosive energy and embodiments of the tree/cross upon which the Primal Serpent slithered to Earth, the Dragon Kings of Mesoamerica were known to be capable of channeling copious amounts of serpent power onto the physical plane. To stimulate this flow of creative energy, the Mayan Kings would pierce themselves with sharp obsidian blades in excruciatingly sensitive areas of the body, such as the genitals and tongue. This mutilating rite apparently had the effect of transporting the Dragon Kings into an altered state of awareness from which they could most easily channel the life force into their surrounding kingdoms.

When the Mayan Dragon Kings died it was believed that some of their serpent power was still retained within their decomposing corpses. In order to utilize this power, the Mayans buried their Dragon Kings underneath temples, thereby infusing these sacred structures with royal life force. Sometimes buried along with a Mayan Dragon King was his double headed serpent staff and serpent scepter, symbols of his serpent power.

THE DRAGON KINGS OF GREECE

Dragon Kings ruled in Greece throughout much of the country's ancient history. They were full of life force, androgynous, and often depicted with human male torsos (Spirit) attached to serpentine lower extremities (matter).

The first Dragon Kings of Greece came from Egypt or were taken to the Aegean area by the Atlantean Pelasgians. Their numbers grew slowly in Greece until they became especially prolific during the Mycenaean Age. In Mycenaean Athens, for example, most kings were, according to Jane Harrison, "regarded as being in some sense a snake."[25] They insured abundance for their subjects while disseminating prodigious serpentine wisdom. Cecrops, the first Mycenaean Dragon King of Athens, is remembered in history as having arrived as an initiate from Egypt while toting under his arm a compilation of spiritual laws for the Athenians. He is depicted as a handsome male king with a very long serpent tail. Erectheus, the fourth Dragon King of Athens, arrived in the city during a major famine and brought renewed prosperity to the people. Possibly of the Thoth-Hermes lineage, he helped establish a mystery school tradition in Greece, the Eleusinian Mysteries, which had many parallels with the Osirian Mysteries of Khemi. Because of his renowned spiritual wisdom he was later venerated as a live snake on the Athenian Acropolis which guarded an olive tree (the tree of wisdom) next to a temple bearing his name, the Erechtheion. One additional Mycenaean Dragon King of note, Kadmus (with K sound of the Serpent), ruled over the "Seven Gated" Thebes, the "Dragon City" of Greece, as its wise priest king. When he died, Kadmus is reputed to have turned himself into a live snake.

5. DRAGON-CREATORS OF THE UNIVERSE

Commonly, within most Dragon Cultures worldwide a serpent or dragon was venerated as the Creator of the Universe. The unfolding cosmologies of such cultures began with the emanation of a creator dragon out of the pure Spirit, followed by its condensation into the multitudinous material forms which henceforth populated the physical cosmos (see Appendix 1, Creation of the Universe).

Within the Mesopotamian Dragon Culture of the Sumerians, the Creator of the Universe was venerated as Enki, the dragon which called forth the universe through Mumu, his divine word. Similarly, the members of the Dragon Culture of upper Egypt recognized the Creator of the Universe to be the dragon Ammon Irta (Lux or) or Ammon Kematuf (Karnak), while their siblings of the lower Egyptian Dragon Culture knew it to be Atum, "the All and the Nothing" (both transcendental Spirit and manifest Serpent). The temple priests of the thriving Dragon Cultures within ancient Greece and Mesoamerica daily paid homage to stone effigies, as well as live, writhing snakes, which they conceived of as earthly representatives of the Creator of the Universe. In Greece such sacred snakes represented the Creator Dragon Agathodeamon, or perhaps Soispolis, the serpent form of the Spirit Zeus, which was venerated as a live snake at the foot of the Hill of Knossos and daily fed honey cakes by a temple priestess. In Middle America the live, reptilian icons were considered to be the earthly forms of Quetzlcoatl, the Plumed Serpent creator, or Huracan, the Primal Serpent Creator with the spiralling, hurricane-type body. Within the Dragon Cultures of India and China the Creator of the Universe was known as the primeval serpent Shesha and the Azure Dragon respectively. In both countries imposing effigies of creative dragons and serpents commanded the place of honor in many sacred temples.

6. THE DRAGON NAME OF UNIVERSAL SPIRIT

According to the "Dragon Cosmologies" promulgated within the various Dragon Cultures, once the universe was created the creator dragon proceeded to nuture its physical "progeny" the way a mother protects and nourishes her young. In order to summon the nuturing and protecting presence of the Dragon Creator, the Dragon Culture priests invoked their serpent deity with sacred, esoteric names. Such names summoned the eternal power of Spirit (the Dragon Creator *is* the projected power of Spirit), and ingeniously reflected the Dragon's andrognynous name and/or its seven principles or aspects.

THE SEVEN LETTERED NAMES OF THE SERPENT

Within the Dragon Communities surrounding the Mediterranean the holy name of the Dragon Creator was often composed of seven vowels, each of which represented one of the seven principles comprising the Primal Serpent. An example of this septenary dragon name was chanted by the ancient priests of Egypt who invoked the power of Spirit by rattling off seven vowels in rapid succession. The Dragon Communities of the Greek Gnostics similarly called forth their version of the power of God, the Serpent Agathodeamon, with a name of seven vowels and, in their iconography, placed these seven vowels over the seven points of the primal beast's golden crown. The seven principles of the power emanating from the Jewish high god, YHVH, was also invoked with an ancient name of seven vowels. According to Robert Graves, this holy name was a version of IAOOUAI, a name discovered by Clement of Alexandria in Jewish-Egyptian magical papyri.29

ANDROGYNOUS AND TRIUNE NAMES OF THE SERPENT

Many Dragon Communities called forth the power of the unseen Spirit with a serpent name of two letters or syllables, thus acknowledging the dual nature of the Dragon and the Dragon's Twins. In India, Chaldea, Egypt and Greece the name of the God's power was written as two hills (symbolizing two cosmic mountains) or two capital A's placed side by side. This name represented the Dragon as both the "first born" of heaven (symbolized by the first letter of the alphabet, A) and the union of the two Twins (the double AA). Some Dragon Communities would unite the two A's or two hills to produce another symbolic name of the Dragon, the letter M, which was sometimes drawn as a snake with two curves to its body In the Greek Dorian alphabet the letter M was referred to as San, meaning "the light of the One," i.e., the power projected from Spirit, as well as "holy." San provided the root for such "holy" words as sanctus, sanctum and saint.[59]

The two lettered name by which the power of Spirit was summoned in Dragon Communities also took the form of Io and AO. Io was one of the names of the Cow/Serpent Goddess of the Mediterranean. It was also a name of the God/Goddess among the Maoris of New Zealand and the Mayas of Mesoamerica who recognized the name to mean "the Spirit of the universe. "59 Among the Greek cultures the title AO represented the first and last letters of the Greek Alphabet, Alpha and Omega, as well as the Dragon's Twins and their powers of creation and destruction. In Chaldea the name AO evolved into Aos and from Aos evolved Chaos, a name for the primeval form of the Dragon. Also evolving out of AO was Tao, the Chinese Taoist name for the Way of the Spirit, the symbol for which was two fishes or serpents superimposed upon a circle. AO was also the basis for the Mediterranean IAO, a name used to invoke the power of the high god of the Greek ş Zeus, and which represented the God's triune powers as embodied within the Dragon. A derivation of IAO, Kiao, became a name for one species of mythological dragon in China.

Other Triune names of the Dragon united AA or M and AO to produce the Egyptian Ammon, the Hindu AUM, and the Jewish Amen. These three names of the Primal Dragon denote both "the first and last" (the Twins) and the Primal Serpent's triune powers of Creation, Preservation and Destruction. The name of the Theban Creator Serpent, Ammon, contains the letter A (power of creation) in its beginning syllable, the letter O (power of destruction) in its ending syllable and the letter M (the Twins' power of preservation) in the middle. The Judeo/Christian Amen has A at its beginning, Min the middle and finishes with "en", implying "end." Each of the three letters of AUM corresponds to one of the Dragon's three powers.

THE UNIVERSAL SOUND AND NAME OF THE SERPENTS OF WISDOM

Dragon Communities around the world also commonly referred to their Serpents of Wisdom by sounds and names associated with the Primal Serpent. Some which have already been mentioned include Quetzlcoatl, Lung, and epithets which begin with or incorporate the universal K sound of the serpent, such as Kumara, Kahuna, Kaberoi, and Kukulcan. However, another name of the Primal Serpent and variations of it was more widespread than these as a designation for the Serpents of Wisdom. This universal name was Naga.

Within the Dragon Communities of India and Mesoamerica the wise Serpents and teachers of the mysteries were addressed as Nagas and Naga Maya. In Australia a close relative to Naga, and perhaps deriving from it, was Nagatya, an order of wise Serpents and shamans whose function it was to initiate the medicine men of the Wotjobaluk tribe. On Fiji another relative of Naga, Nanga, denoted the secret societies of wise men which conducted their meetings in megalithic, pyramidal temples. Within the Fang tribe of Gabon, Africa, a close approximation of Naga was Nganga, the name for a powerful serpent master of their tribe who was the embodiment and teacher of all branches of magic. In nearby Sudan Naga appears to have been the root of Nagua, the name for all magic and those magicians who practiced it. Also derived from Naga is Ngai, the name of the African god who initiates magicians within the Akikuyu tribe of Kenya.

According to Helena Blavatsky the version of Naga adopted by the Mesopotamians and Mexicans was similar. In *The Secret Doctrine* she writes: "The Nargal was the Chaldean and Assyrian chief of the Magi and the Nagai was the chief sorcerer of the Mexican Indians." Today the descendants of the Nagals, the Nagauls of Mexico, continue to serve their people as shamans and adept healers. The title Nagai was also common among the shamans of Uruguay where it meant "chief, teacher and Serpent." In North America the name Naga supplied the root for Naganid, the title of the chief initiating officer of the Midewiwin, the "Great Medicine Society" of the Ojibwas, a native tribe of the Great Lakes Region.

In many cultures not only did Naga and its derivatives denote serpent, but so did N, the beginning letter of these esoteric names. For example, four cultures which claimed to have had a rich serpent tradition, the Egyptian, Etruscan, Pelasgian and Mayan, all inscribed their letter N in the form of a serpent or dragon.

7. YOGIC DISCIPLINES BY WHICH AN ASPIRANT COULD BECOME A SERPENT OF WISDOM

The yogic disciplines of the Worldwide Dragon Culture by which one could become a Serpent of Wisdom will be covered in the following chapters. The lineages of masters who became Serpents of Wisdom within each Dragon Culture will be expounded upon as will the various alchemical disciplines used by them to achieve enlightenment.

THE SERPENTS OF WISDOM
IN
ASIA

A Naga of India

CHAPTER 5

THE NAGAS OF INDIA

The Serpents of Wisdom of India's Dragon Culture were called Nagas, meaning "Serpents." Their symbol, the golden R oyal Cobra, is a version of the "evolved serpent" that represents Spirit (gold color) united with, and accelerating the vibratory frequency, of matter (the snake). While serving as priest kings and hierophants in Bharata Varsha (India's ancient name), these Nagas preserved sacred traditions which stretched back to the very dawn of time. Some of their predecessors had arrived as missionaries from the Motherlands, while others had received divine inspiration directly from Spirit while meditating in solitary retreats within their native India. With their timeless wisdom, the Nagas formulated many of the spiritual philosophies and practices of the current cycle, such as Yoga and Buddhism, which n have since led much of the world's population down a path to enlightenment.

THE NAGA EMPIRES OF BHARATA VARSHA

The Nagas of Bharata Varsha's Dragon Culture divided their country into a patchwork of Dragon Empires and city-states. Two of the first and most important of their city-states were the Kingdom of Kashi on the Ganges and Nagpur, the "City of the Nagas." Nagpur was built in the center of Bharata Varsha thus making it a strategic location for Nagas monitoring the panoply of Dragon Communities throughout the Indian sub-continent. Other important city-states of the Nagas were founded within the Indus River Valley and included the metropolises of Harrappa and Mohenjo-Daro, both of which had running water, public baths and a sophisticated sewage system. Mohenjo-Daro, a city of 35,000 people, was the site of a major college which offered a curriculum of both mundane and spiritual studies taught by a faculty of enlightened Nagas. In the nearby city-state of Lothal the Nagas founded a port city on the Arabian Sea which carried on frequent trade with Dragon Empires around the world while using a universal currency of cowries. Close to Lothal was the city-state of Takshasila, referred to in Greek records as Taxila. This great city of Nagas, named after the mythological serpent Taksha Naga, became a renowned center of theology and academic learning. Greek historians maintain that Alexander the Great visited Taxila on his march across Asia and was both startled and impressed by the size of a huge live snake, a living image of Taksha Naga, which was kept in the principal temple in the city.

110

To the north of the Indus Valley the Nagas established a Dragon Kingdom in what is now Kashmir. According to the two main historical texts of Kashmir, the *Ni/amata Purana* and the *Rajatarangini,* this northern territory of Bharata Varsha was originali y too cold and wet to support life, but a group of Nagas, lead by Nila Naga, drained the region's marshes and lakes and thus made it inhabitable. Kashmir was quickly settled thereafter by waves of colonizing Nagas who made Srinagar (Sri-Nagar, Great Serpent) their capital city. B y the time of the Third Buddhist Council in Srinagar, circa 253 B.C., there was rumored to be over 84,000 Nagas living in Kashmir. Ruling over this proliferation of Nagas was a series of Naga Kings, the most famous of which were descended from a semi-mythical ruler with renowned magical powers, the Naga Karkotaka.

Naga Kingdoms were also established throughout the Ganges River Valley and eastern India. One eastern Dragon Kingdom was founded in Magadha, the modern Bihar, and ruled by a lineage of Naga Kings known as the Shishunagas. Their neighbors and allies were the Naga Kings of nearby Manipur (a region situated in modem B engal and Burma) who claimed descent from a Naga called Pa-kung-ga. To the west of these two kingdoms was ano ther Naga Kingdom which chose as its capital the famous city of Mathura. The royal family of this empire, the Y adavas, were serpent worshippers and the nobles of the family were intimately associated with serpents. The Yadava prince Balarama was an incarnation of the Primal Serpent, the mythical Shesha Naga, and his brother, the Avatar Krishna (with hard K sound of the Serpents), was considered to be one of the wisest Dragon Kings to ever rule in India.

Indian Naga Kingdoms ruled by Dragon Kings also spread throughout the southern portion of Bharata Varsha. One gro up of Kashmirian Nagas colonized a region just below the Vindhya Mountains and therein established a lineage of Naga Kings called the Shatavahana Nagas. While claiming descent from the Primal Serpent, Shesha, the Shatavahana Nagas expanded their dominion until it encompassed the present states of Maharashtra, Andra, and Karnataka. ln nearby Orissa a southern Naga kingdom was founded and ruled by Naga kings of the Vairata Dynasty who claimed descent from a mythical serpent goddess. South of them, at the southern most tip of Bharata Varsha, the Nagas founded the kingdom of Pratishthana and set over it a series of Naga Kings, the most famous of whom was the legendary king Salivahana, reputed son of the mythical serpent Ananta. In adjoining Kerala another Dragon Kingdom was created by a tribe of Nagas calling themselves Nayas. The Nayas became famous in southern India for coiffuring their hair in the shape of a cobra.

THE MAHANAGAS AND SIDDHAS

Other prominent Nagas of the Naga Kingdoms, i.e, those who were not governmental administrators, assumed the roles of spiritual teachers and hierophants. They were aligned with a hierarchy of spiritually evolved Nagas at the top of which were the Mahanagas, the "Great Nagas," and the Siddhas, the "perfected human beings."

The Mahanagas and Siddhas were true masters and teachers of human evolution. They were the caretakers of a vast body of esoteric wisdom which had been handed down to them through lineages of adepts since the arrival of the Pleiadian Master Sanat Kumara, and they were unique in having realized the truth of this knowledge directly. While fully embracing the spiritual practices of their predecessors, they had awakened the Kundalini, the evolutionary force which normally lies dormant at the base of the spine, and then moved it through seven chakras or power centers to the crown of the head, thereby merging with Shiva, the transcendental Spirit. As the fruit of their profound accomplishment some Mahanagas and Siddhas remained in immutable physical bodies for hundreds or even thousands of years. Many acquired supernatural Siddhis, or powers of the Serpent Shakti, such as the power to become as small as an atom or as large as a planet, the power to make the body as light as a feather or as heavy as a mountain, the power to fly through the air, and the power to appear in two or more places at once.

While living in caves, ashrams (monasteries) or roaming the length and breadth of their beloved Bharata Varsha, some Mahanagas and Siddhas elected to remain anonymous servers of humanity and transmitted their wisdom to only a handful of disciples. Others became Jagadgurus or World Teachers and commanded great armies of devotees.

SHIVA, THE LORD OF THE NAGAS

The highest deity of all Nagas was Shiva, also known as Nagadev, "Lord of the Nagas." Shiva, meaning "The Auspicious," was invoked at the beginning of many ceremonies enacted by the Nagas for material and/or spiritual prosperity.

Shiva is a dual deity. He is both transcendental as well as immiment. In his transcendental manifestation he is the Infinite Spirit. In his imminent form he is Spirit birthed & clothed in matter (Shakti, female principle) and is, therefore, his own Son, Murugan or Sanat Kumara. This is why the trident-wielding imminent form of the fire god Shiva so closely resembles the Atlantean King Neptune-Volcan and his Egyptian counterpart Ptah-Osiris.[61] They are all forms of imminent Shiva or Sanat Kumara, the ancient Priest-King of the World.

The characteristics and legends of Shiva, Neptune and Ptah-Osiris reveal striking similarities. Shiva and Neptune-Volcan are both fire gods who wield tridents. Shiva and Ptah-Osiris were both reputed to ride upon a bull (King Osiris encircled the globe on a bull) and both deities had a female consort who manifested as a fiery serpent (Ptah-Osiris's consort was Sekhmet and Shiva's was Shakti). Both gods were, of course, also intimately associated with fire and destruction. The destructive aspect of Ptah-Osiris evolved into the volcano dwelling Roman god Vulcan, the manufacturer of the deadly weapons of war, who in turn was a prototype for the Devil. Like Shiva, the favorite weapon of the fiery, destructive Devil is a trident.

The Greek historian Diodorus claimed that Ptah-Osiris and his bull traveled from Egypt to India in 10,000 BC and would have then merged with the thriving cult of Shiva on Bharata Varsha. When the Greek conqueror Alexander the Great stopped to visit Nysa in India (the modern Nangehar near Jalabad in the Kabul Valley)62 he was amazed to hear from the citizens of that city that Dionysus, the Greek counterpart of Osiris, had anciently visited there and left his teachings. Alexander and his men also discovered that their Dionysus and the Hindu Sanat Kumara are the same deity.

SHIVA AND THE PATH OF YOGA

Within the esoteric schools of the Mahanagas and Siddhas the goal of existence was complete spiritual union with the transcendental aspect of Shiva. The classic image of transcendental Shiva they meditated upon is a male yogi with long matted locks with snakes dangling from his arms and neck and wielding a trident. The snakes represent the serpentine power that emanates from the "male" transcendental Shiva at the beginning of the universe and then crystalizes into all material forms. The trident denotes the three powers wielded by Lord Shiva, that of creation, preservation and destruction of the universe. Meditating Shiva's focus is directed inwards. He is meditating upon himself, the Infinite Spirit that exists within everyone's heart.

A Naga unites with Shiva through Shiva's power, Shakti, which manifests within a yogi as the serpent Shakti Kundalini,which rises up the spine, the yogi's Tree of Life, to finally merge with Lord Shiva at his seat at the apex of the head.

To precipitate the cosmic union with Shiva certain spiritual disciplines called Yoga were observed by the Nagas. The practices of Yoga, meaning union, united Shiva and Shakti, Spirit and matter, as well as all other manifestations of the polarity as it exists within the human form, including the Ida and Pingala

Nadis, the male and female hormones, and the left and right sides of the body (this will be explained later in the book). This comprehensive polarity union was catalyzed by such yogic practices as asanas (stretching postures), pranayama (breath control), alchemy, celibacy, fasting, chanting and meditation.

BECOMING THE ANDROGYNOUS LORD OF YOGA

In order to facilitate their merger with Shiva, the Nagas practiced the disciplines of Yoga while striving to fully emulate and identify with the "Lord of Yoga." They would grow their hair in thick matted locks and often sit in meditation with their legs crossed in padmasana, the "full lotus" position, for many hours at a time. They might also unite their hands and/or hold them in special special meditation-enhancing positions known as mudras. Every position, every action they practiced was alchemical and calculated to unite the inner polarity, activate the Serpent Power, and culminate in union with Shiva. This included the repetition of the mantra Om Namah Shivaya, meaning "Salutations to Shiva," which included within it words and syllables associated with both the elements of fire, "Shiva," and water, "Ma." After many years of Yoga practice, those aspirants who fully merged with the Lord of Yoga by permanently raising the fire serpent, Shakti, to the apex of the head became enlightened Siddhas and Mahanagas. They were, thereafter, recognized by their contemporaries to be the embodiments of Shiva and vehicles of the highest wisdom and most prodigious Serpent Power. Such God-Realized saints were known as Sat-Gurus, "True Gurus," in contra-distinction to the flock of lesser, un-realized, gurus. The title "Gu-ru" unites a syllable of the female, material principle, "Gu," meaning "darkness," with that of a syllable for the male, spiriual principle, "Ru," meaning "light," thus reflecting the union of the polarity these adepts had achieved within themselves. States the *Guru Gita,* "the Guru is Shiva without a doubt."

114

Shiva, the Lord of the Nagas

SHAKTIPAT GURUS, WIELDERS OF SERPENT POWER.

Once achieving union with Shiva, the Sat Gurus naturally gained control over Shakti. Having united with Spirit, the universal power of Spirit was at their command and under their control. Because of their influence over the Shakti, many Sat Gurus chose to become Shaktipat Gurus, Yoga Masters with the ability to awaken the dormant force within sincere seekers of wisdom and initiate their path to union with Shiva.

In order to awaken the Shakti Kundalini, a Shaktipat Guru would transmit a particle of his or her own serpent power or Shakti into a disciple through a process called Shaktipat, meaning "falling Shakti," or "transmission of grace." This transmission of spiritual power occurred through the vehicle of the Master's thought, word, look or touch. Then, once the inner Kundalini was awakened in the chosen devotee, the Shaktipat Guru had the ability of monitoring and controlling the serpent power as it ascended the spine and purified that disciple's physical, emotional, and mental bodies. When the time was right, the Guru would catalyze the Kundalini's final ascent to the top of the head, thus making the disciple an enlightened Mahanaga. This Guru-monitored-yoga has been called Siddha Yoga, the "Yoga of the Perfected Ones," and Maha Yoga, the "Great Yoga."

THE PASHUPATI YOGIS

The earliest traces of both Yoga and the esoteric cult of Shiva and Shakti have been discovered in Harappa and Mohenjo-daro, two of the Nagas' earliest Indus Valley settlements. Excavations within these sites have turned up clay seals and vessels which are decorated with images of Shiva in his Neolithic manifestation of the horned nature god Pashupati, the "Lord of the Animals." Seated in his traditional cross-legged yogic position, this Indus Valley version of Shiva is flanked by his "subjects," wild animals & serpents. Upon his head are perched matted locks and two horns which together form the shape of a trident, the symbol of the nature god's triune powers. His phallus is erect and points upwards, symbolizing that the way to union with transcendental Shiva is through transmuting the seminal fluid into Shakti and moving it up the spine. Pashupati is another form of imminent Shiva, i.e., his Son, Sanat Kumara.

According to early Vedic references to them, the Indus Valley followers of Shiva/Pashupati were a group of long-haired, god-intoxicated ascetics who covered their bodies in sacred ash, practiced pranayama and became transmuted by the fiery Kundalini. They are referred to in the Rig Veda as Keshin and the yogic process of Kundalini transmutation is apparently referred to as Lord Vayu's (the life force) pounding or purifying of the Kunammama, a yogic term for the physical body.[63] The only thing lacking among these early ascetic Shaivites (followers of Shiva) was uniformity and cohesiveness.

In the second century B.C Lord Shiva himself chose to take up physical form in order to codify, solidify and reform the lineage of Shaivite/Pashupati yogis. His opportunity arose when a yogi died while undergoing severe austerities. After entering the fresh corpse and bringing it back to life, Shiva arose as the Siddha Laukulisha, "the Lord of the Club," and a cohesive Pashupati sect was soon born. From out of this sect emerged the 28 Siva Agamas, the sacred scriptures which would become the definitive texts on Shaivite Yoga for the following 2000 years.[64] This new sect made Ka-shi, the "City of Serpents" and "City of Shiva," its headquarters and eventually there were more than 10,000 Pashupati Yogis residing there.

Under Laukulisha (often depicted with a big club and erect phallus) the Pashupati Yogis became an eccentric and ascetic gro up of yogis. Many sought to emulate their beloved Lord of Yoga by wearing matted locks, tiger skins or loin cloths, carrying a begging bowl, a trident, and living a solitary existence. Some like the homed Pashupati even cultivate d the ability of getting erect penises "without any sexual sensations or intentions. "[65] A unique feature of the Pashupati sect was, however, the gross and outl andish behavior which defied social customs and logical reasoning. Many wantonly covered their bodies with filth, exhibited inappropriate singing and dancing, made obscene sexual gestures, walked as if crippled and let their hair and nails grow to repulsive lengths. Because of such reprehensible behavior the cult garnered for itself the title of the Order of the Lunatics. But regardless of whatever judgements it accrued from the populace, such disgusting behavior proved to be a powerful springboard to union with Shiva. By practicing it, the Pashupati Yogis eventually tra nscended the rational world with all its social conventions and dualities and rose to union with their unseen god.

THE KALAMUKHAS, KAPILIKAS, AND AGHORIS

After Laukulisha's time the Pashupati Order of Lunatics gave rise to a number of sub-sects around India. These spinoff branches included the Orders of the Kalamukhas, Kapilikas, and Aghoris.

The name Kalamukha, meaning "black face," is a reference to the big black streak the members of this lunatic sect wore across their face as a mark of death and renunciation. The Kalamukhas cultivated some of the Pashupati's perverse behavior but, as the least extreme of the three lunatic sects, they also strove to cultivate some of the virtues in Siddha Patanjali's Yoga Sutras. In contrast to the Kalamukhas, the Kapalikas abandoned all social and moralistic considerations in favor of cultivating non-dual awareness. While emulating a perverse form of Shiva known as Kapaleshwar, the "Lord of the Skull," each Kapalika or "Skull Bearer" carried a skull which served the manifold functions of begging bowl, pot and ceremonial implement. While living and meditating in frightening cemeteries amongst the dead, the Kapilikas sought to unite with the transcendental aspect of Shiva which is beyond the grave.

The Aghoris, worshippers of a form of Shiva called Aghora, or "the Non-Terrible," were the most extreme group of the three lunatic sects. In order to completely establish themselves in non-dual awareness the Aghoris cultivated the exact opposite behavior of whatever was considered socially acceptable and virtuous. Similar to the Kapilikas, the Aghoris inhabited grave yards, wore garlands of bones and both ate and drank out of human skulls. They performed such repulsive acts as consuming the flesh of corpses, sitting upon garbage piles or dung heaps, and even consuming their own excretion. Their main hangout was the burning ghats on the Ganges in Kashi. The ghats have since moved and now Baba Keenaram Ashram, Aghori world headquarters, occupies their place.

THE MAHESHVARA SIDDHAS

During the time of the Pashupati expansion in northern India, another lineage of perfected masters known as the Maheshvara Siddhas (Maheshva ra is a name of Shiva) established a school of Shaivism in the southern part of country. This school was organized by Agastya, the dwarfish descendant of the Kumaras and ancient sage of the Pandyan Kingdom. When most of the Pandyan Kingdom broke off from the southern tip of Bharata Varsha and sank into the Indian Ocean, Agastya took the ancient teachings of the Kumaras north, subsequently settling in South India's Pothigai Hills (near modem Trivandrum). Here he established the lineage of Maheshvara Siddhas and an academy for the dissemination of both science and spirituality. Under his guidance the Maheshvara lineage flourished and eventually numbered 18 members.4

The teachings of the Maheshvara school of yoga were centered around a trinity of deities: Shiva, the universal "male" principle, Shakti, the universal "female" principle, and their forever-young Son, Kumara. The goal of a Maheshvara yogi was to unite the polarity, Shiva and Shakti, and thereby become the androgynous Son, the Kumara. The yogic practices adopted for accomplishing this union were known by the Maheshvaras as Kaya Kalpa, meaning "Cultivation of the Body," and their goal was Kaya Siddhi, physical

Aghori Sadhus of India

Baba Keenaram Ashram in Kashi-Varanasi
World Headquarters of the Aghoris and Avadhuts

MURUGAN/ SANAT KUMARA/ SKANDA
THE SERPENT SON OF SHIVA

In order to worship and fully identify with the Kumara, the Maheshvaras created images of the divine boy. He was venerated as Skanda, the seven-headed serpent, and Murugan, the peacock-riding savior. He was also identified as Karttikeya, "Son of the Pleiades," and depicted as a boy with six heads, which representedthe six visible stars of the Seven Sisters.

Sanat Kumara was the ancient Savior and Sat-Guru of all yogis. Most Tantric schools of alchemy and yoga in India can be traced back to him. As previously mentioned, it was he who was sent to Earth to enlighten humanity to its divinity. He brought with him his special symbol, the Vel Spear, which according to exoteric legend he used to slay the early beasts that threatened humanity. Esoterically, the Vel represents the special wisdom that Sanat Kumara, as the Savior, brought to humankind. The Vel represents the human spine (shaft) through which the Serpent Kundalini rises up to the Third Eye of Gnostic Wisdom (the blade), thereby revealing to a person their true nature as Spirit incarnate in a physical form. Through the work of Sanat Kumara and his students, including the Maheshvara Siddhas, the knowledge of Kundalini and how to activate it was codified and became the Tantras and Agamas. In that form it then became the foundation of most schools of yoga.

MAHANAGA BOGANATHAR AND THE
PATH OF ALCHEMY

From their headquarters in South India, the teachings of the Maheshavaras eventually spread throughout Bharata Varsha. This wisdom was taken to various parts of India by disciples of Agastya, each of whom focused and expanded upon some aspect of Kaya Kalpa and developed a school based upon it. One such pioneering disciple of Agastya was Boganathar or Bogar, the founder of an esoteric school based on the principles and practices of alchemy.

According to one record of his long life, the Mahanaga Boganathar was born in India and, at a young age, became a student of Agastya. He later left the country in order to travel to China and study under Kalangi Nathar, an immortal Siddha and a world renowned teacher of alchemy. During his many years in India's sister country Boganathar reputedly transmigrated his soul into the body of a dead Chinese man and was henceforth known as Bogar or Bo-Yang.

Sometime around 400 B.C. Boganathar left China and, after traveling across the snowy summits of the Himalayas, returned to his beloved India.

During this long journey he is reputed to have waxed poetic and composed 700,000 verses on spiritual life. These verses were subsequently condensed into 7000 and lovingly presented at the feet of his Guru, the M ahanaga Agastya, at a forum of Siddhas in South India. Taking leave of his M aster Boganathar crossed the Indian Ocean and traveled to Sri Lanka in order to visit the sanctuary of Lord M urugan at Kataragama, "the place of Kartikeya."Here he steadfastly performed yoga for a period of time before succeeding in attracting the blessings of the Divine Son. From that moment onwards Boganathar was firmly established on the mostancient path of the Kumaras.

While in Sri Lanka Bogar supervised the construction of a famous yantra shrine in honor of Murugan Inside the shrine Bogarnath placed the yantra form of Karttikeya - a six pointed hexagram - which was set into a block of alchemical substances created by Bogar. Following the shrine's construction, Boganathar left Sri Lanka and retired to Palani Mali mountain in Palani, South India, to complete his spiritual practices. Finally, after many moons, Boganathar attained Samadhi, spiritual absorption with Shiva's tra nscendental aspect, and was thereafter an immo rtal Kumara. Afte r his enlightenment, a temple and sanctuary dedicated to Murugan was built where hi s final transformation had occurred and it soon became Siddha Boganathar's school of Alchemy in India.4

UNITING THE POLARITY WITH RASAYANA

The alchemical path to immortality (Siddhahood or Kumarahood) as promulgated by Boganathar was known in India as Rasayana, the "Path of Essence" or the "Path of the Elixir." This yogic path spawned a sub-group of M aheshvara Siddhas, called the Rasavara Siddhas - adepts who had achieved immortality mainly through the practices of alchemy.

The goal of the Rasayana path was to produce an androgynous essence or elixir of immortality either within or outside of the yogi's body and then circulate this purifying essence throughout the body. Such a substance was considered to be the essence and seed of the androgynous Kumara. It had the power to unite the polarity within the body, awaken the Kundalini, and eventually transmute one into an immortal Kumara. This it could do because the essence of the Kumara and the Kundalini are synonymous. They are both manifestations of the Serpent Fire. Kumara and Kundalini both begin with the K or Ku sound of the Serpent, and to each is ascribed a serpentine nature The Kundalini is venerated as the androgynous, fire serpent and the Kumara is depicted as an androgynous seven-headed serpent Skanda (kan is the universal sound syllable of the Serpent) or as an androgynous pre-pubescent boy.

To produce the transformative essence, the Rasavacara (practitioner of Rasayana) united substances which reflected the nature of Shiva, the male principle and father of the Kumara, with those which carried the essence of Shakti, the female principle and mother of the divine Son. For example, those Yogis who created the immortal essence within their bodies observed celibacy to unite Shiva and Shakti as their male and female hormones. When a yogi's gender specific hormones became strong enough, they would naturally attract those hormones of the opposite polarity and create a spark. This spark would then travel to the base of the spine and sympathetically awaken the Kundalini.66 To create the inner elixir by this approach could be a long process, however, and potentially require many years to accomplish. Therefore, some Rasayana Yogis chose to expedite the process by employing sexo-yogic techniques. During an act of "spiritual" intercourse some male Rasavacaras would use Vajroli Mudra to suck the female essence up their penises and unite it with their own seminal fluid. Some of the female Rasavacaras would similarly draw the male essence into their vaginas and unite it with their female sexual fluids.

Those Rasavacaras who elected to produce the essence outside of themselves through synthetic means represented Shiva and Shakti with two primary ingredients, usually a metal and a mineral. These materials were alchemically united together through certain esoteric processes to produce the essence of the Son. The two most common substances used in the alchemical recipes were mercury and sulfur or mercury and mica. Mercury was called the sperm of Shiva and represented the male spiritual essence. The fiery red sulfur corresponded to the female essence. United they created the androgynous Kumara.

The scriptures of the Rasayanas were full of injunctions concerning the proper proportions in which to mix the ingredients of the elixir as well as the correct alchemical processes to employ. If the directions were not followed impeccably, a toxic substance might be produced and the Rasavacara could achieve instantaneous death rather than the coveted prize of immortality. There were also certain injunctions as to the appropriate time, place and ritual to employ in the ingestion of the substance. Finally, and perhaps most importantly, the grace of Murugan or Sanat Kumara and the blessings of one's own Guru were essential to achieve ultimate success on the path of Rasayana. The guidance of a Guru, the embodiment of the Lord of Yoga, was considered invaluable for achieving success in any branch of Kaya Kalpa.

MAHANAGA BABAJI NAGARAJ AND THE PATH OF BREATH CONTROL

Another Maheshvara Siddha responsible for founding a school of yoga based upon the ancient teachings of the Kumaras was the Siddha Babaji. Also known as Nagaraj, "King of the Nagas," Babji was a student of both Agastya and Boganathar. Babaji's school of yoga, called Kriya Yoga, was based upon the Kaya Kalpa science of pranayama or breath control.

One of the more authoritative versions of Babaji's life was communicated directly to two of the Mahanagas close disciples, Yogi S.A.A. Ramaiah and V.T. Neelakantan, from Babaji himself. According to this authorized version of his life as found in *Babaji and the 18 Siddha Kriya Yoga Tradition* by M. Govindam, Babaji was born in 203 B.C. to a priest of the Shiva temple in Parangipetttai, southern India. Within his father's temple was a life-sized image of Lord Murugan, an image which had originally been that of a huge Shiva lingum before transforming into the Divine Son. Babaji spent much of his earliest years assisting his father in the temple and immersing himself in the worship of this image of the Kumara.

At five years of age Babaji was kidnapped, but then set free again soon afterwards. Rather than return to his home and family, however, Babaji decided to renounce worldy life and travel throughout India as a mendicant and renunciate. During his subsequent wanderings Babaji encountered many enlightened Siddhas and Mahanagas, each of whom taught him some facet of Yoga. At one point his travels led him to the shrine of Murugan in Sri Lanka where he met the Siddha Boganathar and gained instruction in both alchemy and meditation. Then, following six months of intensive spiritual practice under Boganathar's adept guidance, Babaji achieved a deep state of transcendental absorption or Samadhi during which he achieved spiritual communion with the forever young boy.

After leaving Sri Lanka, Babaji journeyed to the Pothigai Hills with the goal of receiving the spiritual blessings of the Siddha Agastya. With great determination Babaji camped at the Courtallam Falls which were nearby the sage's secluded ashram and vowed to undergo severe austerities until he was blessed with the divine presence of the diminutive sage. Following forty-eight days of rigorous tapas (austerity) Babaji's resolve bore fruit and the tiny Siddha spontaneously appeared from behind a tree. Agastya blessed Babaji and initiated him into that branch of Kaya Kalpa known as Vasi Yoga, the science of breath control. Following this initiation, Agastyar gave Babaji instructions to travel to the Himalayas and master pranayama.

Babji immersed himself in intensive yoga within the Himalayan caves before founding an ashram near the sanctuary of Badrinath. In due time he achieved immortality and became patriarch of his own school of Vasi Yoga called Kriya Yoga. Through the dynamic yogis who subsequently achieved enlightenment through his school, such as the Siddhas Lahari Mahasaya, Shri Yukteshwar, and Paramahansa Yogananda, Kriya Yoga eventually spread throughout the world. Babaji Nagaraj currently anchors the high frequencies of Spirit within an immutable physical form as he continuously oversees the upliftment of humankind from his Himalayan retreat.

KRIYA YOGA, IMMORTALITY THROUGH BREATH CONTROL

Kriya Yoga or Vasi Yoga, i.e., the science of breath control, is based upon the ancient yogic philosophy which maintains that each incarnate soul is allotted a certain number of inhalations and exhalations over the course of a life time. Once this number has been exhausted, the physical body dies. Therefore, in order to live longer or develop an immortal, physical body, a yogi needs to slow down the rate of breathing or suspend the breath indefinitely. When complete cessation of the breath is accomplished, a yogi becomes immortal and a master of Vasi Yoga.

Through the breathing exercises promulgated by Babaji's school of Kriya Yoga, a yogi gradually learns to suspend the breath for greater and greater periods of time. These techniques cause the breath or prana to circulate in such a way so as to clear out all the 72,000 energy channels or nadis within the Dragon Body and thereby transform the physical vehicle into a super-efficient conduit for the universal life force. Eventually the Kundalini is awakened (its seat is within the Dragon Body) and entry and exit points for the prana other than the nose and mouth, such as the chakras and the extremities of the spine, become fully functional. In this way the Vasi Yogi succeeds in reaching the stage of permanent cessation of breath and the goal of Kriya Yoga, immortality, is achieved.

MAHANAGA PATANJALI, INCARNATION OF THE PRIMAL SERPENT

Another prominent Maheshvara Siddha was Patanjali, a sage who lived around 200 B.C . The Mahanaga Patanjali is listed in Hindu records as both a disciple of Laukulisha, the famous reformer of the Pashupati sect, as well as one of the 18 Maheshvara Siddhas. He taught the principles of Maheshvara Yoga while simultaneously living among the Pashupatis in his ashram in Kashi. With

Patanjali's assistance the Shaivite lineages of north and south India became united.

Patanjali was such a highly esteemed Mahanaga that he was worshipped as an incarnation of the great seven-headed Primal Serpent Shesha. According to the accepted legend of his birth, the soul of Shesha fell (pat) from heaven into the palm (anjali) or womb of a virtuous woman named Gonika and took a physical incarnation as Pat-anjali.

As an initiate of multiple Shaivite lineages, Patanjali was the beneficiary of many yogic teachings which had been passed down word of mouth among the Siddhas for countless ages. His destiny on Earth was to be one of the first scribes of the current cycle to organize these ancient yoga teachings, which he referred to as Anusasana, "directions coming down from traditions, "67 into a scriptural format. His most synthesizing and enduring text, the Yoga Sutras, was a comprehensive exposition on the eight successive stages of yoga which culminate in union with Shiva. Since its publication, this text has served as a road map for many aspiring yogis seeking to unite the polarity and unite with Spirit.

THE NATH SIDDHAS AND HATHA YOGA

Around the 10th century A.D., the Maheshvara lineage spawned a brotherhood of mystical yogis called the Naths. Under the leadership of the Siddha Matsyendranath and his premier disciple, the Siddha Goraknath, the Naths united all the previously hidden yogic practices of the Mahanagas into one cohesive system and called their "new" school Hatha Yoga. Just as Patanjali had codified the stages of yoga, the Naths standardized and popularized many of the ancient yogic practices of the Siddhas.

The founder of the Nath brotherhood, the Maheshvara Siddha Matsyendranath, supposedly received the sacred teachlngs of yogic immortality directly from Shiva while he was immersed in a deep yogic trance. The secret teachings of the Lord of Yoga (referred to by the Naths as the Adi Nath or First Nath) were then passed to Matsyendranath's premier student Goraknath and thence to a multitude of aspiring yogis.

According to legend, Matsyendranath first met Goraknath when his future disciple was one day strolling through the hilly Srisadam woods in Southern India. Without warning Matsyendranath, in his immortal Dragon Body, stepped out from behind a tree right in front of Goraknath. Startled at the sight of the phantom Siddha, Goraknath jumped back, but his fear quickly abated upon experiencing the divine love radiating from the etheric Master. With his new student at ease, Matsyendranath proceeded to verbally and telepathically instruct him in the ancient yogic science which leads to the state of the immortals. [68]

Goraknath enthusiastically embraced the teachings of his Siddha Guru and steadfastly embarked upon a twelve year quest for immortality. At the conclusion of his sadhana, or after he had finally attained the immortal state of a Siddha, Goraknath composed the *Siddha Siddhabta Paddhati,* the "Text on the Final Conclusions of the Siddhas," as proof of his spiritual accomplishment.

Matsyendranath authorized Goraknath to take the secrets of the Maheshvaras to North India and amalgamate them with the wisdom of the Pashupatis and its sub-sects, the Kapalikas, Aghoris etc., thereby founding the school of Hatha Yoga. Included within this "new" school were all the ancient Siddha practices including asanas, pranayama, alchemy, and meditation as well as certain postures called Bandhas or Locks which were specifically designed for the awakening of the Kundalini. As part of its curriculum the school also taught the esoteric anatomy of the human body (the "anatomy" of the Dragon Body) which consists of 72,000 nadis, seven power centers or chakras and the serpent power or Kundalini coiled 3 1/2 times at the base of the spine. The textbooks of this school were *Hatha Yoga* and the *Paddhati,* both composed by Goraknath.

The Hatha Yoga movement began in the foothills of the Himalayas and, as it merged with the Pashupati cult, it eventually spread throughout all northern India and Nepal. Many Hatha Yoga monasteries and temple complexes subsequently came into existence and an order of monks, called Kanphatas, was founded by Goraknath to administer to the sacred compounds. The Kanphatas, meaning "Split-eared Ones," were distinguished by the large gaping holes which were specially cut into their earlobes to accommodate their huge golden earrings. Like traditional Shaivite Yogis they were also known to emulate the Lord of Yoga by adorning themselves with matted locks, covering their loins with tiger skins (upon which they also meditated), hanging rudraksha beads from their necks and arms, covering their bodies with vibhuti or sacred ash (symbol of the "dead," transcendental Shiva), and carrying a trident. To honor the goddess Shakti and their Naga lineage, they also carried little brass or bronze images of royal hooded cobras. Many Kanphatas and descendants of Goraknath were closely associated with the serpent, such as his chief disciple, Guga, who was worshipped by his devotees in the form of a royal cobra with expanded hood.

Numerous Naths and Kanphatas eventually achieved complete immortality. When Yogi Svatmarana wrote the *Hatha Yoga Pradipika* three hundred years after Goraknath's journey north, he claimed that many ancient Siddhas of the Nath tradition, including Goraknath and Matsyendranath, were still roaming the planet in physical bodies. When the immortal Naths and Kanphatas finally ascended in their Dragon Bodies to the upper paradise realms of the immortals, they had their immutable physical forms entombed in the classical padmasana or "full lotus" position. Three hundred years after the Nath Siddha Jnaneshwar M aharaj left his immutable body, his tomb was opened by the Siddha Eknath Maharaj, who found the ancient yogi's body as fresh as if it had been interred the day before.

UNITING THE POLARITY AND ACTIVATING THE SERPENT FIRE WITH HATHA YOGA

Goraknath's Hatha Yoga became one of India's foremost paths for polarity union and raising the Serpent Fire. The Sanskrit word Hatha implies this union. Ha denotes "Sun" or the male principle, and Tha denotes "Moon" or the female principle. Together Ha-tha means Sun-M oon, male-female, or Spirit-Matter and denotes their alchemical union within the human body.

A student of Hatha Yoga employed numerous techniques to catalyze the union of opposites within his or her body. The union was effected through a regimen which included a special diet and the disciplines of alchemy, asanas, and pranayama techniques performed in conjunction with three Bandhas or body locks. Jalandara Bandha, a neck lock, and Mulabandha, a perineum lock, assisted a yogi in holding prana in the abdomen and thus creating a "spark" of "androgynous" fire. This spark was then pushed to the base of the spine by Uddyana Bandha, a stomach lock, where it sympathetically ignited the dormant Kundalini fire and opened the "door" of the Sushumna, the central nadi running up the middle of the spine.

When the door of the Sushumna was opened, the prana flowing within the polar opposite nadis, the Ida and Pingala, would be withdrawn from these divergent channels and made to move into the central nadi. Its upward movement, along with the fiery Kundalini, would then precipitate the union of all polarities within the body as well as the opening of the six lower energy centers or chakras (see Appendix 1, II.12), the most important of which was the "androgynous" Heart Chakra. Only with the development of love which emerges with the activation of this chakra, can the lower and upper or "male" and "female" chakras function harmoniously in their fully awakened state. Finally, the dramatic conclusion of Hatha Yoga would occur when the "female" Shakti Kundalini reached the top of the head and united with her lord, the "male" Shiva, within the seventh power center, the Sahasrara Chakra.

YOGIC IMMORTALITY: CREATING THE IMMUTABLE PHYSICAL BODYAND THE IMMORTAL DRAGON BODY

Accordingto the Nath Yogis, during its ascension, the awakening of Kundalini through Yoga would culminate in the creation of an immutable physical body as well as both a higher and lower Dragon Body. The immutable physical body was known among the Naths and Siddhas as the Swarna Deham, the "Golden Body," because it radiated a golden glow. The Dragon Bodies were known as the Pranava Deham, the "Prana Body", and the Jnana Deham, the "GnosticBody" of supreme wisdom and bliss.4 The Pranava Deham was alternately known as the Kumara Body because those who purified it became eternally young.

All three bodies were purified and activated by the awakened Kundalini as it passed through the esoteric anatomy of 72,000 nadis and 7 chakras. With the activation of each would come certain powers and abilities. With thepiercing of the chakras (their complete opening) situated in the etheric Dragon Body all supernatural powers would come to the yogi. When the Jnana Deham, the higher Dragon Body, became fully functional, the Siddha would acquire the ability to ascend to the highest dimensions or Lokas of the universe. A fully enlightened Siddha might, for example, choose to travel within this DragonBody to Siddha Loka, the paradise realm of the Siddhas, which exists on the etheric plane which overlays the planet Jupiter.

AVADHUTS, NAGA BABAS, KAULAS AND PARAMAHAMSAS, DIVINE MAD MEN OF INDIA

A result of uniting the Maheshvara or Nath Siddha tradition with that of the Pashupatis and their sub-sects (the Kalamukhas, and Aghoris) was the creation of other "lunatic" sects of yogis. These sects were popularly known as the Avadhuts, the Naga Babas, the Kaulas and the Paramahamsas. Similar to the ancient Pashupatis, these other lunatic yogis also strived to live in a state of non-dual awareness and spontaneous freedom.

THE ECCENTRIC AVADHUTS

Perhaps the most aberrant and respected of the Nath lunatics were the Avadhuts. Intimately connected to the Aghoris, the Avadhuts began with the Avatar Dattatreya, a divine Avadhut who lived many hundreds or even thousands of years ago. The tradition he started was later reformed in the tenth centuryA.D. by the Nath Siddha Matsyendranath. Today, the official head of both Avadhuts and Aghoris is Avadhoot Gautama Ram, head of Baba Keenaram Ashram in Kashi-Varanasi.

The first Avadhut, Dattatreya, is recognized to have been a joint incarnation of Shiva, Vishnu, and Brahma, the three powers of God. While on

Dattatreya, with the three heads of Brahma, Vishnu & Shiva

Akkalkot Swami

*Avadhut Siddharth Gautama Ramji
Lord of all Aghoris and Avadhuts*

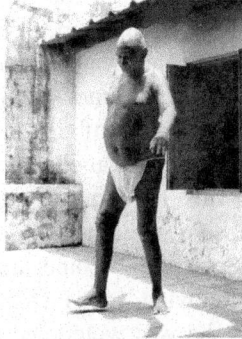

Avadhut Bhagavan Nityananda

Naga Babas

Earth this divine madman lived like a typical "lunatic" yogi. He covered his body with sacred ash, wore matted locks, draped a tiger skin over his body, hung rudraksha beads around his neck, carried a damaru, begging bowl, and trident His penchant for constantly moving from town to town may have begun the itinerant Avadhut tradition of ceaselessly roaming throughout the countryside without any apparent destination.

The Avadhuts who followed Dattatreya adopted even more extreme and unconventional behavior than had their patriarch. One of these later extremists was the Avadhut Akkalkot Maharaj, a madman who was venerated as a Dattavatar, an actual incarnation of Dattatreya. Akkalkot Swami, as he was normally called, was first discovered in the Himalayas imprisoned within a huge anthill. After being released from his cocoon by a woodcutter, the Avadhut descended into the lowlands of India and roamed throughout the countryside and hills while wearing nothing but a scanty loin cloth. With a huge protruding belly and long arms dangling down well below his knees (a typical feature of Avadhuts), Akkalkot gave the comical appearance of a hairless ape to most observers. As he moved he could be heard repeating unintelligible mantras or grunting in ecstasy. His eyes were normally directed inwardly in Shambhavi Mudra, the transcendental state of bliss of the Avadhuts, and a glow of radiant light emanated from his spiritually transmuted body. If a person blocked his path he was known to continue onwards by rising straight up and walking through the air! [69] If a supplicant approached Akkalkot he might shower the person with blessings, but he was also known to become abusive, sometimes striking the startled person with sticks or throwing rocks at them. When the abused devotee returned home, however, he or she was welcomed by great, good fortune. During his long life Akkalkot Swami healed the blind, raised the dead and gave Guru Diksha or initiation to many deserving yogis. Soon after his passing, Akkalkot demonstrated his victory over death by appearing physically to a group of devotees on the outskirts of the town of Nilgaon. [69]

Another famous Avadhut, Bhagavan Nityananda, is reputed to have performed "monkey sadhana" during the early part of his life and lived like an ape in the trees of the Himalaya Mountains. After descending from the mountains, Nityananda roamed around India in a simple loin cloth and lived in jungles and caves infested with snakes and scorpions before finally settling down in an ashram in Ganeshpuri in Maharashtra State. Nityananda always retained his eccentric behavior, however, and was known to spend many hours in Shambhavi Mudra while laying upon a hard flat board or stiff bed and issuing forth occasional grunts of ecstasy. He rarely spoke and when he did so it was in broken sentences. When arising from his deep meditation he could be found moving at a very rapid pace to a nearby river or some an unknown destination. As he walked his fingers were normally fully extended, symbolizing his non-attachment to the phenomenal world. If a devotee approached him for a blessing, Nityanada might hurl a rock or coconut at the unsuspecting supplicant, but this abuse would later turn out to be a great blessing for the person.

Nityananda eventually became renowned for possessing many miraculous powers such as walking on water, materializing objects out of thin air, and appearing in two places simultaneously. Many people claimed to have seen the Avadhut cross the Pavanja River in southern India by walking upon its rapidly moving water. Sometimes while hitching rides in trains, Nityananda would materialize thousands of tickets out of thin air when asked for his own, much to the amazement of the startled conductors. During one of Nityananda's treks around India the Avadhut was jailed for vagrancy. Later, while lying peacefully in his cell, Nityananda was simultaneously spotted by a jail guard casually strolling down the street directly in front of the prison! Nityananda's intense Shaktipat was also renown. His chief disciple, Swami Muktananda, received the Avadhut's Shakti as two beams of brilliant light which emanated from the adept's divine eyes.

THE NAGA BABAS, THE SERPENT FATHERS

The Naga Babas, meaning "Serpent Fathers," are a class of extreme ascetics founded with the help of the great Shaivite Shankaracharya (considered by some to be an incarnation of Shiva), the Naths, the Pahsupatis and their associated sub-sects. Although at some point during their history they were a class of warrior yogis fighting against India's Moslem invaders, the Naga Babas have for most of their existence lived in isolated hermitages or under the open sky.[65] They are naked year-round and daily cover their entire bodies with sacred ash and rudraksha beads. They are distinguished by growing their matted hair down below their waists and then coiling it high upon their heads in the tradition of their beloved deity, Shiva, the Lord of the Nagas. Occasionally the Naga Babas come out of isolation in order to travel on pilgrimage to holy Kashi or for certain special religious festivals, such as Kumbha Melas. Kumbha Melas are convocations of yogis which occur every twelve years at the Ganges and Godavari Rivers and involve immersion in their purifying waters. After arriving at the festival, they unite with their beloved gurus and often receive initiation into the higher ranks of their austere orders. They are always given the honor of entering the water ahead of their brethren, i.e., the other holy men, renunciates and sadhus attending the special event.

THE ANDROGYNOUS KAULAS

Another ancient group of divine madmen spawned by the Naths are the androgynous Kaulas. A Kaula is simply another name for a Siddha, a Perfected Master who has united the male (Akula) and female (Kula) principles within him or herself and become an androgynous adept. One of the first schools of the Kaula Marga, the path leading to Kaulahood, was the Yogini-Kaula school of Kamarupa founded by the Nath Siddha Matsyendranth.

To achieve Kaulahood a yogi is required to progress sequentially through eight stages of spiritual disciplines. During the early stages he or she observes orthodox Vedacara (right hand) practices, i.e., the traditional, conservative disciplines of purification which were espoused by the authors of the Vedas. In the latter 4 stages of the path, however, the yogi adopts the unorthodox, Vamacara (left hand) disciplines, which includes the extremist practices of the ancient Pashupatis and yogis of the various lunatic orders. One popular Vamacara practice of the Kaula Marga is known as "the 5Ms" because it involves the consumption or indulgence in "five forbidden things" -grain, wine, meat, fish, and intercourse-whose Hindi or Sanskrit names began with the letter M. Through the consumption of that which would normally be repulsive, "dense," or prohibited to a spiritual aspirant, this ritual assists the yogi in developing equality consciousness and the non-dual state of Shiva.

Once a yogi progresses through the eight stages and fully unites with transcendental Shiva, he or she becomes an androgynous Kaula and disconnects from the ephemeral world. When commenting upon the profound detachment of a Kaula, the Visva-sara Tantra asserts: "For him (the Kaula) there is neither rule of time nor place. His actions are unaffected either by the phases of the Moon or the positions of the stars. The Kaula roams the Earth in differing forms. At times adhering to social rules, he at other times appears, according to their standard, to be fallen. At times again, he seems to be as unearthly as a ghost. To him no difference is there between mud and sandle paste, his son and an enemy, home and the cremation ground."[71]

PARAMAHAMSAS, GREAT SWANS

The Paramahamsas, "Great Swans" (Hamsa is Sanskrit for swan), are a group of superior Siddhas who have transcended duality and united with Shiva. In contrast to other lunatic yogis, many Paramahamsas have distinguished themselves by conforming to social conventions and are thus more approachable than their aberrant brothers and sisters. Included in this list of Paramaharnsas are

130

the Jagadgurus (world teachers) Muktananda Paramahamsa (chief disciple of Nityananda), Yogananda Paramahamsa (Kriya Master in the lineage of Babaji), Ramakrishna Paramahamsa, and Mata Amritanandamayi Devi of South India.

Ramakrishna and Muktananda were both Sat Gurus and renowned Shaktipat Masters who could transmit their serpent power through a thought, word, look or touch. Muktananda was the first Jagadguru of the present age to transmit Shaktipat enmasse to large gatherings all over the world. As he walked along the isles of such gatherings, he would touch each person between the eyes, at the heart chakra, at the base of the spine, or he might even blow shakti into the mouth of a favored aspirant. Upon completion of his transmissions, Muktananda would return to his seat and the new initiates would then begin to display classic signs of Kundalini awakening. Some would feel pressure, pain or burning at the base of their spines as the inner serpent was aroused from its seat. Others might feel intense heat or shaking (kriyas) as the serpent fire traveled throughout their subtle Dragon Bodies and purified the vast network of nadis and chakras. Still others might assume spontaneous Hatha Yoga asanas, commence rapid breathing, roar like a lion or even hop like a frog as the Kundalini transformed various parts of the physical body. Some fortunate initiates might astral travel to etheric dimensions or lokas while others would transcend into deep meditative states and perhaps have inner visions of saints and gurus. Possibly the greatest of all visions was the sight of the Blue Pearl, a very tiny, blue point of consciousness which normali y resides within the Sahasrara or crown chakra and is a manifestation of pure Spirit or Shiva within the body. Many people were known to see the Blue Pearl with their eyes closed, while in others it would travel out of the head via the eyes and float in front of them. Muktananda used to say that at the end one's spiritual journey the Blue Pearl would exit the body and become as big as the universe, thereby permanently immersing the yogi in transcendental Shiva while surrounding him or her in the blue light of consciousness.

Currently the Jagadguru Amritanandamayi travels the world transmitting Shaktipat and uplifting seekers with her wisdom. "Amma" or "Mother," as she is affectionately called by her devotees,was born with blue colored skin and seated in the cross-legged lotus position, traditional signs of an Avatar or direct incarnation of Spirit. Her mission is to unite the polarity and activate the inner Kundalini within sincere seekers through the transmission of shakti and by teaching Bhakti Yoga, the path of love and service. Another active Shaktipat Guru is Swami Chidvilasananda or "Gurumayi," the successor of Muktananda and wielder of the power of his Siddha lineage.

THE MAHANAGASOF BUDDHISM
THE MAHANAGABUDDHA,FOUNDER OF BUDDHISM

One of the greatest of all Hindu Mahanagas was the Shakyamuni B uddha, commonly known in history as Gautama Buddha or simply "the Buddha," "the enlightened one." This Jagadguru and his disciples were responsible for spreading the ancient wisdom of the Siddhas to approximately one third of the world's population.

Buddha was born in the fifth century BCE as a prince of a royal Naga family. His family was part of the lineage of Shakya Kings who governed the kingdom of Kapilavastu (now part of Nepal) in the northeast part of Bharata Varsha. The Shakya Naga Kings were descended from the lineage of the ancient Solar Race, perhaps the same one which had existed on ancient Mu. Their family symbol, the golden cobra was found in the casket of one of Buddha's family members who succeeded him on the throne.34The Shakyas held alliances with other Naga Kingdoms, such as the nearby Shishunaga Dynasty of Magadha.

When the news of Buddha's entrance into the world reached India's Naga Kings many of them rushed to Kapilavastu for a glimpse of the divine child. Their arrival is documented in the Pali Cannon, the ancient authoritative text on Buddha's life, which states: "The Naga Kings earnestly desiring to show their reverence ... as they had paid honor to former Buddhas ... scattered before him (the new Buddha) mandara flowers, rejoicing with heartfelt joy to pay their religious homage. "72 Joining these kings were many great Mahanagas who had also come to pay their respects to the future Siddha. Once in view of the radiant child one visiting Mahanaga, the Siddha Asita, is recorded to have proclaimed: "The king of the law has come forth to rescue from bondage all the poor, the miserab le,the helpless. "72 Following his announcement, Siddhartha was baptized into the Naga lineage by Nagas which, the record asserts, "gave Buddha his first bath."

Being a natural bomSiddha, an epithet which was incorporated into his given name (Siddha-rtha), Siddhartha soon felt unfulfilled with the mundane life of a prince, and resolved to find a deeper, more spiritually satisfying existence. Eventually renouncing any claim to the throne of the Shakyas, Siddhartha adopted the lifestyle of a wandering mendicant, and set off to find "the truth."

Siddhartha's search for wisdom eventually brought him into contact with many of the prominent Mahanagas and Siddhas of his time. At some point during his wanderings he is reputed to have studied the Shamkya philosophy of the Siddha Kapila and practiced a certain form of yoga called Asphanaka Yoga, the "Yoga of Psychic Expansion."[68] Finally, after many years of spiritual seeking, Siddhartha sensed that his enlightenment was near and trav eledto a rural location near Kashi, the principal seat of the Hindu Mahanagas. His destination later became known as Bodh Gaya, the "Place of Wisdom."

In Bodh Gaya Siddhartha positioned himself under the now famous Bodhi Tree and began a period of int ense meditation. During the ensuing days and nights it is recorded that he was repeatedly tested by Mara the Tempter, a manifestation of the Dark Lord (see Appendix 1, The Twins), who continually placed sensual enticements at his feet. Siddhartha's concentration remained unshaken, however, and he remained steadfastly focused upon the goal of enlightenment.

When he felt close to achiev ingthe sought after goal of Siddhahood, Siddhartha arose from his seat and went to a nearby riv erto refresh and purify himself. Legend has it that he was met there by a celestial Naga Queen, the protectiv enature spirit of the riv er who recognized in Siddhartha a future Mahanaga Emperor in the making and materialized a jeweled throne for him to sit upon. Siddhartha acknowledged the throne, but not feeling worthy to lay claim to it just yet, thanked the queen and retraced his steps tothe Bodhi Tree. On his return he encountered a great Siddha, the Naga Kala, who blessed him with shakti and adv isedhim to stay focused as he would soon be attaining "the truth."

Reclaiming his seat under the Bodhi Tree, Siddhartha descended into a deep trance and soon achiev ed the state of Nirvakalpa Samadhi, total immersion in transcendental Shiva, which is also known among the Buddhists as Nirvana, the "cosmic void." In this state the limited self is completely dissolv edinto the infinite ocean of the unlimited Self or Spirit. Siddhartha continued in this state of Samadhi for sev endays during which a manifestation of the Primal Serpent, the seven headed cobra Muchilinda, expanded its hoods over his head and thereby protected him from all untoward elements and inimical intruders. The Primal Serpent Goddess always attends to the needs of those united with her lord, Shiva.

Eventually feeling called to return to the world and serve humankind, the newly enlightened Siddhartha assumed the state of Sahaja Samadhi, the "natural" samadhi, which is also known by the Buddhists as Bodhicitta, the "mind" and consciousness of a Buddha. In this state the outer world which had previously appeared so unattractiv eand painful to Siddhartha was now perceived to be a joyful manifestation of Shiva. And since he fully identified with Shiva, the world was now perceiv ed to be a reflection of his own Self. Finally arising from his seat, Buddha set out to fulfill his destiny as a Mahanaga Emperor.

Upon traveling north to the famous Deer Park in Sarnath, a spiritual retreat on the outskirts of Kashi, the Shakyamuni - Muni (sage) of the Shakyas - began his spiritual ministry by sharing his newfound enlightenment with a small group of itinerant sadhus. While surrounded by four struggling ascetics, Buddha proceeded to outline his new path, the Middle Path, which could more easily and rapidly lead one to the exalted spiritual state of nirvana than could the path of total abstinence. Comprised of the Four Noble Truths and the Eighthfold Path, Buddha's new yogic regimen was free of the extreme austerities adhered to by the ascetics, but disciplined enough to insure eventual enlightenment.

Leaving his first disciples behind at Sarnath to practice and spread the new religion of Buddhism, Buddha set out on a proselytizing mission throughout India. During the ensuing 50 years he made thousands of converts to his Dharma or teaching, many of whom were Mahanagas, Siddhas and Naga Kings who continually flocked to hear to his high wisdom. One Naga King of the Shishunaga Dynasty of Magadha was so transfixed by the teachings of the Buddha that he made Buddhism the new religion of his kingdom. Other Naga Kings followed suit and soon the Buddha's teachings had united the Naga Kingdoms into one cohesive Naga empire with Buddha himself as its honorary Mahanaga Emperor. From that point onwards, or until the eventual collapse of the Naga Kings' political power, Buddhism had a solid backing in India and remained strong on the sub-continent.

During his reign as the Mahanaga Emperor of India, Buddha founded a brotherhood of Buddhist monks called the Sangha. Of those accepted into the Sangha, some were specially selected to become part of the Buddha's inner circle and receive the most esoteric teachings of the Siddhas. These elite Buddhists gathered in secluded groves or mountaintop retreats to listen to the Shakyamuni discourse on meditation, pranayama, asanas, and the path of the serpent fire. Some of these ancient Siddha teachings, such as those compiled upon the summit of Vulture Peak by Buddha's eventual successor, Mahakashyapa, were later incorporated into the Buddhist Tantras, the most esoteric of Buddhist texts.

After having become a wise old sage of eighty years, Buddha decided his time on the planet was nearing completion. Soon afterwards the great muni died a yogic death and achieved the final state of absorption into Spirit known among the Siddhas as Maha Samadhi and among the Buddhists as Maha Nirvana, the "great" and final absorption. A grand funeral followed as Buddhist monks, Naga Kings and Siddhas from all over India and Asia arrived at Buddha's side to pay their last respects to the Jagadguru. The funeral service was conducted by Mahanaga priests and the cremation of Buddha's body was supervised by the Mallas, a group of Nagas which had been the Shakyamuni's steadfast devotees.

Following his funeral, Buddha's sacred "relics" (possessions, teeth, hair) were divided into eight parts and given over to representatives of eight countries within which Buddhism had spread. These relics were taken to special places in Asia by Naga Kings and Mahanagas who then constructed a small temple or stupa, symbolizing the body of the Buddha, over each. In Burma, for example, the Nagas took 8 hairs from the Buddha's head and built the country's most sacred stupa over them, the Shwe Dagon, or "Temple of the Golden Dragon." In later years the Buddhist king Ashoka is reputed to have traveled to some of these Asian stupas in order to retrieve the relics and return them to India. His mission proved successful except in the ancient Naga Kingdom of Ramagrana where the relics were protected by Naga guardians.

THE MAHANAGA NAGARJUNA

Hundreds of years after the Maha Samadhi of Buddha, a schism occurred within the Sangha thus causing Buddhism to divide into Hinayana and Mahayana sects. The Hinayanists remained faithful to the orthodox Pali Cannon, the first collection of Buddha's teachings compiled soon after his death, while the Mahayanists included within their sacred cannon many of the secret Siddha teachings which the Buddha had left in the safekeeping of certain disciples and Mahana gas. One of the principal figures responsible for revealing these exclusive Siddha doctrines of the Buddha was the great Buddhist patriarch Nagarjuna.

Nagarjuna, the "Naga Arjuna," was born around the first or second century A.D. to a South Indian family in Andhra. Since Andhra was ruled by kings of the Solar Dynasty at the time, many of whom had married Naga princesses, Nagarjuna was probably indoctrinated into the worship of Shiva at an early age. The details of his formative years are fragmentary, but he apparently spent a vast amount of time amongst the southern Indian Mahanagas and assimilated much of their ancient Siddha teachings. He reputedly mastered the path of Rasayana and composed the first authorized scripture on the art of alchemy, the *Rasaratnakara.* He also authored or co-authored numerous scriptures which contained detailed instructions concerning the Siddha disciplines of breath control, asanas and meditation. He is especially renown for mastering the ancient science of mantra or Mantrayana, the path of mantra repetition. It was Nagarjuna who introduced what was to become the most popular of Tibetan Buddhist mantras, Om Mani Padme Hum, which means the "the jewel in the lotus of the heart (which makes the sound of) Hum." Hum, like Kum or Kumara, is the sound of love created by the union of the polarity in the heart.

135

After his initiation into the Sangha, Nagarjuna proceeded to rise to its highest office of Patriarch. Then as the Thirteenth Patriarch (the first was Mahakashyapa, the second was Ananda, Buddha's cousin etc.) , Nagarjuna presided over numerous Buddhist councils, the most famous of which was the Buddhist council of Sri-nagar (Great Serpent) in Kashmir. It was within the assemblies of this renowned Buddhist conclave that the foundational doctrines and tenets of Mahayana Buddhism were clearly and conclusively defined for the first time.

Eventually Nagarjuna attained enlightenment and joined the ranks of the immortal Mahanagas. The Tibetan Buddhist records maintain that he lived for 600 years while other Buddhist traditions assert that he still resides within an immutable physical form. Some substantiated evidence indicates that he lived at least until 700 A.D. and is the Nagarjuna who served as abbot of Nalanda University at that time. Current images of Nagarjuna depict the great Mahanaga with a huge multi-headed cobra sheltering his body with itsexpanded hoods.

THE TANTRIC YOGA OF THE BUDDHIST SIDDHAS

Perhaps Nagarjuna's greatest contribution to Mahayana Buddhism was his development of Tantric Buddhism, a branch of esoteric Buddhism which is based upon the yogic practices and doctrines taught by the Buddha and other Mahanagas. In this work Nagarjuna was assisted by many Buddhist Siddhas, including the Siddha Asanga, found er of the Buddhist school of Yogacara, the Buddhist cara (path) of yoga, which was an evolution of the teachings of the Siddha Patanjali. Together this group of devoted Buddhists composed a series of Buddhist Tantras, the scriptures of Tantric Buddhism, within which the Siddha practices of alchemy, pranayama, mantra repetition, meditation, and Kundalini Yoga were translated into a Buddhist vernacular. This Buddhist Tantric movement eventually culminated in the formation of a variety of Buddhist Tantric schools including Vajrayana or Tibetan Buddhism.

THE BUDDHIST ESOTERIC ANATOMY

Part of the work accomplished by Nagarjuna, Asanga and the other Siddhas of Tantric Buddhism involved the development of a Buddhist esoteric anatomy. The ethe ric sheath or Dragon Body the y eventually agreed upon and popularized in their Tantras was composed of 32 nadis, four chakras, and a version of the serpent fire. The first chakra, called the Nirmana chakra, was located at the navel, and recognized to be the seat of Candali, the Buddhist term for the Kundalini. The second chakra, called the Dharmachakra, was positioned at the heart; the third chakra, Sambhogachakra, was placed at the throat; and the last and highest chakra, the Usnisakamala, was situated at the crown of the head, and corresponded to the Sahasrar. The goal of the Tantric Buddhist yogis was to reunite the dual nadis, Prajna (Ida) and Upaya (Pingala), awaken the Candali, and then move it up the middle nadi, the Sahaja or Avadhuti. Eventually the serpent fire would merge into the Usnisakamala, thereby producing full enlightenment within the yogi.

THE NAGAUNIVERSITIES

After literally hundreds of Buddhist Tantras were composed, Buddhist universities staffed with Siddha professors were established for their dissemination and study. The greatest of these institutions of spiritual learning were the Buddhist universities of Vikramasila and Nalanda, both of which were named after mythical Nagas.

Nalanda, the larger of the two colleges, was located in the Naga Kingdom of Magadha. During its heyday, this university housed over 10,000 Buddhist monks from all over Asia and contained such a prodigious library that it required the shelf space provided for by four large buildings. Its teachers included the famous Mahanagas Naropa and Nagarjuna as well as the Siddha Padmashambhava, the founder of Tantric Buddhism in Tibet.

THE 84 BUDDHIST SIDDHAS

Ultimately Tantric Buddhism produced its own tradition of Siddhas, commonly known as the 84 Buddhist Siddhas. Beginning with Nagarjuna, these Buddhist Siddhas had achieved perfection and even physical immortality through the practices promulgated by the Buddhist Tantric sects. Most of these Buddhist Mahanagas lived in northeast India and had been born into the underprivileged lower classes, i.e., the Vaisyas, Sudras and Untouchables. As sweepers, potters, cobblers, washermen and women, they had been excluded from the Vedic spiritual tradition but openly welcomed into Tantric Buddhism.

Most Buddhist Siddhas were initiated into their respective Tantric Buddhist sects by an acknowledged Siddha Master of the sect. Perhaps the most popular of these sects was that of the Havajra Tantra, an esoteric tradition based upon the direct awakening of the yogic fire or Candali. Once initiated into this or any other tantric tradition, most Buddhist Siddhas achieved enlightenment in 3, 6, 9 or 12 years. Many achieved both physical and spiritual immortality and their biographical sketches often conclude with the passage: "and he went to the realm of the Dakas (the immortals) in this very body (the transmuted physical body or etheric Dragon Body)."

CHAPTER 6

THE LUNG DRAGONS OF CHINA

In China the ancient immortals from Kun Lun, P'eng-lai, and other vestiges of Mu spawned a Dragon Culture within which the priest kings and spiritual masters were called Lung, "Dragons," as well as Hsien, "Immortals." The symbol of the Lung, the mythical azure or golden colored Lung Dragon, was considered to be the highest evolved species of dragon in China. It was a winged, heaven-dwelling species of dragon as opposed to the Li and Kiao, the lesser evolved Earth-bound dragons which dwelt in the sea and mountains respectively. In their attainment of spiritual wisdom and power, the Chinese Serpents of Wisdom personified the heaven-dwelling Lung. Their affiliation with this highly evolved creature was represented by the multi-colored dragon motifs they embellished their sacred vestments with.

THE WU DRAGONS

Possibly the first concentrated manifestation of China's Dragon Culture occurred in the ancient provinces of Ch'u (now Hunan, Anhwei and Szechuwan), which was adjacent to the Kun Lun range, as well as in its neighboring province of Ch'i (now Shentung). At the eastern end of Ch'i was the Gulf of Chihli, an area which anciently swelled with shamans practicing yoga, alchemy, and sorcery. The Gulf of Chihli is opposite the Islands of the Immortals so these shamans could have acquired their secrets from the adepts residing upon P'eng-lai and the other sacred isles.

The Serpents of Wisdom or Shamanic Lung of China's Dragon Culture are traditionally referred to as the Wu. The Wu are described as magician priests and priestesses who possessed supernatural abilities and knew the secret of making the Elixir of Immortality. The Wu were sorcerers, mediums, exorcists, rain makers, healers, alchemists and soul travelers with the power of disengaging their Dragon Bodies from their material sheaths and traveling interdimensionally at will.

Apparently a good percentage of the Wu were women who were renown for their ability to channel both the words and power of their deities on to the Earth plane. According to Mircea Eliade, these trans-channeling shamans could speak the pure language of the gods, become invisible at will, swallow swords, spit fire, and be "carried off on a cloud that shoe as if by lightning."[38]

The most important deity of the early Wu shamans was Hsi Wang Mu, a Dragon Queen whom legends claim resided with in the Kun Lun Mountains on what Taoist historians have called "Dragon Mountain," "Snake Wu Mountain" and Mount Wu, the "Mountain of the Wu." Hsi Wang Mu was an extremely ancient goddess who rode upon a five-color dragon and sat upon a dragon throne. Her veneration may have originated on Mu and then taken to China by Lemurian immortals. She was a version of the primal creatress who governed both life and death on Earth and throughout the cosmos. She could take away life, but it was also Hsi Wang Mu who could bestow the greatest prize of immortality to worthy seekers. Her name was perpetually on the lips of shamans striving for success on their paths to enlightenment and eternal existence. Many Chinese adepts who achieved immortality during their lifetimes eventually retired to her paradisiacal mountain retreat, including the famous Immortal Lao Tzu, the founder of Taoism, who was stopped by a border guard on his way to the Kun Lun Mountains and requested to write down his wisdom for future generations. Many others - both immortals and normal humans - followed Lao Tzu into the mountains of central China. With great hope and anticipation kings, queens and determined human seekers covered hundreds and thousands of miles on foot in hopes of finding the paradise of Hsi Wang Mu and receiving her divine blessing. While there, if they were extremely fortunate they might also be gifted with one of the legendary peaches of immortality that grew on a towering tree in the middle of the Land of the Immortals.

Hsi Wang Mu was the foremost patroness and teacher of the Wu, who sought her blessings in all their spiritual work and reached ecstacy by emulating her spiral dance. While wearing long robes and with their arms extended outwards while their sleeves dangled in the wind, a Wu would continually circle around in a graceful spiral. Through the spiraling motion a Wu could raise the Kundalini Serpent up the spine to the upper chakras in the head and thus achieve gnostic awareness, supernatural powers and transcendance. Many Wu also danced holding two live snakes, one in each hand, to represent the polarity that they would unite internally to resurrect the inner Serpent Power.

The numerous sects of Wu Shamans eventually evolved into the many orders of priests, priestesses and Lung Immortals of historical Taoism. The ancient Wu wisdom regarding yoga, alchemy, and immortality was inherited by the Dragon Kings and Feng Shih (Prescriptioners) of Taoism. And along with it the very ancient medical wisdom of the Wu regarding herbs - and what would late be known as acupuncture - was transferred to an order of Taoist doctors known as the Sai Kung.

Hsi Wang Mu on her Dragon Throne

While holding snakes, a Wu shamaness dances.
Wood engraving from Chu Dynasty.

A Lung Dragon Emperor

THE GOLDEN AGE AND THE DRAGON KINGS

As a national religion Taoism officially began in China around 3000 BCE at the beginning of a Golden Age, an era which lasted for much of the next 500 years. During this age of peace and wisdom the patchwork of autonomous Dragon Kingdoms within China were synthesized into one cohesive Dragon Empire. Lines of communication were established and a spirit of national unity began to flourish.

The central motivating force behind China's unification movement was the immortal priest king, known as the "Dragon" and "the first born Son of Heaven." As descendants of the early Lung Shamans these Dragon Kings governed China with the ancient wisdom they had inherited from their distinguished predecessors.

Five prominent Dragon Kings ruled during the Golden Age of China: Fu Shi, Shennung, Huang Ti, Yao and Shun. They are known historically as "The Original Five." Collectively these five emperors represented the five elements of the Dragon's five-fold body (known in China as metal, wood, fire, water, and earth) although by themselves each was a holistic embodiment of the archetypal Dragon. Each Dragon Emperor reflected the physical appearance of a dragon, wielded Ling or serpent power, and incarnated the Divine Mind.

THE   DRAGON   EMPEROR   HUANG   TI

Of the five Dragon Kings perhaps the one which had the most influence on the development of early Taoism was Huang Ti, the Yellow Emperor, who is sometimes referred to as the Father of Taoism. Huang Ti is associated with the fifth and uniting element of the five elements, earth. As an incarnation of the Divine Mind he wore vestments of yellow gold, the color of the earth element and what it engenders: practical wisdom and philosophical contemplation.

According to the traditional legend of his origins, Huang Ti was conceived by a ray of golden light which emanated to Earth from the Big Dipper (seat of the cosmic Dragon) and pierced the womb of his mother. At birth he had a dragon-like countenance and quickly exhibited precocious serpentine wisdom far beyond his years. Huang Ti could speak by the time he was two months old and by his fifteenth year he had mastered all the known sciences

Upon acquiring the reigns of government Huang Ti adopted a golden gown emblazoned with a large dragon and proceeded to continue the work of his predecessors by further developing Chinese culture. He made his court into a locus for the fermentation of both spiritual and practical ideas and invited to it the most advanced intellectuals. The tenants of Chinese Medicine crystallized at the Yellow Emperor's court during conversations between Huang Ti and his court official Ch'i Po, the transcripts of which became famous as the eighteen volumes of the *Nie Jing,* "The Yellow Emperor's Classic on Internal Medicine," which is still today the definitive textbook on Chinese Medicine. Wholistic medicine was practiced at the court by the physician Yu Fo, who is today often regarded as the first historical practitioner of acupuncture, massage and herbal medicine.

While furthering the codification of Taoism Huang Ti's court became a mecca for the study and practice of spiritual disciplines. The ancient shamanic practices of yoga, meditation and controlled breathing were introduced and practiced daily by the residents of the court for both health and spiritual enlightenment. Sexual yoga or Dual Cultivation was taught to Huang Ti by three female immortals of the Shamanic Dragon Culture-the simple maid, the mysterious maid and the chosen maid-and religiously practiced by the Yellow Emperor and his assistants. The science of Alchemy was also implemented at the court and Huang Ti himself became a renowned adept of the art after succeeding in distilling the Elixir of Immortality. The golden cauldron he distilled the precious liquid within became a good luck charm and was passed down to future generations of Dragon Kings, thereby endowing China with continued prosperity. Only once, during the reign of the megalomaniac Emperor Shih Huang-ti of the Chin Dynasty, was the cauldron lost, thus heralding a dark period in the history of China.

According to one legend, after achieving the ripe old age of 111 Huang Ti boarded a dragon and ascended into heaven. According to an alternate myth, at the end of his life he transformed himself into an etheric dragon and in that form "winged his way to the realm of the immortals."

THE LATER TAOISM OF LAO TZU

Around 500 B.C. the path of "the Way" or Taoism (living in harmony with the will of Spirit), diverged into two paths via the reformation work of the sages Confucius and Lao Tzu. Confucius established "the Way" of right relationships, the social path of Taoism through which the Chinese people could achieve alignment with the will of Spirit while embracing their worldly lives. His branch of social Taoism subsequently became known as Confucianism. By contrast, Lao Tzu, a representative of the ancient reclusive immortals, maintained that "the way" could best be intuited by pursuing yoga and meditation within isolated hermitages and mountain-top retreats. Lao Tzu's "new" branch of reclusive Taoism precipitated the creation of secluded monasteries, lonely mountain retreats and lineages of historical Taoist immortals.

According to legend, the paths of Confucius and Lao Tzu are reputed to have once crossed. Supposedly after being in the presence of Lao Tzu for a short time Confucius declared: "This day I have seen Lao Tzu. Today I have seen a Dragon."

THE HISTORICAL DRAGON IMMORTALS

Lao Tzu and his lineage of historical Hsien or Immortals inherited the ancient secrets of immortality from the shamen of the early Dragon Culture and the Dragon Kings of the Golden Age. These secrets subsequently became embedded in the Taoist cannon, a sacred body of literature which eventually overflowed with over 1,120 yogic and philosophical texts.

Through faithfully adhering to the yogic practices of their predecessors, the historical Taoists developed incredible magical abilities, immutable physical bodies and immortal Dragon sheaths. The unusual abilities of these immortals were sometimes alluded to by historical Taoist writers such as Lao Tzu and Chang Tzu. Chang Tzu maintained that the Taoist Immortals could walk through fire, move through solid rock or jump off of high cliffs without being harmed. Other Taoist authors alluded to the Immortals' ability to walk on clouds, ride upon the wind or live in an immutable physical body for thousands of years.

THE EIGHT DRAGON IMMORTALS

Of all the historical Taoist immortals, perhaps the most famous are the legendary Pa Hsien or "Eight Immortals." These enlightened Masters lived at different times between the reign of the Emperor Yao and the beginning of the second millennium A.D. Some lived hundreds and even thousands of years, such as the Immortal Chang Kuo who reputedly lived for nearly three thousand years. Collectively the Pa Hsien achieved the status of Taoist patron saints and their lives became models for all seekers on the path of immortality.

One interesting legend concerning the Eight Immortals claims that together they once visited the paradise of the immortals in the Kun Lun Mountains. They came to Hsi Wang Mu to attend a birthday celebration of the ruling queen and presented to her as their gift a silk scroll containing 76 characters written by Lao Tzu. This scroll was graciously accepted by the queen of heaven and honorably placed within the royal library of her legendary palace.

THE DRAGON IMMORTAL LI T'IEH-KUAI

The first of the Eight Immortals, Li T'ieh-kuai, felt drawn to a spiritual life at an early age and eventually decided to retreat from the mundane world to seek the isolation of a lonely mountain hermitage. For the better part of the ensuing 40 years Li sat cross-legged upon a simple reed mat while daily practicing intensive yoga and meditation. So consumed was he with the desire to become an immortal that he often forget to eat or sleep.

One of Li's teachers during his period of solitary practice was the great Immortal Lao Tzu. Lao Tzu would occasionali y leave his residence in one of the paradise realms of the immortals and travel within his Dragon Body to Li's hermitage. While there, Lao Tzu's principal instructions to his student consisted in the methodology for enlivening the immortal Dragon Body and traveling within it interdimensionally.

As part of Li's experiential training, Li and Lao Tzu would occasionally disengage their Dragon Bodies from their physical sheaths and together travel within them to distant paradise realms. During one of their interdimensional journeys, Li left his physical body in the care of one of his own devoted followers. When he failed to return to it after a requisite number of days, the devotee decided Li had permanently abandoned his physical sheath and proceeded to have it cremated. As fate would have it, Li returned just in time to catch the last glimpses of his body smoldering upon the embers. Nonplussed, Li caught the sight of a lame beggar's fresh corpse nearby and entered it. Arising in his new crippled body, Li found he required a staff to walk and was henceforth known by his contemporaries as Li T'ieh-kuai, "Li of the Iron Staff." Future iconographic images of Li would represent him as a lame beggar supporting himself with his famous iron staff.

THE DRAGON IMMORTAL LU TUNG-PIN

Before committing himself to the path of the way, another of the Eight Dragon Immortals, Lu Tung-pin, is believed to have been assigned the position of chief magistrate of Te-hua, which is now the city of Kiu-kiang in Kiangsi province. While serving in this post Lu had a dream which completely changed his life. Although only lasting a few minutes of earth time, the dream covered 18 years worth of experience and gave Lu the opportunity to learn some important lessons regarding the impermanence of existence. Upon awakening, Lu firmly resolved to seek the everlasting state of the Immortals.

Lu eventually retired to Stork Peak in the Lu Mountains and embarked upon the life as a Taoist recluse. Legend states that during his ensuing long period of isolation Lu encountered a fire dragon who gifted him with a sword. With the help of this sword Lu was able to perform many miracles and eventually achieve immortality. The fire dragon referred to appears to be a metaphor for Lu's inner serpent fire which "gifted" the fortunate yogi with magical abilities while spiritually transforming him (via the sword) and thus assisting him in his quest for immortality. Current iconographic images of Lu depict the immortal wielding his magical dragon sword.

After achieving union with the Tao, Lu occasionally descended from his mountain top retreat in order to heal the sick, make converts to the path of Taoism and teach important lessons to those entrenched in worldly existence. For one of his lessons Lu traveled to the village of Yo-Yang and disguised himself as a common oil seller in order to test the spiritual evolvement of the town's people. During the ensuing days Lu watched as each consumer tried to undermine his operation by paying less for his oil than they knew it was worth. When a righteous old woman finally stepped up and offered a fair price without even attempting to bargain for the oil, Lu was so pleased with her that he rushed to her house and threw magical rice into her well. The well water immediately transformed into precious wine which the old woman bottled and sold for a high price at the market. She subsequently become very wealthy.

TIIE DRAGON IMMORTAL IAN TS'AI-HO

For most of his life, the Dragon Immortal Lan Ts'ai-ho was a street singer and musician. Periodically, while singing or listening to the sweet, evocative melodies of spiritually inspired music, Lan would drift into a semi-conscious state of ecstatic union with the Tao. Eventually he became permanently established in unity awareness and attained immortality.

Later in his life Lan revealed his spiritual androgyny by often wearing the clothes of a woman while speaking in a low pitched, male voice. He became a musical guru and gifted many seekers with spontaneous spiritual awakening through the power of his uplifting ballads, the best known of which was a commentary on the transitory nature of ex istence.In iconography Lan is always depicted with some form of musical instrument, usually a flute. Sometimes he is portrayed as entertaining the other Immortals, Lu, Li and Chung.

TIIE DRAGON IMMORTAL CHANG KUO

The Dragon Immortal Chang Kuo was reputedly bom during the reign of the Emperor Yao, one of the Dragon Emperors of China's Golden Age. Not much is known of his long life ex cept that he attained immortality and lived for thousands of years. One official record maintains that C hang was still alive and a guest at K'ai Yuan's court sometime between 713-742 A.D. which would have made him close to three thousand years old at the time.

During his yogic training and even after achieving immortality, Chang Kuo spent most of his time as a recluse on the Chung T'iao Mountain in Shansi province. Occasionally he would come down from the mountain and could be found passing a village or casually drifting along a peaceful country road while spreading blessings to all those around him. He was usually perched upon his self-created donkey, a creature he had reputedly made out of paper and magically animated with his supernatural powers. Current iconographic images of Chang depict the immortal riding upon his donkey while holding in his hands phoenix feathers and a peach of immortality.

One interesting story which reveals Chang's complete transformation into a Dragon I mmortal has a reigning emperor of his time inquiring from the scholarly recluse Yeh Fo-Shen as to the true nature of the Immortal. Without hesitation, Yao proclaimed that Chang was the "original vapor" or Chi, the etheric form of the Primal Dragon.

THE DRAGON IMMORTAL HAN HSIANG

The Dragon Immortal Han Hsiang was the nephew of Han Yu, a famous scholar and poet of the eighth century A.D.. Han yearned for true wisdom and the everlasting bliss of union with the Tao. His spiritual search brought him into association with Lu Tung-pin and he quickly mastered the magical arts and the yogic sciences under the guidance of the Immortal. Afterwards he performed some astonishing miracles such as materializing wine out of thin air and causing flowers to spontaneously open with poems written in golden characters upon their leaves. These miracles so impressed his uncle that they became the theme of some of Han Yu's verses. In iconography Han Hsiang holds a gourd filled with the peaches of immortality in one hand and a bouquet of the flowers he magically opened in the other.

THE DRAGON IMMORTAL TS'AO KUO-CIDU

The Immortal Ts'ao Kou-chiu was born into a royal family and is remembered as the brother of the empress Jen Tsung who reigned between 1023-1064 A.D. Possessing a spiritual bent, Prince Ts'ao became disenchanted with his wealthy, mundane life. He then gave away all his possessions to the poor and retired to the mountains to seek immortality.

After practicing yoga and meditating in a lonely mountaintop hermitage for many years, Ts'ao finally achieved his goal. Legend has it that soon afterwards he was visited by the I mmortals Chung-li Ch'uan and Lu Tung-pin who proceeded to test Ts'ao's level of spiritual attainment. In response to one of their probing questions, Ts'ao stated that he had realized that the heart was the true abode of Heaven. I mpressed by his poignant reply the Immortal Chang added: "the heart is Heaven and Heaven is the Way." Convinced that he had united the polarity, awakened the heart (the center of polarity union), and reached unity with the Tao, the two visiting immortals had Ts'ao inducted into the organization of immortals which had become scattered throughout the mountain highlands of China. Afterwards, Chung- li Ch'uan and Lu Tung-pin assumed their glorious Dragon Bodies and escorted Ts'ao to the paradise regions of the Immortals as their guest. In current iconography Ts'ao is depicted wearing his royal robes and carrying the royal insignia of his biological family.

THE DRAGON IMMORTAL HO HSIEN-KO

The Immortal Ho Hsien- ko is the only female of the Pa Hsien. According to one version of her biography, Ho had a dream at the age of fourteen in which she learned that the powder of mother of pearl would grant her the prize of immortality. Upon awakening from the dream she proceeded to consume a large, and potentially toxic, quantity of the substance. The result of her indiscriminate consumption was, however, not death, but the development of an immutable physical body and an immortal Dragon Body within which she could travel interdimensionally. In the years that followed she was occasionally spotted reclining upon billowy clouds and dancing joyously upon rainbows.

THE DRAGON PRESCRIPTIONERS

Many of the first immortals associated with the later Taoism of Lao Tzu were part of an order called the Feng Shih or "Prescriptioners." Many of the Feng Shih were direct descendants of the immortal Lung Shamans of the early Chinese Dragon Culture and inherited many of their ancient rites and secrets.

Around 400 B.C. the Feng Shih came down out of their secluded mountain retreats and commenced to proliferate throughout the towns and villages of China. Some Feng Shih became itinerant medicine men noted for arbitrarily wandering from town to town while spreading the wisdom of yoga and concocting herbal recipes or prescriptions for healing. Many gained renown for their knowledge of longevity, alchemy and immortality and were even summoned to the royal palace to set up a laboratory and produce the Elixir of Immortality for the incumbent emperor. This proved to be a risky occupation indeed. Should the imperial prescriptioner fail to produce the requisite elixir he was likely to undergo extreme torture or even invite upon himself the sentence of death.

The Prescriptioners helped to organize the "new" path of Lao Tzu and are therefore considered to be the patriarchs of modem Taoism. By bringing many of the ancient shamanic secrets of herbalism, breath control, meditation and alchemy down from the mountains, they made this wisdom more accessible

The Eight Immortals of Taoism

Uniting the polar opposite Dragon and Tiger

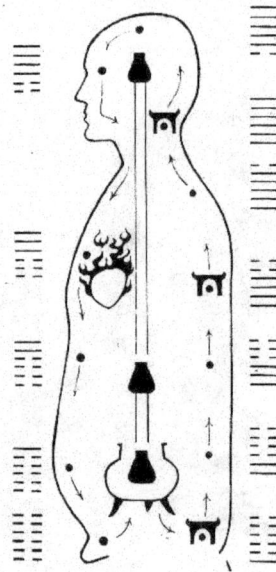

Sending Heart Fire to heat up Kidney Water and produce Serpent Fire

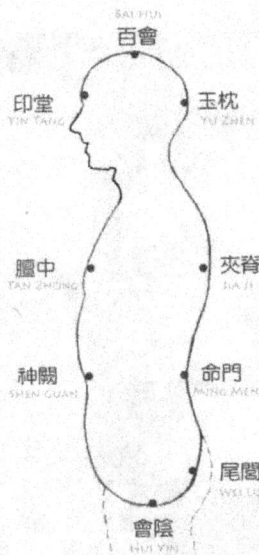

百會
BAI HUI

印堂　　　　玉枕
YIN TANG　　YU ZHEN

膻中　　　　夾脊
TAN ZHONG　JIA JI

神闕　　　　命門
SHEN GUAN　MING MEN

尾閭
WEI LU

會陰
HUI YIN

The Microcosmic Orbit: Circulating the Serpent Fire

for future Taoist seekers. The Feng Shih synthesized the ancient wisdom and translated it into a vernacular which could be readily understood by all sincere aspirants.

THE DRAGON IMMORTAL TSOU YEN AND ALCHEMY

One of the best known of the early Prescriptioners was Tsou Yen. An immortal of the fourth century B C., Tsou Yen was born and brought up in Shentung province among a thriving Dragon Culture of magicians, sorcerers and immortals. After applying himself to years of spiritual studies amongst these adepts, Tsou Yen achieved immortality and then amalgamated the ancient secrets and philosophies of alchemy into a coherent, modern system.

Tsou Yens's synthesized philosophy maintained that at the beginning of time the polarity, yin and yang, emanated out of the unlimited sea of consciousness, the Tao. Yin and yang united to give birth to the androgynous Dragon and its five-fold body which in turn divided to form the five elements of fire, earth, metal, water and wood. According to Tsou Yen, the secret of creating an "androgynous" Elixir of Immortality-the essence of the androgynous Dragon-lied in reuniting the five elements and/or the two opposites into a wholistic, primeval essence.

THE OUTER OR SYNTHETIC ELIXIR OF IMMORTALITY

From hls Shamanic mentors Tsou Yen learned numerous secret recipes and alchemical processes necessary for creating a physical "pill" or Elixir of Immortality. These ancient formulas utilized such ingredients as cinnabar, gold, sil ver, mercury, arsenic, lead, jade and pearls. In order to create the "and rogenous" elixir, Tsou Yen united the requisite ingredients, each of which corresponded to one the five elements or one of the two opposing principles, and then put them thro ugh "9 transforma tions," symbolic of the cycle of spiritual transmutation. The two metals used most frequently in his recipes to represent the male and fem ale principles (or "the dragon and tiger" as the alchemists called them) were mercury and lead.

Tsou Yen's alchemical movement eventually attracted many zealous seekers anxiously pursuing the treasure d goal of immortality. Those seekers who truly understood the philosophy and mechanics of alchemy as delineated by him ultimately succeeded in manufacturing a pill which both awakened their psychic powers and promoted their physical and spiritual immortality. Those who proceeded blindly, however, often suffered fatal reactions due to metal toxicity.

THE DRAGON IMMORTAL HSU
AND THE INNER EUXIR OF IMMORTALITY

Many --Prescriptioners believed that the true pill or Elixir of Immortality was not a synthetic, outer pill but one created inside the body of a spiritual seeker. The members of this contrasting group of adepts founded the path and school of internal alchemy. One of the outspoken constituents of the school was the immortal Hsu. Before he became an internal alchemist, Hsu was a synthetic alchemist who spent many years in the lonely mountains of China while fruitlessly attempting to create the outer pill. One day as he stoked his fire and prepared to create the synthetic pill one more time, Hsu was unexpectedly paid a visit by an immortal sage who claimed to have been attending the birthday festival of a Dragon King on P'eng-lai when he intuitively sensed Hsu's frustration. After arriving in Hsu's camp, the immortal proceeded to survey all of Hsu's assorted vials, herbs, minerals and half-baked mixtures. The wise sage then turned to the struggling alchemist and declared: "The only effective furnace is the one you carry behind your navel and the only safe receptacle for the completed pill lies within your skull a few hairs breaths' from the crown. "[74] The immortal followed up this definitive statement with instructions in the yogic practices of the ancient Lung which were designed to culminate in the creation of the inner pill or Elixir of Immortality (the transmuted essence) and lead it, via the spine, to the apex of the head.

THE HYGIENE SCHOOL AND
TAOIST ESOTERIC ANATOMY

Eventually a school was founded which synthesized all the practices espoused by the Prescriptioners for producing both the inner and outer pill. This was the Interior God's Hygiene School.

The basic text of the Hygiene School, written in the first century A.D., served as a vehicle for the Prescriptioners to coherently amalgamate and catalogue all the practices of the ancient Shamanic Lung. Along with these timeless disciplines, the Feng Shih incorporated into the text their version of the human esoteric anatomy, complete with etheric power centers and meridians. As a microcosmic reflection of the universe, the teachers of the Hygiene School maintained that the human body was home to 36,000 gods, the same number of gods which governed the cosmos. These inner gods were said to reside in cavities or centers of the body, many of which corresponded to the Hindu

Chakras. One of the most important of these gods was Tai I (the counterpart of the Hindu Shiva), an ancient god of the Shamanic Lung who resided in the Niwan, the Taoist counterpart of the Hindu Sahasrara or crown chakra. Other less important gods resided in other parts of the body and other centers, such as "the mysterious square inch" which corresponded to the Ajna Chakra or third eye, and the two Cinnabar Fields. The Cinnabar Fields were situated at the regions of the solar plexus/heart lower abdomen and corresponded to the Manipura and Svadisthana Chakras respectivel y. These two lower centers were also referred to as "cauldrens," thus reflecting their yogic functions as crucibles of the inner pill.

THE DRAGON IMMORTAL KO HUNG

Al ong with the founders of the Interior God's Hygiene School a number of outstanding independent Prescriptioners also synthesized the discipl ines of the ancient Shamanic Lung and organized them into l engthy tomes. The greatest of this genre of pioneering Prescriptioners was the Immortal Ko Hung.

Ko Hung spent most of his very active life as a mountain recl use When not fending off wild animals or disarming inimical dark spirits seeking to obstruct his spiritual progress, he was painstakingly pursuing all the known yogic and alchemical disciplines of the earl y Lung Shamans. After living many years alone while experiencing the efficacy of the various yogic practices first hand , Ko Hung achieved immortal ity and composed the *Pao P'u Tzu,* ancycolpedic reference guide for the mountain recl use and solitary practitioner. Finally, having retained his youthful appearance well into his eighties, Ko Hung sat down in a cross-legged yogic posture and projected his Dragon Body to the real ms of the immortals.

All together, Ko Hung's encyclopedia included 149 secret formulas and 116 vol umes, each of which was overflowing with both spiritual and practical advice for the solitary mountain hermit. To hel p make the hermits' camp safe Ko Hung included in his text efficacious incantations for repelling wild animals, such as tigers and snakes, as well as mantras for fighting the etheric demons which threaten to sabotage an aspirant's spiritual progress. To assist the solitary seeker in making fast spiritual advancement, Ko Hung also incorporated into his book lengthy instruction on controlled breathing and offered numerous al chemical recipes for producing both the inner and outer pills of immortality. Other miscellaneous information supplied in the text included: mantric formulas for getting the God of the Stove, one of the internal gods, to remove the seeker's name from the Book of Death and copy it into the Book of Immortality, as well as a description of medicinal herbs and mantras for healing, some of which were even used for raising the dead.

Ko Hung's encyclopedia became the "Bible" of many solitary hermits. Through its assistance some recluses, including the famous hermit T'ao hung-ching who retained his youthful appearance into his mid 8 0s, are reputed to have achieved both physical and spiritual immortality. For his contribution in synthesizing the wisdom of the ancient Lung and composing such an invaluable text, Ko Hung is generally regarded today as one of the founding patriarchs of modern Taoism.

UNITING THE DRAGON AND TIGER AND ACTIVATING THE SERPENT FIRE

Rounding out Ko Hung's and the other the Prescriptioners' formulary of disciplines for creating the inner and outer pill were yogic practices passed down from the ancient Lung Immortals which were specially designed for uniting the male and female principles, called the Dragon and Tiger. These yogic practices joined the areas of the body where opposing principles have their seats, such as the right (male) and left (female) sides of the body, the right and left eyes, the back and front, and the upper and lower extremiti es of the torso. When adhered to faithfully, such practices would eventually culminate in the union of the Dragon and Tiger, the activation of the serpent fire, and the creation of the immortal Dragon Body.

In order to unite the Dragon and Tiger in their seats within the upper and lower torso, where they exist as fire and water in the lungs/heart and kidneys respectively, specific practices, such as controlled breathing patterns, were developed by the Taoists in order to push the yang fire down in the body and unify it with the lower dwelling yin water. Meditational techniques were also employed to send the fire down to the Dantien, the name of the seat of water directly below the navel. Once the fire was successfully lowered by either of these means, the element would mix with the yin fluids in the lower torso, especially the Jing or seminal essence, and "cook" them into a fiery essence (the Taoist serpent fire).

For uniting the Dragon and Tiger from their other seats in the body, i.e., the left and right arms, the left and right eyes, the front and the back, certain Taoist meditational postures were utilized by the Prescriptioners. These meditational positions were believed to be normal to the human body as they were supposedly adhered to in the womb by an unborn fetus as it experienced unremitting union with the Tao. One popular meditational pose used by the gestating fetus and adopted by the Taoists involved crossing the eyes. Since the right eye corresponds to the Dragon and the left to the Tiger, their crossing or union would naturally elicit a union of opposites in the body. Another meditational pose used by the fetus and adopted by the Taoist yogi consisted of holding the tongue against the upper palate of the mouth, thereby uniting the Ren Channel, the major yin meridian which runs up the front of the torso with the Du Channel, the major yang meridian which runs along the back of the torso. In this way the front (female) and back (male) are united. Finally, the meditating yogi would unite the Tiger and Dragon from their seats on the left and right portions of the torso by simply crossing or touching his left (female) and right (male) hands and feet.

Taoist yogis also employed practices to unite the Dragon and the Tiger in their manifestations within the body as the male and female sexual fluids. These practices fall under the heading of Dual Cultivation, the Chinese term for sexual intercourse with a yogic intent. During Dual Cultivation the male transmitted the male essence or Dragon into his partner via his own seminal fluid and she transmitted the female essence or Tiger into him via her sexual fluids. The opposing fluids would then unite within the lower parts of each partner's body and produce the fiery essence.

CREATING THE IMMORTAL FETUS OR DRAGON BODY

Once the Dragon and Tiger were fully united by any of the above methods, the transmuted, fiery essence was awakened and the Taoist Yogi could then employ certain breathing and visualization techniques for moving it into the Du Vessel. Within this dorsal vessel the Chinese version of the Kundalini could easily ascend up the back to the top of the head. Once there, the radiant essence would be transferred from the Du Vessel into the Ren Meridian (the two vessels connect in the head) and then brought down the front of the body and returned to the base of the spine. This circular pathway of the transmuted essence was called the Microcosmic Orbit.

After continually circulating the fiery essence through the Microcosmic Orbit for a prescribed period of time, thereby purifying the physical body; the Taoist yogi proceeded with the creation of the immortal Dragon Body. To create this etheric body, the yogi withdrew the transmuted essence out of the Microcosmic Orbit and stored it within the lower abdomen. In time this store of purified essence accumulated to a point of critical mass and spontaneously metamorphosed into an "Immortal Fetus," a name for the immortal Dragon Body. This Dragon Body was termed a fetus because it matures in the abdomen, the area in which a pregnant mother carries her developing child.

Once the gestation period of the Immortal Fetus had been completed and the Dragon Body of life force was fully matured, the Taoist yogi learned how to detach it from its physical sheath and move it in and out through the top of the head. Then, over time, the Taoist yogi acquired the ability to move interdimensionally and travel within the Dragon Body to far off planets and universes. Finally, at the end of the yogi's life, the Dragon Body was permanently separated from its physical sheath and the yogi traveled to his eternal home in the heavenly regions of the Immortals.

THE DRAGON IMMORTAL BODHIDHARMA AND THE CHAN SCHOOL

Existing as it did alongside of Taoism, Buddhism also produced its own tradition of Immortals in China. The best known of these masters was the Dragon Immortal Bodhidharma, also known as Da Mo by the Taoists.

When Bodhidharma first arrived in China in 552 A.O. he traveled directly to Peking, the country's capital. This acclaimed Siddha and master of Tantric Buddhism is then reputed to have resided in a cave outside of the imperial city where he commenced to disseminate the Chan School of meditation. Similar to other paths of Tantric Buddhism, the Chan School prioritized rapid spiritual progress and direct ex perience over abstract philosophical speculation. The foundational practices of the Chan School involved long, lonely hours of meditation, often in front of a blank wall, which would ultimately culminate in sudden spiritual revelations and complete union with the Tao. When Bodhidharma eventually relocated to the monastery of Cho-ling as its abbot, he became the ideal role model for the Chan School by spending the majority of his time meditating in front of a wall of rocks.

To supplement his students' long hours of meditation, Bodhidharma incorporated into the Chan School an assortment of yogic techniques, including asanas and pranayama, which he had brought with him from India. These practices were eventually compiled into two tex ts called *The Muscle Tendon Changing Classic* and *The Marrow Washing Classic*. The yoga disciplines of *The Muscle Tendon Changing Classic* increased the health and longevity of the monks and naturally prepared them for the practices of the more esoteric *The Marrow Washing Classic*. The disciplines of this second tex t were designed to transmute the seminal fluid through fire, raise it up the spine to nourish the brain, and eventually culminate in both divine wisdom and immortality.[75] The yogic practices of both these tex ts were eventually assimilated into the Taoist school of breath control, Chi Kung.

THE SERPENTS OF WISDOM
IN
THE AMERICAS

A Snake Clan dancer

CHAPTER 7
THE AMARUS OF PERU

The Serpents of Wisdom of Peru's Dragon Culture were the Amarus, a Quechuan name for snake or serpent. As wise men and priest kings they administered the mystery schools and Dragon Empires which had been founded by the earliest Lemurian and Atlantean Serpents in the Andean highlands, the lowland jungles and the Pacific coastal regions. Two of the best known Dragon Cultures they governed are known historically as the Chimu and the Inka.

CHIMU AND CHAN CHAN, CITY OF THE SERPENT

The civilization of Chimu was perhaps the greatest of the coastal Dragon Cultures in Peru. Chimu developed in close proximity to the Cupisnique and Mochica civilizations, two historical cultures which had been intimately influenced by the highland Dragon Cultures of Tiahuanako and Chavin. Consistent with its ancient neighbors, Chimu was founded around a serpent/dragon theme, a theme which was especially noticeable in the name and serpentine ambiance of its capital city, Chan-Chan, meaning "Serpent-Serpent" (Chan or Kan is the universal name for serpent).

During its heyday Chan-Chan, the City of the Serpent, was home to approximately 50,000 inhabitants. Throughout this bustling serpent city ornamental snakes were either carved or painted on the walls of many public and religious buildings, including the surviving Huaca El Dragon, the "Temple of the Dragon." Live snakes, many of which played an integral role in the performance of the daily religious rites in Chan-Chan, were lodged and fed within the sacred temples. The facilitators of these serpent rites, the shaman priests and priest kings or Chimus, utilized serpent inscribed instruments while adorning themselves with headdresses with the images of snakes slithering across the front. During an official ceremony trained temple shamen would emit snake sounds and recite sacred snake mantras in order to invoke the presence of their beneficent serpent gods.

CHIMU'S DRAGON HERITAGE

Although the founders of the Chimu culture were greatly influenced by their neighbors, they also claimed to have had an origin which was independant of these civilizations. According to their own historical texts, some ancestors of the Chimu anc iently arrived along the South American coast in vessels covered with the images of serpents. They came as a band of traders and colonists from an alien Dragon Culture located somewhere to the north. They were probably kin to a Central or North American Dragon Culture. The North American Hopi Snake Clan, for example, believes it may share an ancestor with the Chimu.55

THE SERPENTS OF CHAVIN DE HUANTAR

One of the principal influences on Chimu was Chavin de Huantar, a compound of pyramids that, according to contemporary Peruvian shamans was built by colonizing Dragons from Mu. The pyramids of Chivan were covered with human stone heads that exhibited the feature s of condors, snakes and puma s, the three sacred animals that the Primal Dragon divided into when creating the universe. These three animals governed the three worlds for their cosmic dragon parent. The stone heads are believed to represent the ancient occupants of Chavin who had mastered the three worlds and their associated animals, thus becoming living Dragons. Their attainments are also represented by the top knot- symbol of an open crown chakra-found on many of the stone heads.

The Dragons of Chavin achieved union with their Dragon Creator through the consumption of a sacred cactus, Wachuma or San Pedro, that shamans claim was brought with the colonists from Mu. They point to an enclosure within the Chavin compound that is said to be the only known temple in the Andes designed and used solely for the purpose of W achuma consumption. There, a glyph on the inside wall of the circular temple reveals the Lemurian origin of the plant. It depicts a Dragon Master carrying the cactus in his hand from Mu to ancient Peru.

Under the pyramids of Chavin a network of tunnels were built for the observance of sacred rites. In the middle of the tunnel labyrinth is the center of the Chavin vortex, where the ancient builders planted a monolith with the features of the Primal Dragon carved into it. The monolith serves as the World Tree in the center of the Chavin dragon's lair. For ages, shamans have traveled in their Dragon Bodies to "climb" the tree to other dimensions.

THE SERPENT INKAS

The Inka s (a name which incorporates the universal K sound of the Serpents) comprised the greatest of inland Dragon Cultures. As a civilization they officially commenced with Aramu Muru, previously a high ranking member of the Solar Brotherhood and Seven Ray Order on Mu, who migrated to the Andes Mountains with his consort, Arama Mara. After landing their light ships in

The Serpentine Walls of Chan Chan

A Dragon Master brings the sacred Wachuma cactus to the Andes from Mu.

El Lanzon: An image of the Primal Dragon in the center of the Chavin labyrinth of tunnels

The flattened 2D dragon form of El Lanzon. The Primal Dragon unites Heaven & Earth.

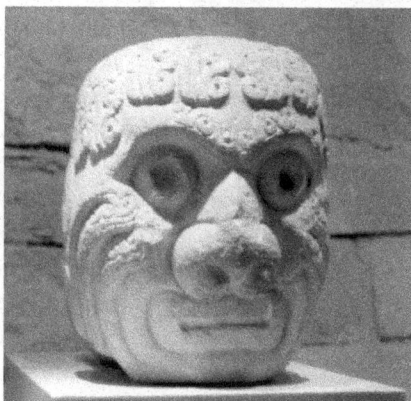

Stone heads of the Chavin Dragon Adepts. They were Masters of the 3 Worlds and their 3 corresponding animals. The 3 Worlds are: The Upper World (Sky, Heaven), Middle World (Earth), and Lower World (Inner Earth, Lower Dimensions). The 3 corresponding Sacred Animals are: Condor, Puma, Snake.

an Andean valley they helped establish a branch of the Seven Ray Order in South America. One legend asserts that these early Amarus eventually founded a lineage of enlightened priest kings and queens known as the Inkas. As the first Inka king and queen, they became known as Manko Kapac and Mama Ocllo.

When Manko Kapac and Mama Ocllo left their incipient port-of-call at Tiahuanako on Lake Titicaca they were covered in "tassels, sashes, and belt ornaments-all in rainbow colors."7 This regalia denotes their membership in the ancient Order of the Seven Rays. Together they led an entourage of builders, the Kapac Cuna, to a powerful vortex in the Andes, the center of which was chosen to be the capital of a new empire. Over this dragon's lair the Serpents from Mu built a great city they called Cuzco, the "navel," and laid it out in the form of a gigantic puma, one of the three sacred animals of the sub-divided Primal Dragon. The puma governs the middle of Earth plane represents its kings and queens. In Cuzco, it also denotes puma energy that radiates outward from the city's underlying vortex. Dynamic Cuzco became the center of the Inkan kingdom known as Tawantinsuyu, Empire of the Four Directions.

CORICANCHA, MAIN TEMPLE OF THE INKAN AMARUS

Near the center of Cuzco Manko built his kingdom's principal temple, the Intiwasi, the "Place of the Sun," in honor of the Solar Spirit Inti, patron deity of the Intic Churincuna, the "Children of the Sun." He then proceeded to found a cohesive empire based upon the timeless spiritual principles of the Solar Brotherhood and Seven Ray Order of Mu. While wearing the Mascaypacha, ancient diademof the Solar Brotherhood, as well as garments that reflected the colors of the Seven Rays, Manko ruled over an empire that eventually spanned much of South America.

Manko's Intiwasi became the nerve center of his new kingdom and the chief temple for the worship to Inti and the other deities of the Inkan empire. It was a huge temple, larger than a city block, covered both inside and out with thick sheets of shimmering gold. Lining its interior golden walls was the magnificent seat of Manko and the other incumbent Inkas, a solid gold throne. This throne was slowly joined by a long line of other golden thrones which were occupied by the of mummies of deceased Inkas, until there were thirteen in number. Whenever a ruling Inka made a crucial decision regarding the future of the empire and/or performed an important ceremony, he would always consult the spirits of these past Amarus for guidance and assistance.

The interior of Intiwasi was divided into cubicle-like sub-temples, each dedicated to one of the principal nature gods of the Inkas, i.e., the lightning, the rainbow, the planet Venus etc. The largest and most important of these sub-temples was the Temple of Viracocha, a sanctuary dedicated to the spiraling serpentine Creator of the Universe (Viracocha denotes "churning fat" or "spiraling waters.") Within this temple hung one of two huge golden sun discs which were kept within the Intiwasi. The most important of these discs had been brought by Aramu Muru or Manko Kapac from Mu, where it had been a power object of the Seven Ray Order, and then stored in the Monastery of the Seven Rays before being transported to the Intiwasi. This sacred disc was seldom seen and only removed from its hidden chamber "in transcendental times or occasions of a cosmic character."[7] When Peru was later conquered, the lesser important of the two discs was carted away by the avaricious Spanish conquistadors while the Lemurian disc was returned to to the region of Lake Titicaca and is now reputed to lie at the bottom of the sacred lake.

Following the invasion of Peru, the Spanish renamed the Temple of Intiwasi the Coricancha, the "Temple of Gold," and carted away most of its valuable gold. Today parts of the old temple provide the foundation for the Spanish cathedral which later arose in its place, the Church of Santo Domingo.

THE CENTRAL PLAZA OF THE INKAN SERPENTS

Nearby the imposing Intiwasi was the sacred plaza of the Inkas, known by them as Huacaypata, the "Place of Crying." Huacaypata (now called the Plaza de Armas) was once surrounded by temples and ornate palaces of the Inka priest kings. At one end of the plaza (where the Cathedral now stands) was the Temple Palace of the Inka Viracocha. This palace was built over a network of water channels which served to amplify the energy of a pre-existing dragon's lair and promoted the temple's function as an important center for sacred rites and initiations. At another end of the sacred plaza was the Amaru Kancha, the "Temple of the Serpents" or the "Place of Wisdom," where the Church of La Compana now sits).The Amaru Kancha functioned as both temple and ancient university, a citadel for indoctrination into all aspects of serpent wisdom. It also functioned at one time as the Temple/Palace of the Inka Huayna Kapac.

TAMBO MACHAY, THE RESTING PLACE OF THE SERPENT

Some of the most sacred of Inkan temples were built by the Amarus in the hills surrounding Cuzco. While ascending the trail leading to some of these megalithic temples, the Inkas were known to stop at a sacred baptismal fountain called Tambo Machay, the "resting place of the serpent," to purify themselves before entering the holy temples. The pure water of Tambo Machay originated from a hidden spring located in the mountain it sat upon and was imbued with the healing and transformative powers of the serpent life force. According to one probable scenario, to activate the vivifying power of this holy water mantras were recited by the Inkan priests as they sprinkled the sacred water over each person as they stood for a cleansing baptism. Watching over these purifying rituals as they occurred were images of Inkan deities, or perhaps the mummies of past Inkan royalty, which stood directly over the fountains. They occupied four stone niches or cubicles which presumably corresponded to the four directions of Tawantinsuyu, the Land of the Four Directions or Quarters.

As it was in ancient times, it is currently the custom of many Peruvian shamans to cleanse themselves in the purifying waters of Tambo Machay before proceeding to Sacsayhuaman and the other hilltop temples.

Sacred Sites Journeys ©2016

The massive stone blocks of Sacsayhuaman

SACSAYHUAMAN, THE SERPENT/LIGHTNING TEMPLE

Beyond Tambo Machay was Sacsayhuaman or Sacahuma, the "Puma's Head," the greatest of the hilltop temples surrounding Cuzco.The temple of Sacahuma was situated at the head of the Cuzco puma and constructed in the shape of a gigantic puma's head.

The Temple of Sacahuma was dedicated to two of the Inkas' most explosive nature deities, the lightning and the serpent. The massive blocks of the temple, the "Puma's teeth," were arranged in zigzag patterns to delineate the path of the lightning as it traveled as a serpent from the heavens to Earth and across the Sacahuma compound . The officiating Inkan priest would theoretically summon the lightning into the Temple of Sacahuma and use its explosive power for purposes of a sacred nature. The Inkas believed that the lightning had the power to transform one into a shaman or wise serpent. Some Andean guides suggest that the Serpent/Lightning Temple may have been used by the Inkan Solar Brotherhood for initiation purposes. This seems probable considering that frequent lightning storms tend to occur around the Summer Solstice, a traditional day for Inkan initiations. Many Andean guides further theorize that the goal of the lightning ceremonies at Sacahuma was the awakening of the inner lightning serpent, the Kundalini. To substantiate this notion they point to a conspicuous carving at the top of the main staircase leading into Sacahuma, which may indicate the raison d'etre of the temple. This symbolic carving is that of a vertically ascending snake which contains six successive round scallops and terminates in a "head," an apparent representation of the course of the Kundalini up the human spine to the top of the head. This Sacahuma "Kundalini" motif, which in size closely approximates the length of the human spine from base to skull, is believed to have once been filled with six or seven crystalline spheres representing the sequential chakras and perhaps with gold filling out its "head." The golden head would have represented the seat of golden wisdom which becomes activated with the wisdom which becomes activated with the opening of the crown chakra. Supposedly the Kundalini serpent was well known among the Inkas and referred to by them as the Kori Machakway, the "Serpent of Gold." The chakras were known as the seven Wakas, meaning "sacred energy," or as the seven Intis, points of light.

The most powerfully energetic points of the Earth's serpent power at Sacahuma were three tall stone towers on the top of the hill temple which possibly represented the three Inkan world. Surrounding the towers were concentruc stone circles that were divided into a network of water channels.

The water, a natural conductor, would have significantly amplified the power of these megaliths and supported the observance of dynamic rituals and initiations within their interior. Legend has it that ruling Inkas and their high priests once observed sacred rites within these nearly four-story high towers. Even today some of the most dynamic shamanic rituals are still observed within the stone remains of these once dominating structures.

The "Kundalini" Serpent symbol at Sacsayhuaman.
It is the same size as the Human Spine and Head.

160

MACHU PICCHU,
"CITY OF THE BIRD OF LIGHTNINGS"

Deep within the Urubamba Valley, the Sacred Valley of the Inkas was another very holy temple, the temple of Machu Picchu. Built upon the summit of a steep hill, Machu Picchu was the Temple of the Condor and "City of the Bird of Lightnings" with each of its streets "a feather."11 Current research in the Andes has revealed that Machu Picchu and many of the major Inka sites were built in the form of one of the 3 sacred Andean animals: a condor, snake, or puma.

Designated to be an astronomical observatory by most Andean researchers, Machu Picchu is also sometimes referred to by the local shamans as the "crystal city" because of the high concentration of resonating quartz crystal within its granite blocks. This unique feature, as well as its lofty geographical location, may have promoted the megalith's function as a receiving/transmitting station for both planetary and extraterrestrial communication. Furthermore, as a natural "condor's nest" it certainly would have provided visiting Extraterrestrial Serpents with an ideal landing pad for their interdimensional birds of flight. During her first visit to Machu Picchu my wife, Andrea Mikana-Pinkham was blessed with the vision of a fourth dimensional, extraterrestrial craft which landed directly in front of her in the center courtyard of this Inkan "nest."

Legends suggest that Pachacutec, the ninth and one of the most spiritually evolved Inkan priest kings, made Machu Picchu his spiritual sanctuary and both revived and further developed the temple compound. Since most of the mummies found at Machu Picchu were female, it is believed that during his reign an order of priestesses who played a pivotal role in the administration and ceremonies at Machu Picchu was active.

The initiations at Machu Picchu were probably performed during the spring equinox when the diamond shaped stone marker in the Temple Plaza pointed directly at the constellation of the Southern Cross, symbol of polarity union. According to guide Dr. Jose "Pepe" Altamirano, former Director of the National Institute of Culture in Cuzco, the spring equinox was the premier time for initiations at many Inkan sites.

According to Dr. Altamirano and other informed guides, the initiation rites were probably administered in either the upper or lower main temple plazas.

Since these temples were united by the zigzagging body of a "serpent" staircase, the goal of the initiations at Machu Picchu may have been to awaken the serpent at its upper and lower seats within the human body, i.e., the base of the spine and the third eye, which are united by the zigzagging Kundalini serpent. As possible confirmation for this theory, after leaving the lower temple one must pass by a room with thirteen windows in order to climb the serpentine staircase. Thirteen is the number of death and rebirth, the experience one must undergo before the awakened Kundalini can fully rise up the spine and merge into the crown of the head. Initiations in the lower temple to awaken the Kundalini could have occurred in proximity to or upon the huge "serpent head" rock which resides there. It presently lies on the temple floor while pointing directly at the serpent staircase or "spine."

The "serpent head" in the Temple Plaza

Rites to awaken the third eye would have taken place in the upper temple over its finely cut stone block, the Intihuatana or "Hitching post of the Sun," which has a serpent rising from its summit and was once surmounted with a round disc. From above, the serpent and the disc would have given the appearance of a serpent eye or a Third Eye of Wisdom. Perhaps in the tradition of the Andean ancients, until recently shamans and visitors to the Intiwatana ceremonially touched their foreheads to the carved stone in hopes of activating their inner psychic vision.

Other powerful rituals at the Intihuatana apparently occured during the sunrise hours on certain sacred days. Carved into the stone block is a shelf or bench which was probably used as a meditation seat and/or as an altar for the images of deities. Today this platform is fully illuminated by the rising Sun during much of the year.

A modern visitor to the Intihuatana will find the contoured block perfectly aligned to the 4 directions. It unites dragon lines running to it from all directions and then moves the dragon force down its upraised "serpent head." Like an etheric snake, the spiraling force slithers around the Intiwatana and then down the natural pyramid it sits upon, finally dispersing throughout the Machu Picchu complex.

Sacred Sites Journeys ©2016

The Intihuatana and its upraised "serpent head"

THE WANKAKILLI YOGIS

Patronizing the Inkan holy sites during their heyday were certain groups of seekers who practiced many of the traditional techniques of Yoga, such as controlled breathing, stretching postures, meditation and sexual tantra. One such group, the Wankakilli or "Andean Yogis," observed such disciplines to awaken the Kori Machakway and then proved their mastery over the inner fire by sitting upon blocks of ice and completely melting them with the power of their inwardly generated heat alone. This amazing feat can only be accomplished when the serpent fire has been thoroughly spread throughout the entire body of a yogi adept. The Wankakilli Yogis are famous in history for their spiritual accomplishments, as well as for having placed a hex on the gold given to Pizzaro and the conquering Spanish Conquistadors as ransom for the Inka priest king, Atahualpa. This curse created many future difficulties for the country of Spain.

HISTORY OF THE 7 RAY/SOLAR BROTHERHOOD IN PERU

After Manco Kapac and a series of enlightened priest kings, bearers of the Mascaypacha, had ruled the kingdom for many years, a degeneration occurred among the Inkan monarchs. Some of the later rulers lost their alignment with Inti, the Spirit, and sought spiritual power solely for themselves rather then for the upliftment of their subjects. When this occurred, the Elders or spiritual adepts of the Solar Brotherhood, who were at that time high-ranking priests of the Inkan empire, took matters into their own hands by withholding power from the Inkan kings and keeping it among themselves. When the Inkan monarchs attempted to acquire their denied power through intimidation and persecution, the Elders were forced to flee the empire and seek refuge within the hidden valleys of the Andes Mountains.

Initially the Elders relocated to a secure valley near Cuzco which was protected by majestic snow-covered peaks. They called their valley Chupani or Pumacchupan, the "Tail of the Puma," and safely lived there for many years. Eventually, however, a group of avaricious Spaniards learned that there was something of great value in the valley (it was the spiritual wisdom of the Elders) and came seeking gold nuggets. Forced to flee a second time, the Elders then marched on foot for four days until they arrived at a remote Andean plateau which they decided was suitable for a village. Here they built a self-sufficient community for themselves and then waited patiently for many years until some spiritually inclined Inka kings, such as Pachacutec, acquired the throne and demonstrated a willingness to serve Inti again. Some Elders were then assimilated back into the Inkan fold but many chose to remain in the secret village. They and their descendants have continued to exist there down to the present time.

Recently the surviving Elders revealed their existence and secret history to Antón Ponce de León Paiva of Cusco, Peru, who has since shared their story in his two books *The Wisdom of the Ancient ONE* and *In Search of the Wise ONE.* Antón's father had been a member of the Intic Churincuna (Quechua for Solar Brotherhood) and it was partly through his influence that Antón, at the age of 37, was taken blindfolded to the hidden village and accepted into the Brotherhood. After seven days of in-depth instruction Anton was taken underground and, in the presence of the mummy of one of the past Elders was initiated into the order.

Following his initiation into the Solar Brotherhood, Antón began the long process of ascending through seven degrees of enlightenment. The grandmasters of the Intic Churincuna, which included the ancient adept Aramu Muru, had reached the seventh level and become Illac Umas, "heads shining with wisdom."[76] These renowned masters, who were also called Amarus or Serpents, possessed supernatural powers and lived to a very old age. It was the mummified body of one of these Illac Umas, the Amaru Yupanqui Puma, which was present within the subterranean tunnel Anton received initiation in. Amaru Yupanqui Puma is reputed to have lived to the age of 135 years and been such a powerful Illac Uma that while alive he had been seen flying through the air and appearing in two places simultaneously. He was a descendant of Tupac Inka Yupanqui, the son of the Inka Pachacutec and the tenth Inka of the Second Dynasty. While at the hidden village, Anton's teacher was Amam Yupanqui Puma's successor, the Illac Uma Nina Soncco, whose name means "heart of fire." When Antón met Nina Soncco he was 100 years old and possessed powerful telepathic and clairvoyant abilities. He could easily read all the thoughts which passed through Antón's inquisitive mind. With Nina Soncco's passing Anton's teacher has become Amaru Cusiyupanqui, the current Illac Uma, who has lived at least 100 years on Earth, but gives the appearance of a man half that age. Also possessing supernatural powers, Amaru Cusiyupanqi has spontaneously appeared in front of Anton at different locations throughout Peru in order to further his spiritual training. Once during a rendezvous at the "Place of Monkeys," an interdimensional vortex near Cuzco, Amaru surprised Antón by suddenly appearing unannounced in his transparent, Dragon Body!

Antón was eventually instructed by his teachers at the hidden village to found a home for abandoned children and old people which would serve the dual purpose of outer retreat for the Solar Brotherhood. At Samana Wasi near Cuzco, Peru, Antón now gives initiation intothe Intic Churincuna while training the young people who will be the spiritual guides of the New Age.

165

An actor wears the ceremonial regalia of an Inka. The Inkas wore symbols of Inti, the Sun God, over their royal breasts and Third Eyes. They also adorned themselves with clothing dyed the 7 colors of the 7 Rays, and they typically wore 3 feathers in their headdresses that were often colored blue, yellow, and red to represent the first 3 Rays, the 3 Worlds and the 3 Sacred Animals they were masters of.

One of the headdresses worn by the Inka Atahualpa had two serpents intertwined, symbolizing high wisdom

166

CHAPTER 8

THE QUETZLCOATLS
& KUKULCANS
OF
MESOAMERICA

The descendants of the first Serpents of Wisdom in Mesoamerica and the administrators of the Middle American Dragon Culture they founded were the Quetzlcoatls and Kukulcans, distinguished titles which meant "Feathered" or "Plumed Serpents" in the Nahuatl and Mayan vernaculars respectively. These Plumed Serpents served in the roles of priest kings, spiritual teachers, and culture bearers to the Middle American people. They introduced and taught the language, sacred calendar, theology and many of the practical arts. They were also responsible for designing and overseeing the construction of many of the pyramids and temples which eventually dotted the Mesoamerican landscape.

THE OLMEC QUETZLCOATLS

As previously mentioned, the legendary first settlement of the Plumed Serpents in Middle America was Tamoanchan, a name which means "the place where the People of the Serpent landed." Located in what is now the state of Veracruz, Mexico, Tamoanchan was the "Garden of Eden" for many native tribes of Mesoamerica.

According to *People of the Serpent* by Edward Thompson, an initiate of numerous secret brotherhoods of the Maya, some of the early Quetzlcoatls from Tamoanchan eventually departed on missionary expeditions in order to found colonies in other parts of Middle America. One of their spin-off cultures is known historically as the Olmec, a civilization founded in the jungles of Veracruz which was based upon direct experience of the Great Serpent.

In order to study the Serpent, i.e.; its shape, movements, and habitat (as well as awaken the inner serpent fire), the Olmecs ritually consumed hallucinogenic psilocybin mushrooms which they reverently referred to as "the flesh of Quetzlcoatl" or "the flesh of the Plumed Serpent." While in a drug-induced fifth dimensional state of awareness, the Olmecs witnessed the Serpent travel along its principal "highway" just below the surface of the ground, as well

167

as in and out of volcanic mountains, its true home and entrance to the upper world. The geometrical patterns ornamenting the Serpent's fifth dimensional body were duly recorded and these shapes provided the basis for many of the Olmecs' cult symbols and serpent effigies.

At La Venta the Olmecs worshiped their serpent deity in its natural habitat by constructing a life-sized reproduction of a volcano out of stones carried from the Tux la volcanic range 60 miles away. They also used green jade collected from quarries 50 miles away to construct huge serpentine masks which they buried ten to twenty feet underground along their deity's subterranean "highway." These masks, as well as other Olmec dragon effigies, united the serpent with another power animal, the jaguar, to produce a serpent-jaguar mix similar to the serpent-puma mix carved by their southern neighbors, the Amarus of Chavin, Peru. The jaguar represented the raw earth energy that moved above the ground, so its union with the serpent was a powerful representation of the currents of life force which flowed both above and below the surface of the Earth.

THE OLMEC SERPENT PEOPLE

With the serpent/jaguar the theme of their jungle civilization, the Olmecs evolved into a quintessential Dragon Culture. All their art, architecture, rituals, calendars and ceremonial costumes in some way reflected the influence of their androgynous dragon deity. They were truly a Mesoamerican serpent people.

The Olmecs were eventually immortalized as a serpent people by their ancient artists. Images recovered from certain Olmec excavations represent these serpent people as having snake-like heads, serpentine facial features and/or dragon-like bodies. A large deposit of snake-headed men, possibly depicting a secret conclave of the Olmec Quetzlcoatls, was recently recovered among the ruins at La Venta, while another serpentine sculpture, also found at the same site, depicts a shaman wearing a serpent embellished headdress and sitting in the posture of an upraised rattlesnake. Perhaps more evocative than these images are the colossal human heads with flat serpent-like facial features which have been discovered around La Venta and other sites in the Olmec heartland. These gigantic stone heads of the Quetzlcoatl priest kings, some of which are 10 feet tall and possess distinct caps or "helmets" along with flat lips and noses. Some academic researchers like the German anthropologist Karl Lukert, see in these helmets the scales found on a snake's head and believe their flat noses and wide flat lips reflect a snake's flat facial features.77

Serpentine images of the Olmec Serpent People

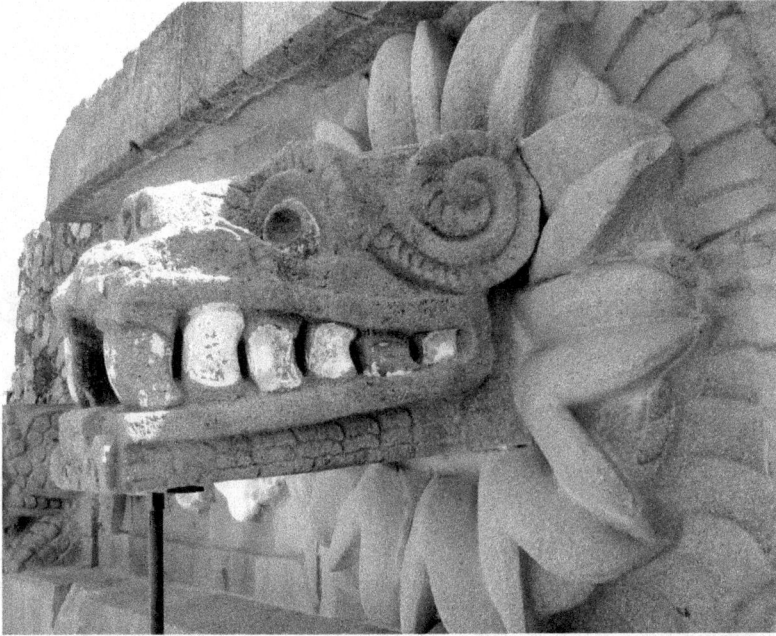

TEOTIHUACAN,
THE CITY OF THE QUETZLCOATLS

According to the records of both Bernardo de Sahagun and Edward Thompson, another spin-off branch of the colonizing Tamoanchan Quetzlcoatls, the Toltecs, hacked through the dense jungle to a choice location in the south where they built a glorious city called Teotihuacan, the City of the Plumed Serpent. Eventually this wondrous city of light became home to over 200,000 inhabitants, many of whom, states Sahagun, were the greatest craftsmen, scholars and artists to ever set foot on Mesoamerican soil. Administering the religious rites and ruling as the city's priest kings was the ancient lineage of enlightened Quetzlcoals.

One of the functions of Teotihuacan was that of an initiation center where favored Toltec seekers were transformed spiritually and inducted into the order of Quetzlcoatls. For this reason it has been called the place "where men became conscious of their (supernatural) bodily powers."[78] It was where the polarity, the snake and the bird, united, or, as the authoritative Mexican archaeologist Laurette Sejourne eloquently puts it, "the serpent learned to fly."[79]

According to Sejourne's detailed reconstruction of the initiation rite as presented in her book *Burning Water, Thought and Religion in Ancient Mexico*, the event began with a candidate observing a purifying fast of up to three or four days in length within the Temple of Quetzlcoatl. This rite was followed by a long, solemn walk down Miccoatli, the "Street of the Dead," a straight tract of roadway connecting the Temple of Quetzlcoatl with the Pyramid of the Sun. As the candidate ceremoniously ambled down the street of the dead, he or she was, for all intents and purposes, officially "dead" to the profane world.

Upon arriving at the Pyramid of the Sun the candidate climbed the long steep stairway which led up to the edifice's apex. Once at the summit, the candidate was, says Sejourne, soon engulfed by a "redeeming fire" as he or she "penetrated into the luminous consciousness of the heavenly bodies."[79] This "redeeming fire," the Kundalini, united the polarity and catalyzed a re-birth within the candidate as it precipitated a "luminous consciousness," the awareness and enlightenment of the illustrious Quetzlcoatls.

TULA, THIRD CITY OF THE PLUMEDSERPENT

Sometime around the eighth or ninth century A.D. a large fire or some other cataclysm put an end to the thriving metropolis of Teotihuacan. But even though many of its magnificent enclosures were singed or reduced to ashes, its ancient spiritual culture survived and was adopted by the citizens of Tula, another city of the Plumed Serpent and Teotihuacan's "sister city."

The founding and construction of the city of Tula began soon after Mixcoatl, chief of the Chichimecas, swept down from the north of Mexico with his band of marauding Nahuatls around the tenth century A.D. Mixcoatl arrived when Teotihuacan was disbanding and the opportunistic chief quickly conquered the dispersing peoples and set himself over them as their new king. Mixcoatl was, however, defeated and murdered by one of his own men soon after commencing his self-appointed rule; but not before fathering a son, Ce Acatl Topiltzin, who later gained vengeance for his father by destroying Mixcoatl's assassins. Topiltzin completed his father's work by building Tula and reviving the lineage of Quetzlcoatl kings. He also helped design and complete the construction of other sacred cities, such as Mitla, the "City of the Dead," which remained intact until the Spanish conquerors destroyed it and savagely murdered its resident Quetzlcoatl priest. The bones of this later Mitla Quetzlcoatl now rest within the roots of the famous "Tree of Life" at El Tule, Oaxaca.

With Topiltzin as its first Quetzlcoatl priest king, Tula flourished for many years and its surrounding area became one of the most prosperous territories in all Mesoamerica. In time, however, Quetzlcoatl Ce Acatl Topiltzin realized that in order to keep the ancient culture of the Quetzlcoatls untainted he would need to reform a Nahuatl people which had developed a tendency to behave very warlike and unrighteous, His reformation movement was moderately successful for awhile, but when his people continued to revert to their unholy ways the frustrated Quetzlcoatl abdicated his throne and permanently departed from Tula. One legend maintains that he proceeded to the Mayan city of Chichen ltza on the Yucatan Peninsula where he resurrected the Teotihuacan culture a second time and ruled over it as its priest king, Kukulcan.

THE AZTECS, DISTORTION OF THE QUETZLCOATL CULTURE

Years after the demise of Tula, the Aztecs revived the Teotihuacan culture by accepting a member of the Culhua tribe, believed to be a direct descendant of the Quetzlcoatl kings, as their honorary ruler. Although the Aztecs adopted much that was truly spiritual about the Teotihuacan culture, they also grafted on to it the bloodthirsty rite of human sacrifice. Although, as some historians claim, there may have been some incidents of human sacrifice at Teotihuacan during its heyday, the Aztecs took the rite to a fanatical extreme and made it the very centerpiece of their culture.

THE SACRED PLAZA AND THE SERPENT'SHILL

The headquarters of Aztec spiritual life was the temple precinct, a district covering 500 square yards and demarcated by a square wall richly adorned with serpent motifs. Inside this serpent wall were eight or nine magnificent temples and pyramids situated around a sacred plaza. The most important and largest of these temples was the great pyramid of Coatlicue (the "Serpent's Hill") and the Temple of Quetzlcoatl.

Ascending 150 feet in the air, the pyramid-temple of Coatlicue easily dwarfed all the other pyramids and temples around it. Here, at the north end of the sacred plaza, the Aztec priests performed their sacred duty of keeping the Sun on its course by daily sacrificing human victims and presenting their beating hearts to their solar deity. Their obsessive fervor reached its peak during religious festivals when 5000 or more victims were sacrificed in a single afternoon.

The design and placement of Coatlicue and the Temple of Quetzlcoatl located on opposite sides of the sacred plaza, revealed profound occult wisdom on the part of the Aztecs. The serpent pyramid was divided at its summit into two twin chapels, each of which was dedicated to one ofthe Serpent Twins, Huitzilopochtli and Tlaloc, the Aztec's chief gods. The chapel on the right or "male" side was painted fiery red and dedicated to the male twin, Huitzilopochtli, the deity of the Sun. The temple on the left or "female" side was dedicated to Tlaloc, the female twin and god of water, and painted with blue bands reminiscent of the blue shade of water. These twin temples were strategically aligned so that during the spring and autumn equinoxes, pivotal times of the year when the polarity naturally united, shafts of light from the Sun would pierce the common area between them. The solar beams would then alight on the opposing Temple of the Plumed Serpent, symbol of the twin's union.

Once the pyramidal, semi- circular Temple of Quetzlcoatl was fully illuminated, the rays of the equinox Sun would stimulate the movement of the serpent life force down and around the temple's exterior and up through its spacious interior. The temple of the Plumed Serpent would then become a natural life force resonator and capacitor with the power to awaken and move the inner spiritual energies within an aspiring Quetzlcoatl. During the time of this equinoxal activation, the Temple of Quetzlcoatl was presumably used as a temple for initiations into the Quetzlcoatl Brotherhood.

THE AZTEC QUETZLCOATLS

Like its parent culture of Teotihuacan, the greatest goal of Aztec life was the achievement of the office and consciousness of a Quetzlcoatl. This was accomplished through years of study, unselfish service to the chief Aztec god, Huitzilopochtli, and a steady climb up the ladder of the Aztec priesthood.

Candidates for the Aztec priesthood were usually the sons of nobles. They entered the college of priests, the Calcemac or "College of Quetzlcoatl," at a young age and, while learning both the mundane and spiritual sciences, were given certain apprenticeship positions such as temple sweepers and preparers of sacrifices. During a long and tedious training period these aspiring priests were often forced to sleep on the temple floor, consume a sparse diet or completely fast, observe celibacy and take daily ritual baths in the school's pools. As part of their spiritual regimen some Aztec chelas also wandered late at night into nearby forests to "deposit in a ball of grass maquey spines stained with their (own) blood and dedicated to the honor of one particular god."[80] These sharp spines, which had been sacrificially stabbed into differentparts of a chela's body, apparently assisted the budding priest in achieving statesofspiritual awareness.

On his way up the hierarchal ladder, the Aztec Plumed Serpent-in-training would first be ordained a Tlamacazton or novice priest. If he proved himself capable in this office he might then be promoted to a Tlananacac or a Tlamacazqui, two orders of priests with greater power and responsibility. If after undergoing extensive purification and thoroughly distinguishing himself at this level, he might finally rise to the top of the hierarchal ladder and become a chief priest and Quetzlcoatl.

Traditionally there were only two Quetzlcoatl high priests presiding over the Aztecs' religious life. These two Plumed Serpents were assigned caretakership over one of the "twin" gods of Coatlicue. The Quetzlcoatl Totec Tlamacazqui administered to the rites of Huitzilopochtli and Quetzlcoatl Tlaloc Tlamacazqui oversaw the rites of Tlaloc. According to the historian Sahagun, these highly regarded Quetzlcoatls were the most righteous and the wisest of all ordained priests. Each was "of pure heart, good, and humane; (one) who was resigned; who was firm and tranquil, a peacemaker, constant, resolute, brave ... (one) who had awe in his heart."[42]

Above the high priests was the priest king, a living god and a ruler in direct line to the ancient Quetzlcoatls of early Mesoamerica and, perhaps ultimately, Atlantis. As proof of their descent fro m the earliest Quetzlcoatls the Aztec priest kings wore the sacred q uetzal feathers in their headdresses and the jaguar gloves of power over their hands.

THE EAGLE AND JAGUAR KNIGHTS: UNITING THE POLARITY

While much of Teotihuacan's spiritual ity was lost or distorted in its Aztec translation, some mystery schools were able to preserve the ancient rites and teachings of the Quetzlcoatls in their original purity. One such school, the Academy of Malinalco, was founded high in the Mexican mountains by Quetzlcoatl missionaries. It became a training ground for the Jaguar and Eagle Knights, two orders of initiate s who zealously guarded the authentic teachings of their Plume d Serpent ancestors.

The Malinalco Academy consisted of a group of temples and dormitories richly ornamented with serpents and other sacred motifs. The main temple, an imposing circular temple carved directly out of rock which held the power of a pre-existing vorte x, was guarded at its entrance by two gigantic serpent heads, the Serpent Twins. The walls within thi s temple were covered with symbols associated with the three worlds, as well as numerous motifs explaining how to master them. One of the most theologically instructive temples in the complex possessed a doorwa y in the shape of a huge serpent and contained images of the jaguar and eagle within. Such occult symbology suggested that within the body of the Primal Serpent exists the Twins, the eagle (male heavenly twin) and jaguar (female earth twin) [81]

As part of the secret spiritual training they had inherited from the Quetzlcoatls, the Eagle and Jaguar Knights learned to perform ancient hieroglyphic dances which represented the unfolding drama of the male and female principles as they interacted within the cosmos. The dances often commenced with the harmony and/or conflict of the polarity and ended with their reconciliation and reunion, the goal of creation.

Spiritual initiation at Malinalco involved the observance of severe austerities over a designated period of time. If the candidates remained firm and succeeded in completing these austerities, they were "knighted" and entrusted with the caretakership of the secret teachings of the Quetzlcoatl lineage. While commenting on the secret initiation process of the Knights, Munoz Camargo, a Spanish historian, remarked: "... first of all they were locked for forty or seventy days in a temple of their idols; and they fasted all the time and communicated with none but those who served them; at the end of that time they were taken to the Great Temple and were given important doctrines of life which they must keep and guard ..."

THE MAYAN KUKULCANS

According to the notes of Edward Thompson, a third branch of the Tamoanchan Quetz doatls traveled to the Yucatan where it mixed within the indigenous civilization to produce the Mayan culture. The resultant city-states it thus engendered were administered by priest kings and sages known as Serpent Priests or Kukulcans (Plumed Serpents).

One of the primary headquarters of the Mayan Kukulcans in the Yucatan was the holy city of Chichen Itza. According to Thompson, the temple compound at Chichen Itza was first built by Mayan Canob or "Serpents" who had arrived from Tamoanchan.[43] They were assisted by the great patriarch of the Itza Maya, the Kukulcan Itzamna, and his entourage of Serpent builders. Sometime later in its history, the city was rebuilt and enlarged by the Toltec king Quetzlcoatl of Tula, thereby becoming the official meeting place of the Quetzlcoatls and the Kukulcans.

Constructed in the center of Chichen Itza was the Temple of Quetzlcoatl/Kukulcan, one of the most important temples of the Yucatan Kukulcans. Twice a year the centrally located pyramidal temple became the birthing place of a seven-faceted serpent. During the spring and fall equinoxes, when the polarity united as the androgynous Serpent, the shadow of a snake could be seen (and can still be) as seven united triangles slithering down the steps of the pyramid of Quetzlcoatl. Since it was common to conduct initiations and special rituals in Mesoamerica during the equinoxes, it can be assumed that initiations into the lineage of Kukulcans took place either within or upon the summit of the temple during this sacred time of the year.

THE MAYAN SERPENT CULTURE

Paralleling their sibling cultures, the Olmecs and Toltecs, the Maya regarded the Primal Serpent as an integral part of their lives. According to the accepted philosophy propagated by the Kukulcan priests, the universe was created by the Primal Serpent and its "progeny," i.e., the sea, the Earth, the sky, and the cycles of nature, were intimately associated with the great beast. The Earth was formed on the back of a great aquatic reptile; the sea with its undulating waves was called Can or Serpent; and the cycles of time reflected the birth, growth and death of the Serpent.

Since the universe was a reflection of the Primal Serpent, the Maya acknowledged that to be in harmony with the cosmos required aligning with the shape, movement, and cycles of the cosmic Serpent. In their quest to achieve this goal they studied the designs found on physical snakes and patterned their creations accordingly. States the Mayan scholar Jose Diaz-Bolio: "Mayan art, architecture, geometry and religion all derive from the ☐ Mayan rattlesnake, Crotalus Durissus Tzabcan. Its skin pattern, the four-vertex Canamayte which in Mayan means "Four-Corner Square," shows a basic symmetrical design. Coinciding with its rhomboid pattern are the outlines of the Mayan thatched roof house, the pyramid, the temple roof vault or "false arch," the design on a Mayan blouse, and even the flattened forehead of the Maya himself. "[81]

THE MAYAN SERPENT PRIESTHOOD

Like the Aztecs, the Mayas had a stratified priesthood. And similar to their neighbors, the goal of Mayan life was to ascend to the upper ranks of the sarcedotal hierarchy and become a Serpent Priest and Kukulcan.

Near the bottom rung of the Mayan hierarchal ladder were two classes of priests intimately involved with Mayan sacrifices, the Nacoms and Chacs. These priests superintended the sacrifice of plants, minerals, and animals. They also oversaw the sacrifice of the supreme offering, the human heart. During this most holy and efficacious, but unsavory of sacrifices, the Chacs held down the legs and arms of human victims while the Nacoms proceeded to cut out their beating hearts and offer them to the high gods.

Above the Nacoms and Chacs were the Balams, the Jaguar priests. The Balams were keepers of the sacred records; their historical recollections were compiled into a series of sacred texts known as the *Books of Chilam Balam*. The Balams were also pre-eminent wielders of the raw explosive power of the jaguar which they used for both soothsaying and healing. They were a branch of the Serpent-Jaguar People which once inhabited an area stretching from the Olmec heartland to Chavin in central Peru.

Near the top of the Mayan sarcedotal ladder were the chief priests, known both as the Ahua Kan Mai or "Serpent" Priests and the Ah Kin Mai or "Solar" Priests. These priests embodied the light and wisdom of the Solar Spirit while wielding its ex plosive, serpent power. They were the main officiants of Mayan religious ceremony and oversaw all sacrifices and initiations.

At the pinnacle of the Mayan spiritual hierarchy was the priest king, a descendant or official representative of the lineage of Kukulcans which stretched back to Tamoanchan and perhaps Atlantis. The Mayan ruler was an androgynous Dragon King, a unifier of Heaven and Earth, and an embodiment of the serpent power of Spirit. To symbolically designate himself as the androgenous union of the Twins, the priest king wore representations of Hunapu and Xbalenque, the mythical Mayan twins whose polar opposite principles he had merged within himself. Upon his head sat the colorful quetzal feathers, symbolic of Hunapu, the spiritual twin, while covering his hands were the distinctive jaguar gloves of Xbalenque, the jaguar and material twin. When functioning as a cosmic tree and wielder of the serpent/jaguar power, the Kukulcan priest king was believed capable of channeling through his body the highest and most ex plosive frequencies of life force. He could either use these frequencies for his own spiritual transformation or radiate them into the surrounding area for the material prosperity of his subjects.

INITIATION INTO THE ORDER OF KUKULCANS

Initiation into the Order of Kukulcans was administered within the Mesoamerican temple/pyramids and occurred during the solstices and equinoxes or other pivotal holy days determined by the Tzolkin or sacred calendar. Following a fast and, often, a purifying sweat lodge ceremony, the candidates would be escorted between the monstrous dragons and/or gaping serpent mouths which flanked the entrance to an initiation temple/pyramid. Upon arriving within the edifice's inner sanctums they would be taken before an image of the world/cosmic tree, the road connecting Heaven and Earth, which would rise up above or in back of the main altar. Then, following the recitation of mantric chants and rites by the Kukulcan priests, the candidate's inner K'ulthanilni[82] (Mayan for Kundalini) would awaken. As it moved up the spine the fire serpent would pierce the seven choklahs[82] (Mayan for chakras) and completely activate the dormant Dragon Body, the vehicle through which the new initiate would eventually be able to travel the Kux amSuum, the intergalactic grid "leading to the umbilical cord of the universe."[54] When it finally reached its destination at the top of the head, the K'ulthanilni would merge into the crown choklah and fully awaken within the initiate the enlightened consciousness of the Kukulcans.

177

A model of the Aztecs' TwinTemples of Coatlicue, the "Serpent's Hill," and the circular Templar of Queztlcoatl across from them.

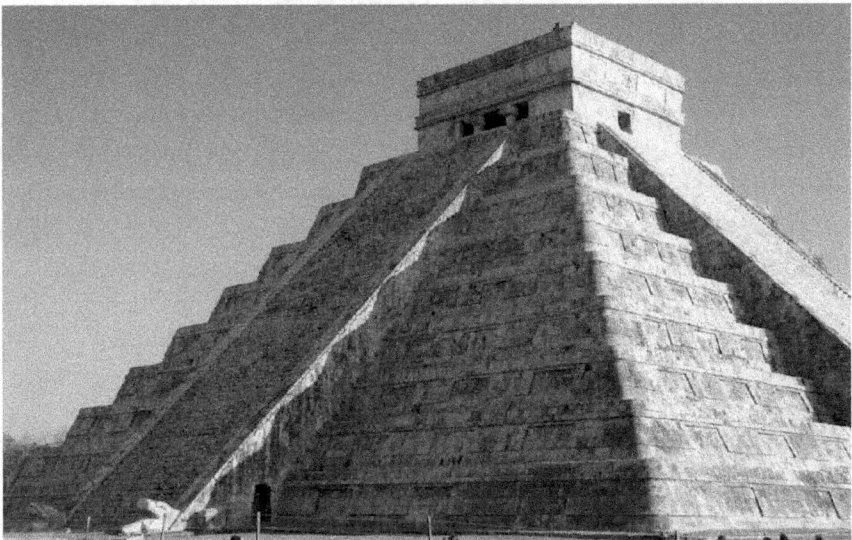

The Temple of Kukulcan at Chichen Itza at the Vernal Equinox when the serpent of seven triangles descends down it.

Mayan Temple of the Two-Headed Serpent at Tikal, Guatemala

Stelae of a Mayan Kukulcan King as the World Tree
Like the World Tree, Mayan Kings were Heaven/Earth unifiers

CHAPTER 9

THE SERPENT CLANS AND TRIBES OF NORTH AMERICA

According to ancient Native American records, when the colonizing Serpents of Wisdom arrived in North America they organized themselves into numerous tribes, appointed a Sun as leader over each and then migrated to various parts of the North American continent. [11] Some of the migrating Serpents, such as the Shoshone, Iroquois and Sioux, subsequently banded together into tribes which venerated serpentine patron deities and/or became known by names denoting Snakes or Serpents. Other Serpents of Wisdom cloistered together into Serpent Clans or societies after being assimilated into tribes which venerated multiple animal deities. Two of the principal Serpent Clans they founded are known as the Snake and Thunderbird Clans.

SERPENTS OF THE SNAKE TRIBES AND CLANS

As members of the North American Snake Clans or Tribes the Serpents became very highly regarded and even feared by their tribal brethren and contemporaries .. Many acquired the reputations of being veritable snakes in human form and were cautiously approached the same way one would draw near a dangerous reptile. They were reputed to wield the lethal power of a live snake and display both the intimidating temperament and appearance of the unsavory beasts. As a sign of their viperous power, Snake initiates would often adorn their body with snakeskins or snake tattoos and hang snake fangs from around their necks. They also conveyed poisonous snake venom within a medicine bag and/or armed themselves with a serpent-embellished rattle which would hiss eerily like a coiled snake when shaken. The tendency of such snake initiates was to be secretive, like a stealthy reptile, and some even developed apenchant for seeking out dark secluded dwellings or living nocturnally.

The serpent power wielded by members of the Snake Clan or Tribe possessed the three traditional qualities of the life force, i.e., creation, preservation and destruction. Which aspect was utilized by them depended upon the motivation of the Snake. Those Snakes who functioned within their respective tribes as healers, magicians and rainmakers wielded the creative or preserving aspect of the serpent power. They also functioned as protectors of the tribe and might, like the Cherokee Serpents, dispatch their protective power in the form of dragons (called Ukdena by the Cherokee) to patrol the countryside and protect the tribe from inimical trespassers." By contrast, those Snakes who channeled the destructive/ transformative aspect of the serpent power functioned as nefarious black magicians and sorcerers, but also as Kundalini Masters and dowsers. In these latter roles they would awaken and move the transformative serpent power within another aspiring Snake or within the Earth's Grid.

As embodiments of serpent wisdom, an additional function of the Snake initiates was that of caretaking and disseminating esoteric wisdom. Many Snakes were part of a long line of Serpent Masters who had preserved the most secretive, occult wisdom-some of which had been passed down word of mouth since the time of the Motherlands. Often this wisdom was interwoven into the rituals which the Snake Clan or Tribe initiates performed during their tribes' religious festivals.

INITIATION INTO THE SNAKE CLAN

To become a member of a Snake Clan often necessitated undergoing an intense and sometimes terrifying initiation involving "bonding" with deadly, live snakes. These dangerous rites were calculated to make one a brother or sister of all snakes by releasing any fear for the scary beasts and/ or by being fully consumed by them.

Initiation into some Snake Clans or Tribes required that the candidate remain alone in a snake infested desert or occupy a darkened room or pit swarming with poisonous snakes. Initiation into the ancient Anasazi or Hopi Snake Clan, for example, required a candidate to sit calmly in a room full of venomous rattlesnakes while allowing the threatening creatures to slither all over his or her body. If the candidate survived this frightening ordeal he was considered favored by the Great Spirit and promptly ordained into the Clan. Initiation into other Snake Clans or Snake Tribes required a candidate to be repeatedly bitten by venomous snakes and thereby fully assimilate the snake's power and essence. In *Indian Medicine Power,* Brad Steiger describes such an initiation into the Shoshone or Snake Tribe: "... the candidate, after thorough purification, goes high on a mountain top and permits himself to be bitten over and over by a rattlesnake. According to the (Shoshone) Indian, if the candidate has power and has been properly prepared, he will recover, absorbing the mana (power) of the snake and thus become a brother of the snake."

One gruesome initiation into some Snake Clans or Tribes required candidates to be physically eaten and consumed by a snake. Initiation into the Snake Tribe of the Gros Venture Indians, for example, called for the candidate to cut off parts of his body, such as an ear or finger, and feed them to a live snake. Then, according to one account of the initiation, after consuming the body part the snake supposedly says to itself: "I pity this man. I will give him power and make him strong." The snake (or essence of the snake) would then proceed to enter the man's mouth and move throughout his whole body, completely consuming him. From then on the tribe's newly initiated "snake" was fully endowed with serpent power and "had become unkillable."[83]

THE HOPI SNAKE CLAN

Of all Snake Clans, the Hopi Snake Clan is the best known and possibly one of the first to have set foot on the North American continent. According to the Hopi records, the Snake Clan has been a part of the Hopi tribe for three precession cycles or Worlds. If each World is 26,000 years in length, then the Hopi Snake Clan has been in existence for at least 78,000 years and was probably a branch of the Serpents from the Motherlands.

Members of the Hopi Snake Clan maintain that during the current Fourth World a new dispensation of snake rites were introduced into the clan by a Hopi boy who learned the rites directly from the Snake People at their House of Snakes. Apparently this lad was floating down the Colorado River one day when his raft was suddenly swept away by a strong current which carried him all the way to the sea. After landing on an island paradise the boy was met by Spider Woman, one of the Hopi creator gods, who escorted him through a secret passageway and into the underworld land of the Snake People. Here, in the House of Snakes, the boy was fully initiated into the snake rituals and then instructed to return home and teach them to his tribe.

This myth of the Hopi boy, believed to be at least partly symbolic, has over time justifiably solicited numerous interpretations. The Snake People of the island paradise were probably Snake initiates and their underground civilization and "House of Snakes" are presumably references to the tunnels and caves used by them for their mystery rites. Because of the resemblance of the Hopi Snake Dance to traditional Mesoamerican snake dance rites previously observed in the Mayan settlements of Copan and Chichen Itza, it is possible that the island's Snake People were part of the organization of Plumed Serpents which had inhabited Middle America from very early times. One conspicuous similarity between the Mesoamerica Serpents and the Hopi Snake Clan is their common veneration of the horned and plumed serpent.

THE HOPI SNAKE DANCE:
UNITING THE POLARITY AND AWAKENING
THE SERPENT FIRE

The most esoteric mysteries of the Hopi Snake Clan, including the ascent of the Kundalini, have for many years been symbolically enacted during an annual sixteen day Snake Dance festival. Thanks to the interpretive work of Frank Waters, author of *The Book of the Hopi* and one of the first Caucasians allowed to study the ancient Hopi rites, the esoteric wisdom underlying the rituals of this festival has recently come to light.

The beginning of the Snake Dance festival begins when the Snake Clan members venture into the scorching southwestern desert to gather up a requisite number of live rattlesnakes. Their slithering clan brothers are then taken back to camp and set in the middle of a subterranean meeting room, the clan's kiva. Then, as initiates of the clan sit in a circle surrounding the rattlesnakes, the poisonous beasts are allowed to roam freely throughout the dimly lit kiva while arbitrarily climbing over each clan member's body. A fearless rapport between the snakes and the clan members is subsequently established and soon some Snake Clan members are daringly picking up the live rattlesnakes and holding them in their hands or even clenching them between their teeth.

Following the gathering ritual is a foot race event which has undeniable esoteric undertones. Those involved in the race run along a straight track of desert before ascending sharply to the top of a steep bluff. The leader of the group of runners carries a bundle of sticks, each of which is painted a different color. According to Frank Waters, the bundle of colored sticks represents the colors of the seven chakras and the runners symbolize the ascent of the Kundalini as it travels up the human spine and pierces the seven power centers. The final ascent of the serpent power and its merger into the crown chakra is represented by the runners' final ascent to the summit of the steep bluff.

Following the foot race an esoteric rite symbolizing the union of the polarity or "sacred marriage" is ritually enacted by the Snake and Antelope Clans. During this mysterious rite a young girl representing the Snake Clan is joined in "matrimony" to a young boy representing the Antelope Clan. With all the trappings of an actual marriage ceremony, the two are formally wed. According to Waters' interpretation of the event, the Snake Clan and the young girl are symbolical of the female principle while the Antelope Clan and its young male representative denote the male principle. Therefore, their union denotes the sacred spiritual union of the polarity. Waters further suggests that the Snake and Antelope Clans are intimately associated with the Kundalini and Crown Chakra respectively, so their union is also symbolic of the merger of the serpent power into the apex of the head.

The climax of the sixteen day festival occurs at its conclusion during the famous Snake Dance, a rite which incorporates all the esoteric symbolism of the preceding days. During this engrossing event, the Snake Clan members paint themselves vermillion red, the color of the serpent fire, and then dance alongside members of the Antelope Clan who cover themselves with silvery grey paint, the color of the crown chakra. As the two clans come together in the dancing arena, the union of the polarity and the merger of the Kundalini within the crown chakra are both symbolically enacted.

The culmination of the Snake Dance happens when the Earth's Kundalini is awakened and sent upwards into the sky. This phenomenon is precipitated by a representative of the Snake Clan who brings to life the planetary fire serpent by stamping his foot loudly upon a board placed over a hole, symbolic of the Earth's Root Chakra. Once the Earth's Kundalini is awakened and begins to ascend heavenward it is felt perceptibly by all the members of both clans. As it moves through the bodies of the dancers they "sway left and right like snakes."[8] Then, when the energy has finally risen to their heads, the members of Snake Clan become ecstatic and fearlessly pick up the live serpents they had previously gathered and dance with them between clenched teeth. Later, at the conclusion of the dance, the snakes are set free and the dancers consume an emetic to empty their stomachs. "Otherwise," claims Waters, "their bellies would swell up with the power (of the serpent) and burst."[8]

SNAKE CLANS OF THE GREAT LAKES AND THE GREAT HORNED SERPENT

One of the most prolific gathering places of the northern Snake Clans has been the Great Lakes region. The patron deity of these clans has been the Great Horned Serpent, a monstrous dragon believed to inhabit the deepest parts of the lakes. Although extremely frightening to behold, this beast was regularly propitiated by intrepid Snake Clan members. One eyewitness account of the dragon depicts the creature as possessing "a head with a pair of pronged deer horns, a large mouth breathing fire, a huge body covered with fish scales, and a reptilian forked tail."[84]

According to the legends of the northern Snake Clans, by its underwater thrashings the Great Horned Serpent was known to precipitate the occurrence of turbulent waves and dangerous spiraling whirlpools in the Great Lakes. If not prepared for, such phenomenon could easily catch a native fisherman unaware and drag him down to a watery grave. In order to appease the Great Serpent and

Hopi Snake Clan Initiates

Hopi Snake Clan Dancers

The Great Horned Serpent

An Heyoka Shaman

obviate such disasters, Snake Clan members regularly offered oblations and prayers to the monstrous creature. At other times the beast was summoned by the Snakes in order to harness some of its formidable power for themselves or their tribes. The most courageous of Snakes might even attempt to capture one of the beast's horns as legends maintained that it was saturated with supernatural serpent power. Should a Snake Clan member, or a member of any other clan, capture this prized charm, he was considered invincible and victory was assured to him in all his conquests.

The Wynadots, cousin to the Serpent Iroquois, once inhabited the Great Lakes region and succeeded in establishing intimate relations with the great underwater Homed Serpent. Through psychic lines of communication, the Great Serpent taught the Wynadot Elders how to worship it through fifteen ritual songs and an annual feast of thanksgiving. For their meticulous attention to these rites, the Wynadots received both protection and prosperity from the Great Homed Serpent.

THE THUNDERBIRD CLAN, CHANNELERS OF INTENSE SERPENT POWER

A second branch of the North American Serpent Clan is the Thunderbird Clan. The patron deity of this clan is the mighty Thunderbird, a North American version of the Chinese rain dragon. Like the rain dragon, the Thunderbird is conceived of by Native Americans to be a winged form of the Great Spirit. It is a manifestation of the Primal Dragon and an "aspect" of the serpent. For this reason members of the Pacific Northwest Snake and Thunderbird Clans dance together in ceremony.

Initiates of the Thunderbird Clan are, like their brothers and sisters of the Snake Clan, intimately associated with rain and possess special rainmaking abilities. In order to generate bountiful precipitation, members of the Thunderbird Clan either invoke the spirit of the Thunderbird through mantras and vocables or summon aspects of the Thunderbird's extended body, the "Thunderbeings."

Many members of the Thunderbird Clan also acquire the ability to channel the serpent power of the "Bird of Lightning" through their own bodies and then utilize it for healing and spiritual transformation. This power is received directly from the Thunderbird and is very concentrated and deadly, like an explosive bolt of lightning. When handled appropriately, however, this awesome energy can be transmitted into others to elicit a spontaneous healing or to awaken the Kundalini, the inner "lightning serpent." One group of lightning bolt channelers are known as the Heyokas, a branch of "contraries," who channel the transformative currents of the Thunderbird into others to "reverse the negative trend of man and nature"[85] by awakening the inner spiritual energies and impelling humankind on a path to spiritual enlightenment. According to the Heyoka traditions, the spirit of the Thunderbird originally manifested to the Clan Elders and taught them the proper technique for receiving and projecting its potent energy.

THE SERPENT PROPHET

Throughout time there have been many Serpents of Wisdom in North American, but one fair skinned or "pale" prophet stands apart from the rest. This wise teacher is remembered in tribal legends as having once traveled the length and breadth of the continent while spreading important religious rites and spiritual wisdom to many native people. He visited the early Algonquins and is remembered by them as Emeeshtotl, the "Feathered Serpent." The Choctah received him as him Ee-me-shee, the wind god. The Iroquois called him Hia-wa-sah, the "Plumed Serpent," and recognized him as one of the Masters ·who have served them for many ages as their respected spiritual teachers. The Pawnees remember him as Paruxti and the Dacotahs still refer to him as Waicomah.[55]

According to most tribal legends, when the prophet first appeared to a tribe he was clothed in a long white robe and wore sandals upon his feet. Upon his hand was inscribed the Tau cross, symbol of the androgynous Serpent Sons. Wherever he went he rallied around him twelve disciples and was, therefore, always associated with the number thirteen, the number of the Dragon/Phoenix. When he departed, the natives continued to venerate him as Venus, the Celestial Phoenix.

In *He Walked the Americas* L.Taylor Hansen compiled all the legends of the mysterious pale prophet into one book. After thoroughly reviewing these legends, Hansen concluded that he was Jesus Christ or an Essene Master of the same Order of Serpents.

EXPERIENCES WITH AN ANASAZI SNAKE

From 1989-91 my wife and I had a first hand experience with a member of the Anasazi Snake Clan. The Snake initiates of the Anasazis, meaning the "Ancient Ones," were intimately related to and ancestors of those comprising the Hopi and Navajo Snake Clans. Our Anasazi Snake, we were to find out, had lived around 1200 A.D. on what is now Second Mesa of the Hopi Reservation in Arizona.

For weeks leading up to our initial "encounter" my wife, Andrea, had been receiving subtle messages from a disembodied spirit calling itself "Thunder Eagle" who desired to speak through her. Feeling naturally apprehensive about lending her body out to a foreign entity, she resisted the idea until one cold December night on Orcas Island. While four of us huddled around the wood stove in my brother Sahar's house and discussed the "channeling" dilemma, Andrea suddenly recanted her fixed position and volunteered to serve as the desired vehicle for the petitioning spirit. Not wanting to postpone the inevitable any longer, she then closed her eyes, did a little invocation to call forth the "light," and quickly slipped into a meditative trance. In almost the very next second, to the great surprise and concern of those of us in the room, the ethereal facial features of an old man seemed to descend from above and superimpose themselves over Andrea's. Since I was sitting directly in front of her at the time I could clearly distinguish a phantom face with dark coloring, deep set wrinkles, a large nose, and thinning, grey hair. If this floating face was that of Thunder Eagle, I decided, then he had certainly led a hard, rugged life. When the hard, phantom features suddenly dissolved into Andrea's softer visage, we all waited anxiously to greet the entity which now presumably inhabited her body. Slowly opening his borrowed eyes wide, the spirit of Thunder Eagle stared directly at me and enthusiastically announced, "My Son, it's so good to see you again!" Our adventure with a disembodied Anasazi spirit had officially begun.

Over the weeks and months that followed we learned from Thunder Eagle that the three of us, he, myself and Andrea, had lived together near Second Mesa around 1200 A.D. Andrea had been his wife and I his son. During our joint incarnation together, my former "Dad" had been an initiate of the Anasazi Snake Clan and the possessor of immense serpent power-a kind of Native American Kundalini Guru. When Andrea and I as his wife and son were judged ready, we too had become Snake Clan initiates and Thunder Eagle's serpent power had been transmitted into both of us. Apparently our Snake initiation, which had culminated in the awakening of the Kundalini, had not been an easy one—according to Thunder Eagle, it had even included a death-defying rite within a deep, dark pit swarming with poisonous snakes.

Later, perhaps on another dimension, we three Snake Clan members had made a soul pact to work together to help awaken serious spiritual seekers. To fulfill this destiny, Andrea had agreed to channel the voice of Thunder Eagle and I was to be the vehicle of his serpent power. This is why our Anasazi Snake was now re-entering our lives.

I clearly remember when Thunder Eagle first activated my channel and moved his formidable energy through me. I was in a room in our house where I normally see clients for acupuncture and other natural healing therapies. My hands were positioned on a client when I felt a sobering jolt of electricity shoot through my body. More jolts followed and soon it felt as though I was sitting on a live 220 volt wire. My entire body, both inside and out, was bathed with a silvery glow while an electrifying sense of euphoric bliss flooded my being. In order to share this power and its accompanying bliss with my wife, I took my hands off the client and placed them on Andrea, who was then sitting on the floor next to me. Together we shook in unison as the lightning bolts pierced her heart and transported us into a united ecstasy.

Soon after my channel was opened, Andrea and I began to fulfill our destiny by traveling around Western Washington State, giving workshops within which she was the voice and I the hands of Thunder Eagle. While also utilizing acupressure and controlled breathing patterns for added effect, we soon witnessed many participants in our seminar having what I had come to recognize as classical Kundalini awakenings. Some people felt energetic throbbings at the base or along the course of their spines and within the seven chakras. Others were overcome with "kriyas," contorted body movements catalyzed by the purifying influence of the serpent fire as it moved through their etheric bodies. Still others reported the whole gamut of psychic experiences, from astral travel to viewing past lives or future events. It did appear as though the transforming power of the Snake Clan was having a profound effect on these people.

One of the last experiences we had with Thunder Eagle was at Second Mesa on the Hopi reservation where we three had decided to return "home" one more time. When we arrived a special Hopi ceremony was in progress and the sound of ancient chants filled the air. Andrea and I immediately positioned ourselves on a high bluff overlooking the sprawling Arizona desert and then allowed the rhythmic chants to gently rock us into a comfortable trance. Soon Thunder Eagle spontaneously "popped in," as he was accustomed to doing by then, and while using Andrea's arms began pointing out to me an area two or three miles in the distance where he said we had all lived together as a family. The sight of his former home quickly became an emotional catharsis for Thunder Eagle and thick tears welled up in his eyes before spilling down over his cheeks. Soon he and I were both crying as we reminisced about a lifetime which had, over the previous months with our Anasazi Snake, become almost as real as the present one.

THE SERPENTS OF WISDOM
IN
ASIA MINOR AND
THE MEDITERRANEAN

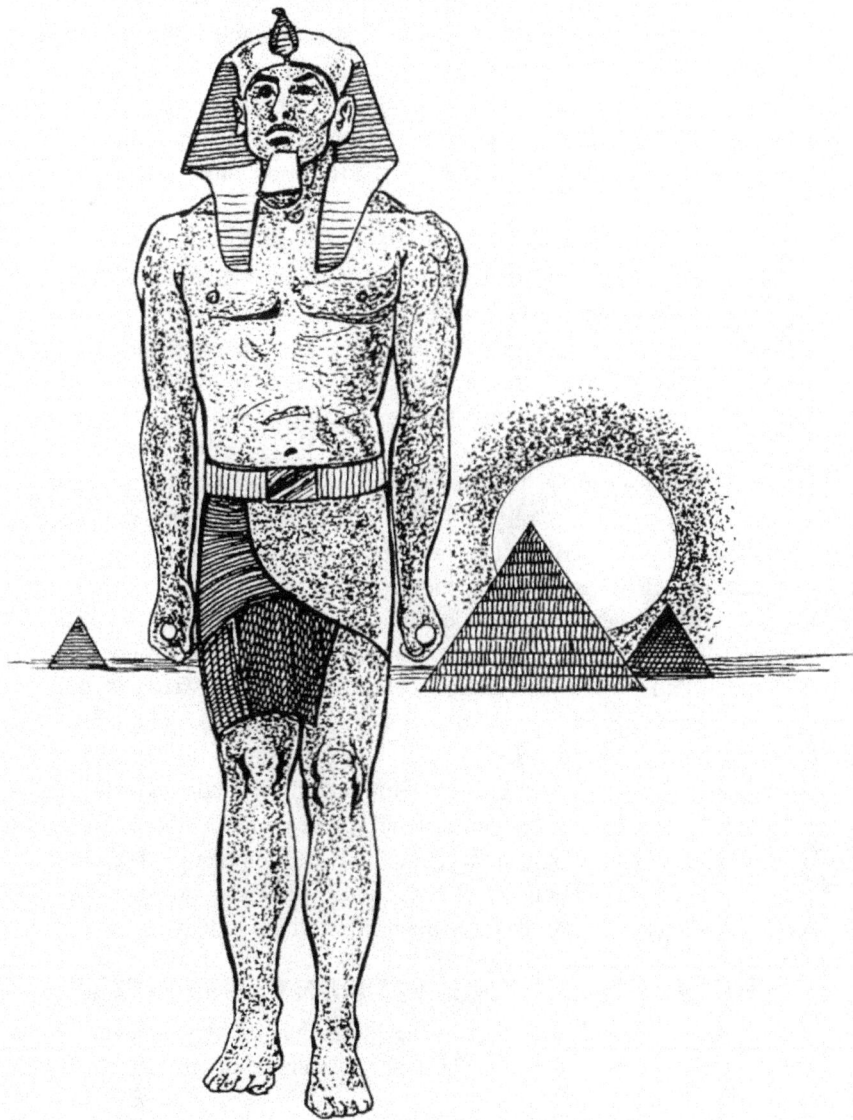

A Djedhi of Egypt

CHAPTER 10

THE MESOPOTAMIAN ANUNNAKI

Following the establishment of a Dragon Culture in Mesopotamia, the Serpent People of Enki, the Anunnaki, meaning the "Progeny of Anu" or "Sons of God," became assimilated into a Middle Eastern branch of the Serpents of Wisdom. Contained within this hierarchal organization were the Mesopotamian priest kings and the Shangu, a priestly fraternity of magicians, diviners and exorcists called the Ashipu, Baru and Kalu. All members of the organization embodied the Primal Dragon and/or had access to its protection and explosive power.

THE DRAGON KING, GRANDMASTER OF THE MESOPOTAMIAN SERPENTS

As the Grandmaster of the Mesopotamian Serpents, the priest kings of Sumeria, Akkadia, and Babylonia were the principal officiants at most important religious ceremonies. At these sarcedotal functions they were recognized to be the hands and voice of Anu, the great Spirit, and the vehicle of his serpent power on Earth.

Upon ascending the throne of Mesopotamia, the throne of Tammuz, the ancient nature god and "serpent deity who emanated from the heaven god Anu," the priest kings inherited the immense creative power and wisdom of Anu's manifest aspect. Then, in order to keep their power strong during their respective terms in office, they received a continuous supply of serpent power from the bull gods Enlil and Marduck whose representatives (or incarnations) on Earth they were esteemed to be. The celestial bulls Enlil and Marduck both wielded and passed on the creative power of the Dragon. Marduck inherited the power from his father, the Dragon Enki, and Enlil acquired it through the star group associated with him, the Celestial Serpent, the Pleiades. Beginning with Sargon of Akkad, the early Mesopotamian kings designated themselves bull delegates on Earth by adopting bull seals as their official emblems. They also wore horned tiaras to stately functions and into battle in order to symbolize the creative serpent power which flowed to them from their bull patrons.

THE ASHIPU, THE SERPENT PRIESTS OF ENKI

Below the priest king in the hierarchy of Mesopotamian Serpents were the Ashipu magician priests. The Ashipu were children of the Dragon Enki and descendants of the earliest Anunnaki missionaries. A traditional declaration of an Ashipu priest was: "I am the Ashipu who was created at Eridu."[86] Eridu was Enki's capital city and the ancient Mesopotamian headquarters of the Anunnaki.

The Ashipu priests were a part of all temple staffs in Sumeria, Babylonia and Assyria. They were called upon to exorcise spirits and control the forces of nature whenever they threatened the land and people of Mesopotamia. To perform their work, the Ashipu would invoke the assistance of their patron deity, Enki, and then communicate directly with the offending gods and demons. They also utilized powerful incantations which were extracted from certain magical texts passed down from the pre-diluvian Anunnaki. With these books as their guides and Enki's assistance at their beck and call, the Ashipu could produce almost any kind of magic.

While performing their duties, the Ashipu priests would dress in ceremonial outfits covered with fish scales, reminiscent of the water-dragon Enki. To begin their rites, each one would take a wand made of cedar wood and inscribe a circle around himself while chanting: "In my hand I hold the magic circle of Enki, in my hand I hold the cedar wood, the sacred weapon of Enki, in my hand I hold the branch of the palm tree of the great rite." Then, in order to invoke Enki's divine presence, the Ashipu would describe the Dragon's primeval form:

> "The head is the head of a serpent
> From his nostrils mucus trickles
> The mouth is beslaved with water
> The ears are those of a basilisk
> His horns are twisted in three curls
> He wears a veil in his head band
> The body is a sun fish full of stars
> The base of his feet are claws
> The sole of his feet has no sole ... "[86]

Following this propitiation, the Ashipu priest would wait quietly for his mantric words to bear fruit. Soon the spirit of the Dragon Enki wound respond and surround the magician with his awesome but supportive presence. Then, with the appropriate incantations, the Ashipu would confidently proceed with his important work.

THE BARU AND KALU, CHANTERS AND DIVINERS

The other two categories of priests in the Mesopotamian hierarchy were the Baru, the diviners, and the Kalu, the chanters. The rites and mantras practiced by these priests were believed to have been passed down from King Enmenduranki, one of the Seven Elders or priest kings who reigned before the flood. King Enmenduranki, the "serpent king" of pre-diluvian Mesopotamia, may have been part of the same lineage which produced the Egyptian Thoth-Hermes and the Hebrew Enoch.

Before being ordained into the priesthood, the Baru diviners were required to undergo a long period of academic training. During this time they were expected to memorize all forms of divination including the interpretation of the lines on the livers and lungs of sacrificed animals, the symbolism of dreams, and the astrological interpretation of star and planetary positions. The Baru also learned to read the omens of nature and to recognize the appearance of certain animals or weather patterns which presaged specific future events. Then, once ordained, the Baru balanced his academic training with spiritual disciplines involving concentration and deep meditation. In this way he acquired the ability to psychically communicate with the Sun god Shamash who, from his high vantage point in the sky, knew all events on the Earth, both past and future.

The Kalu priests were masters of the science of mantra. It was their duty to know the appropriate mantras for each religious function and to become adept at their proper intonation. Their conscientious repetition of the ancient formulas insured the protection and success of the rites. As the Kalu chanted their mantras they sometimes also danced or played special drums, cymbals or harps, some of which were decorated with little bulls or a bull's heads and possessed a sound reminiscent of the "bellowing of a bull."[86] Such harps would invoke the creative power of the bull and the Kalu could then use this power to infuse their incantations with additional potency. Thus, the Kalu chanters, like the priest kings, were wielders of the creative power of the Serpent Enki.

THE NERGALS, CHIEF SERPENTS OF CHALDEA

In the later Mesopotamian empire of Chaldea the head of the priesthood of Middle Eastern Serpents became known as the Nergal or Nargal. The name Nergal is an evolution of Naga, the universal name for the Serpents of Wisdom, and also derives from Nergal, the Babylonian version of the god Volcan or Vulcan, the underworld fire serpent. States the author of *The Secret Doctrine,* "The Nargal was the Chaldean and Assyrian chief of the Magi (the Rab-Mag)..."[15] Biavatsky further maintains that the Nergal identified himself with a powerful, sacred animal, and kept a representative of that animal near him in a cage as he worked his magic.

Perhaps the most famous Nergal is mentioned in the Book of Jeremiah in the Bible. This is Nergal-sharezer, the Rab-Mag or chief magician priest who

190

accompanied Nebuchadrezzer (who was possibly his father) into battle against King Zedekiah. When the king of Judah saw the Nergal dressed in his magician's robe, as well as a great band of warriors which surrounded him, it is said that the Jewish monarch fled with great haste in the opposite direction.

The Ashipu priests of Enki wear their dragon-fish magical robes.

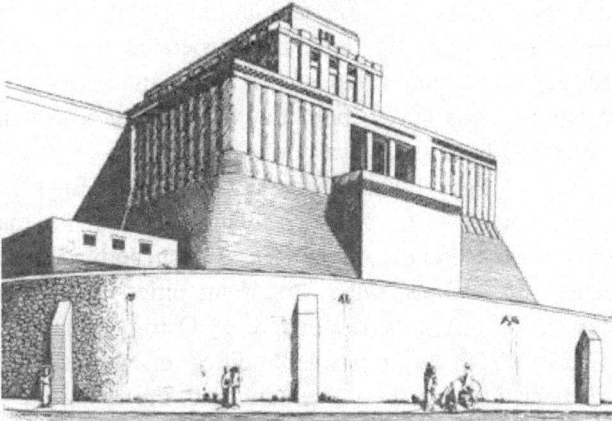

The home of Dragon Enki in Eridu.

CHAPTER 11

THE DJEDHI OF EGYPT

Once established in Egypt, the Dragon Culture engendered a brotherhood of priest kings and spiritual masters called the Djedhi whose definitive symbol was Uadjet, the Ureaus, a golden likeness of the indigenous desert asp. The roots of Djedhi and Uadjet, "Dj" and "Djed," denoted serpent and column respectively, and thus designated a Djedhi as one who had raised the inner serpent (the Kundalini) up the human vertebral column to the spiritual centers within the head and thus become a Serpent of Wisdom. The mark of such an evolved Djedhi was the golden asp or golden band which was honorably worn over the seat of wisdom, the third eye. As Isa Shwaller de Lubicz, one of the foremost authorities on Egyptian mysticism, informs us: "... the victorious rising of this fire (the serpent fire) to the frontal lobe is symbolized by the Ureaus (the golden serpent) on the forehead of the Pharaoh."[87]

THE DRAGON LAND AND ITS SERPENT CITIES

The emissaries of the Dragon Culture in Egypt, the Djedhi, considered their land to be pulsing with life force and venerated it as the living body of Osiris, a nature god or cosmic man and manifestation of the Primal Dragon (Osiris's sacred number was seven; both the word "dragon" and the name Osiris denote "many eyed".) The country was divided into two territories, symbolic of Osiris's higher (Lower Egypt) and lower selves (Upper Egypt). His backbone was associated with the powerful Nile River, and many of the major cities built along the river's course were placed in areas which corresponded to the cosmic man's power centers or chakras. Other important cities were constructed by the Djedhi in vortex areas which corresponded to Osiris's numerous acupuncture points. Collectively, all these empowered cities on the body of Osiris were "Serpent Cities." Each was home to a serpent god, the city's patron deity, which was the inhabitant of the dragon's lair upon which the city was built.

Joseph Jochmans, an author and Egyptian tour guide who is responsible for re-discovering many of the ancient correspondences between Osiris's chakras and the Serpent Cities listed below, believes that special chakra initiations may have occurred in temples built at these power spots. His accumalated evidence

192

reveals that within these sacred enclosures the same chakra a Serpent City corresponded to within the body of Osiris was activated within worthy seekers of wisdom.

PER-UADJET, CITY OF THE SERPENT GODDESS UADJET

One of the earliest and most important of the Serpent Cities in the north of Egypt was Per-uadjet (later called Buto), the "City of Uadjet." Uadjet was a name of the Serpent Goddess and within her sacred city was built one of the most glorious serpent shrines in all of Egypt. Per-uadjet served as the ancient political capital of lower Egypt, Osiris's "Higher Self," and it is said that the early Egyptian kings were crowned by the city's protectress, Uadjet.

Per-uadjet was also the capital city of the 19th nome or territory, which was anciently called Ammt, "the Two Eyebrows,"23 perhaps in reference to the Serpent Goddess's seat between Osiris's eyebrows. In its location in the Nile Delta region the city of Per-uadjet was presumably associated with the nature god's sixth chakra or Third Eye.

ANU/ ON/ HELIOPOLIS, CITY OF THE SERPENT RA-ATUM

Another important northern Serpent City was Anu, also known as On by the Hebrews and Heliopolis by the Greeks. This was the city of Ra, the Solar Spirit and Atum, the infinite Spirit who took physical form as the Primal Serpent. Atum, "the all and the nothing" (both transcendental and manifest), merged with Ra to become the solar god Ra- Atum, with the name Ra designating the early rising of the Sun and Atum denoting the orb's evening descent into the underworld.

The great city of Heliopolis was the principal seat of serpent wisdom during Egypt's earliest ages. As such, both it and the Great Pyramid which sat across the Nile River from it were intimateiy associated with Osiris's sixth and seventh chakras and assisted in their opening within worthy initiates. Stored within the city of Anu was the most esoteric wisdom of alchemy, the science of how to spiritually transmute a person through the purifying influence of the serpent fire, which had anciently been transported from Atlantis by the Thoth-Hermes adepts. The symbol of these masters, the caduceus, was a diagram of the human spine, path of the Kundalini and the twin nadis which spiral along its course. Thoth-Hermes' alchemical wisdom was studied and taughtat Heliopolis by the Djedhi priesthood and used within the Great Pyramid during initiations.

From a planetary perspective the City of the Solar Spirit served as the western headquarters of the entire worldwide organization of Serpents of Wisdom or Solar Brotherhood. It was specially chosen by the incipient Serpent missionaries of the Western Motherland to be their principal Control Central and initiation center for all aspiring seek ers around the globe. Three of the greatest western Serpents of Wisdom to study and undergo initiation there are Plato, Pythagoras and Jesus Christ.

THE SUN TEMPLE AND TEMPLE OF THE PHOENIX

The main temple at Heliopolis was the Sun Temple, a huge structure which served as both temple and academy for the Djedhi priesthood. This colossal, pillared temple had a seating capacity of 13,000, a number of the dragon-phoenix, the bird which anciently emanated from the Solar Spirit. When filled with a sea of enthusiastic chanting priests, the temple virtually exploded with the sacred name of Ra-Atum. Leading the chorus was the "Great One of Visions of Ra-Atum," the chief priest, who sat at the front of the temple near the symbol of the Solar Spirit, a huge metallic disc made of solid gold.

Adjacent to the Sun Temple was another sanctuary of Ra-Atum called the Het Benben or "Temple of the Phoenix." The Temple of the Phoenix was a roofless temple used primarily for calendrical purposes. The Sun's rays would reflect off a large obelisk (one of Atum's forms) which was situated in the center of the temple and its resulting shadows along the ground would reveal the time of year and hour of the day.

MEMPHIS, CITY OF THE FIRE SERPENT PTAH

A third northern Serpent City of renown was Memphis. Along with the pyramid of Sakkara and its adjoining healing temple of sound and color, Memphis is believed to have corresponded to Osiris's fifth chakra, the chakra of sound and communication. As the early capital of Egypt, Memphis communicated with all of Khem as well as much of the known world.

Memphis was the city of the fire god Ptah, an evolution of the ancient fire serpent of Atlantis, Volcan, which was transported to North Africa by the Serpents of Neptune. One popular manifestation ascribed to the serpent Ptah was the primeval mound, an incipient form taken by the Primal Serpent when it first precipitated out of the cosmic sea. In honor of Ptah's mound form, Memphis was built upon an earthen k noll and named Hi-Ku-Ptah, the "Mansion of the Ka (soul) of Ptah."

Ptah ruled in Memphis with his consort, Sekhmet, whose name means "the power" or "the powerful." Sekhmet was Ptah's serpent power, his fiery feminine energy, and therefore referred to by the alterna te epithets of Mehenet, the fire serpent, and Nesert, the flame. Sekhmet's priests were medical doctors who called upon the fire serpent's power to effect a complete and rapid healing within their patients. They and the other devotees of Ptah's consort would also call forth her destructive/ transformative power to destroy evil, annihilate the enemies of truth, and awaken the inner Kundalini.

Ptah's principal anthropomorphic form in Memphis was that of a pygmy-sized man. His diminutive image, which is better known by its later Roman evolution, the dwarfish Vulcan, was worshiped in the south end of the city in a temple adjacent to a library containing countless, valuable scrolls. These buildings were located in front of another very sacred shrine, the temple of the fire god's twin sons, the Kaberoi. Among the priests of Khemi, the Kaberoi Twins were venerated as founders of the Kaberoi Brotherhood whose Atlantean initiates had brought to Egypt both the worship of the Kaberois' "father," Volcan, as well as the priceless records of their western motherland. The Carthaginian historian Sanconiathon referred to the Kaberoi missionaries as the "Seven Sons of Sydyk" who were requested by a member of the Thoth-Hermes lineage to write down their sacred records once they h ad reached Egypt.22 Presumably their records were then stored in Ptah's library.

CROCODILOPOUS,CITY OF THE WATER DRAGON

Twenty five miles south of Memphis the Djedhis constructed a huge man-made lake called Lake Moeris and founded a city of the water dragon or crocodile upon its shores. Later the Greeks of the Hellenic Empire designated this city as Crocodilopolis, "the place of the Crocodile-dragon."

The patron deity of Crocodilopolis was Sobek, a manifestation of the Primal Dragon when it initially emerged from the Cosmic Sea. Sobek, the crocodile god of time and cycles, was intimately associated with an ancient Egyptian cycle of 60 days, a Serpent Cycle based upon the crocodile's 60 teeth. Sobek's celestial constellation was part of the Big Dipper and served as an important indicator of the annual cycles of nature.

At Moeris the dragon god Sobek was worshiped as the numerous live crocodiles which inhabited the depths of the holy lake and occasionally sunbathed upon its sandy shores. According to the historian Strabo, the priests of Sebek treated the crocodiles as pets and affectionately served them a daily ration of bread, meat and wine. When they died, their bodies were mummified and interred in a nearby mausoleum.

THE LABYRINTH, BODY OF THE COSMIC DRAGON

Situated at the east end of Lake Moeris was the famous Egyptian Labyrinth, a glorious monument to the Zodiac, another incipient form of the Primal Serpent after it had expanded to become the physical universe (see Appendix 1). The Labyrinth was a huge cluster of buildings which, according to Pliny, was built in shimmering marble and energizing granite, thus making full use of the vortexual power it was built upon. Strabo commented that the labyrinth rivaled the pyramids of Giza in stature and Herodutus allowed that it was greater in architectural beauty than "all the works and buildings of the Greeks put together."

During the time period that Herodutus visited the Labyrinth, the edifice was a cluster of 12 temples joined together in a circular or horseshoe shape and surrounded by one continuous wall. These 12 temples represented the 12 nomes or divisions of Egypt and the twelve divisions of the Zodiacal Dragon. For this reason, the historian Pliny maintained that the twelve temples were dedicated to Ra, the Sun god, who traveled through the twelve "temples" or divisions of the Zodiacal Dragon during the course of each annual cycle.

While the twelve temples of the labyrinth represented the journey of the soul on the physical or earth plane, another, more secretive labyrinth built directly below it symbolized the journey of the soul in the Duat or "underworld" dimension which lies between Earth and the Heaven or Hell realms. This labyrinth was comprised of a meandering network of water channels, each of which represented one of the various "paths" taken by the soul of the deceased. Within these waterways swam a live crocodile, a living representation of Sobek. According to Egyptian tradition, the deceased soul was destined to encounter Sobek in the Duat and needed to find a way to bypass or defeat the crocodile of time and death if it was to ascend into the paradise realms and enjoy everlasting life.

According to the famous occult researcher and Rosicrucian Lewis Spence the lower labyrinth, as well as its upper counterpart, were important sites for the enactment of initiation rites among the priesthood of Lake Moeris. Here the triumphant initiates would achieve victory over both time and death by defeating live manifestations of Sobek.

HERMOPOLIS, CITY OF THE EIGHT SERPENTS

The principal Serpent City in the middle of Egypt was Khemenu or Hermopolis, the location of Osiris' fourth chakra. This Serpent City was the meeting point of Upper and Lower Egypt, i.e., the polarity, which united at Hermopolis to produce the androgynous Primal Serpent. Near the city was Tell El Amarna, the site of Pharaoh Akhenaten's huge temple which was built in the shape of a cross, the symbol of polarity union.

Hermopolis was the quintessential Serpent City. It was a vortexual "Garden of Eden" and some Egyptian texts even claimed that it was the center of the entire universe. Ancient artists portrayed the city as being situated within the coils of the great Primal Serpent which protected Hermopolis as though it was its premier lair. Legends maintained that it was here that the Primal Serpent was born and then divided into four serpent progeny called Nothing, Inertness, Infinity, and Invisibility. These four serpents further divided into male and female halves to bring the total number of serpents to eight. Together this family of eight serpents swam together and their home, Hermopolis, thus acquired the nickname of Shmunu or "Eight Town."

Herme-opolis, the "City of Hermes," became a city of serpent wisdom and home to many of the greatest philosophical minds of Egypt. It was a mecca for philosophical speculation and, along with Heliopolis, Memphis and Thebes, produced the country's four definitive systems of theology. Throughout its history the city continually distinguished itself as a crucible for the further fermentation of the wisdom brought to Egypt by the lineage of Thoth-Hermes Masters.

THEBES, CITY OF THE SERPENT AMMON

Thebes, the location of Osiris's third chakra, was a southern Serpent City of high regard. It was to this dragon's lair that Ammon, one of the eight serpents born in Hermopolis, founded its own city. In ancient times the city was commonly referred to as No-Ammon or Nut-Ammon meaning "the Town of Ammon." Here the Serpent Ammon was worshipped astwo serpent gods: Ammon Irta and Ammon Kematef. Similar to the Jewish Amen and the Hindu AUM, Ammon was the sound signature of Spirit traveling in the form of a great serpent.

Thebes is sometimes referred to as "the southern Heliopolis." Like its sister city to the north, it was home to a colossal Sun Temple and an important temple/school of the Djedhi priesthood. A second temple at Thebes, now in Luxor, has been called the "Temple of Man" by thebrilliant archeologist R.A. Shwaller de Lubiz. After extensive research, Shwaller de Lubiz discovered that *this* temple of wisdom was built in the exact proportions of the human body, thus revealing that the infinite Spirit, as well as all sacred knowledge, exists right within the human fonn.

KOM-OMBO, CITY OF THE DRAGON SOBEK

The sister city to the northern Crocodilopolis, and Sobek's theological capital in southern Egypt, was Kom-Ombo (both Kom and Om are universal names of the Primal Serpent), location of Osiris's second chakra. It was at Kom-Ombo that the Primal Dragon's priests united Sobek, the crocodile (the Serpent Goddess), with the Solar Spirit Ra (the God) to produce the androgynous Sobek-Ra, the Primeval Mother/Father Serpent. An inscription on one of the temples of Kom-Ombo described the androgynous first serpent: "Sobek-Ra, (the one) who came forth out of the primordial Nu (the Cosmic Ocean), (is) the first of all divinities."

The main temple of Sobek's complex at Kom-Ombo consisted of a large building from which issued out two identical wings, each of which was dedicated to one of the dual aspects of Spirit. One wing was built in honor of Horus, the unmanifest Spirit, and the other glorified Sobek, the Primal Dragon. In proximity to this building was a network of water canals within which swam live crocodiles. In order to gain mastery over time and water (the element of the second chakra) an initiate in training was expected to swim through these channels without getting devoured by the deadly incarnations of Sobek.

INITIATION INTO THE ORDER OF THE DJEDHI SERPENTS

As in many Dragon Cultures worldwide, the goal of an aspiring seeker of wisdom in ancient Egypt was eventual ordination into the Order of Serpents. To gain entrance into the indigenous Order of the Djedhi serious candidates were required to undergo an arduous process of yogic purification culminating in an initiation within the Great Pyramid at Giza.

To begin their respective spiritual quests, the Egyptian aspirants would first travel from their homes to the feet of the Pharaoh, the highest Djedhi initiate, for a preliminary interview. If the aspirant reflected the spiritual qualities sought after by the discriminating priest king he or she would then be sent off to a temple in one of the Serpent Cities in order to serve an apprenticeship and perhaps undergo an initiation in accordance with the city's associated chakra. Intensive purificatory disciplines were thereafter observed as the chosen candidate prepared for a possible future induction into the Order of the Djedhi. For months or even years the lives of the Djedhi candidates were

The "dual" Kom Ombo Temple and
Two Forms of Sobek, the Egyptian "Dragon"

At Abydos: Thoth offers Osiris the symbolism of two opposing snakes in one hand. In the other hand is an ank, the symbol of immortal life that the pharaoh will achieve by uniting the snakes within himself.

At Abydos: The Raising of the Djed Pillar Ceremony.

monitored closely as they underwent a strict regimen which included: daily sweeping the temple floors, bathing twice a day, shaving the entire body every other day, periodic fasts, numerous yogic exercises and hundreds of hours of contemplation and prayer. Academic and scriptural study was also required and the candidates were expected to decipher and memorize the hieroglyphic scriptures which decorated the walls and pillars of temple complexes. Many of these hieroglyphs comprised the 36,000 books of Thoth-Hermes, the greatest of which was *The Book of Thoth,* [24] a book of alchemical secrets believed to have been composed by one of the original Thoth-Hermes missionaries from Atlantis.

THE TWIN NADIS, THE SERPENT FIRE, AND THE DRAGON BODY

Another "book" adorning the walls of Egyptian temples and most likely studied by Djedhi candidates in some form was the Book of Am-Duat. This text was recently found embellishing the tomb walls of the Pharaohs of the 18th and 19th Dynasties and then interpreted by Lucy Lamy, daughter of R.A. Shwaller de Lubiz. Through a series of instructive hieroglyphs the text recounts the journey of Ra, the Spirit, as it takes on a material body and then proceeds to assume the successive forms of larva, cocoon and winged beetle. According to Lamy, this "journey" depicts an esoteric process; its classical symbols of metamorphosis denote the progressive stages of human transmutation. She contends that the Kundalini is represented near the end of the text as the serpent Mehen, Ra's "support" during his final metamorphosis into Khephri, the winged beetle.[88]

Other hieroglyphic Egyptian texts which have recently come to light and were also presumably studied by the Djedhi candidates in training are alluded to in the writings of Isa Shwaller de Lubiz, wife of R.A. Shwaller de Lubiz. Within these texts the twin primary channels, known as the Ida and Pingala Nadis in yogic esoterica, are cryptically referred to as "the Path of the Soul of Osiris" (the Ida) and "the Path of the Soul of Ra (the Pingala)."[23] They are also called Seth and Horus, the "Twin Serpents" or the "Twin Columns" which unite their polarities during the course of spiritual evolution to become the singular Djed column (the spine), path of the serpent fire. The Kundalini, which is also mentioned in many of these texts, is cryptically referred to as Iârt or Aârt, two names of the Ureaus serpent. The roots of its serpentine names, iâr or aâr, mean to "to rise" and, adds Shwaller de Lubiz, "alluded to the rising of the snake of fire along the spinal column."[23]

Certain Egyptian texts also allude to the immutable and immortal bodies. The immutable physical body is referred to as the Djet, and the two etheric Dragon Bodies are alluded to as the Ka (lower Dragon Body) and the Ba (higher Dragon Body). According to Isa Shwaller de Lubiz, the Dragon Body of a fully enlightened Djedhi Master is alternately given the name of Akhu, "the Luminous Spiritual Body."[23]

THE DJED, RAISING THE KUNDALINI

One additional instructive tool used by the teachers of the Djedhi candidates was attendance at the staged production of King Osiris's legend at Sais, Philae, Busiris or Abydos. Osiris, the cosmic dragon-man and life force, was depicted in the drama as an ancient pharaoh who was murdered by Seth, his brother, and then entombed within a coffin before eventually being brought back to life. This poignant allegory represented both the annual death and rebirth of the life force as well as the process of initiation undergone by a Djedhi initiate. The climax of Osiris's drams was the raising of the Djed column, an event which symbolized the rebirth of the life force as well as the resurrection of a Djedhi initiate. Through the lifting up of an actual pillar, representing Osiris's spine and its indwelling serpent power, the actors of the drama symbolized that the archetypal initiate had overcome death through the redeeming power of the Kundalini. The name by which they referred to the column/spine, Djed, includes the root Dj, a syllable that denotes the fire serpent which dwells in the spine as its root and innermost essence.[23]

UNITING THE POLARITY
WITIHN THE GREAT PYRAMID

After years of study and purification some Egyptian candidates were finally judged eligible for initiation into the Order of the Djedhi. They were then escorted from their respective Serpent Cities to the worldwide headquarters of the Serpents at Heliopolis and there awaited initiation within the Great Pyramid.

Following the onset of a powerfully energetic night, the initiation process was consummated as a chosen candidate was led blindfolded to the paws of the Sphinx, which, according to the Egyptian priest Iamblichus, was the "entrance to the secret vaults where the priests held their tests." After a Djedhi priest chanted some mysterious mantra s a hidden door would magically fly open and the candidate would then be ushered into a hallway which ran under the Sphinx and into the Great Pyramid. His or her passage beyond the Sphinx (an image of Anubis, guardian of the necropolis of Osiris), symbolized that the candidate had completed earthly existence and was now ready for spiritual ascension.

Upon entering the inner precincts of the pyramid, the candidate was led to a room either below or above ground to begin the initiation rites. Ancient texts and recent discoveries point to there being a mirror image pyramid below ground as well as numerous chambers yet to be discovered within the Great Pyramid. According to the testimony of the *Crata Repoa,* a Renaissance period text of Egyptian initiation rites compiled from the writings of Herodutus, Plutarch and others, the tests of a Djedhi candidate took place within many of these chambers as well as within their adjoining passageways.

The culminating rite was administered within the Great Pyramid's principal initiation chamber, now known as the King's Chamber. Here the alchemical powers were most potent within the pyramid. Two star shafts inclined at an angle near the sacred thirty-seven degrees, the initiation angle for "meeting the serpent,"[9] led from the room to the outer cosmos and served as passageways for star

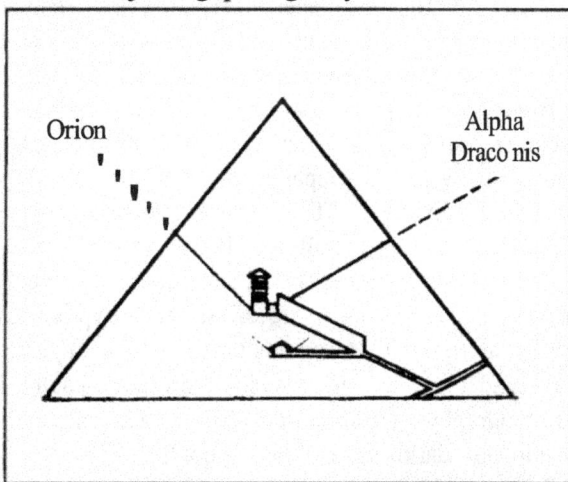

The star shafts connected to the King's Chamber

energies arriving from Alpha Draconis, the heavenly seat of Seth-matter, and from Orion, the celestial abode of Horus-Spirit (Orion was also associated with Osiris who, along with his evil brother Seth, represented the duality of Spirit/matter). Within the King's Chamber these opposing essences united to produce a balanced ambiance which was conducive to the awakening of the androgenous fire serpent. The polarity union of the chamber also precipitated a "zero point" of magnetism, the optimum condition for spiritual awakening.[90]

In the middle of the initiation chamber stood a solitary stone sarcophagus, the "tomb" and alchemical crucible for the candidate's spiritual transformation. Built with dimensions similar to those of the Ark of the Covenant,[90] the Hebrew receptacle designed to capture the essence of androgynous Jehovah, this Egyptian tomb was perfect for uniting the polarity.

OPENING THE CHAKRAS

After a candidate had entered the sarcophagus and its ponderous stone lid was replaced, he or she was declared officially dead by the presiding Djedhi priest. The chief priest would then commence the recitation of the redeeming words of Thoth-Hermes contained within *The Book of Thoth* in order to precipitate the union of the polarity and the activation of the inner Kundalini at the base of the spine. A three day process was thereby consummated as the dynamic fire serpent began its upward march to the summit of the head.

As the awakened serpent fire rose up the spine to pierce each successive chakra, visions and feelings associated with that specific center would flood into the consciousness of the aspiring Djedhi. If he or she was sufficiently prepared for this unfolding process, these evocative visions and feelings would pass in and out of consciousness without any problem. If the candidate was ill prepared however, he or she was likely to become attached or overwhelmed by the inner scenarios. This could stall the ascent of the Kundalini and potentially end the initiation process prematurely.

In recent times Elisabeth Haich, a respected spiritual teacher in Germany, received vivid past-life recall of an Egyptian initiation she had undergone in the Great Pyramid, a remembrance which apparently included the experiences of the Kundalini as it moved through each of her chakras. In her spiritual autobiography, *Initiation,* she writes movingly of having been closed up within the darkness of the sarcophagus in the King's Chamber while visions reflecting the nature of the Kundalini and each chakra moved in and out of her consciousness. When the Serpent Power first stirred at the base of the spine, she described having the vision of a dark, goat-faced, "satanic monster," symbolic of the destructive nature of the serpent fire. Then, as the Kundalini's corresponding chakra, the "Earth Chakra," was opened, she found herself overcome by the distinct sensation of being cold, paralyzed and inert, like a solid rock within the dense Earth. When the serpent fire ascended through her second chakra, the "Water Chakra" and sexual center, she was transported into the middle of a lucid dream scenario in which she and a group of participants embraced each other lustfully while enjoying a sexually explicit, primal dance. When the Kundalini presumably reached the fourth or "Air Chakra," the "Heart Chakra," she experienced a profound love between herself and a visionary lover. And so it went, with each succeeding chakra being pierced by the serpent fire and providing an experience of the elementand emotion it was associated with. [91]

SOARING WITHIN THE IMMORTAL DRAGON BODY

As the Kundalini worked its way up through the chakras, a Djedhi candidate was also likely to experience activation of the immortal Dragon Body and the Ba's separation from its physical sheath. When this occurred, the candidate would arise out the stone sarcophagus within his or her Ba and experience immortality first- hand as it soared around the King's Chamber and up through the star shafts to the heavenly realms of the immortals. There is ample evidence suggesting that during these ethereal flights some of the candidates ascended to certain star bases of the Extraterrestrial Serpents, such as those within the Orion constellation.

In the 1930's the British author Dr. Paul Brunton experienced his own "death" within the King's Chamber and the subsequent release of his eternal Ba. In his book A Search in Ancient Egypt Dr. Brunton recounts in detail this pivotal experience which began by being shut up alone in the forbidding darkness of the Great Pyramid. After succeeding in groping along the pyramid's perilous corridors to the King's Chamber, the doctor initially encountered denizens of inimical spirits which had apparently stationed themselves there to keep intruders out, but the ambiance soon turned peaceful with the arrival of an etheric Djedhi Master. Upon entering the chamber, the phantom guide telepathically instructed Dr. Brunton to lie down in the empty stone sarcophagus before proceeding to catalyze the initiation process through the repetition of the ancient mantras of Thoth- Hermes. Under this adept's guidance Dr. Brunton was quickly engulfed by a death- like catatonic stupor, perhaps the result of awakening the Earth Chakra. This was followed by a sensation of being "caught up in a tropical whirlwind" as the doctor's Ba catapulted out of its physical sheath and floated above the sarcophagus. Then, states Dr. Brunton in his own words: "I was free. No other word will express the delightful sense of liberation which became mine. I had changed into a mental being, a creature of thought and feeling yet without the clogging handicap of the heavy flesh body in which I had been shut up... I knew, at last, why those wise Egyptians of old had given, in their hieroglyphs, the pictured symbol of the bird to man's soul- form (symbol of the Ba). I experienced a sense of increased height and breadth, a spreading out just as though I had a pair of wings."[92]

THE RESURRECTED DJEDHI

At the conclusion of a Djedhi candidate's three days of entombment, the rising serpent fire would finally arrive at its destination within the head and dissolve into pure Spirit. At that moment the candidate would finally achieve the fruit of all his arduous spiritual practices and become an immortal Djedhi and "Stable One," i.e., one who had raised the djed, elevated the serpent, and overcome death. From that point onwards the new Djedhi was known as a Kheper or "Arisen One," a term derived from Khephri, the "resurrected" beetle.

Following the candidate's full illumination, the lid of the sarcophagus was removed. The newly resurrected Djedhi would then arise from the granite coffin and be warmly welcomed by members of the Egyptian Order of the Djedhi who had stationed themselves around the tomb. Stepping forward, the Grandmaster of the Djedhi, the Pharaoh or a member of his royal family, would formally christen the new initiate a high priest or priestess by bestowing upon him or her the symbol of the order, the golden band of wisdom which was honorably worn over the third eye.

THE MAGICIAN PRIESTS, WIELDERS OF SERPENT POWER

As new Serpents of Wisdom, the initiated Djedhi priests and priestesses left Heliopolis with the wisdom, power and tools to perform tasks assigned to them by the Djedhi hierarchy. With the power of the serpent at their disposal and such tools as snake-like staffs, serpentine wands and books of mantric incantations, the new Djedhi priests and priestesses were assigned to certain temple complexes around Egypt within which they would assume the roles of healers, magicians, spiritual teachers and/or temple administrators.

Within their new sacred habitations the Djedhi priests were given certain privileges denied lesser ranking priests, such as access to an esoteric library called the House of Life. Contained within this library were a variety of ancient alchemical texts, such as the books of Thoth-Hermes, and a multitude of magical recipe books full of mantric incantations for amplifying and directing the serpent power. Some of these texts listed prescriptions for casting almost any spell and/or placating almost any god or goddess. They were filed away under such titles as "The Book of Appeasing Sekhmet," "The Book of Magical Protection of the King and his Palace," "The Book of Knowing the Secret Forms of the Deity," and "The Book of Spells for Warding off the Evil Eye." So closely did the Djedhi priests become associated with this library that Seshperonch or "Scribe of the House of Life" became the common coptic term for an initiated magician priest.[93]

With both the power of the serpent and an infinite number of mantric recipes at their disposal, the Djedhi priests and priestesses could effectively enact magic as long as they began their rites with a strict protocol. They were first required to purify themselves by washing out their mouths with pungent natron and then inscribing the symbol of truth upon their tongues with green ink. The magician priests would then proceed to trace a circle or geometrical figure on the ground with their staff or Was Scepter, symbol of their serpent power. Stepping into the center of this figure which was dedicated to a protective god ruling the hour, they would recite an incantation multiple times or until they were convinced that they had evoked the deity of the mantra and their spell had born fruit.

Many adept priests and priestesses became extremely successful with their magic and even gained legendary renown throughout Egypt. According to the "Westcar Papyrus," during the reign of Pharaoh Khufu one magician priest, known simply as "Djedhi," gained notoriety for successfully reattaching severed heads to animals. This same Djedhi was also famous for knowing the "secret chambers of the sanctuary of Thoth" at Heliopolis where the sacred books of Thoth-Hermes were kept. A second initiate and magician mentioned in the Westcar Papyrus was famous for having magically animated a wax crocodile which attacked and devoured his wife's lover, thereby putting an end to their illicit affair. A Greek reference to the power of the Egyptian priests can be found in Lucian's biography of the adventurer Eucrates who traveled from Greece to Thebes and personally witnessed two colossal statues speak seven oracular verses under the animating spell of the Theban priests. Later, during a boat ride up the Nile, Eucrates met an accomplished magician priest who claimed to have studied the magical arts for over 23 years. The priest demonstrated his powers to Eucrates by magically controlling all the fishes in the river and playfully riding upon the back of a dangerous crocodile. Intrigued with the priest's display of powers, Eucrates followed him home. There the surprised Greek adventurer encountered a magically animated broom dressed in human clothing which was busily performing all the priest's household chores.

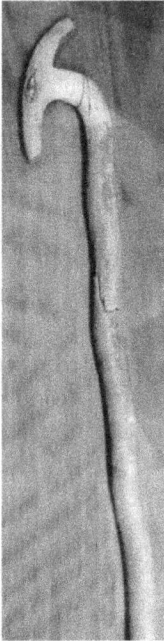

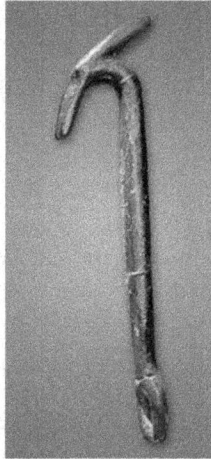

The Was Scepter carried by the Djedhi Priest both represented the source of his Serpent Power and also amplified his Dragon Force. The shaft denoted his spine; the bifurcation at its base represented the twin energy vessels that unite at the base of the spine; and the head denoted the Third Eye of Wisdom activated by the ascending Fire Serpent. The head was the head of Seth, Lord of Death and the destructive Kundalini. The Was could be made of wood, metal or faience, which was a composite of crushed crystal that amplified the Force.

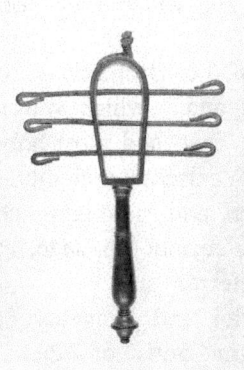

Masks of deities, curved wands, ankhs, sistrums, and even voodoo dolls and crystal balls were used by the Djedhi to amplify and direct the Serpent Power and thereby empower their healing & magic.

CHAPTER 12

THE GREEK AND AEGEAN CHILDREN OF THE SERPENT GODDESS

Once the Dragon Culture had reached the eastern end of the Mediterranean Sea, the colonizing Serpents of Wisdom and their descendants, i.e., the Pelasgians, Danaans, Libyans, Anatolians, Amazons, Cretans and Greeks, established a cohesive Dragon Empire dedicated to their principal deities, the Serpent Goddess and her serpent/bull Son. Set over their Mediterranean kingdom as its temporal and religious leaders were specially anointed priest kings and hierophants known collectively as Sons and Daughters or "Children of the Serpent Goddess."

SAMOTHRACE: HEADQUARTERS OF THE BROTHERHOOD OF SONS

The priests of the Goddess's eastern empire were Her consecrated Sons, the Dactyloi, Kouretes and Korybantes. These matriarchal priests staffed the Goddess's temples, taught within Her mystery schools, and oversaw Her religious rites on the islands of Samothrace, Cyprus, Crete, as well as upon mainland Greece and Asia Minor. They also functioned as warriors and guardians specially trained to protect the sanctity of their mother's mysteries. For this purpose they carried deadly weapons, such as swords and daggers, which they occasionally unsheathed during their symbolic warrior dances.

Apparently the first official headquarters of the Brotherhood of Sons in the Mediterranean was Samothrace, "the Sacred Island," which was alluded to by ancient historians as having been the Goddess's first and most holy shrine in the Aegean. While commenting on Samothrace's extreme antiquity, Diodorus said the island was settled before the great deluge and Herodutus pointed out that the Pelasgian people of the island spoke a very ancient language, called Sai, which pre-existed most all vernaculars in the Mediterranean.

Under the guidance of the colonizing Dactyloi and Kouretes Samothrace became home to temples dedicated to the Twin Sons of the Serpent Goddess, the Kaberoi Twins. The Samothracian Kaberoi, who were also referred to as the Theo Megaloi or the "Great Gods," as well as the "Twin Fires," the two halves of the primal Kundalini fire. They were the original "Twin Flames " and Soul

Mates, and the ubiquitous twin serpents of their androgynous serpent mother. Herodutus referred to them as the sons of Ptah or Vulcan, the fire god and personification of the Kundalini, while Cicero claimed that they were the divine sons of Proserpine, the "First Serpent" Goddess. Symbolic images of them as the twin serpents climbing the shaft of caduceuses were once scattered throughout the sacred isle, although their premier image was that of two twin boys.

The members of the Dactyloi Brotherhood recognized within the images of the Kaberoi a wealth of symbology. The serpentine images of their beloved Twin Flames represented the polarity, known as the Ida and Pingala serpents in the Hindu tradition, which unite as the androgynous fire of transformation. For this reason, the Kaberoi Twins were referred to by their devotees as adept smiths and were invoked for their power to execute a fiery transmutation within a seeker. The statues of the Kaberoi as twin boys also represented to the Dactyloi the patriarchs of their tradition, i.e., the first Sons and Brothers of their ancient brotherhood. In this regard, the twins represented both the primeval split of the Primal Serpent Goddess into twin progeny at the beginning of time as well as the adepts of the Kaberoi Brotherhood of Atlantis who had resided on Earth as the first Sons of the present 104,000 year cycle. It was in the mystery schools of the Atlantean Kaberoi that the secrets of the brotherhood were first promulgated before being transported to the Aegean.

As direct descendants of the Kaberoi, the Dactyloi were referred to by their Aegean brethren as the wielders of fire and "they who invent fire and the use of iron."[25] Like their legendary ancestors, they also knew the process of awakening the inner fire and its ascension. As representatives of the Atlantean Kaberoi Brotherhood in the Aegean, the Dactyloi passed on their esoteric wisdom of the Kundalini to their famous Greek students Orpheus, Kadmus, and Pythagoras, who in turn transmitted the secret knowledge of the serpent fire to others.

INITIATION INTO THE BROTHERHOOD OF SONS

Those prospective candidates seeking initiation into the Brotherhood of Sons on Samothrace were first led into the Kaberoi's centrally located temple soon after arriving on the sacred island. Waiting there to greet them, according to the historian Hippolytus, were the principal statues of the Kaberoi Twins as "two naked boys, having their hands and their genitals elevated towards heaven." The Kaberoi's upraised hands pointed the way to heaven while showering the candidate with blessings. Their erect and elevated genitals symbolized that the "way" to heaven was through transmutation of the seminal fluid and its ascension along the course of the human spine as the Kundalini fire.

Hekate, the Serpent Mother and "Triple Goddess," with destructive weapons, snakes and her sacred dogs.

A Medusa mask similar to the ones used by the Amazons.

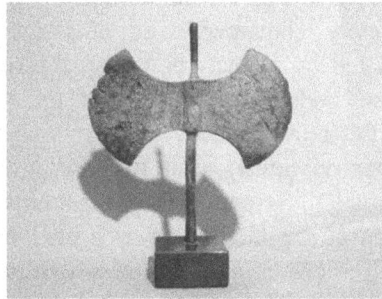

The Cretan Snake Goddess & The Labrys. Symbols of the Goddess's Androgyny.

A Dionysian Baccanalia

A Priestess of Dionysus with Her Thrysus.
Symbol of the Spine and Third Eye

After leaving the holy presence of the Kaberoi, a candidate was escorted into an adjoining temple for preliminary purifications. Following a sincere admission of their most heinous transgression, the candidate was led over a drain and completely showered with holy water to the accompaniment of sacred mantras recited by a Dactyloi priest, the result of which was absolution from all past sins and rebirth as a Son of the Goddess. Arising from his profound cleansing, the new initiate was then ushered into a throne room and given a purple (color of Spirit) sash to wear around his waist and a crown of olive leaves (symbol of Serpent wisdom) as ornamentation for his head. In this regalia the new Son of the Goddess was seated upon an elevated throne and permitted to survey his new empire, the kingdom of the Goddess, which he would now help to administer along with his brothers. Meanwhile, at the base of the throne other ordained priests of the Goddess, the Korybantes and Kouretes, performed a sword dance to the pulsing rhythmic beats pounded out upon ox hide drums. Their hieroglyphic dance symbolized the destruction of any evil or ignorance which could possibly taint the future purity of the new Son. At the conclusion of this rite the initiate was given a special ring of magnetized iron which was coated with gold. The ring accelerated the vibratory frequency of the new Son, empowered his auric field, and promoted the ascension of the Kundalini up his spine. The sacred ring represented membership into the Brotherhood of Sons and guaranteed instant help during times of danger from the Kaberoi Twins.

INITIATION INTO THE SISTERHOOD OF DAUGHTERS

Samothrace was also the site of initiation into the "Sisterhood of Daughters," a rite which was performed in the Zerynthian cave/temple of Hekate (with hard K sound of the Serpent). The temple of Hekate was constructed and cared for by the Amazons, intrepid female Pelasgians from both Libya and Atlantis who also venerated Samothrace as the principal Aegean shrine of the Goddess. They depicted their goddess Hekate, a manifestation of the Serpent Goddess, as snake-footed, snake-haired or three-headed in order to symbolize Her serpentine wisdom and triune powers. Hekate was especially associated with the destructive/transformative powers of the Serpent Goddess and therefore designated patroness of Her most secret mysteries: death and resurrection. During either the full or dark phase of the moon, those accepted into the Sisterhood of the Goddess underwent an initiation in which a representative of Hekate, a consecrated priestess wearing a snake-haired mask of Medusa, used symbols to dramatically enact the mysteries of birth, life and death. Meanwhile dogs, the animals sacred to Hecate, were humbly sacrificed to the Goddess, Finally, at the conclusion of the rites, the new initiated "Daughter of the

Goddess" pledged to guard the mysteries of the Serpent Goddess by adopting a lifestyle and temperament reminiscent of the archetypal Warrior Daughter, Artemis/ Athene. In the same way that the Kaberoi Twins were the archetypal and first Sons of the Brotherhood, Artemis/ Athene was recognized as the first Daughter of the Sisterhood.

Initiation into the Sisterhood of the Serpent Goddess was also conducted within the other sacred temples and upon other islands of the Amazons. Besides Samothrace, their principal initiation centers were the Islands of Lemnos and Lesbos, the temple of Artemis at Ephesus (where she was also called Diana) on the Asia Minor coast, and the citadel of Colchis on the shores of the Black Sea.

CRETE, GOVERNMENTAL SEAT OF THE SERPENT GODDESS

In so far as Samothrace served as the early religious capital of the Aegean, Crete was its ancient governmental headquarters and the principal seat of the Serpent Goddess's temporal powers. Between 2500-1500 B.C. a lineage of Cretan kings called Minos, regal Sons of the Serpent Goddess, ruled over a Dragon Kingdom which included most of the major islands of the Aegean as well as numerous coastal settlements in Greece, Italy and Asia minor. Legend has it that above the throne of the incumbent Minos hung the emblem of his authority, the Labrys or double headed axe. This was the symbol the androgynous Serpent Goddess, the king's true "mother."

THE SERPENT/BULL CULT ON CRETE

Similar to Samothrace, Crete was also an important headquarters of the Serpent Goddess's mystery rites. Her sacred rites had anciently been brought to the island by the early Dactyloi colonists as well as by Her Sons and Daughters who had traveled to Crete from Asia Minor. Once on Crete all these transplanted rites precipitated the formation of both a private and public cult.

The public rites, called the Thiodasia, were officiated by the priest king of Crete. They were held in honor of the nature god Zan, a serpent/bull deity and manifestation of the life force, which legend maintained was reborn in one of Crete's cave/temples each spring only to die the following autumn. His mother was Rhea, a Cretan version of the Serpent Goddess.

Zan's rites were festive affairs conducted in or around the king's splendid palace/temple. Over the course of many days people from all corners of Crete would come together to participate in a series of rituals designed to honor the Bull Son, such as acrobatic vaulting over running bulls and a ceremonial mating between the priest king and his queen who dressed as a bull and cow for the occasion. The high point of the Thiodasia was the feast of raw meat during which the Cretan people were given the chance to commune with the spirit of the serpent/bull Son by consuming a living manifestation of him. A specially chosen bull was ritually slaughtered and pieces of its raw flesh were passed around and eaten by all those in attendance. To wash down their meal, a wine beverage, representing the Son's blood, was decanted out of bull shaped vessels. This celebration of the Son through a meal of meat and wine was the Cretan precursor of the later Christian Holy Communion.

THE DEATH DEFYING RITES OF THE LABYRINTH

Other rites of the public cult included initiation within the Cretan Labyrinth. The design of this famous structure, historically ascribed to the Cretan architect Daidalos, was supposedly modeled after the Egyptian Labyrinth on Lake Moeris and was, therefore, a form of the Zodiacal Dragon or Primal Serpent Goddess. The name labyrinth reflects this esoteric truth. It means "House of the Double Axe" or "House of the Goddess" and is derived from the root "Labrys," the indigenous name for the double headed axe, symbol of the "androgynous" Goddess.

Within the meandering passageways of the Cretan Labyrinth, which was conceived of as the Goddess's "womb," lived Her "dark" bull Son, the Minotaur. The Minotaur was, like the crocodile god Sobek of the Egyptian Labyrinth, a god of time and a version of the "Dark Lord" (see Appendix 1, The Twins). The mission of an aspiring Cretan initiate was to enter the Labyrinth, defeat the Minotaur (possibly an actor playing the part), find the luminous dwelling place of Spirit at the center of the Labyrinth (one of the Cretan maze's names was Da-pu-ri-to-jo, "a Way to the Light"), and then return to its entrance. The victorious emergence of the new initiate from the Labyrinth thus signaled that he or she had defeated time and overcome death.

Possibly the fiercest demons encountered within the Labyrinth were those of an aspiring initiate's own making. It is believed that the Cretan rite, like many initiations in the Mediterranean, may have begun with the consumption of a potent hallucinogenic beverage. An hallucinogenic sacrament was a recognized staple of the Greek rites which evolved out of the Cretan ritual, the Eluesinian Mysteries.

An alternate labyrinth rite was observed in the Knossos palace of the Cretan priest kings, the interior of which was similarly designed in the form of a maze. While performing a dance maneuver known as the Crane Dance, each candidate would wander along the labyrinth-like palace corridors in hopes of discovering a "way to the light." The Crane Dance was based upon the mating dance of the crane which included "nine steps and a leap," symbolic of the evolutionary cycle of nine stages which an aspiring initiate must conquer and leap out of before achieving spiritual freedom. While performing this dance, the candidates would eventually reach a centrally located courtyard framed by seven golden pillars, symbols of the Goddess's seven principles, within which was the dwelling place of "light" or pure Spirit. While communing with Spirit in the center of the palace labyrinth the candidates overcame death and were reborn in "the light of Spirit."

THE SECRET RITES OF THE DACTYLOI: THE THUNDERS OF NOCTURNAL ZEUS

Those Cretan aspirants who felt drawn to participate in the secret initiation rites of the private cult and thereby become members of the Kaberoi Brotherhood on Crete, the Dactyloi Brotherhood, submitted themselves to an arduous purification and initiation process staged within hidden cave temples located upon the upper elevations of Mt. Ida and Mt. Dikte. The mysterious rites performed within these caves have been immortalized by many ancient historians under the epithet of the "Thunders of the Nocturnal Zeus."

The focus and climax of the highly secretive rites of the Thunders of the Nocturnal Zeus was initiation by the Thunderstone, a solidified meteorite with highly magnetic properties. The stone was conceived to be a crystallized form of Zeus's explosive power which, as a flaming serpent, had been thrown down from Heaven to solidify as a rock on Earth. Zeus in his Thunderstone manifestation is mentioned in a chapter of later Greek mythology which alludes to Rhea's presentation to Chronus of the baby Zeus in the form of a "stone wrapped in swaddling clothes."

The Thunderstone initiation was administered in the Cretan cave/temples by vegetarian-consuming Dactyloi priests dressed in long white robes and sandals. After leading a candidate through preliminary purifications, which included communion with the bull Son via a meal of raw bull flesh (the last meal of animal flesh they would ever consume), the priests ceremoniously struck the candidate upon the head and/or back with the sacred rock. As the magnetized Thunderstone interfaced with the candidate's own electromagnetic field it would send subtle electrical currents up and down his body. Because of the interconnection between the electromagnetic field and the etheric Dragon Body, home of the Kundalini, this stimulation would simultaneously activate the indwelling serpent fire and assist in its evolutionary ascension. When the most famous Dactyloi initiate, Pythagoras, was struck by the Thunderstone, he went into a deep mystical trance and lay with his face buried in the ground "as if dead" for an entire night.29 When Epimenides, an initiate of the Diktean Cave, was hit by the stone, he "died" and had an intense dream which encompassed fifty seven years worth of Earth experience. During the dream he learned many important lessons regarding the impermanence of life and communed with etheric teachers and gods of the upper worlds.

Following the candidates' "death" by the Thunderstone, a 27 day (3x9 days-or three cycles of 9) metamorphosis period ensued as the transformati ve energies awakened by the magnetized rock traveled throughout the new initiate's body. During this transmutation period the candidate remained night and day solely within one of the cave/temples while receiving the sacred teachings of the Dactyloi. Then, after having reached the end of his apprenticeship, the candidate was escorted into the presence of an image of Zeus's power, a serpentine thunderbolt, which sat upon a large throne. While kneeling down in front of this throne, the new initiate took his final vows and received full ordination into the Order of the Dactyloi.

THE SERPENT GODDESS TRADITION IN GREECE

THE THREE SEATS OF THE SERPENT GODDESS

During the Mycenaean era the governmental headquarters of the Serpent Goddess's eastern Mediterranean kingdom shifted from Knossos to Athens. Then for the succeeding thousand years this Greek city-state became the Goddess's temporal and cultural seat of power in the Aegean. Concurrent with this development, the Oracle of Delphi became the Serpent Goddess's Aegean seat of divinitory wisdom and Eluesis was chosen as the seat of Her mysteries.

In Her temporal seat at Athens the Serpent Goddess was worshipped as Athene, a goddess from Atlantis and Libya who had arrived in the Aegean via the Pelasgians and Amazons. Once in Athens, Athene's serpentine nature was transferred to her serpent Son and etched upon her body shield and sword as slithering serpents. The androgynous nature of the ancient Serpent Goddess remained intact with Athene, however, and was reflected in her "masculine" authoritarian/ militaristic temperament which coexisted with her "feminine" patronage over the cultural arts and crafts, such as weaving. Following Athene's legendary battle with Neptune for control of Athens (perhaps symbolic of the ancient battle between the Athenians and Atlanteans), the Goddess become the city's sole patroness and protectress When the imperialistic Greek city-state subsequently flourished and expanded well beyond its earliest boundaries, Athene became matriarch over much of the Serpent Goddess's Aegean empire.

At Her divinitory seat at the dragon's lair of Delphi the Serpent Goddess took the form of Delphinia, a phantom pythoness, who spoke her prophetic messages of wisdom through the vehicle of a Pythion Priestess.

The Pythion Priestess on her throne at Delphi

213

Once a month, following preliminary purifications which included a fast of three days and the intake of a special potion of mind expanding herbs, the Pythian Priestess would climb a throne which straddled a large, gaping hole in the ground, the vortexual home of the earth pythoness. After comfortably seating herself, the priestess would proceed to go into a hypnotic trance while staring directly into the eyes of a live snake. Then, once the Serpent Goddess started to speak through her, the priestess would maintain her deep trance by chewing laurel leaves, an herb sacred to the pythoness, and by inhaling cannabis burned on a braz ier directly below her seat.

At the seat of the Goddess's sacred mysteries at Eleusis, the ancient secrets of immortality were transmitted to initiates within a compound which comprised a labyrinth and a huge temple of initiation with 42 (7x6) pillars supporting its roof and a seating capacity of 3000. Within the underground labyrinth a seeker could become a Son or Daughter of the Goddess by re-enacting the sacred mystery of Persephone or Proserpine, the "First Serpent" Persephone was a personification of the Serpent Goddess and the serpent life force which must spend part of the year above the Earth, during the growing season, and part below, during the season of death.

THE HALLUCINOGENIC RITES OF THE SERPENT GODDESS

Persephone's mystery rites were based upon her legendary abduction by Pluto, her captivity in the underworld god's subterranean kingdom, and her eventual return to the surface of the Earth. Her rites were thus divided into two parts, the Lesser and Greater Mysteries, which were celebrated in the Spring and Fall, the times when the serpent life force disappeared from the surface of the Earth and when it returned. Of these two rites, the Greater Mysteries which celebrated Persephone's return to the surface of the Earth were considered the more important. During the Greater Mysteries the Eleusinian candidates would symbolically re-enact the return to life of Persephone by undergoing their own deaths and spiritual rebirths. The rites thus paralleled those of the Djedhi priesthood (from which the Eleusinian mysteries were partly adapted) in which the Egyptian initiates re-enacted Osiris's death and resurrection by experiencing their own.

The rites of the Greater Mysteries officially began after six days of purifying spiritual exercises during which the candidates would travel back and forth between a temple in Athens and the Eleusinian mystery academy. Then, during the darkest period of a specially chosen night, the rites were consummated by the candidates' consumption of a hallucinogenic beverage called the Kykeon. Apparently the active component of the beverage was psilocybin because, as the scholar Robert Graves informs us, "(the) beverage contained ingredients whose first letters could be arranged to spell out "mushroom," the secret ingredient. "29 Such psychotropic mushrooms were known in the Mediterranean area to both precipitate a hallucinogenic trance as well as awaken the inner Kundalini. Their Kundalini-activating effects have been confirmed in recent times by the ethnobotonist Andrew Weil through his studies of contemporary mushroom-consuming societies.

Once the inebriating effect of the hallucinogenic beverage had taken effect within the purified systems of the participants of the Greater Mysteries, they would be ushered one by one through the entrance of the Eleusinian Labyrinth. This maze, a version of the Cretan Labyrinth, was dug out of the hill upon which the Eleusinian Temple stood and designed to simulate Pluto's frightening underworld (a version of Hell) in the same way the Cretan maze simulated the underworld of the evil Minotaur. When the candidates, each of whom played the role of Persephone, entered this maze they quickly found themselves in pitch-black darkness and forced to blindly grope along the damp earthen walls which lined the labyrinth's corridors. As the Kykeon reached its peak of influence, each candidate would unexpectedly be confronted by the terrifying shapes of Pluto's denizens which seemed determined to obstruct their passage through the underworld. If properly prepared for this heart-arresting experience, the candidates would recognize the monsters as phantom-like projections of their own internal demons and "slay" their morbid adversaries along with the corresponding dark aspect of themselves. In this way some candidates "died" many times within these frightening tunnels.

After what must have seemed like lifetimes, the candidates completed their journey through the labyrinth and emerged into what one Greek author referred to as the "light of day in the middle of the night." This luminosity was the light of wisdom which accompanied the new initiates' spiritual rebirth. Then, while witnessing "an ear of com reaped in silence" (Hippolytus, 3rd Cent. A.D.), the initiates completed the Eleusinian rites as well as their own spiritual rebirths. The inner fruit of the com symbolized the "ripened" Spirit within each Eleusinian initiate which was now "resurrected" and released from its husk of limitations, i.e., its fears, ego and physical sheath.

MYSTERY RITES OF DIONYSUS, THE SERPENT/BULL

Another Greek cult which co-existed with the Eleusinian Mysteries and also incorporated the consumption of hallucinogenic sacraments was that of the cult of Dionysus, the serpent Son of Zeus, the Spirit. Dionysus was a composite god synthesized from the Cretan Zan and the Egyptian Osiris to produce a resurrected serpent/bull Son. He was patron of both his own cult as well as the Eleusinian Mysteriesand known by the esoteric name of Iakos, a title derived from Iao and the hard K sound, both of which are ancient sound signatures of the Primal Serpent.

The rites of the Dionysian cult were enacted during high energy periods, such as full moon nights, on top of secluded mountains or within isolated forest glens. After secretly meeting on a pre-arranged night, the participants of a Dionysian ritual would seek to unite with the Son of God by first altering their awareness with strong wine, hallucinogenic mushrooms, or other potent mind-altering sacraments. Then, while meditating upon their beloved deity, they would proceed to sing and dance in the tradition of the legendary followers of Dionysus, the god-intoxicated Maenads. One group of female participants of the rites so completely identified themselves with the legendary Maenads that they even referred to themselves as "the Maenads." During some of the coldest nights in November and December these intrepid women would climb to the frosty summit of the 8000 foot Mount Parnassus while dancing along the course of its knee-deep, snow covered trails. The reward for their efforts was ecstatic union with the transcendental aspect of the Son of God.

Some moonlit rites of the Dionysian cult, which were attended by both women and men, resembled an assembly of the "Lunatic Yogis" of the Hindu tradition. In order to completely transcend the dualistic consciousness of good and evil, right and wrong, the participants of these aberrant nocturnal rites reprised the more savage actions of the mythological Maenads. Many scurried into the bushes and returned with the carcasses of wild animals between their teeth, while others performed perverse sexual acts. Such savage actions were, however, often punctuated by solemn initiations into the Order of the Bacchuses, a Greek branch of the Sons and Daughters of the God/ Goddess. During these initiations, a pine branch shaped like a caduceus and called a Thyrsus was placed upon the backs of candidates by a priest or priestess of Dionysus. This sacred implement had the effect of stimulating the electromagnetic field of the candidates while sympathetically awakening the inner transfonnative fire serpent.

Other secret initiation rites of the Bacchuses were administered within the cult of Sabazios, a branch of the Dionysian cult in Thrace. During these rites union with Dionysus was precipitated by a live snake which was painted gold and allowed to slither throughout the shirt of a candidate, thereby presumably stimulating the movement and ascent of the Kundalini. As the fruit of these rites, the participant was blessed by the Son of God in his serpentine form while uniting with his transcendental aspect.

THE ORPHICS, REFORMERS OF THE SERPENT GODDESS'S MYSTERIES

The orgiastic Greek rites of Dionysus were eventually reformed by the Order of Orpheus, a branch of the Order of the Dactyloi. The founder of this order was the legendary Serpent of Wisdom Orpheus, who, like his Egyptian counterpart, Thoth-Hennes, represented not one person but a lineage of Masters. Some of those in the Orphic lineage were Dactyloi initiates while others were Djedhi adepts of the Osirian mysteries. They all shared a common commitment, however, which was to reform and standardize the Aegean mysteries of the Goddess and her Serpent Son. Because of their extensive work, by 500 B.C. the members of the Order of Orpheus could be found throughout the empire of the Serpent Goddess teaching and administering the reformed rites of the Kaberoi, Cybel, Persephone and Dionysus.

The Orphies' specific influence on the orgiastic Dionysian cult consisted in introducing rites of a more disciplined and yogic nature. The Orphics maintained that the way to permanent union with the Son of God was not through drugs or occasional full moon dalliances in the mountains, but through the adoption of a spiritual lifestyle punctuated with the regular observance of yogic practices. They contended that the only way to permanently unite with the transcendental aspect of Dionysus was through renouncing the selfish and animalistic urges which occupy the material flesh. They taught that through a strict vegetarian diet, occasional fasts, study of the scriptures, service to others and lengthy periods of meditation, a seeker could permanently become a Bacchus.

PYTHAGORAS, INCARNATION OF THE SERPENT

The greatest of the Orphic and Dactyloi initiates was Pythagoras, a wizard and hierophant whose name means "I am the Python" or "I am the Serpent." Pythagoras was an incarnation of the Primal Serpent which took birth to synthesize and reform the mystery traditions scattered throughout the ancient world.

During his upbringing upon the Island of Samos, Pythagoras was exposed to many of the most ancient mystery teachings of the Serpent Goddess. Having been bom into a Pelasgian home he was surrounded by the wisdom of the first colonists of the Aegean, some of whom had arrived directly from Atlantis. Pythagoras also came into contact with numerous Orphic priests on the island and through them learned some of the ancient wisdom of the Dactyloi and Djedhi.

Upon reaching a mature age Pythagoras set out across Europe, Asia and Africa to fulfill his destiny. He is reputed to have first traveled to the western headquarters of the Serpents of Wisdom in Egypt where he spent twenty two years studying with the most renown priests of Memphis, Heliopolis, and Thebes. The culmination of his pivotal time in Khem was initiation within the Great Pyramid, at which point he became a Djedhi and high ranking member of the worldwide Order of Serpents. Leaving Egypt, Pythagoras traveled to Samothrace, Crete, and Eleusis where he gained initiation into the Dactyloi Order as well as all diverse branches of the Aegean mystery academy. Then, traveling in an eastward direction, Pythagoras earned initiation into the Chaldean rites of the Ashipu, the Phoenician rites of Adonis, the mysteries of the Persian Magi and the yogic disciplines of the Hindus. Legend has it that in India, where he was known as Yavancharya, Pythagoras achieved his final initiations in the cave temples of Elephanta, Ellora and Ajanta, subterranean caverns which supposedly connected to a network of tunnels leading to the eastern headquarters of the Serpents in Tibet.

Returning home to the Mediterranean area, Pythagoras founded his synthesized mystery school in Crotona, Southern Italy, and quickly procured for himself a reputation as an incarnation of the Serpent's power and wisdom. Among his new Italian peers it became common knowledge that Pythagoras was capable of controlling the weather, prophesying the future, and even raising the dead. Among his students Pythagoras garnered the additional denomination of a hard task master. A candidate seeking initiation into his school was first required to undergo an austere probationary period of five years during which absolute silence was observed punctuated with a sparse vegetarian diet devoid of beans.

There were three degrees in Pythagoras's school. Following the long probationary period, the worthy student was initiated into the first degree of Mathematicus. In this degree the initiate was exposed to various forms of geometry and mathematics. Pythagoras maintained that the basis of all things is numbers, so he made their study precede all other. If the initiate sufficiently learned the lessons and passed the examinations of this first degree he or she was ushered into the second degree of Theoreticus, meaning theory or philosophy, and taught to speculate about the nature of existence and the origins of the cosmos. Finally, if the initiate passed the tests of the second degree he or she was eligible to become one of the spiritual elect and gain initiation into the third degree of Electus. This final initiation had the power of transporting the initiate "into the light of the fullest illumination"[24] and leading him or her to complete union with the transcendental Spirit. As an Electus, the student became a true Son or Daughter of the God/Goddess and a full fledged member of the worldwide Order of Serpents.

Once a student had risen within the rank s of the Order of the Pythagoreans he or she was given a golden ring upon which was engraved the five pointed star surrounded by an ouroboros serpent (serpent biting its own tail), symbol of both the Pythagorean and worldwide Order of Serpents. Famous initiates of the Pythagorean Order who wore this ring included Epimenides, the Cretan initiate of the Dactyloi who lived 150 years; the wizard Empedocles who could see into both the past and future; and the Master Apollonius who was renowned for his teleportation and dematerialization abilities.

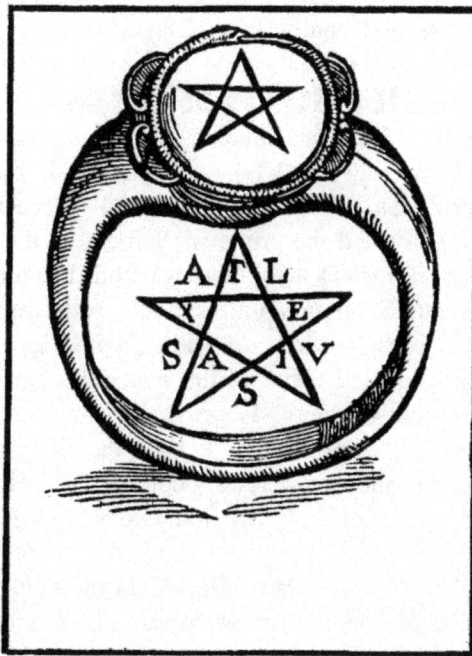

An initiate's ring of the Pythagorean Order of Serpents

CHAPTER 13

THE LEVITES OF PALESTINE AND THE POSSESSORS OF FIRE

Beginning in the second millennium B.C., a Dragon Culture was founded by initiates from the mystery school traditions of the Mesopotamian Anunnaki and the Egyptian Djedhi. A synthesized mystery school tradition, the progeny of these two parent traditions, was thus born. This new Hebrew Order of Serpents reflected its pre-Palestinian roots by including within its lineage of patriarchs the Egyptian Thoth-Hermes (as Cain and Enoch), the Mesopotamian priest king Enmenduranki (as Enoch), along with Abraham, Moses, the Levites, the Prophets, the Essenes and finally Jesus Christ.

YOD HE VAU HE: BOTH SPIRIT AND DRAGON

Like the Hindu Shiva and Shakti, the transcendental supreme god and his power, Yod He Vau He (YHVH), was an androgynous deity whose transcendental presence was the infinite Spirit and whose manifest aspect was the Holy Fire or Holy Spirit and the primeval Serpent on the Tree (see Appendix 1, Part I). Both aspects of YHVH are inherent within his "unspoken" name, Yod He Vau He, which unites Yod, a sound syllable reflecting the transcendental male principle and the consciousness of I AM, with He Vau He or EVE, the three-syllabled and three-lettered name of the material, female principle and the three powers of the Serpent Goddess. Together the two parts of the sacred name unite to form "I am EVE," "I am Life" and "I am the Serpent." In recognition of their deity's two aspects, the early Jews depicted YHVH as a figure with a human male upper body ("male" Spirit) and two snakes ("female" matter) for legs and feet.[94]

YHVH'S dual nature was also reflected in the numerology of his sacred name. According to the Jewish system of gematria, the science which assigns a number to each letter, the numerical equivalent of Yod is 10, a number symbolic of the male principle which manifests as both the transcendental Spirit (0) and the singular awareness of I AM (1). The gematrical reduction of He Vau He is 16 or 7 (1 +6=7), the number of the female principle and the Serpent Goddess's seven principles.

THE PRIMAL SERPENT GODDESS, CHOKMAH AND SHEKINAH

YHVH's manifest aspect was referred to by the Hebrews as Chokmah and Shekinah (hok-mah and she-kine-ah), two names for the Primal Serpent Goddess which both pivot around K, the universal seed sound of the Serpent. Each name reflects qualities of the transcendental god's manifest aspect-Chokmah translates into "wisdom" and Shekinah means "light," "presence," and "Holy Spirit." Shekinah is closely related to the Egyptian and Hindu names for the Serpent Goddess and power of Spirit, Sekhmet and Shakti, and like its counterpart Shakti denotes "electrical sparks."95 Chokmah was closely related to the Serpent Goddess Sophia, its counterpart in the Greek mystery school traditions, which was venerated as the wisdom and power of God. One legend has Sophia manifesting in the Garden of Eden as the Serpent on the Tree.

In the Hebrew sacred literature Chokmah/Shekinah refers to herself thus: "God made me in the beginning of His works, as the first of His acts." "I am the Word which was spoken by the Most High."96 (The Word created the Universe.)

CAIN, THE POSSESSOR OF FIRE

According to the hidden wisdom of the Kabbala (Ka-bbala, Serpent Wisdom), the esoteric tradition of the Hebrews and Jews, after transcendental YHVH projected his manifest aspect and proceeded to create the universe, the androgynous deity divided into two component parts and became Adam (the spiritual, male principle) and Eve (the material, female principle) In this regard, YHVH's translated name "I am Eve" can be expressed as "Ad-am-Eve." Adam and Eve were placed in the "Garden of Eden" to mate (or reunite) in order to produce Cain, the "first born" Son. Cain was thus Adam and Eve reunited as YHVH's manifest aspect, the androgynous Primal Serpent. For this reason Helena Blavatsky rightfully asserts: " ... the lord god (YHVH), or Jehovah, is Cain esoterically, and the tempting Serpent as well..."15

In the Kabbalic mysteries Cain's birth as the androgynous fire serpent was revealed in a mysterious allegory which describes an illicit cohabitation between Jehovah (YHVH) and Eve. Apparently Jehovah, in the form of Sameal, the spirit of fire, secretly seduced Eve during Adam's absence and their union brought forth Cain. Cain, whose name means both "smith," a worker with fire, and the "possessor" of fire, thus inherited the nature of the serpent fire from his father.

The myth of Cain's mysterious birth and fiery nature was apparently adopted into the Hebrew tradition from its earlier parent orders. It appears as

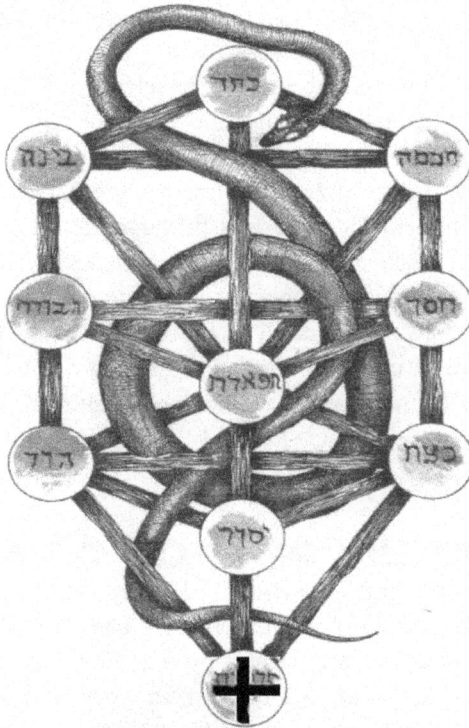

Cain was the Primal Serpent that spiraled down the Tree of Life to Malkuth, "Kingdom," the symbol of which is Cain's Mark, a circle with a cross within it. This symbol became the emblem of the line of Grail Kings who possessed the Serpent Fire.

King Melchizedek was a Grail King who carried the prized cup of immortality. He was "without father or mother or geneology, without beginning of days or end of life." He is a form of the ancient King of the World, who has no parents on Earth and is eternal. He is thus a manifestation of Sanat Kumara, Neptune and Cain. Through him the Holy Spirit flowed to Abraham & the Jewish race. His gift was the Star of David, yantra (geometrical) form of Sanat Kumara.

though he may have been a direct evolution of Volcan, the Atlantean fire serpent, as well as the fire serpent's later manifestation of Vulcan, the Roman smith god. This truth is corroborated by the author of *The Source of Measures* who points out that in *Genesis* one can find Cain introduced as V'elcain or V'ulcain, a title which means "and the god Cain" and bears obvious resemblance to the name Vulcan. Furthermore, states B lavatsky, the name Cain can also be interpreted to mean "(the) inventor of sharp iron tools and smith work,"[15] thus providing additional confirmation for Cain's evolution from Volcan/Vulcan.

"KING" CAIN WAS NEPTUNE AND SANAT KUMARA

If Cain was Volcan or Vulcan and Ptah, and also acknowledged to be the Serpent on the Tree, then he must be the Hebrew version of the Atlantean Neptune and the Hindu Sanat Kumara. This truth is introduced and expanded upon by Laurence Gardner in *Genesis of the Grail Kings,* wherein he presents a Grail King list of planetary monarchs that begins with Cain. In fact, claims Gardener, in the esoteric Midrash and Phoenician canons the Mark of Cain, a circle with a cross within it, is recognized to be an archetypal symbol associated with the Kabbalic Tree of Life that denotes "Kingdom," thus making Cain a Hebrew manifestation of the ancient King of the World. Furthermore, according to one version of his name, Qayin, Cain denotes "a Spear." From this perspective he is synonymous with the Hindus' King of the World, Sanat Kumara, who is often paid homage to solely in the form of his definitive symbol, the Vel Spear.

Also like his counterparts Neptune and Sanat Kumara, Cain is regarded esoterically to be the Kundalini itself. This associates him with the universal fire and endows him with the powers to create, preserve and destroy. This is why he is both a great architect who built a city that bears his name, as well as the murderer of his own brother. As the Serpent Power itself, Cain is a "possessor of fire," and it was he who passed fire down a line of kings and patriarchs called "possessors."

ENOCH, THE TRANSMITTER OF HOLY FIRE

The Master Enoch is either the third or seventh patriarch of the Hebrews depending on which generation list, Seth's or Cain's, one subscribes to. As the third patriarch Enoch would have been a teacher and a manifestation of the Divine Mind of God (three is the number of communication). As the seventh patriarch Enoch would have been the carrier of the power of death and transformation (seven is the number of death). Since he is associated with both numbers, Enoch appears to have been both a true teacher and possessor.

Like Cain before him, Enoch was a possessor and transmitter of fire. His name denotes both "enlightened seer" and "initiator," one who initiates through the transmission of the Shekinah or Holy Fire. Enoch is apparently a Hebrew name for one of the M asters in the lineage of Thoth-Hermes, a truth which becomes nearly irrefutable in light of their identical legends and the fact that in the esoteric records of the Arabs they are both referred to by the same name, Idris. Both Enoch and Thoth-Hermes were manifestations of the Divine Mind of God, and each was a prophet of that aspect of spiritual wisdom known as sacred science (science united with spiritual principles). Each was associated with the design and construction of certain sacred edifices, including the Great Pyramid of Giza. And both are mentioned as pre-diluvian masters who preserved the mystery teachings of the Serpents of Wisdom on tablets or pillars before the onset of a great flood, returning as post-diluvian masters to recover these sacred teachings once the flood waters had subsided.

The figure of Enoch may also be synonymous with the hierophant/priest king Enmenduranki, the Sumerian pre-flood monarch who may have also been a master of the Thoth-Hermes lineage. Both Enoch and King Enmenduranki were masters of sacred science and the uniters of spirituality and science (Enmenduranki means "uniter of Heaven and Earth"). Their intimate relationship is also revealed within the Hebrew and Sumerian pre-diluvian generation lists of kings which list both as the seventh patriarch. It is believed by some that the Hebrew list of 10 pre-deluge patriarchs is a spurious copy of the Mesopotamian list with Hebrew names inserted in place of the more ancient Sumerian. It has been satisfactorily proven, for example, that Ziusandra, the last Sumerian King before the flood, is a carbon copy of the last pre-deluge Hebrew patriarch, Noah.

ABRAHAM, THE MAGICIAN PRIEST AND POSSESSOR OF FIRE

Following the great deluge, the first historical possessor of Holy Fire was Abraham. According to the Hebrew esoteric tradition, this future patriarch of the Isrealites was living as an initiate of the M esopotamian mystery academy in "Ur of the Chaldees" when Yahweh first called upon him to become the "father of many nations." His early whereabouts and spiritual office are mentioned in the Hebrew Torah which claims that Abraham's original home was "Aurkasdeem," a name which denotes both "Ur of the Chaldees" as well as "the light or power (Aur) of the magicians and prophets (kasdeern)."[97] A comprehensive translation of the scriptural passage could thus be rendered as:

223

"Abraham's home was in Ur among the light and power of the magicians and prophets."

As a magician/prophet of Ur, possibly an Ashipu priest, Abraham would have been schooled in the wisdom of the ancient priest king Enmenduranki (or Enoch). As a magician priest surrounded by "light and power" he would also presumably have been a possessor of serpent fire. This, as it turns out, is clearly revealed in the Bible where we learn that his original name was Ab-ram, meaning the "possessor of Ram" or the "possessor of fire."[97] Ram is the universal sound syllable for fire.

Abraham's serpent power was apparently enhanced when he left Ur for Palestine and received the blessings of King Melchizedek, a manifestation of the ancient King of the World who was "without father or mother or genealogy, without beginning of days or end of life." Melchizedek shared wine out of the Grail Chalice he carried, thereby transmitting to Abraham and his Hebrew-Judaic line the blessing of abundant Holy Spirit Fire.

After settling in Palestine, Abraham proceeded to disperse his sacred fire to his children and their descendants. From Abraham, the power passed to Isaac and thence to Jacob or Israel and then to Israel's twelve sons, the leaders of the twelve tribes of Israel. Eventually it infiltrated all the Children of Israel, thus making them a sacred and blessed race. Of the original twelve tribes who received the Holy Spirit those who received it in the greatest measure were the Tribes of Judah and Levi. From out of these two tribes emerged the kings, priests and prophets of the Israelites and the leaders of the Hebrew Order of Serpents.

THE LEVITE POSSESSORS

With their portion of Shekinah or Serpent Power, the "possessors" of the Tribe of Levi respectfully administered YHVH's religious rites. While serving as temple administra tors, priests, judges and prophets, they became the "hands" and "voice" of great Jehovah on Earth. They also becameinveterate worshippers of YHVH's manifest serpent form which they made the centerpiece upon their sacred altars.

Within the tribe of Levites YHVH's manifest aspect was worshipped as Leviathan, a dragon closely related to Lotan or Lawton and Ladon, two versions of the Primal Serpent worshipped in North Canaan and Greece respectively. The name of this dragon, Levi-athan, is thought by some to have been the basis for the name Levite.[98] YHVH's serpent form was also known among the Levites as Nehushtan, meaning the "brazen serpent," and worshiped by them as a golden

A Levite Priest waving incense to the Brazen Serpent

or brass image placed upon the altars of the "high places," i.e., the Hebrew temples. These metallic serpent images survived until the days of King Hezekiah "who broke the images of the serpent which had been in the high places since the time of Moses."₉₉

Along with serpentine images of Nehushtan, the Levites also worshipped mummified or metallic snakes and effigies of the Angelic Orders of Serpents, the Seraphim and Cherubim. Recent excavations in Israel have uncovered copper and bronze images of serpents within the holy sanctums of temples once administered to by the Levites.[73]

MOSES, THE LEVITE

Perhaps the greatest Levite and one of the first to introduce the worship of Leviathan/Nehushtan to the Isrealites was Moses. The Levite Moses is famous for having set the brazen serpent upon a cross in front of a group of wandering Israelites suffering from the bites of deadly snakes which swarmed within the steamy Sinai Desert. According to *The Book of Exodus*, those who looked upon the raised serpentine image received health and life. In this context "life" denoted not just physical longevity, but also spiritual immortality. The brazen serpent was an ancient motif of spiritual resurrection and everlasting life which the Djedhi priest Moses had taken with him out of Egypt.

The Brazen Serpent of Moses

MOSES, THE EGYPTIAN MAGICIAN PRIEST

Moses was bom as a Hebrew Levite in Egypt during a time when the reigning Pharaoh, Ramses, issued a decree in which all the first bom male children of the Hebrews were to be murdered. In order to save the infant Moses, his mother placed him in a reed basket and then set it afloat upon the Nile River. Later, when it came to rest on the river bank, the basket was discovered by the daughter of the Pharaoh whose maternal instincts compelled her to take the baby home and raise it as her own.

While growing up within an Egyptian royal family, Moses was accorded all the privileges of an Egyptian prince, including entrance into the ancient mystery schools of Khem. According to both Strabo and Manetho, part of Moses' training occurred at the Academy of Heliopolis where he received ordination as a Djedhi priest within the King's Chamber of the Great Pyramid. As the result of his initiation, Moses acquired the supernatural abilities of an Egyptian magician and carried a staff or "rod" as the symbol of his power.

Moses's serpent power blossomed until it exceeded that of most magician priests of Egypt. Examples of his superior powers are found throughout *The Book of Exodus*. When Moses was forced to compete with Pharaoh's chosen magicians his staff turned into a live snake and easily consumed their snake-transformed rods, thereby symbolizing the superiority of his serpent power over theirs. While using his immense power, Moses proceeded to create the plagues and disasters which finally convinced the Pharaoh to free the enslaved Israelites. Simply by raising his rod Moses was able to turn the waters of Egypt into flowing blood and compel frogs to emerge out of the lakes and rivers and invade peoples' dwellings. He also magically precipitated a plague of locusts over the land and caused the death of all the Egyptians' first born sons. Later, after leaving Egypt, he parted the Red Sea and drew water from a dry rock in the desert of Sinai with but the slightest wave of his magical rod.

THE TABERNACLE, UNION OF THE POLARITY

When Moses left Egypt for Palestine he took with him all the ancient wisdom, instruments, and rites of the ancient Djedhi priesthood. With this knowledge he began his tenure as a high Levite priest of the Hebrews by designing a temple modeled after the Egyptian temples of the Djedhi. His temple is referred to in the Bible as the "Tabernacle" in the desert.

As the counterpart of an Egyptian prototype, Moses's Tabernacle had 60 pillars, the number of an Egyptian cycle, and opened to the east like an Egyptian solar temple. It also reflected the function of an Egyptian initiation chamber by serving as an alchemical crucible for the union of the polarity. The columns of the tabernacle united Heaven and Earth (the roof and floor), as did and the two cherubs (manifestation of the Twins) which were draped over the Ark of the Covenant. To insure that every facet of the tabernacle promoted balance and the union of the polarity, Moses hired a representative of the tribe of Dan, whose

Moses and Aaron defeat Pharoah's priests with their stronger Serpent Power

The Twin Cherubs of the Ark of the Covenent represent the universal polarity that emerges in and out of the androgynous Infinite Spirit.

Solomon's Temple: The perfect Alchemical Crucible for polarity union.

The Caves of Mt. Carmel, homes of the Essene & Nasorean Serpents.

symbol was the snake (female principle), and one member of the tribe of Judah, whose symbol was the solar lion (male principle), to oversee the temple's construction. [99]

The later Temple of Solomon reflected Moses's Tabernacle and similarly united the polarity. Besides possessing columns and cherubs similar to the Tabernacle, Solomon's Temple further precipitated the union of the polarity by incorporating strategically-placed, metal rods into its design. The rods united water channels (representing the female principle) which ran under the temple to golden spires (representing the male principle) on the temple roof, thereby completing the fusion of Heaven and Earth.[52]

THE SCHOOL OF THE PROPHETS

Because of the spiritual guidance offered by Moses, as well as the arcane legacy of Abraham, a Hebrew Order of Serpents called the School of the Prophets eventually crystallized. The secret wisdom of this school, the Kabbala or secret mysteries, coalesced as a synthesis of the knowledge Moses had acquired in Egypt and on Mt. Sinai along with the wisdom which Abraham had brought out of Chaldea.

The School of Prophets is first mentioned in the Bible as a group of itinerant prophets who occasionally met to prophesy together under the watchful eye of their Master, the Levite Samuel. This roaming band of prophets eventually acquired a fixed location for a school upon the summit of Mount Carmel where they built a compound of buildings. Some of their buildings served as monasteries for the resident prophets while others were used as teaching facilities and temples of initiation for the prophets-in-training. Famous prophets who studied and/or taught at the school include Elijah, Elisha and Jesus Christ.

From their seat on Mount Carmel, the Hebrew Order of Serpents sent and received communications from other branches of the Serpents of Wisdom around the world. According to ancient Rosicrucian records, the prophets on Mt. Carmel would occasionally exchange communiqués with the Djedhi priesthood of Heliopolis, Egypt. Supposedly at one time some very valuable records were transferred from the Sun Temple at Heliopolis to the School of the Prophets for safekeeping. Later these records were carried to the eastern headquarters of the Serpents in Tibet and supposedly continue to exist there in a hidden, underground vault.[100]

THE ESSENES: "SONS OF ZADOK," THE LEVITE

One important offshoot of the School of the Prophets was the Essenes. This branch of the Hebrew Serpents of Wisdom served as a vehicle for bringing the ancient mystery teachings of the Hebrew Serpents down from Mt. Carmel as well as for founding communities based upon their spiritual principles.

The reason for the formation of the Essene Order was three-fold. First, the Essenes were founded to revive the teachings of the prophets and Levites. In their time the members of the Jewish priesthood, i.e., the Sadducees and Pharisees, had degenerated into hypocrisy and power mongering. The Essenes distanced themselves from this sarcedotal community and chose instead to handpick their religious leaders from among the direct descendants of the Levite Zadok, King David's high priest. As self- appointed revivers of this pure Levite strain, the Essenes referred to themselves as "the Sons of Zadok."

The second reason for the founding of the Essene Order, which naturally follows the first, was to create communities in which the members would scrupulously adhere to the law of Moses and the spiritual codes of the School of Prophets. In order to accomplish this cherished goal the Essenes separated themselves from the common, profane man and established communities either on the outskirts of towns or in obscure, isolated regions. While living peacefully in such remote areas as the shores of the Dead Sea and Lake Moeris in Egypt, the Essenes were able to pursue an existence which was in accordance with the will of YHVH and immune from interference or censure of the Jewish hierarchy.

With the spiritual principles handed down within the School of Prophets, the Essenes developed a daily regimen which was a healthy balance of spiritual study and practical labor. The Essenes would begin their day with meditation and prayer followed by the worship of the Sun, a representative of the transcendental Solar Spirit, as it rose above the horizon. Then, after traveling to their respective fields and workshops, they would spend the daylight hours involved in some useful occupation, such as carpentry, pottery, sewing, and farming. Many Essenes also became adept healers and herbalists with a profound knowledge of fasting and nutrition. Because the wisdom of healing was eventually dispersed throughout the entire group, the Essene sect in Egypt became known as the Therapeuts (related to "therapeutic"). By itself, the name "Essene" is reputed to have evolved from a Syrian word for healer.

At the completion of their day, the Essenes would once again worship the Solar Spirit before devoting the evening hours to meditation and the study of their scriptural texts, the *Kabbala, The Torah,* and *The Book of Enoch.* Although they avidly studied these ancient texts, the focus of the Essene movement was not philosophical speculation but union with their guardian angels (Higher Selves) and YHVH. Within the Essene Order guardian angels were probably conceived of in the forms of cherub dragons as they had been within the traditions of their ancient ancestors, the Kaberoi Masters of Atlantis and the Ashipu priests of Mesopotamia. In order to purify themselves and effect a cosmic union with these etheric guides, the Essenes consumed a pure vegetarian diet, occasionally fasted (for up to 40 days), and meditated frequently. Sometimes during their deepest meditations they would unite with their Angelic Selves and journey interdimensionally to the highest heavens via their Merkabah vehicles, the Jewish term for light or Dragon Bodies. The root Mer translates into "light," and the syllables Ka and Ba refer to the higher and lower Dragon Bodies.

JESUS CHRIST, THE ESSENE NASOREAN

A third and very important reason for the creation of the Essene Order was to act as a vehicle for the birth of a divine Son a Messiah, who was destined to be born among the Jews. Since the days of the Prophet Isaiah the immanent birth of a teacher and savior who would establish YHVH's kingdom on Earth was spoken about and anxiously awaited by the initiates of the School of Prophets. For the reception of this divine leader on Earth, the Essenes, a name which also denoted "expectancy, " were specially founded.

Actually, two messiahs were awaited. According to the *Dead Sea Scrolls,* one messiah was prophesied to be born into the Tribe of David and serve as the King Messiah. This would be Jesus Christ. The second messiah was to be born into the Tribe of Levi and then serve as the Priest Messiah. This would be John the Baptist. Both Jesus and John were Essene Nasoreans. They had both been born into an Essene sect that was the synthesis of Jewish Essenes & Gnostic Mandeans who had originated in the Far East on the Island of Sri Lanka when it was the Garden of Eden and occupied by the Serpent on the Tree: he who is known as the great gnostic teacher Sanat Kumara. They brought Sanat's gnostic teachings west, successively uniting with the Sumerians, Persians, Egyptians, and finally with the Essenes, whom they taught the true rite of baptism that culminates in Kundalini activation. The most powerful of the Mandeaens were the Nasurai, a cousin to Nasorean that also contains the prefix Nass, meaning "Serpent." The Mandean Nasurai and the Essene Nasoreans were Serpents of Wisdom who fully embodied the gnostic wisdom of the First Serpent, Sanat Kumara.

When just thirteen years of age, the age when a Jew officially becomes a man, Jesus left Palestine and set off to study the mystery traditions of other branches of the Serpents of Wisdom around the globe. His subsequent adventures are currently mentioned within various records, including the travels of "Issa" (Asian Name for Jesus) which were discovered in 1887 by the Russian adventurer Nicholas Notavich in a monastery in Ladakh, "Little Tibet."

The first leg of Jesus's journey, a two years passage through the arid deserts of Asia, ended safely in India. In the land of Bharat Jesus proceeded to become a faithful student of the ancient Vedanta philosophy and learned the path of yoga from numerous Mahanaga Siddhas. Jesus also went on pilgrimages and visited many of India's holy cities and shrines, including the holy city of Serpents, Kashi, and the famous Jaganath temple in Orissa. At some point he is reputed to have traveled to a Buddhist monastery in the Himalayas and studied the doctrines and philosophy of the Shakyamuni.

Leaving India at the age of 26, Jesus traveled first to Persepolis, the capital of Persia, where he studied the teachings of Zoroaster under the tutelage of the Magi priesthood. Continuing west, he journeyed to Athens in order to study with the renowned Greek philosophers and from there passed into Egypt via the port of Alexandria. Once upon the soil of ancient Khem, Jesus was escorted by high ranking Djedhi initiates to Heliopolis where he learned the wisdom of the Thoth-Hermes while preparing for his final initiation within the Great Pyramid.

JESUS THE CHRIST, GRANDMASTER OF SERPENT WISDOM

Jesus's pivotal Egyptian initiation occurred on a pre-arranged, auspicious night. While members of both the Extraterrestrial and planetary Orders of Serpents watched with great anticipation, Jesus was escorted through the paws of the Sphinx and into the Holy of Holies, the King's Chamber. Here he was directed by the presiding Djedhi to lay down within the ancient sarcophagus while the mantras of Thoth-Hermes were recited over his "corpse." The fiery transformational process of the upward Kundalini was then officially consummated.

When Jesus finally arose from his "tomb" three days later he did so as a resurrected Djedhi Adept. Surrounding Jesus's sarcophagus were the most powerful Djedhi Masters in all of Egypt. They fully acknowledged Jesus's attainment and then welcomed him into their elite order as a fully awakened Khepher. Years later, according to certain documents recovered by the Knights Templar, the great power and teachings that Jesus received in Egypt passed to John the Divine, who with Mary Magdalene was his prime successor.

From their etheric realm, the immortal Kumaras also acknowledged Jesus's newly acquired high spiritual status. From their omniscient perspective, however, Jesus's enlightenment was not new—he had simply removed the veil of igno rance which separated him from his true soul vibration and identity, that of the Avatar Sananda Kumara. As an Avatar, an eternally illuminated Son of God, Jesus had taken numerous physical incarnations for the spiritual upliftment of Earth's inhabitants. One of his embodiments during the current 6 million year cycle was that of the Lemurian Avatar Sananda Kuma ra who, after arriving on Earth with his brother Sanat Kumara and other Kumara adepts, proceeded to work for the spiritual salvation of humanity. Since tha t time, while Sanat Kumara has remained on Earth as King of the World Sananda has returned in a series of physical incarnations. A ray of Sanat Kumara has, however, also come into physical incarna tion on special occasions, such as during the lifetime of Jesus when Sanat was embodied as the Mandeaen and Essene prophet John the Baptist. A prophecy of his inevitable incarnation was held by the Essene adepts whose ancestors learned of it while in captivity in Babylonia. From the Middle Easterners the Jewish Rabbis learned that Sanat Kumara, whom the Sumerian descendants knew as Enki, was due to be reborn as the "Fish Avatar" at the beginning of the Piscean Age. He would be a co-Messiah with Jesus and identified by being born into the Tribe of Levi. He would be a baptizer who, like Enki, became known from spending half his day in water and the other half on land.

THE GRANDMASTER OF THE NASOREAN SERPENTS

Upon his return to Palestine, Jesus's first order of business was to mobilize the fragmented Essene Order, which during his absence had been outlawed by King Herod. Then, during a pre-arranged rite in the River Jordan which was attended by many high ranking Essenes, Jesus was baptized by John the Baptist and anointed a grandmaster of the Nasorean or Nazarene Order of Serpents, According to the clairvoyant Edgar Cayce, John the Baptist had previously been in attendance in Heliopolis during Jesus's initiation within the Pyramid of Giza.

Following his Palestinian coronation, Jesus rallied around him twelve apostles. The twelve apostles symbolized the twelve signs of the Zodiac and the twelve phases of soul evolution. When added to this group of twelve, Jesus was thirteen, the number of the resurrected Dragon/Phoenix, the number of the planet Venus, and the esoteric number of the androgynous Sons of God.

TEACHING THE WISDOM OF THE SERPENTS

During his ministry Jesus the Nazarene transmitted to his disciples pure gnostic teachings that had begun on Earth with the arrival of the Kumaras. He taught that within each person's heart is the indwelling "Kingdom of Heaven."Jesus also revealed that it was the destiny of all people to develop the powers of a God or Goddess and indicated that his disciples would eventually "do even greater things" than he had. His final instruction as he sent his apostles outo preach the gospel was: "Be wise as Serpents and harmless as doves."

KABBALIC YOGA

As heir to the wisdom of many branches of Serpents, Jesus the Gnostic Nasorean was well schooled in the art of yoga and the secrets of awakening the inner serpent fire. To assist in the spiritual awakening of his disciples, Jesus taught them a form of Kabbalic Yoga which had been handed down word of mouth fro m the Nasorean Essenes, the School of Prophets, and the Levites. He also tra ined them in the esoteric doctrines of the Kabbala which outlined the awake ning of the Shekinah or serpent power and its ascent up the spine

The secret yogic practices and Kabbalic doctrines taught by Jesus were not publicly revealed to the world until the 13th and 14th centuries A.D. In 1305 A.D. Moses de Leon, a rabbi living in Spain, published the Kabbalic Sephirothic Tree which was a diagram of both the universe and man, and included a map of the human power centers, or chakras, and the course taken by the Kundalini up the human spine.

This geometric tree was depicted with a serpent slithering along its 22 limbs or "paths" which, with its seven lower and three upper Sephiroth (representing the power centers), added to 32, the approximate number of vertebrae lining the spinal column. Other Kabbalic mystics of the time revealed that the spine and serpent fire were discretely encoded into the Bible as the "Tree of Eternal Life" which was protected at its base by a cherub with a flaming sword. The biblical tree was symbolic of the human spine the "yogic tree of life," and the cherub (angelic dragon) with the flaming sword was a manifestation of the fiery Kundalini serpent which perpetually guards its base.

While Moses de Leon was creating a sensation in Europe, back in the Middle East Abraham Abulafia was creating perturbations of his own by publicizing the ancient Kabbalic Yoga taught by Jesus and the Essenes. This form of yoga included special postures for stretching, as well as breathing techniques for clearing the etheric Dragon Body. It also involved special meditational practices focused upon the ten Sephiroth, a Jewish rendering of the chakras. While meditating upon each Sephiroth successively, the practitioner of Kabbalic Yoga was able to move the inner flame to each sequential energy center until it had risen to the apex of the head. It would then unite with Kether/Ain Soph, the highest Sephiroth and chakra, at the top of the Sephirothic Tree or spine.

AWAKENING THE SERPENT FIRE
THE DAY OF PENTECOST

Although Jesus's disciples achieved much purification and activation of the Kundalini through the practice of Kabbalic Yoga, their greatest awakening occurred during the "Day of Pentecost" when the Master transferred his serpent power to them. Jesus had previously prepared his Apostles for the sacred event by proclaiming that he would he would baptize them with not only water but also with "fire."

On the Day of Pentecost the Apostles were gathered together in a room at a pre-arranged location. After a short time into the room came "a sound (like) a rushing mighty wind." The very next moment the Apostles experienced the descent of the Shekinah as "cloven tongues of fire" which "sat upon each of them'" (this has its counterpart in India as the descent of grace or Shaktipat of the Hindu Siddhas). Accompanying this descent of serpent power was the manifestation of the "gifts of the Holy Spirit" which compelled the Apostles to talk in "tongues" and channel healing energy for the benefit of others. Such "gifts" are classical manifestations of the awakening and upward movement of the Kundalini. Currently they are sometimes displayed by the members of the Pentecostal Church when the congregation prays for the descent of the Holy Spirit.

JESUS CHRIST, THE WORLD TEACHER

Following Jesus's transmission of power to his disciples, it is believed by some chroniclers that he lived until an old age as a teacher of the School of the Prophets. The gnostic teachers Mani and Basilides, two keepers of the hidden wisdom regarding Jesus's life, both claimed that the Messiah did not die on the cross and continued to live long after his legendary "resurrection."

The tomb of Yuz Asaf in Srinigar, Kashmir

According to the testimony of other secret records, after completing his time in Palestine Jesus became a world teacher and traveled throughout the globe. Numerous legends held by Native American tribes and those documented in The *Book of Mormon* claim that he came to America to both spread the Gospel and "do his father's business." Following his sojourn in North America, the natives continued to remember Jesus by his symbol in the sky, the planet Venus, the sacred planet of the Kumaras. One compelling Asian legend asserts that Jesus spent the last few years of his life among the Mahanagas of India and Tibet. According to this legend, the Messiah's final resting place is the tomb of Yuz Asaf near Srinagar, the capital of Kashmir and ancient stronghold of the Hindu Nagas. The people of Kashmir currently maintain that Jesus arrived in their country two thousand years ago and was known among them as Yuz Asaf (compare to Jesus's Hebrew name, Yazu, and the name Jo-seph). He performed many miracles and healings among them before his death and entombment in 109 A.D.[35]

SANANDA KUMARA, INTERPLANETARY SERPENT

According to esoteric sources, since his ascension Jesus Christ has continued to watch over Earth from an etheric realm. According to the Atherius Society founded by George King in the 1950s, Jesus continues to reside on the etheric dimension of the Kumaras' sacred planet, Venus. During the last two thousand years he has appeared physically to select individuals on Earth, such as the late Sister Thedra, who he spontaneously healed from terminal cancer. After the miraculous healing, Jesus told Sister Thedra "call me by my right name, Sananda Kumara" and then gave her the assignment of serving as his prophetess on Earth to help prepare humankind for the coming New Age. Until her death in 1992 (she lived another 40 years after her healing), Thedra ably accomplished her mission through the vehicle of *The Association of Sananda and SanatKumara* which was based at Mt. Shasta, California and then Sedona, Arizona, two headquarters of the Kumaras in North America. On June 1, 1961 Jesus as Sananda Kumara also made an appearance at Chichen Itza, Yucatan, and was photographed there by an archaeologist working at the site. Sananda instructed that the photograph be given to Thedra. It has since become the possession of *ASSK* and graced the walls and altars of many aspiring Kumaras throughout the world.

The above reproduction is from a photograph taken on June 1, 1961, when Sananda (Jesus) appeared in tangible form at Chichen Itza. At that time he instructed the archeologist taking the photo to give it to Sister Thedra.

The late Sister Thedra and Anton Ponce de Leon Paiva.
Both Thedra and Anton have headed American esoteric organizations that had their roots in Lemuria with the Order of the Seven Rays and the Kumaras

CHAPTER 14

THE NAASENI & OPHITE GNOSTICS

Following the final ascension of Jesus Christ, the teachings of the Apostles and the Kabbalic & Nasorean mystics diverged into two distinct schools. The teachings of the first school, those which became the foundation of the Christian Church and designed for the masses, were based upon Jesus' "Christ Myth" that recounts the birth of a Divine Son of God to a virgin; his ministry to save humanity; his crucifixion; and his promise to return. This legend was adopted by St. Paul although it had existed since very ancient times when it was the primal legend of Sanat Kumara, the Green Man (see my book *The Truth Behind the Christ Myth*). According to this school, there was only one Son, one Christ and one Savior, Jesus Christ. The teachings of the second school subscribed to the Serpent Wisdom of the Mandeaens and Kabbalists which equated Christ with the Serpent Son coiled upon the tree/cross. This second school, the school of Gnosticism designed for initiates, maintained that Jesus was indeed a Serpent who had fully awakened the Christ within, but it also contended that every human is a budding Son or Daughter of God with the same potential to fully incarnate Spirit and wield the wisdom and power of the Serpent.

During its heyday the school of Gnosticism gained wide acceptance and eventually spread throughout Palestine, Alexandria, and within the centers of the early mystery school traditions, such as Antioch, Epheusus, Athens and Rome. Its membership included Serpents of Wisdom called Naaseni and Ophites, names denoting Serpent in the Hebrew and Greek languages respectively.

THE LINEAGE OF GNOSTIC SERPENTS

Since Gnosticism was the foundation of both Kabbalism & Mandeaenism, the Gnostics claimed that the wisdom of their school was as old as the primeval Garden of Eden and had been transmitted to Adam and Eve. They maintained that the original preceptor of Gnosticism was the Serpent on the Tree, which had been "a type of Jesus Christ."[29] The Primal Serpent transmitted the teachings of Gnosticism to Adam, Adam passed them to Seth (Thoth-Hermes) and Seth in turn passed them to the "Sons of Seth." Through the Sons of Seth, which the Gnostic historian Iamblichus identified as the descendants of the first Thoth-Hermes (builder of the Great Pyramid), the wisdom of gnosticism eventually spread throughout the Earth.

JESUS CHRIST, INCARNATION OF THE EDEN SERPENT

Like Serpents around the globe, the early Gnostic Serpents of Egypt and the Middle East believed that the 1st Savior had been sent to Earth by his mother Sophia and manifested as the Serpent on the Tree. And like their Gnostic counterparts these "Christian Gnostics" also recognized this first Serpent Savior was incarnated as their later personal savior: Jesus Christ. Although the Hindus would have referred to the First Serpent as their Sanat Kumara, their seminal gnostic doctrines agree with their western counterparts. The Serpent Wisdom and Power of the Primal Serpent - call it Christ or Sanat Kumara - is the same spirit that overshadows all true Saviors.

According to the Gnostics, when Christ walked the Earth his message to humankind was quintessential gnostic wisdom. His gnostic teachings, such as "the Kingdom of Heaven exists within," were carefully preserved by the Gnostics in a series of "Gnostic Gospels," dialogues with Christ, which were subsequently banished from the Christian Church and secretly hidden. In one of these "heretical" Gospels, the *Gospel of Phillip,* Jesus is quoted as stating that whoever achieves Gnosis is "no longer a Christian, but a Christ." In another forbidden Gospel, the *Gospel of Thomas,* Christ expresses the traditional gnostic sentiment that all humans can be the Sons of God by proclaiming "When you come to know yourselves, then you will be known, and you will realize that you are the Sons of the living Father."101

SIMON MAGUS, WIELDER OF SERPENT WISDOM AND POWER

After Christ's passing, the mantle of Gnosticism passed to co-disciple, Simon Magus. According to the early Church Father Ireanus, Simon was, like Jesus, a disciple of the Mandeaen prophet John the Baptist. John, a god-intoxicated soul, was, like the eccentric madmen of other traditions, given to irrational and even destructive behavior. With his sole article of clothing a camel hair tunic, John lived alone in the woods while subsisting on a diet of "locusts and wild honey." Under his tutelage Simon Magus learned that all humans can rise above the veil of mundane existence and evolve into divine gods and goddesses.

While adhering to the yogic path outlined by John, Simon Magus eventually developed profound gnostic wisdom and supernatural powers. He discovered the Christ within his own soul and then proclaimed himself a living God. Following his enlightenment, he wandered around Palestine and attracted many disciples while ostentatiously displaying his formidable serpent powers. While surrounding himself with large crowds of spectators, Simon would materialize objects, raise the dead, fly through the air and even change his physical shape into that of an animal.

Simon Magus eventually traveled to many countries outside of Palestine and availed himself of the gnostic wisdom contained within their mystery school traditions. Much of his accumulated wisdom was later incorporated into the philosophy of his gnostic sect, the Simonians. Eventually Simon traveled to Rome and was hired as the court appointed sorcerer of the Emperor Nero. Legends claim that he lost his life soon afterwards during a magical duel with the first Christian Pope (referred to as "Bishops" initially) Saint Peter.

Following the death of Simon Magus, many of the Gnostic Master's teachings were preserved and popularized by his chief disciple, Menander, another god-intoxicated soul and magician. According to the Church historian Eusibius, Menander proclaimed himself to be a god/savior and publicly advertised that any sincere seeker could become a god or goddess through his guidance. Like the early patriarch of his gnostic lineage, John the Baptist, Menander was also famous for initiating his disciples through baptism.

Menander passed the grandmastership of the gnostic lineage to his disciples Basilides and Saturnalis. Saturnalis took the gnostic teachings to Antioch and Basilides transported them to Alexandria, Egypt where they achieved their greatest popularity. Then, under Basilide's premier student, Valentius, the school of gnosticism flourished as never before. Valentius, a theological genius and perhaps the greatest reformer of gnostic doctrine who ever lived, synthesized many divergent gnostic philosophies into one coherent system. Having served an apprenticeship to Plotinus, the celebrated Neoplatonic philosopher, Valentius grafted many of the concepts of Neoplatonism to the gnostic catechism.

With the passing of Valentius the flame of Gnosticism in Alexandria and throughout the ancient world began to weaken as the school approached its final extinction around 400 A.D.(see Chapter 16: City of the Serpent's Son). Today the sole surviving Gnostics in Asia are the Mandeaens, the baptisers of south Iraq, who hold Jesus and John the Baptist as ancient Nasurai of their tradition.

NAASENI AND OPHITES: THE JEWISH AND GREEK GNOSTIC SERPENTS

According to Hippolytus, a Church Father and historian who composed a Christian history of "heretical" sects, many of the very first Gnostics who traveled to Egypt were known as the Naaseni, or the "Serpents" (from Naas or Nahash, Hebrew for "serpent") The Naaseni were descendants of the School of the

Prophets and continued the ancient worship of their predecessors by worshipping Nahustan, the golden or "brazen" Primal Serpent, which they adoringly placed upon wooden crosses. They also venerated live snakes as manifestations of the Serpent and incorporated these slithering beasts into many of their rituals. During the daily ritual to bless their food, for example, the early Gnostics were known to cajole a live snake to crawl over loaves of bread and then kiss the beast squarely upon the mouth.

The Naaseni movement eventually engendered teachers who separated from the parent order to form their own gnostic schools, each of which was at least partly committed to the worship of the Primal Serpent. Many Gnostics, however, remained purely Naaseni in belief and worship were later known more commonly as the Ophites (Ophir and Ophite is Greek for "Serpent").

GNOSTIC LIBERATION FROM JALDABAOTH, THE DARK DRAGON

The seminal gnostic doctrine and myth as promulgated by the Gnostic Patriarchs maintained that at the beginning of time Chokmah or Sophia, the Serpent Goddess, created the physical universe and then became its benevolent patroness. Soon after the completion of the cosmos, however, one of Sophia's Seven Sons, the Dark Dragon Jaldabaoth, usurped the reigns of government for himself and proceeded to set himself over the universe as its evil dictator. Jaldabaoth, who was a personification of that aspect of Jehovah which was an ex acting and stringent lawgiver, eventually bequeathed a group of limiting karmic rules by which the people on Earth were forced to live. Ever since implementing his decrees the human spirit has been perpetually chained to the physical world and the illusion of reality it engenders. The path of Gnosticism, as set forth by the Serpent on the Tree and other Gnostic liberators, was formulated so that the inner spirit could awaken from this illusion, ex tricate itself from physical form and return to its rightful home in the heavens.

Many of the gnostic schools which arose espoused yogic disciplines as a means to spiritual freedom. During the era of the Egyptian Gnostic cults, for ex ample, it was common for a gnostic seeker to procure a regimen of yoga from an authorized Gnostic Master before retiring to a quite monastic cell or venturing out into the lonely desert in search of a cave sanctuary to practice these disciplines. Then, while seeking to unite with his Angelic Guide or Higher Self as their Essene predecessors had once done, the gnostic seeker would observe celibacy, consume a sparse diet, occasionally fast, study the traditional gnostic tex ts, and spend countless hours lost in contemplation and meditation.

241

intuitive faculties would begin to awaken within a gnostic aspirant and the illusion of the material world would gradually diminish. Under the purifying effects of the activated serpent fire, which was venerated as Sophia as well as Chnouphis, the androgynous lion-headed serpent, the subtle and spiritual bodies would slowly become awakened and the bonds of physical existence broken.

Within his or her awakened Dragon Body, a gnostic seeker would learn the secrets of astral traveling out of Jaldabaoth's kingdom and into the higher heavenly realms, ultimately ascending to the highest plane, the Pleroma, the "Fullness of God." To assist in these interdimensional excursions, the aspirant would use as a guide *The Book of Enoch* and the Neoplatonist Iamblichus's schematic of Aeons or stratifications of the universe. Such texts would inform the aspirant concerning what to expect upon any given plane while also instructing him or her in the appropriate mantras to use in order to bypass the dimensional gate keepers. The seeker was, of course, also assisted and protected during these astral flights by his or her Angelic Presence.

Eventually the veil of illusion would completely dissolve and gnosis would fully blossom within the heart of a dedicated seeker. The aspirant could then permanently unite with his or her Angelic Presence or Higher Self and function fully out of the Angelic or Dragon Body even while residing within a physical form. All supernatural powers would be at the new Gnostic Master's disposal and the awareness of "I am unlimited Spirit" or "I AM GOD" would continuously resound within their hearts like the ring of a finely tuned bell. As a fully enlightened god or goddess, the new adept had the option of ascending to the upper paradise regions or remaining on Earth to serve as a guide for other aspiring Gnostics.

Chnouphis, a Gnostic version of the Kundalini Serpent

THE SERPENTS OF WISDOM
IN
NORTHERN EUROPE

A Druid Adder

CHAPTER 15

THE DRUID ADDERS OF BRITAIN

" I am a Druid, I am an architect, I am a prophet, I am an Adder."
- declaration of a Druid.

The Serpents of Wisdom of the British Dragon Culture were known   as Naddred or Adders. They were more commonly known as Druids, a title which in the Gaelic language of early Ireland signified a wise man, sorcerer and Serpent. Among the later Celts the designation of Druid denoted a priest, an enlightened spiritual master, a judge or even a priest king.

THE PEOPLE OF THE SERPENT GODDESS DANA

"All who are adepts in Druidical and magical arts are the descendants of the Tuatha de Danaan." —From an Irish manuscript.

As previously mentioned, the Druids arrived as part of the earliest waves of colonists to settle in Britain. They were especially concentrated in Ireland and Wales where they existed as magicians and masters of the Pheryllt, Nemedians, Fomorians and Firbolgs. Their greatest proliferation in the British Isles occurred, however, during and after the arrival of the Tuatha de Danaan.

The Tuatha de Danaan, the "People of the Serpent Goddess Dana" were a branch of the ancient seafaring Danaans of the Mediterranean, who, beginning in the second millennium B.C., abandoned some of their coastal territories in the Aegean Sea and Asia Minor coast to conduct a series of migrations to the windswept regions of northern Europe. One wave of these migrating Danaans was led by Brutus, a citizen of Troy, who founded Caer Troia or New Troy, later to be known as London. He and his Danaan compatriots named early Britain "Albion," an epithet derived from Albina, the name of the eldest of the fifty daughters of Danaus, the ancient prince who led a migration of Danaans to Greece from their home in Panopolis, Egypt. Another wave of Danaans, the largest, were led to Ireland in the fifteenth century B.C. by the mythological hero Dagda, a Herculean figure who is represented in iconography as a club wielding patriarch. Accompanying these Danaans were three Arch Druids, Brian, Iuchar and Iucharba and two Arch Druidesses, Becuill and Danaan.

Upon reaching the shores of Ireland, Dagda, the Druids and the magical Tuatha de Danaan began a series of incursions into the island by cloaking themselves in a mist and appearing unexpectedly in front of the Firbolgs, the established occupants of the country. Once the Firbolgs had been conquered, the Danaans spread themselves throughout their new land, some electing to found colonies while others chose to establish themselves as sorcerers and/or head mystery schools. The Dagda built a palace/temple for himself at Brugh na Boinne or Newgrange, a strategic vortex point from which he could effectively rule his new kingdom. The Danaan Mananan founded a mystery school on an island off the coast of Ireland which now bears his name, the Isle of Man. Mananan was a legendary magician who reputedly used his powers to build a community out of huge blocks which he magically transported many miles through the air. He is also averred to have confused his enemies by manifesting simultaneously as 100 persons, none of which bore any resemblance to his actual physical form.

Once their colonizing efforts were complete, the Tuatha de Danaan were themselves conquered by another wave of immigrants known as the Milesians, a kindred people of Asia Minor who founded the Gaelic culture in Ireland. Following the defeat of the Danaans, the Milesians reportedly drew up an armistice agreement which stipulated that the People of Dana were to henceforth leave the surface of the Earth and inhabit an underground kingdom entered solely through sidh-mounds, the "hollow hills" of Ireland. The Tuatha de Danaan acquiesced to the demands of their conquerors and subsequently became a magical population of subterranean dwelling fairies, elves and dwarfs.

THE DRUID ADDERS

According to one rationalization, the Tuatha de Danaan never completely left the surface of the Earth, but remained as the Druids. F ollowing the banishment of the Danaans, their secrets, and some of their Druid priests, were assimilated into an amalgamated order of Druids which was also comprised of the surviving adepts of the ancient Pheryllts of Wales, as well as those of the

Milesians and Firbolgs. Because of the existence of this order, those Danaans who had been exiled underground were later able to return to the upper world by reincarnating as Druids, thereby allowing them to once again teach their magical secrets and rule their beloved Ireland as one of its priest kings. Such was the case with the Irish King MacGreine, the "Son of the Sun," and King Mongon of Ulster, who proclaimed himself to be an incarnation of the Danaan Fionn.

When the Celts later arrived in Britain those Masters of the order of Druids were assimilated into the Aryan culture as priests, judges, and kings even though they continued to preserve the religious outposts of their ancestors, the Pheryllt and Tuatha de Danaans, and teach their ancient secrets in mystery academies. During this period Mananan's community on the Isle of Man became one of the Druid's principal teaching facilities and the headquarters of an Arch Druid, one of the three grandmasters of the Druid Adders. The sanctity of New Grange and the sidh hills were also preserved and the Druids would occasionally lead the Celts in full moon rituals at these holy retreats. Some sidh hills were natural vortexes, so ceremonies conducted in their proximity were especially efficacious. The word sidh is apparently related to the Latin sedes and the Sanskrit siddha, both of which mean power, thus making sidh mound mean "power" mound or vortex mound. Some prominent sidh mounds were recognized to be interdimensional doorways with the function of transporting one directly to and from the "underground" or otherworld kingdom of the Tuatha de Danaan. When seeking guidance from their ancestors at the sidh mounds, the Druids either communicated with them psychically or traveled directly to their "underworld" realms in their Dragon Bodies.

THE KINGDOM OF THE DRUID ADDERS

Eventually the kingdom of the Celts grew in size until it spanned the length and breadth of Europe. Druid missionaries were then dispatched throughout the sprawling continent to supervise the construction of earthen temples, stone circles and mystery schools for the enactment and dissemination of their ancient rites and mysteries. Of all the temple sites thus established the most numerous were groves of oak trees and as early as 200 B.C. hundreds of such nature temples covered the European landscape. Some ofhese oak groves were considered to be especially sacred and venerated theway a Christian would exalt a major cathedral. One magnificent grove/temple in the center of Gaul, for example, annually attracted hundreds of Druids from all over western Europe to witness important rituals administered by the Arch Druid of the province. Another especially holy grove, located in Galatia, the eastern most part of the Celtic kingdom, annually hosted religious gatherings which were presided over by 12 high Druids called Tetrachs and attended by a multitude of lesser Druids. Because of their association with these European oak groves the Druids eventually garnered for themselves the denomination of "Oak Men."

OAK GROVES, HOMES OF THE SERPENT GODDESS

The oak grove temples were often created around one dominant tree which the Druids were known to strip of all its branches and then attach the largest limb horizontally across the tree's center, thereby fanning a cross. In this shape the oak tree was venerated both as the archetypal tree/cross which unites Heaven and Earth, as well as the body of the Primal Serpent Goddess (see Appendix 1). This form of goddess/tree worship may have had its roots in Atlantis or at the oracular shrine of Dadona in Pelasgian Greece where Danaan priestesses worshiped Oaks as manifestations of the Goddess Dione, Dana or Diana.29

Since the central oak tree was the temples' main altar and the Druids' link to Spirit, anything which grew upon it was considered to be especially holy and charged with supernatural power. One parasitic herb in particular which grew on the tree, the mistletoe, was believed to be saturated with serpent life force and handled only by the high Druids.

According to the historian Pliny, the ceremony in which the sacred mistletoe was cut from the central oak was the most holy of Druid rituals. The rite was enacted six days after the new moon, a time of the month when the serpent life force was at its most potent. With a gold scythe made in the shape of a crescent moon, the precious plant was carefully severed from its tree and immediately caught in a white apron by the presiding high Druid, thereby retaining the plant's purity (white is the eternal color of purity). To complete the ceremony, two white bulls, the purest of all bovines, were sacrificed to the Goddess and their blood poured on the ground to fertilize the mother Earth.

Once cut, the life giving mistletoe became part of certain Druidical potions. Since it carried the preserving life force, or as Lewis Spence calls it, "the essence of life,"32 it was considered efficacious for healing and fertility. Because of its profound healing effects the Celts referred to the plant as "all heal." Mistletoe was also commonly added to potions of other herbs to increase their potency. It was, for example, mixed within herbal potions ingested for the purpose of promoting alchemical transformation.

TRAINING TO BECOME A DRUID ADDER

In order to become a Druid Adder, a sincere seeker would, after careful consideration by a counsel of adepts, be accepted into an accredited school of wisdom. He or she might then be sent to a temple grove or to one of the mystery schools scattered throughout Britain for intensive study and initiation.

According to one ancient manuscript, the earliest of Druid schools in Britain was founded by the Pheryllt in an area near Oxford University. A second important school of Druidism in Britain, and perhaps the greatest, was later established on the Island of Anglesey, which was anciently referred to as

Muinendh, "the Island of Teaching." Anglesey was located directly across the water from Emrys, the "Ambrosial City" of the Pheryllt alchemists, so its curriculum was no doubt strongly influenced by these early adepts. Another renowned mystery academy of the Druids was eventually founded on Innis nan Druidhneah (later called Iona), the "Island of the Druids." This school was later inhabited by the order of Culdees and converted into a Christian monastery by St.Columbo.

Perhaps the most authoritative information regarding the general curriculum taught within the Druid schools was that brought back to Rome by the famous conqueror of the Gaulish Celts, Julius Caesar. The Druid Diviciacus, a Celtic priest whom Caesar befriended in Gaul, told the Roman general that Druid training sometimes required up to 20 years to complete and included a curriculum of mythology, grammar, law, philosophy and poetry. Of all these subjects, the most important was poetry. The Druids encoded all the secrets of the universe, including the origins of the cosmos and the path to salvation, into their poetic verses. Supposedly at one time there were as many as 20,000 of these sacred verses. Since writing was discouraged, these sacred verses required memorization by the student of Druidism.

OVATES, BARDS AND DRUIDS

As a student progressed through the mystery school training, he or she ascended through three primary degrees called Ovate, Bard and Druid. At each stage the student was taught a specific curriculum, given a specific task to perform and required to wear a colored robe which corresponded to that level.

In the first stage of Ovate, the Druid in training was given a green robe, the color of learning, and a course schedule stacked with certain foundational subjects, such as grammar, mathematics and philosophy. He or she was also given the special function of diviner. To perform this role the Ovates learned how to interpret bones or "omen sticks" which were tossed into the air and then read according to their arrangement once they landed on the ground. The Ovates also learned to predict the future through the interpretation of the flight of birds and the sound of certain bird calls. Finally, the Ovate learned to prognosticate events from the most unsavory of divination tools, the entrails extracted from the bowels of an animal or even a human victim.

After reaching the degree of Bard, the Druid in training wore a long sky blue gown, the color of harmony, truth, and the higher levels of intuitive wisdom which he or she had the potential of aspiring to. While assuming the special function of poet he or she was required to memorize copious numbers of Druidical verse, recite them verbatim at religious gatherings, and then attempt to unlock their inherent metaphysical meanings. According to the *Illumination of Rhymes,* while seeking to decipher a poem's spiritual import a Bard might travel to the picturesque location alluded to within the poem, such ali a mountain peak, a cave, or a body of water, in order to receive direct inspiration.

Finally, having passed the tests of an Ovate and Bard, the student was initiated into the third degree of spiritual adeptship, the Order of Druids, and given a long white robe to wear. The white color represented the pristine purity which the new Druid was expected to reflect in all his or her thoughts, words and deeds. Having become a Druid he or she would merit the utmost respect from the Celtic community while serving his or her brethren as a high priest and judge. The new Druid initiate would also serve as a teacher of the mysteries and a guide to all aspiring Druids in training.

INITIATION INTO THE SACRED ORDER OF DRUID ADDERS

Initiation into the high rank of a Druid Adder was a secret affair and conducted within underground tunnels and chambers and within solitary places where the Earth currents united to produce the androgynous serpent life force, such as dragons' lairs, stone circles and sidh mounds. The time of Druid initiation usually corresponded to pivotal periods of the year when the celestial energies were conducive to the yogic reunion of the polarity, such as the solstices, equinoxes, and the new and full moons. Such "androgynous" times and places provided the ideal environment for the activation of Keridwen, the androgynous Serpent Goddess, whose rites were administered by her priests, the Priests of Pharon or Pheryllt alchemists, and their Druid descendants.

According to Lewis Spence's scholarly reconstruction of a Druid initiation in *The Mysteries of Britain,* the sacred event would begin at a Temple of Keridwen where a Pheryllt adept or Druid priest, along with three attendants, would ceremoniously meet the candidate at the entrance. Spence claims there was an important Temple of Keridwen approximately one mile from Emrys, the legendary city of Keridwen's Dragons, but he also maintains that since she was a manifestation of the Primal Serpent, all stone circles in Britain were temples of Keridwen.

After perfunctory introductions, the Druid candidate was sent to the nearest body of water to purify the physical body, after which he or she was given a transformational beverage called the "Cauldren of Keridwen." Within this cauldren or chalice were mixed stimulating ingredients, such as hyssop, vervain, wort, and sea water, which had been distilled into the androgynous essence of Keridwen and therefore possessed the alchemical power of awakening the

Serpent Goddess at her seat at the base of the spine. Supposedly this "Cauldren" or essence of Keridwen had, according to *The Spoils of Annwn,* a Welsh text, originally been discovered in an underworld place called "the four-cornered castle" in the "Isle of the Active Door." This sounds like a metaphorical description of the four petaled root chakra, home of the serpent fire, and the door to the Sushumna Nadi under which it sits.

After the Druid candidate had imbibed the Cauldren of Keridwen from out of its vessel, a crescent moon shaped chalice, Spence asserts that he or she would "remain for a season in one of the mysterious cells or caves of the Druidic cult, where he was subjected to a rigid course of discipline, and where he studied the rites and imbibed the secret doctrines of Keridwen, lastly emerging reborn into the outer world."[32] After this intensive period of training, the candidate would then submit to at least one more trial before officially being anointed a Druid. That concluding rite was the famous "trail-at-sea." During the darkest and coldest part of a night, the Druid candidate would be set adrift on a turbulent sea while laying fully exposed upon a raft without oars. If a candidate could keep from being swallowed up by the tumultuous waves and survive a full night upon the icy, windswept water, the incumbent Druids took it as a sign that he or she had been specially chosen by the gods to achieve the hallowed station of a Druid.

One additional initiation rite may, among certain branches of the Druids, have been administered within the oak groves and stone circles, the "Temples of Keridwen." It is conceivable that considering their predilection for attracting lightning, these open-air temples could have served as powerful alchemical crucibles for spiritual transmutation. While laying upon a stone altar, an aspiring Druid could conceivably have been struck directly by a lightning bolt and thereby become, like the Peruvian A marus,a shaman or Serpent. Perhaps a potion made of the sacred mistletoe, which the Druids conceived of as a manifestation of the lightning, played a role in such transformative rites.

THE SEVEN DEGREES OF THE DRUID ADDERS

After fulfilling the required tests to become a Druid, an initiate still had seven degrees of mastership to ascend through before he or she became an Arch Druid, the highest of all Adders. With each successive degree, the Druid was given a different colored sash to tie around his or her white gown and a Gleiniau Naddred, or "Serpent's Egg," to hang from his or her neck. The "egg," a blue-green glass bead set in gold, was strung on leather and indicated the level of serpent wisdom and power attained. The most powerful Druid Adders

250

revealed themselves by displaying the most Serpent Eggs over their breasts.51

An Adder who succeeded in acquiring seven "eggs" became an Arch Druid, a fully perfected Master. Such a Druid had united the polarity, merged with the transcendental Solar Spirit within, and become a clear vessel of serpent power and wisdom. The ceremonial regalia of these Arch Druids reflected their power and androgynous nature. Upon their heads was set a golden crown with projecting rays to represent the Sun, symbol of the Solar Spirit, while within their hands was a Moon-shaped scepter, symbol of the female principle and serpent power which emanated from their hands.

At any given time the office of Arch Druid was held by only three divinely elected seekers and each had his headquarters in the "Magical Isles" which surrounded Britain. One Arch Druid had his seat on the Isle of Anglesey; another was established upon the Isle of Man; and the third was situated upon the Isle of Wight, anciently known as "the Dragon's Isle."

Stonehenge, an initiation temple of Keridwen, the Serpent Goddess

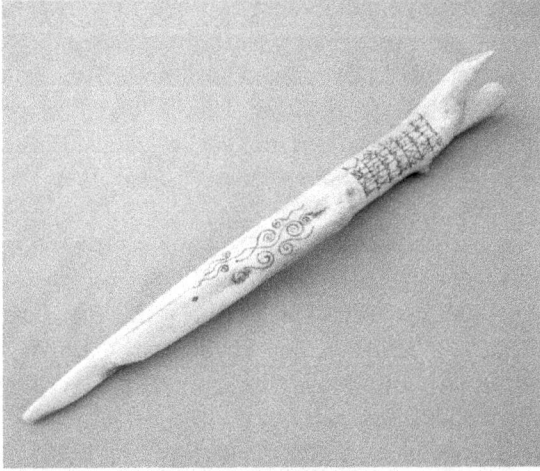

A Druid Yew Wand

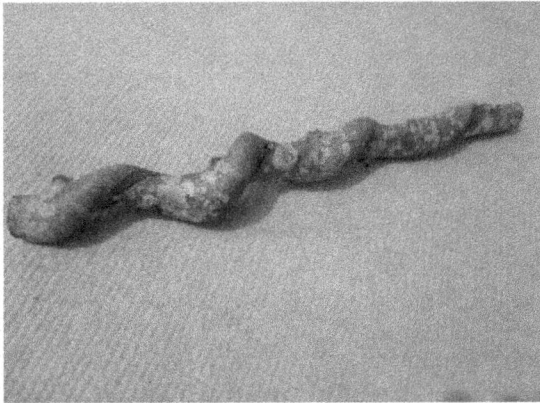

A Druid Oak Wand. A serpentine shape was more powerful.

A Serpentine Oak Staff of a Druidess.

Keridwen, the Serpent Goddess of the Druids

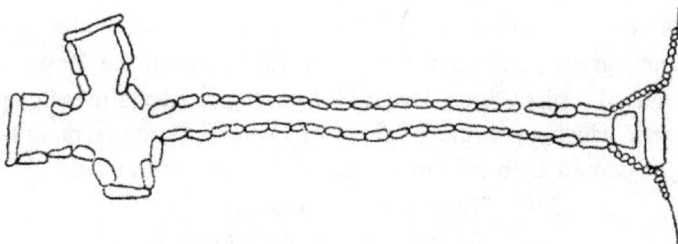

Inner Earth Initiation Chamber of the Druids.

THE DRUID MAGICIANS, WIELDERS OF
SERPENT POWER

Like the Egyptian priests of the Djedhi, the Druids received instruction concerning how to summon, store and direct the serpent power. During their initiations they acquired rods or wands and learned certain efficacious incantations and symbols which had been passed down from their magical predecessors, the Tuatha de Danaan. One such incantation allowed the Druids to summon a foggy mist similar to the one created by the ancient Danaans to deceive and defeat the Firbolgs. Another popular incantation was the Feth Fiada, a spell which had been passed by the magician Mananan and empowered the Druids to become completely invisible or shape shift into any desired animal or human form. While utilizing this spell, the legendary Druid Fer Fidail regularly assumed the form of a woman and the Druid magician Taliesin was able to appear in the likeness of a vulture, an eagle, or even an inanimate sword. Other Druids used the same spell to transform themselves into menhirs, the standing stones of Britain, and supposedly have remained in that inanimate shape down to the present time. Two additional important spells acquired from the Tuatha de Danaan, called Teinm Laegha and Imbas Forosnai, enabled the propitiating Druids to magnetize to them any knowledge contained within the universe. Finally, rounding out their formulary, the Adders inherited incantations which allowed them to change the weather, fly through the air, prophesy, see into the future, speak directly to the gods and even raise the dead. It is recorded that when the Romans and Christians landed in Britain the magical Druids used some of their ancient spells to create deadly tempests, floods, and heavy snowfalls in order to repel the invaders.

In order to fully empower their magic, the rites of the Druid Adders were often enacted during full moon nights, and possibly during lightning storms, within the parameters of vortex areas, sidh mounds or sacred groves. The magical rites would commence with the presiding Adder summoning the life force or Dragon by tracing a circle upon the ground with an oak or yew wand. Within this circle the adept would draw symbols of the Dragon, such as "Druids Feet" or pentagrams, symbols of the five-fold body of the Dragon. Or he might inscribe into the dirt some "Druids's Eyes," the two dimensional symbols of tetrahedrons, which were the symbols of fire, the Dragon's preeminent element. The Dragon would then be summoned to the spot with a mantric chant such as this: "Cum saxum saxorum

In dversum montum oparum da

In aetibulum

In quinatum - Draconis!"[51]

Soon a mist, a lightning bolt, or currents of high frequency energy would arrive and move through the Druid's body. The Druid's wand (or sword) was then held high in the air while his or her magical commands were loudly and forcefully pronounced in each of the four directions. Such commands were greatly empowered by the serpent power and, in this way, the summoned Dragon assisted the Druid in bringing into manifestation all his desires. Sometimes the raised sword would afterwards be planted upright into the center of the vortex, thus acting as a kind of lightning rod to send the currents of Dragon's power into the Earth and throughout the British Grid.

At other times, the Druids acquired the creative power of the Dragon by consuming the flesh of bulls and/or by wrapping themselves up in bulls' hides. While wearing their bull cloaks these Druids were known to enter into battle and decimate entire armies. The Druid Mog Ruith, for example, is famous for entering his battles with a bull's hide cloak wrapped around his shoulders and a white speckled bird headdress upon his head. The Druids also received divinitory visions while sleeping within the folds of a bull's hide. During one period of Irish history the Irish king was selected in accordance to the prophetic dream of a Druid who had spent a night wrapped up in bull's hide.

UNITING CHRISTIANITY WITH DRUIDISM

Christianity was first introduced into Britain when Pope Gregory I approved a law which sanctioned the fusion of Celtic and Christian belief. Soon afterwards, many British kings, such as King Diarmuid MacCeurbhail, accepted Christianity and declared that both it and Druidism should co-exist as co-operative religious faiths. As a result, some new sects arose which were an amalgamation of the two traditions.

The Druid-Christian synthesis eventually engendered the formation of certain sects like that of the Culdees. The Culdees pursued a daily regimen of both Druid and Christian spiritual disciplines while living as a cloistered group of monks upon the ancient Danaan Island of Iona. After genuflecting in front of the cross and chanting Christian devotional hymns, they would commune with Druid nature spirits in the fields or recite the magical incantations of the ancient Pheryllt and Danaans. Many Culdees who mastered the Danaan magical rites were known to have achieved the power to shape-shift, become invisible and even summon blistering storms on demand. Their ultimate goal, however, was to achieve the state of Jesus Christ, a renowned ascended adept who was both a Christian Master and the greatest of all Arch Druids.

ST PATRICK CHASES THE SNAKES OUT OF IRELAND

In the fifth and sixth centuries A.D. two of the most influential Christian missionary sent to the British Isles, St. Patrick and St. Columbo, succeeded in stamping out Druidism in Ireland and other parts of Britain. St. Patrick's eviction of the Druid Adders is symbolically referred to in the Christian missionary's biography as his having "chased the snakes out of Ireland." Following their forced dismissal, the Druids became a secret, "underground" organization in Ireland or took refuge in other parts of the British Isles.

THE REVIVAL OF THE DRUID ADDERS

After its decimation by zealous Christian missionaries, Druidism became circumspect but still continued to survive as the Order of Bards in Wales. The Welsh Bards were an enlightened group of soul seekers who religiously studied the Barddas, a compendium of ancient Druid verse, and secretly consumed an elixir out of the Cauldron of Inspiration, a version of Keridwen's Cauldron, which assisted them in awakening their dormant psychic and prophetic abilities.

In 1245 during a gathering of all Bards and remaining British Druids a new organization or "grove" of Druids, called the Mount Haemus Grove, was founded. Later, in 1717, John Toland founded the Universal Druid Bond. The present Order of Druids in Britain is descended from this Order. In 1964 the Order was reformed and became the Order of Bards, Ovates, and Druids.

PART II:

ECLIPSE AND REVIVAL
OF THE
SERPENTS OF WISDOM

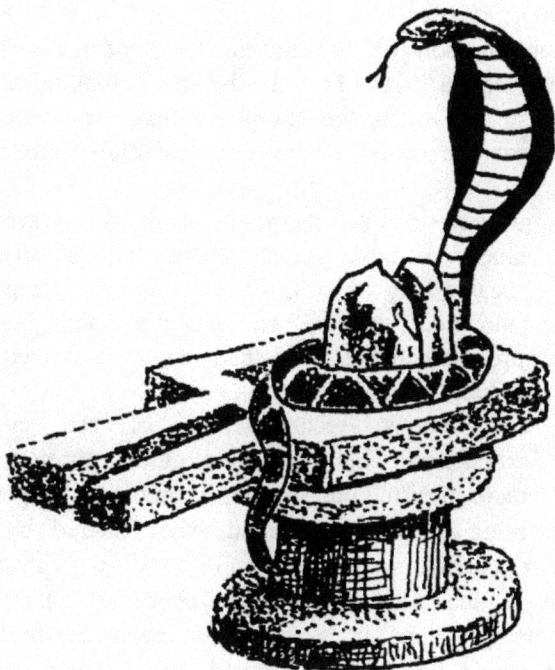

CHAPTER 16

ALEXANDRIA: CITY OF THE SERPENT'S SON

Beginning in the fourth century B.C., a port city on the Mediterranean coast of Egypt sent out a call to the Serpents of Wisdom throughout the world to come and share their mystery teachings in an atmosphere of familial love and acceptance. This burgeoning city of light was Alexandria, the "City of the Serpent's Son." Its open invitation triggered a mass migration of spiritual teachers to North Africa and helped establish Alexandria as a worldwide headquarters for the Serpents of Wisdom.

THE SERPENT'S SON

The catalyst, whose vision of a one world kingdom had originally inspired the creation of Alexandria, was Alexander the Great, the port city's founding father. At his death, this illustrious Macedonian patriarch, who was also known as the "Serpent's Son," was interred within a golden sarcophagus near the center of the city and daily remembered by its adoring citizens.

Alexander's identity as the Serpent's Son was revealed to him early in his military career when the young general traveled to the Oracle of Ammon in Egypt. Located at the Oasis of Siwah deep within the Egyptian desert, the renowned oracle was second only to Delphi in the authority of its pronouncements and had been patronized in the past by such famous Greek heroes as Hercules.

According to the famous reconstruction of the event by the historian Ptolemy, Alexander and his men were guided through the Egyptian desert to the remote oracle by "talking serpents," probably Serpent initiates of the Djedhi. Upon arriving at Siwah, Alexander was ushered by the presiding priests into the inner chambers of the temple and the presence of their god Ammon, a deity which was both the transcendental Spirit and manifest serpent god. After being seated in a specially prepared throne, Alexander watched in amazement as an oracular priest's body began to shake and a deep groaning voice issued from his trembling lips. "Welcome, my dearly beloved Son," spoke Ammon, "You have a special mission ahead of you, you will rule a great kingdom on Earth, My kingdom." Following this startling announcement, Ammon proceeded to instruct Alexander in the direction he should lead his army and in specific mantric incantations and rituals he should perform in order to stabilize and amalgamate the various parts of his huge empire. Later some of Ammon's rituals were performed by Alexander off the coast of India when the Macedonian conqueror reached what he believed was the edge of the world.

When Ammon's detailed instructions to Alexander were complete, the great god became silent. Then, while showering Alexander with blessings, the deity sent his Son off into the Egyptian desert to fulfill his glorious destiny. From that point onwards, the accepted legend was that Alexander's rightful father was the highest god, Zeus-Ammon, who as a serpent had mysteriously slithered into the bed of his mother and helped conceive the future world emperor.

Word of Alexander's meeting with Ammon and his designation as the Son of God spread quickly. When the Macedonian general eventually entered the Egyptian capital of Memphis a celebration in his honor was already in progress. Then, amid shouts of "God" and "King," Alexander was anointed Pharaoh in the tradition of the ancient god-kings. Following his coronation, Alexander began to make plans regarding the capital city of the worldwide empire he was destined to rule. It was to be called Alexandria, a city built upon the foundations of the ancient port city of Rhakotis and its sacred temple of Osiris.

ALEXANDRIA, CAPITAL OF THE WORLDWIDE DRAGON CULTURE

Alexander died before his projected capital city was built, but one of his devoted generals, Ptolemy Sotor, completed the ambitious project. Following in his commander's footsteps, Ptolemy Sotor was installed as Pharaoh of Egypt and then proceeded to make the "City of the Serpent Son" into the capital city of the Worldwide Dragon Culture.

For three hundred years Ptolemy Sotor and his descendants, collectively known as the Ptolemies, continually added to Alexandria's prestige as a planetary cultural center by playing host to some of the greatest spiritual and philosophical minds on Earth. They also greatly embellished the beauty of Alexandria by inviting world famous architects and artists to create ornate temples, sculptures, fountains and magnificent gardens within the city's boundaries. In order to appropriately welcome the Serpents of Wisdom as they arrived from all parts of the globe, one of the Ptolemies constructed a lighthouse on the Island of Pharos.

SERAPIS, THE DRAGON OF ALEXANDRIA

Out of Alexandria's ideological synthesis arose Serapis, a composite god and the city's principal deity. In Serapis, many of the nature gods, creative deities, and underworld demons which had evolved out of the Atlantean Fire Serpent were reunited. Volcan of the Old Red Land of Atlantis was, in a sense, resurrected and worshiped anew. The eclectic god Serapis was specially created by Ptolemy Soter and his staff of mystery school hierophants to be a synthe sized deity which both the Egyptian and Greek citizens of Alexandria could mutually accept and adore. Using Osiris-Hapi or Osiris-Apis of Memphis, a bull-headed form of Osiris as their base, they added the features and characteristics of the Egyptian Imhotep, as well as those of Dionysus, Zeus, and Asclepius of the Greek tradition.

In its completed form god Serapis was both an unseen, transcendental deity as well as a manifest serpent god. Serapis's serpentine nature was encoded within his name which was an amalgamation of Osiris and Apis or Serpent and Apis. His name was commonly translated by his Alexand rian devotees as "the sacred serpent" or the "fire serpent." The Hebrews, for example, recognized the name Serapis as a version of their word Seraph, which meant "burning" or "fiery" and served as the basis of the word "Seraphim," the name of the fiery serpents which flew above the throne of YHVH.[24] They and their Alexandrian compatriots associated the seven letters of Serapis's with the seven principles of the Primal Serpent and referred to their god as Theon Heptagrammaton, "the god of seven letters."

Throughout Egypt images of Serapis as a human male god (his transcendental aspect) straddling a dragon or crocodile or with a reptile at his side (his manifest aspect) were eventually placed within numerous "Serapeums," the temples of Serapis. The greatest of these temples, the Serapeum of Alexandria, was so magnificent that it was listed by the classical Greek historian Rufinus Toranius as one of the Seven Wonders of the World. Within its pillared corridors Serapis was worshiped as a colossal male statue composed of "all kinds of metals and woods" (says Toranius) which stood upon a crocodile and leaned against a serpent encoiled staff. At the top of the staff blossomed the thre e heads of a lion, dog, and wolf symbolizing the deity's thre e powers of creation, preservation and destruction.

Serapeums with installed images of Serapis were also built in many other parts of the Greek/Hellenistic empire. In the Greek islands and the Mediterranean rim countries the venerated god's form either leaned against a serpent staff or was wrapped within the slithering folds of a monstrous snake.

Sometimes Serapis could be found with a serpent tail and intertwined with the serpentine form of his consort, Isis. He was also often depicted carrying upon his shoulders the cornucopia, a basket full of fruits and vegetables which symbolized the gifts of the serpent life force, and wearing a golden crown of seven points, representing the serpent's seven principles.

INITIATION INTO THE CULT OF SERAPIS

The rites of Serapis crystallized into an eclectic synthesis of the rites of initiation administered within the Greek and Egyptian mystery schools. To assist in the amalgamation of these rites, Ptolemy hired Manetho, an Osirian priest of Heliopolis, and Timotheus, an initiate of the Eleusinian mysteries who worked in tandem to unite the rites of Osiris and Isis with those of the Eleusinian Demeter. The resultant mystery school they created was stratified into the Greater and Lesser mysteries (patronized by Serapis and Isis respectively) and included rites which precipitated an internal death and resurrection within the candidate.

In Alexandria initiation into Serapis's mystery tradition took place within a maze of tunnels dug into the hill upon which the city's Serapeum was built. Similar to the Eleusinian mysteries, the tunnels were designed to simulate the experience of Pluto's underworld. Also similar to the rites of Eleusis, a candidate prepared him or herself with days of fasts, meditation and other purifications before entering the labyrinth. Finally, he or she was declared "dead," given an hallucinogenic beverage to consume and then released into the dark forbidding corridors of the gloomy maze.

As the effect of the potion reached its climax, the inebriated candidate would find him or herself groping along the walls of the labyrinth while simultaneously being assaulted by legions of blood curdling apparitions. Similar to other Mediterranean initiations, these demonic phantoms created a deterrent to the candidates passage through the dark "underworld" while also dredging up his or her most paralyzing fears. These imagined obstacles were supplemented by "strange mechanical contrivances," actual physical gadgets, which were strategically positioned throughout the tunnel system and designed to accentuate a candidate's terror. There was also a perilous chasm at least fifteen feet across, which, if not safely leaped across, would send the candidate plunging hundreds of feet to his or her death.[24]

After what must have seemed like an eternity, those who survived Serapis's treacherous labyrinth reached an opening to the "upper world," a door at the end of the underground maze which led to the upper temple area. Like a reborn *initiate* of the Eleusinian mystery school, the initiate then emerged resurrected from the underworld. To complete the initiation, a high priest would greet the new initiate and lead him or her into the presence of the statue of Serapis in the center of the upper temple. While communing with the old Dragon and Creator of the Universe the initiate received final blessings and ordination as a priest or priestess of Serapis's Order of Serpents.

LUCIUS APULEIUS AND THE ORDER OF SERPENTS

Serapis's mystery rites eventually spread throughout the Mediterranean region and spawned numerous Orders of Serpents in many countries. One extant account of these rites in Italy and the order they engendered can be found in the classical text *The Golden Ass,* a semi-autobiographical account written by Lucius Apuleius, an initiate of Serapis's temple in Rome.

According to Lucius's stirring description of his own initiation, after being accepted for induction into Serapis's lesser mysteries he was led into the presence of the presiding hierophant who "brought out of the secret place of the temple" a sacred text illustrated with snakes and dragons and describing the ancient rites of the Great Goddess Isis. With text in hand, the priest then guided Lucius through a series of purifying baths during which he demanded "pardon of the gods" for the candidate's past transgressions. Afterwards, while commanding Lucius to fast for ten successive days, the priest transmitted to him "certain secret things (about the Order of Isis) unlawful to be uttered."

Upon the arrival of Lucius's initiation night, the high priest escorted him to "the most secret and sacred place of the temple." Then, states Lucius in his own words, "I approached near unto hell, even to the gates of Proserpine, and after that I was ravished through out all the elements, I returned to my proper place: about midnight I saw the sun brightly shine, I saw likewise the gods celestial and the gods infernal, before whom I presented myself and worshipped them."[102]

On completion of his dramatic initiation experience, Lucius was ordained as a priest of Isis and a member of the Order of Serpents. As part of his investiture, he was given the ceremonial robe of his new serpent order, a floor length gown embroidered with "beasts wrought of divers colors, as Indian dragons, and Hyperborean griffins." Then, following a short stint as priest of the Goddess, Lucius had his head shaved, underwent another ten day fast, and experienced the apparently more secretive Greater Mystery rites of Serapis/Osiris which he was forbidden to divulge.

CHRISTIAN INTOLERANCE OF THE SERPENT'S WISDOM

Initially the Christians of Alexandria were eclectic in their beliefs and tolerant of both Serapis and the synthesized doctrines being promulgated within the port city. Two of the outstanding members of this early Christian community were Clement of Alexandria, a Christian mystic, and Origen, a student of Ammonuis Saccus, the teacher of Plotinus. Clement and Origen were avid students of the mysteries and even attempted to amalgamate the ancient esoteric wisdom into the fledgling Christian Church. These two patriarchs occasionally worshipped within the Serapeum and gave the temple a church-like ambiance by having inscribed upon its walls their most sacred Christian symbols, such as the monogram of Christ.

Eventually the Catholic doctrines crystallized and the winds of Christian non-acceptance towards the ancient Serpent Wisdom began to blow hard in Alexandria. Finally, in 389 A.D., the fundamentalist Church Fathers inflicted a major assault upon what they judged to be "heretical" and "paganistic" ideology. With "God on their side," a group of fanatical Christians led by the patriarch Theophilus, climbed the sacred hill and destroyed the Serapeum which had, by that time, inherited the Museum's extensive library and become the center of Alexandria's rich cultural life. By ransacking the Serapeum and destroying the indwelling golden statue of Serapis, the Christians struck directly at the jugular of all ancient mystery school traditions.

Fortunately, however, just before and during the attack on the Serapeum many of the sacred texts of the ancient Serpents of Wisdom were clandestinely carried off and hidden. Perhaps the most esoteric and priceless of all scriptures, the *Book of Thoth,* was preserved by the priests and priestesses of Serapis who managed to flee with the text under the cloak of darkness. Once in new lands, these initiates extracted the archetypal images contained within Thoth's book and arranged them into the Major Arcana of the Tarot.

THE SERPENT'S WISDOM IS NEARLY EXTINGUISHED

After the attack of the Serapeum the torch of serpent wisdom in Alexandria became but a flicker. Then, in 415 A.D., it was all but completely extinguished. During that fateful year Christian mobs murdered Hypatia, the reigning head of the Neoplatonic school, as she was walking home from the Museum. A mass exodus ensued as initiates of the various Alexandrian mystery schools, fearing for their lives, fled to Europe or the East in hopes of finding lands sympathetic to their beliefs. A dark period of ignorance had descended upon the West, but the timeless Serpent Wisdom proved resilient and refused to die.

CHAPTER 17

LATER ARABIC AND EUROPEAN BRANCHES OF THE SERPENTS OF WISDOM

THE SUFIS

Following the downfall of Alexandria, many Serpents of Wisdom found refuge within the surviving mystery schools of Greece and Rome, such as the academy of the Neoplatonist Proclus in Athens. Other gnostic masters and seekers found asylum in the deserts of Egypt, in central Europe, or in the Middle East, where they came into contact with the vestiges of old gnostic orders, alchemists, and groups of desert dwelling Arabic adepts known as the Sufis. Collectively, the Sufis comprised an elite Middle Eastern branch of the Serpents of Wisdom. They possessed their own secret traditions and an ancient lineage of masters extending back many thousands of years.

THE ARABIC ORDERS OF SUFI SERPENTS

The earliest Sufi Serpents of Wisdom were an order of solitary mystics who roamed throughout the Arabian desert in search of secluded caves and isolated oasises. Referred to by the ir brethren as the Mugarribun or "Near Ones," " and as the Sufis, the "people of the wool," because of their custom of wearing only rough cut woolen garments, these earl y nomads were exalted spiritual masters renowne d for their elevated states of consciousness and their magical powers. In his commentary on these earl y desert dwelling sages the modem Sufi Idris Shah remarks: "The Sufi ancients could walk on water, describe events taking place at vast distances, experience the true reality of life... When one Master spoke, his hearers went into a state of mystical rapture and developed magical powers. Wherever Sufis went, mystics of other persuasions, often of great prominence, became their disciples-sometimes without a word having been spoken."103

With the founding of the Moslem empire the Sufis were divided into sub-groups of mystics within which they abandoned their traditional camel wool robes in favor of more conservative cotton caftans or "patched frocks." Many of the new Sufi Orders thus formed espoused the reclusive lifestyle ofo their predecessors. They devoted themselves to the pursuit of inner wisdom & founded monasteries or desert hermitages to support their solitary predilections. The other new Sufi Orders were also committed to the advancement of spiritual wisdom, but their members chose to integrate themselves into Moslem society rather than retreat from it. The members of these mainstream Sufi Orders dedicated themselves to uplifting society by becoming professors, doctors, astronomers, alchemists and philosophers. Many lived and taught in the huge Moslem universities of Baghdad, Kufu, Cairo, Basra and Cordoba.

As Mohammed's empire expanded, the Sufi Orders became dispersed throughout Asia and North Africa. But whatever part of the empire they eventually settled in, these groups of mystics unbiasedly assimilated the mystery traditions of the conquered people, be they Egyptians, Hindus, Buddhists, Persians, Gnostics, Kabbalics, or Christians. The enlightened Sufi Masters recognized the same universal truths uniting all these diverse traditions and they even acknowledged the true spiritual teachers of each path to be "Sufis." For this reason, many of the greatest Serpents of Wisdom of other traditions, such as Christ, Zoroaster, and Thoth-Hermes (known as Idris among the Sufis) were assimilated into the Sufi tradition as Sufi patriarchs. The teachings of these Masters were translated into Arabic and thereby contributed to the development of Sufi doctrines and libraries.

BARAKA, THE SUFI SERPENT POWER

As proprietors of a very ancient lineage of Serpents, the Sufis possessed great wisdom and power which had been handed down from teacher to disciple for countless generations. They called their serpent power "Baraka," meaning the "Blessing" and the alchemical power that accompanies a saint's blessing. The grandmasters of each Sufi Order normally possessed immense amounts of Baraka which allowed them them to accomplish almost any supernatural feat. From them Baraka dispersed throughout the lower ranks of each Sufi Order.

When an aspiring Sufi was ready to receive Baraka, he or she would respectfully approach an acknowledged Sufi Master. Then during a sacred initiation ceremony in which the candidate pledged unremitting allegiance to the respective Sufi Order, the Baraka would be transmitted from Master to disciple. Upon transference, the power would awaken the inner fire serpent within the new Sufi initiate and consummate a rapid process of alchemical unfoldment.

To increase Baraka and accelerate its movement following the initial transmission, a Sufi initiate would devote him or herself to serving both his or her own Master, as well as the greater Sufi Order. The initiate would also adopt a regimen of intensive spiritual disciplines such as fasting, chanting, yoga and meditation besides occasionally embarking upon a pilgrimage to Sufi holy lands and the tombs of past Sufi masters, sacred places where Baraka was believed to continually bubble up like an etheric artisan well. Within the Sufi Order of Dervishes, swirling dances might also be prescribed for the activation and ascent of Baraka. During such a stimulating dance, a Sufi would whirl around in a circular, spiraling fashion. This movement would ex cite the inner Baraka and assist in its ascent up the spine, eventually culminating in a mystical union with Allah, the transcendental Spirit.

As Baraka moved throughout the subtle body of an awakened Sufi initiate it would activate and purify seven etheric centers called Lataif, which roughly correspond to the seven Hindu Chakras. Of these seven Lataif, one is located below the navel in the vicinity of the Svadisthana Chakra, one is situated in the area of the heart in the vicinity of the Anahata Chakra and another resides between the eyes in the vicinity of the Ajna Chakra. With the activation of each successive Lataif, a corresponding increase in wisdom and intuition would awaken within the evolving Sufi. Finally, with the activation of the seventh Lataif, Ma'rifat or full gnosis would blossom within the enlightened Sufi master and he or she would ex perience Fama, a losing of the limited self in the vastness of Allah.

THE SUFI SERPENTS, GODS INCARNATE

When a Sufi finally succeeded in achieving lttihad, union with Allah, he or she was henceforth considered by his or her peers to be a perfected Master, a Serpent of Wisdom, and a god-realized soul. Such esteemed Sufis were known to publically announce their ex alted state of godhood to the world at large. While lost in spiritual ecstasy, some Sufi Masters would occasionally cry out "Anal Hagg," "I am God," or "Subhani," "glory be to Me alone." This was the declaration of the god-realized Sufis Mansur al-Hallaj, Bayazid Bistani, Mansur Manstana, Abu Yazid, and Rabia.

According to the accepted wisdom of certain Sufi Orders, the greatest of all god-realized Sufis was the Prophet Mohammed. In their estimation he was the most ex alted Sufi Master, a "perfected man" and an ex ample of the archetypal initiate. Testimony of his supreme state of enlightenment is embedded within the "Hidden Traditions," the secret sayings and discourses of Mohammed. In one passage of these Sufi tex ts Mohammed is recorded as having proclaimed: "he that hath seen me hath seen God."[104] But the enlightened Mohammed was also quick to allow "whoso knows himself knows his lord"[104] thereby leaving the path to godhood open to all seekers.

THE KNIGHTS TEMPLAR, HEIRS TO THE SUFI AND HEBREW SERPENTS

Eventually the Wisdom of the Serpent passed into Europe via waves of missionaries who had studied with the Sufi Serpents of Wisdom and imbibed their ancient, eclectic wisdom. One wave of European missionaries were known as the Knights Templar, a group of Christian Knights who had ostensibly banded together to ensure safe passage to Christian pilgrims traveling between Europe and the Holy Land. Their true origins were, however, more personal. They came to recover sacred temple treasure and scrolls that their Jewish ancestors had left behind when fleeing the invading Romans in 70 A.D. and then marrying into the noble families of Europe. They also journeyed to Palestine to reclaim the throne of Jerusalem. They, and many of their cousins who marched with them, were direct descendants of the marital union between Jesus and Mary Magdalene.

While in Palestine the Knights came into contact with the Sufis soon after moving into the al-Aqsa Mosque, which was built on the Temple Mount next to the Dome of the Rock which sat upon part of the ruins of Solomon's Temple, the eventual symbol of their order. Their Sufi teachers were adepts of an Order called the Al-banna or "the Builders," a sect formed by the Nubian Sufi and alchemical adept Dhu Nun, a Master who had traveled throughout Egypt while extensively studying the Books of Thoth-Hermes and the Djedhi priesthood which decorated the walls and columns of the surviving temples.

Through their pivotal association with the Sufis, the Christian Knights learned the mysteries of Solomon's Temple, as well as the esoteric wisdom of the Greek, Egyptian, Persian, Chaldean and Hindu mystery academies which was preserved in the vaults of their mentors. They mastered the Arabic language and subsequently poured over many of the priceless scriptures which had been collected from all over the Moslem Empire and translated into the language of the Sufis. Within these texts they discovered the secrets of Alchemy, Hermeticism, Astrology, Gnosticism, Magic, Yoga, Sexual Tantra, etc. Their alchemical wisdom was further embellished upon when, while digging around the foundations of Solomon's Temple, they are reputed to have found a text on alchemy composed by King Solomon himself.

Of all the esoteric mysteries introduced to the Knights, however, that which intrigued them most was the secret life of Jesus Christ and a gnostic sect founded by his Master, John the Baptist, known as the Johannites. The Johannites evolved out of the Mandeaen tradition that had arrived in Palestine from the east with the gnostic wisdom of the First Serpent on the Tree, Sanat Kumara, whose names included Jnana Pandita, meaning the "Teacher of Gnosis" - which as the original Serpent on the Tree he truly was. When the Mandeaens came west Jnana evolved into the Hebrew Yohanan and the English John. Many of the Mandeaen prophets, including John the Baptist, were recognized as equal to, and even incarnations of, the Jnana Pandita, and given the honorable title of "John." John was not a name but a title meaning "He of Gnostic Wisdom and Power."

When the Templars first united as an order in 1118, their first grandmaster, Hughes de Payen also accepted an offer to become head of the Johannite sect headquartered in Jerusalem. Following his acceptance of this office Hughes de Payen and his Templar Knights could claim descent not just from John the Baptist but from a long line of Mandaeans that extended back to Sanat Kumara and the Garden of Eden.

THE TEMPLARS IN EUROPE AND DRAGON BAPHOMET

With the rites and mysteries they assimilated during their sojourn in Palestine, the Knights Templar returned to Europe and founded a new branch of the Serpents of Wisdom on their native soil. This would be ome known as the Underground Stream, as well as the Johannite and Holy Grail Church.

With their principal headquarters in Paris and southern France, a haven of gnostic Christians, alchemists, and secrets regarding the family of Jesus and Mary that legends claim once lived there, the Knights Templar moved freely around the country while transforming numerous castles into ornate temples and constructing cathedrals according to the principles of sacred geometry. In accordance with the wisdom they acquired from the Sufi al-Banna, the Templars constructed Gothic Cathedrals that were gnostic temples designed to generate the alchemical force and activate the inner Serpent Power. On the central altar of these edifices sat Black Madonnas, images the Templars brought back with them from the Holy Land that symbolized & generated the destructive/transformative power of the Goddess. Nearby, painted upon the floor in most Gothic Cathedrals, were labyrinths, which through the far right and left movements imposed upon a seeker walking along their twisting passageways balanced and united the brain hemispheres, thereby generating gnostic consciousness. In order to identify that their cathedrals were indeed alchemical crucibles, the Templars and their trained masons coverd both their exteriors and interiors with alchemical symbology. At the entrances of both the Notre Dame Cathedral in Paris and the Cathedral of Amiens, for example, one can still find alchemical symbols that reveal the entire alchemical process. Another popular symbol of the Knights Templar was that of an imposing black dragon named Baphomet, meaning "Baptism of Wisdom." Baphomet was a representation of the Kundalini itself - the Serpent power whose activation and alchemical influence was the true baptism. Dhul Nun had brought Baphomet's image with him out of Egypt, the ancient country which is known to have produced a black "philosophers stone" and to have associated the color black and the firey goat with transformation, immortality and gnostic enlightenment.

According to the 19th century Freemason and Templar descendant, Eliphas Levi, Baphomet was synonymous with the Goat of Mendes, the goat-headed version of fiery Volcan which had been anciently transported by initiates of the Motherland to Khem, and to Sumeria where it became Enki.

The essence of Baphomet, which Lèvi claimed was the life force and the transformative Kundalini, was apparently transmitted via the famous "Templar Kiss," a secret ritual during which a Templar Master kissed a new initiate below the navel, at the base of the spine and on his mouth. It was also reputed to have been awakened within the order through practices of Alchemy, Sexual Tantra and Yoga.

Since many of the Europeans who eventually became Templars were wealthy nobles, large sums of money and land eventually poured into the organization's treasury. Consequently the Templar's were soon acknowledged to be one of the richest and

The Primal Dragon Baphomet on a French Church.

most powerful branches of Serpents in the world. Then fate placed two impassable road blocks in front of the Templars in the form of the Catholic Church and King Philip the Fair of France. King Philip needed money to finance

BAPHOMET
KNIGHTS TEMPLARS' GOD

Baphomet represents the androgynous Primal Dragon and Creator of the Cosmos that is the union of the polarity. This is why it unites Heaven and Earth by having one hand up and another down, and also why it features both a male phallus and female breasts. As the Primal Dragon, it is an embodiment of the Serpent Power, the Alchemical Force and the Kundalini. As such, it destroys all things that keep a seeker from knowing his or her divine nature, a function evinced by its forbidding dark black color.Its association with alchemy is plainly evident. The words "Solve" and "Coagula" on its forearms are the names of two important stages in the alchemical process.

Thoth-Hermes-Mercury is the anthropormorphised Primal Dragon. He is both the patron of alchemy as well as its goal, the creation of the Alchemical Fire. His fiery transformative essence is contained within - and emanates from - the Emerald Tablet. Just by being in the presence of the tablet alchemy occurs within a person.

the expansion of his kingdom and decided to usurp the Templars' wealth for himself. To do so he dispatched a communiqué to the Catholic Pope in Rome in which he included a list of heretical charges against the Templars and demanded their imprisonment. The Templars were attacked soon afterwards by the Inquisition and their incredible wealth and land was seiz ed by the French authorities.

During the subsequent rapid demise of the Templars many knights were imprisoned. Many would then die under torture or by burning, including the last Grandmaster of the Order, Jacques de Molay. Some Templars managed to escape, however, and took refuge in England and Scotland where they proceeded to help lay the foundation of modern Freemasonry. Other brothers flocked to the safety of certain sacred Mediterranean isles which had anciently been occupied by the Atlantean Serpents of Wisdom. Some became sea pirates; others vanished into the European countryside. Wherever they fled the Templars vowed to one day re-group and establish God's holy kingdom throughout all the countries of the Earth.

THE EUROPEAN ALCHEMISTS, CREATORS OF THE SERPENT FIRE

Following the lead of the Templars, other waves of truth-seeking Europeans flocked to study with the Sufi sages and then returned home overflowing with esoteric wisdom. Of the occult knowledge thus transported by them, the most popular was that pertaining to Alchemy, the science of uniting certain ingredients together in order to produce a "Philosophers Stone," a manifestation of the Serpent Fire which could turn base metals into gold or humans into gods and goddesses. Those who transported this ancient wisdom into Europe helped precipitate the formation of a European Order of Alchemists.

CREATING THE SERPENT FIRE WITH THOTH-HERMES'S 13 PRECEPTS

In their cold, damp laboratories scattered throughout Europe the practitioners of alchemy labored night and day to create a physical manifestation of the Serpent Fire which would speed up the evolution of matter and thereby make them either rich or immortal. With this goal in mind, they separated and reunited the male and female components of a substance, which they cryptically referred to as Philosophical Sulfur and Philosophical Mercury, in order to create the "androgynous" Serpent Fire. In its resultant form of either a powder or liquid, their version of the Serpent Fire became commonly known by cryptic epithets such as the Alchemical Mercury, the Animated Mercury, the Dragon, the

Philosophers Stone, and the Holy Ghost. According to the British researcher John Michell, it was also recognized to be the power "enshrined within the initiatory chambers of the pyramid. "52

The purpose of the Alchemists' textbooks was to outline the stages involved in the production of the Serpent Fire. The most popular of these texts, and key to them all, was the Emerald Tablet of Thoth-Hermes, the ancient Atlantean patriarch of alchemy. The writing on this tablet delineated 13 stages of alchemical transmutation in the form of thirteen precepts. Thirteen is, of course, the number of death and the resurrected Dragon/Phoenix.

THE SERPENT FIRE AS A RED POWDER

In the form of a fiery, red powder (color of the serpent fire), the Alchemists would sprinkle their synthesized Serpent Fire on top of base metals such as tin, lead, mercury, silver or any other pure metal. Under its influence an alchemical reaction would quickly unfold as the base metal was transmuted into pure gold.

Such material transmutations were known to have been accomplished by numerous Alchemists working within many of the countries in Europe. While conducting his alchemical experiments in a castle tower of the reigning English King Edward, the famous Spanish alchemist Raymond Lully is reported to have transmuted 5 0000 pounds of mercury, tin and lead into solid gold. In Austria, the alchemist Wenzel Seiler is on record for having transmuted large quantities of tin into gold in the presence of the Emperor Leopold. Testimony of his accomplishment is preserved today within the imperial treasury of Vienna in the form of one of Seilor's partly transmuted pieces of silver. In Bohemian alchemist named Labujardiere transmuted two and one-half pounds of mercury into gold in the presence of the Emperor Ferdinand. The occasion was duly commemorated by a coin which still bears the inscription: "Divine metamorphosis caused in Prague January, 15, 1640 witnessed by his Imperial Majesty Ferdinand III." A successful French transmutation wasaccomplished by the alchemist Nicholas Flamel who used the transmuted goldto finance the construction of 14 hospitals, 3 chapels, and 7 churches.

THE SERPENT FIRE AS THE ELIXIR OF IMMORTALITY

When produced in the form of a liquid, the synthesized Serpent Fire was referred to as the Elixir of Immortality and consumed daily by spiritually inclined alchemists seeking to accelerate their own evolution and become a living God or Goddess, This "androgynous" elixir had the power to facilitate the reunion of the polarity and promote the awakening of the inner Kundalini.

271

Ascended Master who works primarily on the etheric planes but occasionally assumes a physical form if his work of uplifting humanity requires him to do so.

THE HERMETIC ORDERS, BRANCHES OF THE EUROPEAN SERPENTS

Many of the branches of European Serpents governed by St. Germain were comprised of spiritually inclined alchemists who had united during the late Renaissance period to produce numerous Hermetic Orders. Since Hermes "signifies a Serpent,"24 these Hermetic Orders were essentially "Serpent Orders." Their members adhered to a regimen which included the daily study and practice of the alchemical techniques and gnostic doctrines of their ancient patriarch, the legendary Serpent Thoth-Hennes. The founding of these various Hermetic Orders eventually led to the formation of a well defined network of Serpents throughout Europe.

THE CORPUS HERMETICUM, THE SURVIVING BOOKS OF THOTH-HERMES

The doctrines of Thoth-Hennes which were studied within the various Hermetic Orders had been acquired from the Sufis or from the Serpents of Wisdom who fled Alexandria during the city's demise. One prized collection of texts which came directly from Alexandria was the seventeen volume *Corpus Hermeticum,* a compilation of gnostic wisdom believed to contain the last surviving remnants of the 35,000 or so texts authored by the lineage of Thoth-Hermes. Having descended through the melting pot of Alexandria, however, many of these surviving texts had been re-written in the language of Neoplatonic philosophy, Greek and Kabbalic mysticism.

When the Serpents of Wisdom fled Alexandria the texts of the Corpus Hermeticum were transferred to Greece and remained carefully hidden there for the next thousand years. Finally, in the 1400's, the texts resurfaced with a monk named Leonardo da Pistoria who supposedly found them in Macedonia, transported them to Florence Italy, and then laid them at the feet of a noble patron of the arts, Cosimo de Medici. The Florentine noble had the texts translated into Latin by the scholar, Leonardo Ficino, and then published in 1471.

PYMANDER THE DRAGON, LEGACY FROM ATLANTIS

The most important manuscript contained within the Corpus Hermeticum is entitled Pymander or "The Dragon." This uniquely archetypal text presents the sequential phases of the unfolding of the universe beginning with the birth of the Primal Serpent and culminating in spiritual enlightenment. Since it is such a purely archetypal treatise, this text may have escaped the filter of Alexandria and retained the purity of its first Atlantean author. Pymander is written in the form of a dialogue between Pymander, the Primal Dragon, and his first disciple on Earth, Thoth-Hermes. As the text opens Thoth-Hermes is passing though a desolate landscape (symbolizing "desolate" ignorance) in search of spiritual knowledge. After devoting himself to intensive prayer and meditation, Thoth-Hermes was blessed by the divine vision of the Primal Serpent. Spontaneously appearing before him, the "Great Dragon, with wings stretching across the sky and light streaming in all directions from its body," introduced itself as "Pymander, the (Divine) Mind of the Universe, the Creative Intelligence, and the Absolute E mperorof all. "24 The archetypal teacher and Primal Dragon had arrived to teach Thoth-Hermes the mysteries of the universe

. Pymander proceeded to present to his new student a live holographic presentation of the origin and destiny of the cosmos. To begin his elaborate presentation, Pymander changed into pure effulgent light, symbolic of Spirit, "the spiritual nature of the Great Dragon," and the first stage in the creative process. The Primal Serpent then delineated to Thoth-Hermes the succeeding phases of creation: "The Supreme Being (which was)-the Mind-male and female, brought forth the Logos or Word (the Serpent Son) ... The Word moving like a breath (the serpentine life force) through space called forth the fire (the Serpent Fire) by the friction of its motion ... (it) passed as a whirlwind (spiraling form of the Serpent) through the universe, causing the substances to vibrate and glow with its friction .. the Son (the dragon)(then) formed Seven Governors (the seven parts of the Dragon) ...and the Seven Governors controlled the world by the mysterious power called Destiny .... "24

Having completed the first part of his holographic light show, the Primal Dragon then outlined to Thoth-Hermes the evolutionary phase of destruction/transformation and its culmination as human salvation. Through a series of images placed within his student's mind, Pymander portrayed the end of evolution as a reunion of the male/female principles and a "return again to the father (Spirit) who dwelleth in the white light." According to Pymander, a Master who has completed the evolutionary process and united with Spirit becomes an "Hermaphrodite, or male and female (united)."24

At the conclusion of his lengthy presentation, the Primal Dragon transmitted his knowledge and power into Thoth-Hermes, thus awakening within his student the divine mind of wisdom. He then sent away the new Serpent of Wisdom with these parting words: "Blessed art thou, O Son of Light, to whom of all men, I, Pymander, the light of the world, have revealed myself. I order you to go forth, to become as a guide to those who wander in darkness, that all men within whom dwells the spirit of My Mind (the Divine Mind) may be saved by My Mind in you, which shall call forth My Mind in them. Establish My Mysteries and they shall not fail from the Earth, for I am the Mind of the Mysteries and until Mind fai ls my Mysteries cannot fail."[24]

THE ELITE EUROPEAN SERPENTS, THE ROSICRUCIANS

Of all the Hermetic Orders and branches of the Serpents of Wisdom in Europe, the most exclusive was the Hermetic Order of the Rosey Cross or the Rosicrucians. The Rosicrucians were the "cream" of the European spiritual alchemists and could justifiably call themselves the true and authentic heirs of the ancient Serpent Wisdom. They claimed to possess a direct link to the ancient Serpents via the Knights Templar and certain alchemists who had studied directly with the Sufis, such as Raymond Lully, Paracelsus, and Artephuis.

The Rosicrucians first made their existence known as a European organization around 1614 A.D. with the German publication of two documents, the *Fama Fraternalis* and the *Confessio Fratenitatis,* The circulation of these documents in Germany were intended to be both a public declaration of the order's existence as well as a rallying cry to all spiritual alchemists ready to unite in solidarity for the freedom and enlightenment of the world. The *Confessio* claimed the world was on the threshold of new age of Serpent Wisdom. This truth had been symbolically communicated by the Almighty via the recent discovery of "The Messengers of God," the stars in the constellation of Serpentarius, the Serpent.

THE "FIRST" ROSICRUCIAN SERPENT, CHRISTIAN ROSENCRUTZ

The *Fama* claimed that the Order of Rosicrucians had been officially founded 200 years earlier by a German seeker named Christian Rosencrutz or C.R.C. for short. The *Fama* maintained that C.R.C. had acquired the undational doctrines of Rosicrucianism while on a pilgrimage to various Sufi holy cities. In the holy city of "Damcar" (Damascus?) C.R.C. was reputed to have spent three years studying physics, mathematics and alchemy while translating into Latin a book of Sufi wisdom, the sacred book" M." Later, in the holy city of Fez in Morocco, C.R.C. studied the magical arts and the science of necromancy (communication with the dead) under the tutelage of various Sufi magicians.

Following his return to Germany, C.R.C. compiled the esoteric wisdom he had gathered and proceeded to teach it to eight specially selected students. These eight apostles were the first initiates and brothers of the Rosicrucian Order. Later, when C.R.C. felt his students were ready to teach the ancient wisdom on their own, he authorized them to travel as teachers to other countries outside of Germany. The Rosicrucian patriarch died soon after their departure.

Two hundred years after C.R.C.'s death, the descendants of the original eight brothers received an intuitive beckoning to travel to the Master's tomb in Germany for what would prove to be a momentous event. Upon their arrival they jointly opened up the sealed tomb and, amazingly, found C.R.C's body in a perfectly preserved condition. Surrounding the Master's immutable body were the sacred books T, H, and M-the holy texts which C.R.C. had brought back from the Sufi mystery academies. These priceless texts were carefully removed from the Master's tomb and later became part of an expanded Rosicrucianism. Finally, after having paid their respects to the Master, the discoverers resealed C.R.C.'s tomb and then left to begin a new chapter in the Rosicrucian Order. The publication of the *Fama* and *Confessio* followed soon afterwards.

TIIE ROSICRUCIANS, DESCENDANTS OF THE ATLANTEAN SERPENTS

Once the *Fama* had proclaimed the presence of the Rosicrucians in Germany, many affiliate branches of the order throughout Europe followed suit by subsequently disclosing their existence. Concurrent with their "coming out" was an outpouring of new information regarding the history of the Rosicrucians which seemed to suggest that the organization was actually much more ancient than the *Fama* had divulged. The Rosicrucian Order of the Rosy and Golden Cross, for example, traced their lineage back to Noah, Thoth-Hermes (Cain and Enoch) and Adam. The Rosicrucian Ancient and Mystic Order Rosae Crucis traced its lineage back to an Egyptian order presided over by the Pharaoh Akhenaten. The Oriental Rite of Memphis claimed it was founded by an Alexandrian prophet, Ormus, who had united pagan and Christian mysteries to found the Rose-Croix. [105] The Rosicrucian Hermetic Order founded by the American Pachal Beverly Randolph traced its antecedents back to the Essenes and before them to the Serpents of Wisdom on Atlantis. [106]

THE "PHILOSOPHY OF THE FLAME"
THE SERPENT FIRE

The principal alchemical doctrine of the Rosicrucians was known as the "Philosophy of the Flame" and many of the early initiates of the order were referred to as "Fire Philosophers." Their Philosophy of the Flame, the perennial philosophy of all Serpents of Wisdom, maintained that all life originated out of fire, divided into the universal polarity and then finally reunited back in to fire. The referred to fire, states the noted Rosicrucian philosopher Hargrave Jennings, is "not our vulgar, gross fire, but an occult, mysterious or inner supernatural fire (i.e., the Serpent Fire)."87

The roots of the Philosophy of the Flame, claims Freeman Dowd, a prominent Rosicrucian scholar, can be found in ancient Fire Worship, the rites of which, says another Rosicrucian, Manly P. Hall, had their origin on the Motherland of Atlantis. Adds Jennings, these ancient fire rites were of an essentially "sexual nature" since they culminated in the union of the polarity and the awakening of the fire serpent.

The ancient fire rites adopted by the Rosicrucians took the form of alchemy, yoga, prayer/meditation, laboratory alchemy and sexual tantra. Once they had awakened the inner yogic flame through these practices, its transformative influence then unfolded through seven stages that corresponded to the serpent fire's opening of the seven successive chakras. These seven stages were allegorized in *The Chemical Marriage of Christian Rosencrutz* byJohann Valentin Andrea, a Rosicrucian who had studied directly under the Sufis.

THE SERPENTS OF FREEMASONRY

Another Hermetic Order and a close cousin to the Rosicrucian Order was that of Freemasonry, an organization which also spread throughout Europe during the Renaissance period. The Rosicrucian and Freemasonic Orders were closely linked; they claimed similar histories and even traded members back and forth.

THE ANCIENT BUILDERS WERE
POSSESSORS OF THE SERPENT FIRE

According to the order's records, Freemasonry began on the Motherlands as an order of Serpents of Wisdom who were adept builders. Collectively, these builders began with Cain, the "smith" and "possessor" of fire. Legend had it that with the creativity engendered by his fire power, Cain built the first city and named it after his son, Enoch. Cain is apparently synonymous with one of the members of the Thoth-Hermes lineage, whose city was built upon the Giza Plateau in Egypt as the three huge pyramids

Leading up to the flood and the destruction of the Motherlands, Cain's heirs, the Children of Lamech, inscribed as hieroglyphs the secrets of building upon two pillars and then stored them in a place immune from flood damage. These Children of Lamech may be synonymous with a later member of the Thoth-Hermes lineage, as well as the Jewish patriarch Enoch, both of whom are reputed to have inscribed their wisdom on pillars preceding the deluge and then hidden them in a water-tight cavern.

THE WORLDWIDE ORDER OF SERPENT BUILDERS

Following the dispersion of the flood waters, a worldwide order of builders eventually emerged around the globe. Like Cain and Lamech's son, Tubal Cain, the master builders of each branch of this planetary organization were in some way associated with the serpent fire. Within its Egyptian branch the master builders and architects were often adepts of the Thoth-Hermes lineage. Within its Mesoamerican branch many of the master builders were Quetzlcoatls and Kukulcans, the "Plumed Serpents." The master builders of the Southeast Asian branch were often Nagas and Mahanagas, the "Great Serpents." Throughout the Greece and the Hellenic empire the master builders were part of the Order of Bacchuses, the followers of Dionysus, the Serpent Son. These Dionysian Architects were responsible for constructing temples in honor of Dionysus and amphitheaters for the re-enactment of his sacred legend. One of the more famous branches of the Dionysian Architects was founded at Tyre on the Asia Minor coast and presided over by the master builder, Hiram Abiff. Hiram Abiff was known esoterically as Chiram, an ancient name of Thoth-Hermes which denotes "serpent fire." Historically he is recognized as the Master Builder of Solomon's Temple. According to information disseminated by a modem lodge of Templars in London, *The Knights Templar of Aquarius,* Hiram Abiff and his fraternity of builders constructed Solomon's Temple exactly in accordance with dimensions and geometries passed down to them from the Children of Lamech, the ancient builders of Atlantis.

THE SERPENT BUILDERS OF EUROPE, THE FREEMASONS

The Order of Serpent Builders eventually entered into the heartland of Europe through the gateway of Rome. The first European branch of masons was founded in Rome by King Numa, a powerful Serpent of Wisdom and the second king of the city, who could manifest "lightning in a cloudless sky." Numa sent delegations to Egypt, Chaldea and Palestine in order to collect the esoteric secrets and rites directly forom the lodges of Serpents Builders in those countries and then founded the Roman Collegia with him as its inçipient Grandmaster

After many years, when the Lombard's invaded Italy, the initiates of the Collegia disbanded and retreated to the Island of Comacina in Lake Como. When they were finally conquered, these "Comacine" Masons were sent throughout Europe to build castles and churches for their new masters. In these distant countries they succeeded in establishing numerous masonic lodges and esoteric rites which were later embellished upon first by the Templars and then by the Rosicrucians and Freemasons returning from the Sufi citadels of learning.

The official amalgamation of the Templars' esoteric rites with those of masonry occurred under the auspices of the Scottish King Robert the Bruce who formed the Royal Order of Scotland for the knights after they fled Franc e. The official amalgamation is believed to have taken place in 1286 at the Lodge of Kilwinning in Scotland. At Kilwinning the Masonic rites were infused with Templar alchemy and gnostic wisdom acquired from the Sufis and Johannites in the Holy Land. At "Mother Kilwinning," masonry evolved into Freemasonry.

The first Freemasonic Gran d Lodge, known as The Mother Grand Lodge of the World was founded in England in 1717 under the guidance of a group of Rosicrucian adepts who were summoned to the country by Elias Ashmole and the Rosicrucian Robert Fludd. The founding of this Grand Lodge officially marked the beginning of Freemasonry in the modem era and established a model for all subsequent lodges in both Britain and Ame rica.

CHIRAM, THE MASTER BUILDER
PERSONIFICATION OF THE SERPENT FIRE

Under the synthesizing influence of the Masons, Templars and Rosicrucians the goal of modern Freemasonry became the "rebuilding of Solomon' s Temple," an alchemical process by which the physical body was "rebuilt" or transmuted into an immutable body by Chiram, the "Master Builder" and Serpent Fire. The nature of Chiram, the Kundalini, and the process of leading it to the top of the head, were duly allegorized in the principal instructive myth of Freemasonry, The Legend of Hiram Abiff, within which Chiram was personified as Hiram Abiff, the Master Builder of Solomon's Temple.

At the outset of his legend, Chiram as Hiram Abiff is murdered and buried by jealous masons as he attempts to leave the grounds of Solomon's Temple, thus symbolizing the Kundalini' s "death" and "entombment" at the base of the human spine. Eventual ly, however, Hiram is rescued by King Solomon who reaches down into the Master Builder' s grave and pulls him out with "the strong grip of a lion's paw." This last episode of Hiram's drama represents the last stage of spiritual practice in which the Solar Spirit (whose representative animal is a lion) located in the crown chakra uses the attracting force of its positive polarity to pull Chiram, the negatively charged Serpent Fire up to its seat at the top of the head.

THE 33 DEGREES OF MASONRY: 33 SPINAL VERTEBRAE

Once Chiram, the Kundalini, is awakened within the human body and ascends to the seat of Spirit, it progresses through 33 stages, the approximate number of vertebrae comprising the human spine. F or this reason, and also because 33 is the archetypal number of polarity union (3+3 represents the three sides of two triangles which unite as a Star of David), the Freemasons incorporated 33 mystical degrees into their order. To designate themselves Serpents, one advanced degree was named "The Knight of the Brazen Serpent."

THE "DIVINE" CAGLIOSTRO, COMMANDER OF THE EUROPEAN SERPENTS

One of the greatest of Freemasons and a leading figure of all Hermetic Orders was the Count Alessandro Cagliostro. The "Divine Cagliostro," as he was honorably referred to, exemplified the expansive character of a high ranking Freemason of the seventeenth and eighteenth centuries. Like many of the other Master Masons of his time, he was a recognized lineal descendant of the Templars, a pioneering philosopher, an alchemist, an occultist, a world traveler, and a Rosicrucian. At the pinnacle of his life Cagliostro ascended to the highest rungs of the European Order of Serpents and recognized second only to St. Germain in his lofty esoteric wisdom and occult attainments.

According to his own controversial autobiography, leading up to his initiation in a Freemasonic Lod.ge Cagliostro had a spiritual upbringing similar to that of Christian Rosencrutz. In his early years he frequented the holy Sufi cities and was a student of Sufi Masters in Medina, Mecca and Fez. While studying in North Africa Cagliostro also spent years apprenticing Egyptian priests and eventually gained initiation as a Djedhi Adept Then, to complete his spiritual tra ining, Cagliostro tra veled to the Island of Malta to probe the minds of the Knights of Malta, and subsequently become initiated into their alchemical order.

To consummate his ministry, Cagliostro first traveled to England, the principal headquarters of Freemasonry in Europe. In honor of his formidable spiritual accomplishments, the hierarc hy of the Grand Lodge of Britain quickly ushered Cagliostro into their order as a fellow Master Mason.

The Esoteric Seal of Cagliostro revealing his status as an Alchemist & Serpent.

Count Alessandro Cagliostro

Castle of William IX of Hesse-Kassel, site of the Wilhelmsbad Congress uniting the Freemasons and Illuminati was held in 1782.

Symbol of the united Freemasonry-Illuminati Order

Caglisotro traveled to Europe where he received induction into Adam Weishaupt's Illuminati Order which claimed direct descent from the earlier Templars. During his initiation Caglisotro vower to exact revenge for the slain Templars and began by joining a movement to formally unite the Illuminati and Freemasons into one cohesive and very powerful fraternity. He then assisted St. Germain as the great alchemist's second in command in order to mobilize the French Revolution, which ultimately became the vehicle of vengeance for his Templar ancestors by bringing down the French monarchy.

During his ensuing travels in such countries as Prussia, Brussels, the Hague, Germany, France and Italy, Cagliostro helped charter many new lodges as well as evolve those already in existence. He also performed many miracles and garnered for himself a reputation as both an accomplished alchemist and healer. Finally settlin g in Strasbourg, France, Cagliostro quickly became famous for both transmuting base metals into "five to six thousand pounds of gold" and alchemically producing diamonds in the presence of Cardinal de Rohan, Bishop of Strasbourg. Cagliostro also gained renown for performing numerous miraculous healing at Strasbourg and had convalescents from all over Europe flocking to his healing temple. To keep his clients well after their healing had occurred and prevent the scourge of old age, Cagliostro produced numerous vats of the Elixir of Immortality and devised a complete alchemical rejuvenation program. This regeneration program, which was to be observed every 50 years, began on the full moon in May and involved strict diets and special purgatives to remove all toxins fro m the body. If all went as planned, after 40 days the participant would display a newly regenerated body complete with youthful looking hair and even a new set of teeth.

Cagliostro 's downfall occurred in 1789 when he traveled to Rome to present to the Pope his ambitious plan of uniting "The Children of Hiram" (the Freemasons) with the "Sons of St. Peter" (the Christians) into a one world organization. The master mason's mission failed grievously. He was captured by the Inquisition and sentenced to death for heresy. When the Order of Freemasons came to the rescue and revolted on his behalf, the Pope was compelled to commute Cagliostro's sentence to life imprisonment. Poor Cagliostro was then taken in chains to meet an inglorious ending to his amazing life within the castle-prison of San Leo, the most feared prison in Italy where"inmates were known to have been driven mad in a matter of weeks."[87] Here Cagliostro spent the rest of his life in a damp, dark, und erground dungeon. According to one legend, however, Cagliostro escaped from his cell and traveled east to the headquarters of the Serpents of Wisdom in Tibet.

CAGLIOSTRO'S EGYPTIAN RITE: MASTERING THE SERPENT

Cagliostro's greatest contribution to the development of Freemasonry was to fashion masonic rites in accordance with ancient Egyptian and Atlantean models. His most famous creation, the Egyptian Rite, was based upon Cagliostro's own direct experience in Egypt, as well as the *Crata Repoa,* a compilation of Egyptian initiation rites taken from the ancient writings of Herodutus, Apulius, Diodorus, Plutarch and others. To properly house his Egyptian Rite, Cagliostro created a Freemasonic Lodge in the image of Solomon's Temple and ornamented it with statues of certain Egyptian deities, such as Isis, Anubis, and Apis.

Intrinsic to Cagliostro's Egyptian Rite were seven stages or degrees (the traditional number of death and transformation), each of which required a special initiation to enter. Some of the initiation rites were designed to awaken the inner fire serpent and assist in its movement up the spine. During induction into one of the early degrees, for example, the aspirant was taught specific breathing techniques which were calculated to culminate in the awakening of the Kundalini. A candidate of this degree was also required to gain mastery over the fire serpent by being shut up in a darkened room swarming with live snakes, the physical manifestations of the inner serpent. The mastery achieved by this initiation supported the candidate in a later degree during which he or she learned how to consciously manipulate and direct the serpent fire for both healing and spiritual transformation.

THE
RETURN
OF THE
SERPENTS OF WISDOM

CHAPTER 18

THE EUROPEAN DRAGON EMPIRE

Beginning with the collapse of the Knights Templar, the tacit goal of all subsequent branches of the European Serpents of Wisdom, including the Freemasons and Rosicrucians, was to wrestle the dictatorial power out of the hands of the Catholic hierarchy and all self-serving monarchies in order to transform Europe into a Dragon Empire ruled over by wise Serpents. With this goal in mind, the diverse branches of European Serpents eventually mobilized to form a Serpent/Protestant Confederacy.

THE SERPENT/PROTESTANT CONFEDERACY

The dream of a Serpent/Protestant confederacy first began to take tangible form during the Reformation of the Christian Church. Under the disruptive influence of Martin Luther, a fringe member of the Rosicrucians, a schism occurred in both the Christian Church and the "Holy Roman Empire" it controlled, thereby precipitating the formation of two separate churches and two empires. One church and one half of the former empire remained traditional or catholic in doctrine and continued to be ruled either directly or indirectly by the Roman Pope. By contrast, the second church and the other half of the former empire became liberal or protestant and managed to break free from the crippling authority of the old European power complex. Perceiving this schism as a tremendous opportunity to realize their dream, the European Serpents of Wisdom sprung into action and proceeded to align themselves with the new Protestant regime.

Once it became undeniably apparent which monarchies were going to ally themselves with the new Protestant Empire, each was approached individually in order to enlist their support for the fledgling Serpent/Protestant Confederacy. Led by St. Germain and Cagliostro, many high ranking members of the Rosicrucians and Freemasons worked tirelessly in order to create a network of alliances among these European nobles. Ultimately their efforts were well rewarded. Some Protestant kings and queens not only offered their allegiance to the Confederacy but even donated their castles as headquarters for the movement. Eventually many of them went on to become high ranking initiates within the Hermetic Orders of Serpents.

In the Duchy of Shleswig-Holstien St. Germain found support from the country's protestant ruler, Prince Charles of Hesse, who willingly offered his castle as a headquarters for the Confederacy. One part of the Prince's palace was subsequently remodeled into an alchemical laboratory, another wing was transformed into an initiation chamber, and still another wing was converted into a meeting place for members of the Confederacy. In time Prince Charles acquired initiation into Freemasonry and became highly regarded by members of the organization for his powers of communicating with the dead. He was also noted for having had a profound spiritual revelation during which he remembered in detail his past life as Joseph of Aramathea, the uncle of Jesus Christ. In England the Protestant Queen Elizabeth and much of the British government were eventually won over to the Confederacy by the Rosicrucian John Dee. Dee was the occult and esoteric advisor to the queen and also served as her secret liaison, the queen's "007." In this capacity Dee was senton covert missions throughout Europe with instructions to create alliances with other Protestant governments while simultaneously spying on the activities of the Catholic Church. When backin Britain Dee presided over clandestine meetings of governmental officials, such as The Royal Society, an organization whose membership of Sir Walter Raleigh, Sir Francis Bacon and other statesmen were Freemasons who met to discuss affirmative action for the creation of democracy. Their rallying cries for freedom were disseminated throughout Britain and Europe as cryptic massages encoded within the plays of Shakespeare (Sir Francis Bacon is believed by many to be the "real" Shakespeare), as well as Bacon's *New Atlantis*, Sir Walter Raleigh's *World History*, and other ciphered communiqués.

In eastern Europe the Serpent/Protestant Confederacy found a willing participant in the tiny country of Bohemia, a nation often visited by Dee during his undercover missions. Following the rise to prominence of John Hess, the famous rebel who lit up Europe with the idea of democracy, Bohemia became a mecca for progressive minded individuals. The King of Bohemia, Rudolph II, supported the Protestants and transformed Prague, his capital city, into a haven for Alchemists, Hermeticists and Kabbalists. Rudolph's castle was given over to the covert activities of the Serpents and transformed into a fortress of esoterica. Legend states that within the walls of the palace were specially designed chambers embellished with esoteric symbols, secret texts, and unusual, metaphysical instruments. Administering the esoteric palace rites was Rudolph himself along with his staff of high ranking initiates. The king's chief advisor, Pisteria, was a Master Kabbalist and below him were an assortment of alchemical adepts and magicians serving as court officials. King Rudolph and Pisteria promoted the vision of a Protestant Europe of enlightened Serpents and welcomed into his palace Dee, Kepler, Bruno and other famous members of the European Order of Serpents.

The Protestant nobility of Germany, France and Prussia also rallied in support of a Serpent/ Protestant Confederacy. The Protestant ruler of Wurtenburg, Duke Ferdinand I, allied himself with the Serpents of Wisdom and later evolved into an adept alchemist and occultist. Following his affiliation with the Confederacy, the country of Wurtenburg was transformed into a German mecca for European Serpents. In Ingolstadt Germany, a branch of Serpents calling themselves the Illuminati was founded by Adam Weishaupt, professor of philosophy and cannon law at the University of Ingolstadt. The Illuminati was one of the true heirs of the Knights Templar wisdom and was patronized by many intellectuals and nobles involved in the creation of the Serpent/Protestant Confederacy. In nearby Prussia, King Frederick became a high initiate of Freemasonry and an ardent supporter of the Confederacy. In France, Philip Egalite, the Duke of Orleans, was elected as Grandmaster of the Grand Lodge of France. Philip and other French nobles helped found a branch of the Confederacy and then proceeded to set the stage for the ensuing democratic revolution in France.

THE SERPENTS DESTROY THE BASTILLE

Once the Serpent/ Protestant Confederacy was securely in place, the Serpents turned their attention to the overthrow of certain dictatorial monarchies which stood in the way of a unified free Europe. Perhaps the most blatant example of such self-serving monarchies - and the one most influential in the downfall of the Knights Templar - was the French monarchy. In order to bring down King Louis XVI and Queen Marie Antoinette, the European Order of Serpents chose as its principal target the Bastille, a famous prisonwhich was at the time a symbol of political and ideological oppression in France. The attack was orchestrated by members of the Nine Sisters, one of the most esoteric branches of the European Serpents of Wisdom, which boasted a membership of the dynamic revolutionaries Cagliostro, Voltaire and Helvetius. Cagliostro, who had become a popular figure among the French people because of his numerous healings, set the plan in motion by publicly circulating a letterin which he called for the destruction of the prison at all costs. As planned, a copy of the letter ended up in the hand s of King Louis who felt thre atened enough by its contents to have Cagliostro immediately arrested and imprisoned within the Bastille. Quick to exploit the move the Serpents then proceeded to stir up anti-crown sentiment for the injustice Loius had directed against the peoples' hero. Led by Camille Desmoulins of the Nine Sisters mobs of citizens were soon mobilized and together they stormed the

Bastille, razing the building to its foundations. Anarchy followed throughout Paris and soon the king and his queen were decapitated in one ofo the many guillotines set up around the city.

With the destruction of King Louis XVI and his regime the Order of Serpents sent a message to all dictatorial monarchies in Europe. A new era had arrived on the continent and it was only a matter of time before a new, democratic regime would reign supreme.

Queen Elizabeth wears the Serpent of Wisdom on her sleeve.

The Emperor Rudolph II has an audience with an occult adept.

CHAPTER 19

THE NEW LAND OF THE PHOENIX

While the Serpent/Protestant Confederacy was busy solidifying a democratic Europe, many leading Serpent of Wisdom on the continent were quietly drawing up plans for what was to be a model democratic nation across the western sea. Referred to within closed circles of initiates as the "New Atlantis" and the "New Land of the Phoenix,"1 this proposed civilization was to be an ideal democratic republic. It was to allow freedom of speech and belief while being governed by Serpents of Wisdom elected "by the people and for the people." For many years the Serpents spoke secretly among themselves regarding this projected utopia but openly circulated cryptic depictions of it to circles of freedom fighters and intellectuals throughout Europe. In his *New Atlantis*, for example, Sir Francis Bacon described his vision of the western shangri-la as a place across a great sea governed by officials wearing white turbans inscribed with red crosses, i.e. Rosicrucians.

13 COLONIES, NUMBER OF THE PHOENIX DRAGON

Starting in the late 1600s members of the European Order of Serpents began leaving their comfortable lives behind in order to undertake the long, arduous journey across the Atlantic Ocean to become citizens of the New Land of the Phoenix. Once in North America they proceeded to organize a cohesive network of Rosicrucian and Freemasonic Lodges within a nation of 13 colonies, the ancient number of the Phoenix Dragon. In 1694 a Rosicrucian colony was established in Pennsylvania and by the early 1700s Freemasonic Lodges were literally sweeping across the new nation. By the beginning of the Revolutionary period there were a multitude of common lodges and seven (number of the Serpent) Grand Provincial Lodges scattered evenly throughout the Thirteen Colonies. Within these various lodges the Serpents could meet and discuss strategies for the founding of an independent nation unshackled by British rule.

THE GREEN DRAGON TAVERN

In order to throw off the yoke of the British Crown, the Freemasonic Lodges proceeded to found subversive organizations, such as the Sons of Liberty, which were calculated to intimidate British officials and promote the

289

boycott of all British imports. The Masons also attempted to stir up anti-British sentiment among the colonial masses by presiding over pep rallies in taverns and other public meeting places.

One of the favorite forums of the Freemasons in Boston was the Green Dragon Tavern, a popular gathering place which Daniel Webster referred to as "the headquarters of the revolution. "[87] During one frenzied meeting at the tavern a plan was hatched to resist the British tariff on tea by destroying a new shipment of the commodity residing in Boston Harbor. It was decided that on the night of December 6, 1773 a group of Freemasons of Saint Andrew's Lodge would disguise themselves as Native Americans, clandestinely board the tea ships and toss the cargo overboard. This act of s sabotage, known historically as the Boston Tea Party, was to become an unforgiving thorn in the side of the British Crown and a full scale Revolutionary War was declared soon afterwards.

THE MILITARY LODGE

When the war with Britain was finally at hand, the North American Freemasons pooled their resources in order to organize a formidable resistance against their oppressive rulers. They chose the Rosicrucian and Master Mason George Washington to supervise the building of an army, and brought over from Germany the Freemason Baron von Steuben to instruct the virgin troops in the art of battle.

In its final form, the Colonial Army was a "Military Lodge" and a "Who's Who of American Colonial Freemasonry."[107] Over 2000 of its officers were Freemasons and out of these at least 100 were generals working directly under Washington. Many high ranking officers were also Freemasonic Grandmasters. Included in this elite list was Washington, Paul Revere and Joseph Warren, the Grandmaster of the Massachusetts Grand Lodge who became famous for sacrificing his life while leading a battalion up Bunker Hill.

THE "SERPENT" DECLARATION AND CONSTITUTION

Following their victory in the Revolutionary War, two important documents were drawn up by the Serpents of Wisdom in Philadelphia, a city which was ostensibly named after Philadelphes, the "Supreme Secret Society" of Freemasons in France. Their temporary lodge was Independence Hall, an imposing edifice originally built as a masonic temple by the Grandmaster Ben Franklin and his masonic brethren of Saint John's Lodge. The first of their documents, the Declaration of Independence, was authored principally by the Freemason Thomas Jefferson and signed primarily by high ranking Freemasons. Of the 56 signers of the document, 50 were Freemasons, including the Grandmaster John Hancock. Their other famous document, the Constitution of the United States of America, was modeled after the unwritten constitution of the Five Nations of the Iroquois, the native Serpents of North America. Much of the content of this document was acquired by Ben Franklin and other leading Freemasons who attended treaty councils of the Iroquois and learned firsthand their ancient constitution. By incorporating these native precepts into the United States' constitution, the Founding Fathers indirectly composed their own "Serpent Constitution."

THE NEW NATION OF THE PHOENIX

After the successful Philadelphia Convention, the government of the United States began to take concrete form as the country's first President, the Freemasonic Grandmaster George Washington, was sworn in by Robert Livingston, Grandmaster of the New York Lodge. With hordes of attending Freemasons cheering the inauguration, a new "Nation of the Phoenix" was officially born. Following this momentous event, a similar gathering was held in which the cornerstone of the new capital was laid. This ceremony was executed by the Grand Lodge of Maryland and several lodges under the jurisdiction of Washington's Virginia Lodge. As was his practice, President Washington attended the service in full Freemasonic ceremonial regalia, complete with apron.

THE GOVERNMENTAL LODGE

When the wheels of the United States government finally began to turn, the new institution resembled one huge Freemasonry Lodge. Most of the high ranking officials in all three branches of government were either Freemasons or allied with the principles of Freemasonry and they all gathered together within Greek temple-like structures reminiscent of the earliest Mediterranean lodges. While the Grandmaster Washington was presiding over the Executive Branch of government, John Marshall, a brother master mason from Washington's Virginia Lodge, was chairing the Judicial Branch as its first Chief Justice. The majority of lawmakers in the House of Representatives and Senate were also Freemasons.

The Freemasonry monopoly of governmental positions continued for at least the first hundred years of United States history. Following Washington as president were John Adams, Thomas Jefferson, James Madison, and James Monroe, all of whom were Freemasons. The Congress remained solidly Freemasonic until the middle of the twentieth century. According to a 1924 census, even in that year the Senate had a membership which was sixty percent Freemason. [107]

291

THE SEAL OF THE NEW NATION OF THE PHOENIX

The original design for the first seal of the "Nation of the Phoenix" was submitted by the Freemason William Barton to a congressional council in 1782. The design incorporated numerous ancient serpentine motifs, many of which had been utilized by the European Orders of Serp ents. In the upper right hand corner of the design was a pyramid motif based upon the seal used by the European Illuminati. Over this pyramid were thirteen letters, Annuit Ceoptis, meaning: "He (God) hath prospered our beginning" and written upon its base was the inscription Novus Ordo Se clorum, "New World Order," which referred to the planetary democracy being established by the Serpents of Wisdom. In the center of Barton's design was a motif comprised of two Phoenixes, one burning in flames and the other being resurrected from its ashes. On eithe r side of the Phoenixes was a human figure, possibly Barton's rendering of the "Twins."

Barton's design was eventually adopted as the first seal of the United States but with minor modifications; the revised seal contained more incidence of the sacred number of the Phoenix, 13. For example, instead of a solid structure, the pyra mid was divided into 13 courses. Barton's two Phoenixes were united into one long necked tufted Phoenix which carried in its mouth a banner of thirteen letters, E. Pluribus Unum, "out of many, one." In its talons were thirteen arrows and an olive branch (fruit of wisdom) with 13 leaves. Above the Phoenix was set 13 stars arranged in the form of a Star of David, which is another ancient symbol of the androgynous Phoenix. This original Phoenix continued as part of the national seal until 1841 when it was replaced with an eagle.

The Seal of the United States of America

The original flag of the Nation of the Phoenix also incorporated the symbology of the Phoenix. It was a flag of thirteen stars and thirteen alternating red and white stripes which represented the androgynous nature of the Phoenix (red-male, white-female). This flag evolved out of an earlier flag which had been hoisted by the Freemason Sons of Liberty. Their banner had been composed of alternating stripes and a large rattlesnake straddled across them. The snake was cut in pieces, each of which denoted one or more of the 13 colonies, thus revealing that its initial expression the US was the Nation of the Serpent.

SERPENTS OF THE "NEW WORLD"

Of the early Serpents of Wisdom who helped found the "Nation of the Phoenix" the greatest were Ben Franklin, George Washington, and Thomas Jefferson, each of whom was a Freemason and/or a Rosicrucian.

THE GRANDMASTER BEN FRANKLIN

Of all the early American Serpents who laid the groundwork for the new nation, none is more important than Ben Franklin, a Rosicrucian, Freemason and Grandmaster of numerous secret societies. Possessing the unique balance of spiritual insight and fiery ambition, Franklin was able to help the Colonial Freemasons bridge the gap between idealism and action and finally achieve independence. Leading up to the period of independence, Franklin created the Leather Apron Club, one of the earliest of Freemasonry Lodges in America. This organization was more than just a Freemasonic Lodge, however, it also served as a vehicle for "preparing members for citizenship in a yet-to-be-born nation."[108] Following the creation of the Leather Apron Club, Franklin acquired initiation into a Freemasonry lodge in Philadelphia and was later elected as Grandmaster over all lodges within the state of Pennsylvania. In order to make the Freemasonic rites uniform within the 13 colonies Franklin composed and published a series of "masonic by-laws, manuals and constitutions"[108] which served to standardize the rites and philosophies adhered to by the Colonial Serpents. In order to organize his Freemasonic brethren into a cohesive force for independence, he also published numerous treatises within which he encoded Rosicrucian wisdom along with a "call to arms" to all those ready to join in the fight for freedom. One of his occult literary vehicles was the famous *Poor Richard's Almanac*.

Franklin's activity within the Order of Serpents in North America also included membership in the Apollonian Society, an esoteric fraternity founded upon the rites and principles of the ancient Egyptian and Atlantean

The serpent flag of the 13 colonies produced by the Sons of Liberty.

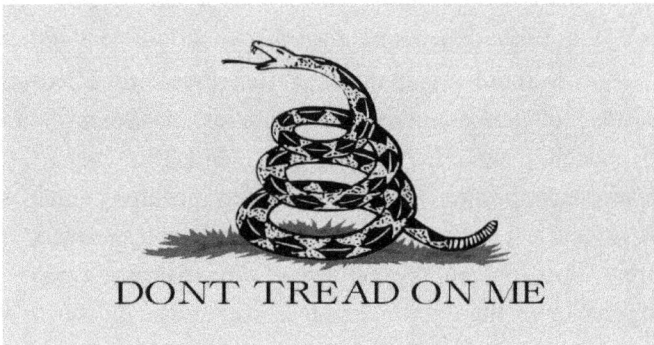

An early serpent flag of the US used by the Continental Marines during the Revolutionary War.

Paul Revere, Grand Master Freemason

George Washington, Master Mason

Benjamin Franklin, Grand Master Freemason

Freemasons George Washington and Joseph Clark, Grand Master of the Maryland Lodge, lay the conerstone of the US Capitol building in 1793.

Serpents of Wisdom. By assisting in the creation of this secret society, Franklin infused the new world with the most ancient Serpent Wisdom. Franklin was also responsible for investing the North American Order of Serpents with the occult principles of the Nine Sisters, an elite branch of European Serpents, which Franklin had been initiated into while on a diplomatic mission in France.

Franklin is well known for making his own life a reflection of the spiritual principles he preached to other masons. He led a pure spiritual life punctuated by vegetarianism and daily meditation. His prodigious philanthropic activities included the creation of numerous libraries, hospitals and firehouses. Franklin was also a crusader for the creation of positive relations with the Native Americans and eventually became an honorary member of various tribes. Through his efforts numerous treaties were created between the North American tribes and the United States government.

THE GRANDMASTER GEORGE WASHINGTON

The Freemason and Rosicrucian George Washington is considered the greatest of leaders during the United States' earliest hours. In the opinion of many Freemasons he was a savior who had taken birth specifically to father a new nation of spiritual adepts. His eventual election as first President of the United States was but titular recognition of his status as "Father" and "First Serpent" of an empire of Freemasons. At his death he was canonized by his Freemasonic brethren as a saint.

Exhibiting spiritually precocious gifts from a young age, Washington was initiated into the Lodge of Alexandria Virginia as an Entered Apprentice when just twenty years old. Two years later he became the lodge's first Master Mason and later ascended to the to the degree of Royal Arch, one of the highest of Master Mason degrees. Washington was also honorably inducted into the Mystics of Wissahickon, the Supreme Rosicrucian Council, which was instrumental in constructing both the Declertion of Independence and the US Constitution.

When Washington assumed the office of president he was simultaneously elected to serve as honorary Grandmaster over all the Freemasonic Lodges in the United States. Faced with the challenges and responsibilities of leading a new nation, Washington was, however, prevented from taking an active role in this unprecedented position.

THE BURIAL OF AN AMERICAN SERPENT

Washington's funeral was an elaborate Freemasony affair. The service was based upon the ancient Egyptian rites of resurrection and presided over

by

three Freemasons from Washington's Alexandria Lodge. At the climax of the service six Freemasonic pallbearers hoisted Washington's "sarcophagus" upon their shoulders and ceremoniously placed the casket in an "underworld" pit. Masonic symbols representing Washington's status as an American Serpent of Wisdom and "immortal" were then placed upon the casket.[87] these esoteric symbols included Washington's masonic apron, two crossed swords (representing the union of the polarity) and sprigs of acacia (an ancient symbol of immortality). In the minds and hearts of many attending Freemasons, the immortal spirit of Washington would thereafter continue to guide the development of the new country from an unseen realm.

Soon after Washington's funeral, a motion was introduced in Congress by Freemason John Marshall to erect a memorial in honor of the first president. It was decided that the most appropriate monument for the deceased Freemason was the Egyptian "frozen snake," the obelisk. Soon afterwards, in 1793, a special ceremony was held in which the Freemason Robert Mills used square, level and plumb, the symbolic tools of Freemasonry, to lay the cornerstone of what was to become a 600 foot obelisk, the tallest structure of its kind in the world.

THE FREEMASON THOMAS JEFFERSON AND THE NEW ALEXANDRIA

A Freemason, Rosicrucian and initiate of the French Order of the Nine Sisters, Thomas Jefferson was another important Serpent and founding father. He was an important contributor to both the Declaration and Constitution and under his guidance the first American university was founded in Virginia. Modeled after the Lyceum of Greece and the Alexandrian Museum, Jefferson's university resembled an ancient mystery academy of the Serpent and offered a curriculum similar to that taught within the Museum.

Jefferson was chosen by the North American Serpents to oversee the creation a "New Alexandria" because of his intellectual and spiritual achievements. He was a recognized adept of most practical sciences including chemistry, botany, anatomy, surgery, zoology, natural philosophy, medicine, mathematics, astronomy, geography, politics and law. He was also an occult genius who had studied the esoteric wisdom and communicated the ancient mysteries through secret ciphers. His work with ciphers or secret codes earned Jefferson the title of "Father of American Cryptography."

In the creation of his "New Alexandria" Jefferson brought together all the most renowned American teachers in both the scientific and religious fields.

To house the classrooms of these adepts and their students, Jefferson constructed a campus of magnificent temples similar to those of the ancient Museum. Through the proper synthesis of sacred geometrical principles, each building was designed to be an alchemical crucible for the fermentation of Serpent Wisdom. Within the walls of these temples such diverse subjects as chemistry, mathematics, religion, philosophy and metaphysics coexisted harmoniously and supportively.

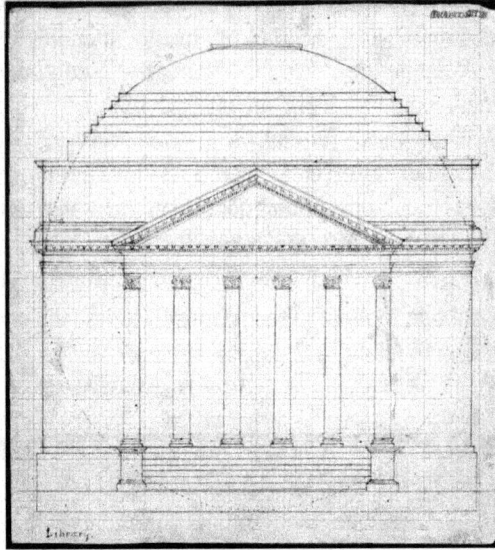

Jefferson's Blueprints

CHAPTER 20

THE NEW PLANET OF
THE PHOENIX

Although the attainment of freedom and democracy in Europe and North America was significant, it was just a stepping stone in the materialization of a "New World Order," a global democratic society. This has been the ultimate goal of all Serpents of Wisdom over the past 2000 years and one which has been continually worked for by them. Its arrival is now on the threshold.

According to a prophecy which has been held by the worldwide Order of Serpents since the beginning of the 104,000 year cycle, following the transition from the Second to the Third Millennium a Golden Age of Wisdom is destine d to dawn upon the Earth. During this New Age a greater number of people than ever before will have the opportunity to ascend to a new level of spiritual awareness and alchemically transform into Serpents of Wisdo m. All terrestrial life on the globe will also experience rapid evolution as the Earth itself is raised up and transformed into the "New Planet of the Phoenix."

COMPLETING THE 104,000 YEAR CYCLE

Collectively, the people of Earth have now finally reached the end of the 104,000 year major cycle. In fact many cycles are coming to completion at this juncture in history, including a long 6 million year cycle and many minor Serpent Cycles of time. (see Appendix 1, Part IV: Cycles of the Serpent). These minor cycles of time include the 26,000 year Precession Cycle, which began with an Aquarian Age and the sinking of Lemuria, along with 13,000 year Cycle of the Phoenix that began with the final destruction of Atlantis.

THE GRAND PHASE OF DESTRUCTION/TRANSFORMATION

Having arrived at the end of a major cycle, we can now expect to experience a grand phase of destruction and transformation which naturally occurs at the end and beginning of all major cycles of time. Such destructive periods are not new to the Earth; there have been many as numerous minor cycles have come and gone during the 104,000 year major cycle. The destructive phase which ended the first 52,000 year cycle (midpoint of 104,000 year cycle) precipitated earthquakes volcanoes and other natural disasters which split

THE WORLD OF VENUS, CHRIST AND THE PHOENIX

Since it is the power of love which unites all things together, the Fifth World will also be known as the "World of Love." The ruling planet of the age will be the planet of love, Venus, and for this reason the Fifth World will additionally be known as the "World of Venus," the "World of the Phoenix" and the "World of the Christ" Venus, the Phoenix and Christ are synonymous-all three are synonyms for love, reunion and resurrection.

The coming Fifth World of Venusian love has been prophesied by many of the major religions and cultures around the world. Numerous Native American tribes, including the Seneca and Hopi, foretell of it.27 Christian theologians conceive of it as the coming "thousand year reign of Christ" while Mesoamericans allude to it as the return of their savior, Quetzlcoatl, whose symbolic planet is Venus and whose sacred number is 13 (number of the Phoenix). The Tibetans maintain that the coming World of Love is a planetary return to the enlightened consciousness of love which has for ages reigned supreme within the mythical land of Shamballa. They, along with the Christians and Hindus, claim that the new World will dawn following the victory of a messiah (Rudra Chakrin of the Tibetans, Kalki Avatar of the Hindus, Christ of the Christians) who will ride upon a white stallion and, while leading an army of spiritual warriors, will cleanse the Earth of the inimical forces of darkness.

In astrological vernacular the Fifth World is known as the two thousand year "Age of Aquarius," an epithet which is the astrological counterpart of the "thousand year reign of Christ." Aquarius is the sign of the Son of God, the androgynous "water bearer" who blesses humankind with "water" (i.e. mana, electricity, the life force and the Holy Spirit). At the commencement of the Fifth World our Solar System will begin a new 26,000 year cycle around the Pleiades by precessing through Aquarius, the Zodiacal sign denoting new beginnings and radical change.

THE RETURN OF THE KUMARAS

The return and reign of Christ as prophesied within the *Holy Bible* also refers to the return of the Avatar Sananda Kumara, as well as the collective return of the Kumaras, the ancient Avatar spirits who were the first to teach the path to salvation during the present 104,000 year cycle.

Of course the Kumaras never completely left the Earth. Sanat Kumara, for example, has remained etherically as the Earth's monarch to monitor the spiritual evolution of humankind, while Sananda Kumara has periodically returned in physical form to act as saviors for the Earth and all her children. The prophesied "return" of the Kumaras, therefore, denotes a time when some Avatar Kumaras will be returning physically to Earth, as well as a time when the trans-physical presence of other Earth-bound Kumaras will be clearly perceived by humans. Such humans will have developed the fifth dimensional senses req uired to see and communicate with the etheric immortals directly.

The prophesied "return" of the Kumaras has one further implication. The "re turning Kumaras" refers to those humans who will become immo rtals in the coming Golden Age. When enough such enlightened humans have transformed into immortal Kumaras, the planet will once again be populated with Kumaras as it was in Golden Ages past, and the World of Venus, the World of the Kumaras, will officially commence.

THE PILLARS OF THE NEW AGE

To prepare for the New Age, both the etheric Kumaras as well as physically incarnate masters on Earth are now working to activate many important dragons' lairs upon the planetary grid. Of these vortexes, certain ones are of special importance and will serve as the foundational pillars for the New Age. These are the ancient chakras, dragon lairs and Courts of the King, the Planetary Logos. They include Mount Kailas in Tibet, the Earth's Crown Chakra, as well as Sedona, Arizona the Planetary Root Chakra. They also include Giza, Egypt, Glastonbury, England and Macchu Picchu/ Lake Titicaca in Peru.

Another "pillar" of the New Age now being activated is the United States of America, a country which has, since being founded by the Serpents of Wisdom, led the world in the fight for planetary democracy. The United States' number, 13, and its earliest symbol, the Phoenix, have designated the country as the place where the Phoenix, the bird of freedom, will initially spread its wings before subseq uently embracing the entire planet. The country is also destined to be a place where the united Atlantean/Lemurian Culture will emerge. Within the United States, Earth's perennial melting pot, all polarities will unite and the androgynous flame for the new World of Venus will be kindled.

303

CHAPTER 21

BECOMING A
SERPENT OF WISDOM

NOW IS THE TIME

Throughout the preceding pages of this text many ancient forms of spiritual practice for uniting the polarity, awakening the inner fire serpent and purifying and fully utilizing the immortal Dragon Body with all its wisdom and power have been introduced. As history reveals to us these practices have been consistently disseminated around the globe by the Serpents of Wisdom to enlighten humanity. Such practices are now becoming increasingly popular as the current Serpent Cycle completes its destruction/transformation phase, and the polarity within the Earth as well as within our own bodies can more easily unite than at any other time. Should we decide to participate in the current trend towards planetary transformation, each one of us has a unique opportunity to take a huge evolutionary step to becoming a Serpent of Wisdom.

DISCIPLINES TO UNITE THE POLARITY AND AWAKEN THE SERPENT FIRE

Many of the spiritual practices mentioned within the text for becoming a Serpent of Wisdom are described in detail in the following pages. To initiate a transformational regimen, a seeker can adopt those yogic practices which are best suited to his or her lifestyle and temperament. For example, a seeker possessing a loving temperament but not especially drawn to a disciplined lifestyle may be attuned to the spiritual rites of the Bhakti Path, the path of love. By contrast, an aspirant with a disciplined temperament may be attracted to those practices which require punctual regularity for their success, such as the yoga disciplines of asana, pranayama and meditation.

UNITING THE POLARITY THROUGH
THE PATH OF LOVE

For reuniting the polarity and awakening the fire serpent, the Serpents of Wisdom have for ages recommended the Bhakti Marga, the path of love, as the quickest and safest route. This path was originally brought to Earth by the

305

Venusian Masters, the Kumaras, and then taught by them throughout the 104,000 year cycle. This path includes chanting, the cultivation of unconditional love through service to humanity, and the worship of a deity. A seeker's deity can be his or her spiritual Guru and/or any Serpent Son of God such as Christ or K-rist, Krishna, the Kaberoi and the Kumara(s).

A Bhakta's daily expression of love for self and others naturally unites the polarity within his or her physical body and awakens the androgynous serpent fire. Such a seeker successfully raises the transformative fire from its seat at the base of the spine and experiences an all consuming "fire of love." To expedite this yogic fire a traveler on the path of love can continuously repeat the name of the Masters of Love, "Kumara," as well as chants which glorify his or her Guru or some incarnation of God.

UNITING THE POLARITY WITH YOGIC POSTURES

Through the asanas of Hatha Yoga the male/female principles naturally reunite and the fire of yoga is kindled. Most any combination of postures, when practiced regularly, are efficacious in clearing the subtle energy vessels and arousing the Kundalini from its seat within the etheric body. Once the Kundalini is awakened, those postures which stretch the spine, such as the cobra, plough, and cat stretch, are effective for strengthening the spine for sitting meditation so the serpent fire can easily move upwards.

UNITING THE POLARITY WITH CONTROLLED BREATHING

Pranayama, or the Yoga of controlled breathing patterns, unite the polarity and awaken the Kundalini at its seat within the Pranamaya Kosha, the sheath or body of prana. Effective pranayama techniques includes alternate nostril exercises which balance and unite the Ida and Pingala Nadis (conduits of the male and female principles) as well as breathing exercises to awaken and fan the inner fire, such as Bastrika Breath (bellows breath) or Breath of Fire.

Alternate Nostril Breathing-With the index and middle fingers of the right hand hold the right nostril closed while inhaling through the left nostril for the mental count of 4. Then close both nostrils (thumb of right hand closes left nostril) for the mental count of 8. Now open the right nostril and, while exhaling, keep the left nostril closed with the thumb for the mental count of 8. While keeping the left nostril closed inhale through the right nostril for the mental count of 4. Continue back and forth between nostrils this way for a couple of minutes.

Bastrika Breath or Breath of Fire—Start by fully exhaling the breath through the nostrils. Then perform short exhalations while forcing the remaining breath out of the lungs. If this part of the exercise is performed right, the stomach should contract with each short exhalation and the nose and stomach together will simulate the action of a bellows. Following 20 repetitions of this bellows breath, fully exhale through the nose once again and then follow it with a long inhale which fills the stomach and abdomen to capacity. Hold the breath for a short time then slowly exhale. Perform this exercise twice, then meditate.

UNITING THE POLARITY
WITH SOUND VIBRATION

The production of inner sound vibrations through the repetition of mantras is another effective way of reuniting the polarity and raising the Serpent Fire. Many mantras, such as Om Namah Shivaya and Om Mani Padme Hum, incorporate syllables and sounds which correspond to the male/female principles and thereby promote their reunion within the body.

Om Namah Shivaya: Om Namah Shivaya is the name of Shakti, the Serpent Goddess, and its repetition works to awaken her from her slumber at the base of the spine. The mantra incorporates words and syllables which correspond to the male/female principles as well as to the five elements, the components of the Goddess's universal body. It therefore has the power to both unite the polarity as well as purify the five elements as they exist within the physical body. Om vibrates the aether element; Na vibrates the earth element; Ma vibrates the water element; Shiva vibrates the fire element; and Vayu or Vaya vibrates the air element. Om Namah Shivaya can be repeated for meditation, while taking a stroll in the woods, exercising etc. During meditation this mantra should be repeated mentali y once on the in breath and then once on the out breath. The more it is repeated with faith, the stronger it becomes as a vehicle for deep meditation and transformation.

Hamsa or Só ham: Both Hamsa and So'ham are composed of two syllables, one for each principle, and can therefore naturally unite the polarity. Both mantras are derived from the Sanskrit Ahamsa, meaning "I am That" or "I am everything," i.e., the consciousness of androgynous Serpent of Wisdom. Hamsa means "swan" in Sanskrit. Through its repetition, the s eeker transforms from an "ugly duckling" into a beautiful "swan."

The mantras Hamsa and So'ham are primarily used for meditation as their repetition is synchronized with the subtle movement of the breath. When mentally repeating So'ham the yogi should breath in on So and out on Ham. When repeating Hamsa, the yogi breathes in on Ham and out on Sa. By their rhythmic repetition the Ida and Pingla Nadis and their associated male and female principles become balanced and eventually unite. After long practice with either mantra, Kumbaka or breath retention spontaneously occurs within the abdomen as So-ham or Ham-sa dissolves into Aum, the name or sound of the androgynous Dragon.

OM Mani Padme Hum: The ancient Tibetan mantra of the Serpent Nagararjuna can catalyze the union of the opposing principles within the physical body. Ma-ni activates the female principle, Pa-dme stimulates the male principle, and Hum unites the two principles at the heart.

Amaru Meru: A fourth mantra for awakening the inner serpent fire is Amaru Meru. Amaru is an ancient Quechuan name for serpent and Meru is an ancient designation for "center." Together they summon the serpent in the center of the body, the Kundalini, to awaken from its slumber and climb the tree of life to the top of the head. The mantra can be repeated mentally at a rapid pace for a couple of minutes at the start of meditation to stimulate the Fire Serpent or it can be synchronized with the in and out breaths for achieving transcendence.

Kumara: The repetition of the mantra of love, Ku-ma-ra, unites the polarity as "ma" and "ra" within the body's center of androgyny, the Heart Chakra, as it awakens the inner fountain of love.

MEDITATIONSECRETSFOR UNITINGTHE POLARITY

Yogic meditation is an easy and effective practice for uniting the polarity and awakening the Fire Serpent. A cross-legged position in which the two legs cross and/or simply touch can be adopted to unite the right and left, male and female halves of the body. When the two sides of the body unite, the inner principles are united and the Kundalini is naturally activated.

Any cross-legged position can be employed for yogic meditation but the most efficacious is the full lotus, the sitting posture in which the left and right feet are placed on top of the opposing thighs. The full lotus is effective because it not only unites the opposites but also locks the life force within the body, heats it up, and then assists in the awakening of the Kundalini. Also, with the left leg on top of the right, the posture promotes control ofthe active side (right side) by the inactive or meditative side (left side). While sitting in this or any other cross-legged posture the yogi can further unite the opposites and control the active by the inactive by placing the left hand on top of the right and resting them in the lap.

Taoist meditative practices for reuniting the polarity perfectly compliment and facilitate the yogic positions. While in a cross-legged position, Taoist Masters prescribe uniting the polarity by crossing the eyes (right eye-male, left eye-female) and touching the tongue to the upper palate. The eyes can be crossed by staring at the tip of the nose or closing them and focusing upon the "mystical square inch" or "third eye" area between the eye brows. Touching the tongue to the upper palate unites the principal yin channel which runs up the front of the body, the Ren Meridian, with the principal yang channel which runs up the back, the Du Meridian, thereby creating a circuit of energy, the Microcosmic Orbit.

Another secret to uniting the polarity through meditation is to meditate between the sacred hours of 4-6 A.M. This time period, known as Brahma Mahurta (the hour of Brahma), is considered by Yogis and Masters around the world as the optimum time for meditation because at this time of the night a person is naturally breathing equally in and out of both nostrils. Normally a person favors the right or left nostril and this causes either the male or female principle to be predominant in the body. By breathing equally through both nostrils, the two principles become balanced and naturally unite.

POLARITY UNION THROUGH HEMISPHERIC SYNCHRONIZATION

New Age meditation technology (audio and video) unites the polarity by balancing and uniting the left (center of male principle) and right (center of female principle) hemispheres of the brain. Normally the two hemispheres are out of synch with each other and produce dissimilar brain wave patterns. By sending rhythmic signals through the auricular and optic nerves, New Age technologies which utilize blinking lights and repetitive sound signals can synchronize the patterns of both hemispheres and thereby unite them. When the hemispheres are united, the entire brain commences to produce Theta brain wave patterns, the patterns associated with deep meditation and union with Spirit.

FIRE PRODUCING TOOLS FOR POLARITY UNION AND KUNDALINI ACTIVATION

Another New Age (or very "Old Age") tool for re-uniting the opposites and awakening the fire Serpent is a pyramid. This geometric structure, whose name means "fire in the middle," unites the three dimensional shape of a triangle, the tetrahedron (symbolizing the male principle), with the three dimensional shape of the square, the cube (symbolizing the female principle), to generate the frequency of the androgynous Fire Serpent. When meditating within a pyramid, the structure's inner, transformative frequencies assist in the union of the polarity and the awakening of the Kundalini.

A good place to meditate is the center of a pyramid, the location of a standing wave in the shape of an upward moving Serpent spiral. When sitting with the back aligned with this ascending spiral, the awakening of the Kundalini and its ascension up the spine naturally occurs. For the quickest results, a metal pyramid made out of copper, silver, or gold should be used.If one chooses to sleep under a pyramid, a structure made of wood should be utilized.

Crystals compliment pyramids and are also excellent tools for uniting the polarity and activating the Kundalini. On the molecular level crystals are "frozen fire serpents" and composed of tetrahedrons arranged in spiraling double helixes. The double helixes represent the male and female principles which are united as fire (the tetrahedron is symbolic of the fire element). Similar to the side angle of the Great Pyramid at Giza, Egypt, the termination angle of a crystal is 52 degrees, a special angle to promote transformation.

When placing crystals upon the body surface, especially the chakra centers, these tools can assist in the transformational process by moving blocked energy, releasing stagnant emotions, and activating the Kundalini. They can also be placed in gridwork patterns around the body and thereby unite the polarity and awaken the fire serpent. One of the best patterns to use for this purpose is the geometrical form of polarity union, the Star of David. In this arrangement the terminations of the crystals would point inwards towards the person.

To enhance the activating effects of both crystals and pyramids, they can united to form simple temples. While sitting or laying down within a pyramid, a person could surround himself or herself with crystals and place one upon each chakra center. Other modalities for awakening and/or moving energy, such as pranayama or mantra, could then be employed.

UNITING THE POLARITY AT DRAGONS'LAIRS

Meditation, yoga, or other spiritual disciplines observed within the parameters of vortexes or dragons' lairs, i.e, power places upon the Earth's grid where the opposing principles unite and produce an upward moving spiral, will catalyze the union of opposites within the body and raise the inner Fire Serpent. Exceptionally powerful dragon lairs include: Sedona, Arizona; Mt .Shasta, California; Giza, Egypt; Chichen Itza or Palenque, Mexico; Glastonbury, Avebury and Stonehenge in England; and Lake Titicaca and Machu Picchu, Peru. Macchu Picchu and the other vortexes in Peru are especially significant for initiations during these end times as they awaken the female principle, the principle which has laid semi-dormant within many souls for thousands of years. When the female principle becomes balanced with the male, the two principles unite and awaken the Kundalini. Mt. Shasta and Boynton Canyon in Sedona are also especially important vortexes at this time in history. Both places are perfectly balanced vortexes (vortexes are usually classified as predominantly yin or yang and work to activate the corresponding principle within a person) and can therefore balance and unite the male and female principles while opening the heart center. Sedona is also efficacious in awakening Kundalini now because as the Planetary Root Chakra it is currently fully activated.

KUNDALINI ACTIVATION THROUGH PRAYER

For activating the Kundalini the power of prayer cannot be overemphasized. When a supplicant prays in earnest to God for wisdom and spiritual growth, the God/Goddess responds by showering the person with blessings in the form of Serpent power, Shakti or the Holy Spirit. If a person's desire for liberation is correspondingly strong, the Holy Spirit will awaken the inner Fire Serpent and lead it to the top of the head.

HOLY MASTERS,
TRANSMITTERS OF SERPENT POWER

If a seeker proves his or her desire and worthiness to God, he or she may be directed to a true spiritual Master, one who has merged his individual identity with Spirit and can guide a disciple to full god-realization. Such a Siddha, or Perfected Master, is a vehicle for God's Shakti or Serpent Power and can easily awaken a seeker's Kundalini via a thought, word, look or touch.. Some Siddhas are also Jagadgurus, or "World Gurus," and have desciples all over the globe. They include Sri Mata Amritanandamayi Devi, one of the greatest living Mahanagas of Kerala, South India, who annually tours the globe and h as an active ashram in San Ramon, California, as well as Swami Chidvilasananda or Gurumayi, the successor to the great Shaktipat Master, Swami Muktananda Paramahamsa, whose ashrams are located in Ganeshpuri, India, South Fallsburg, New York, and Oakland, California.

LIVE WITH BALANCE AND UNITE THE POLARITY

One final way of uniting the polarity is by living in astate of balance. If you are too extroverted and outgoing, strive to become more introverted and reflective. If you are too male (aggresive, rational, dominating), strive to become more female (passive, emotional, caring). You will know when you are out of balance because parts of your self, as well as the activities in your life, will be in continual conflict.

When you live in balance, the male and female principles naturally balance and harmonize with each other and you will eventually become androgynous. With androgyny comes the awakening of the transformative serpent fire and, ultimately, union with Spirit.

311

APPENDIX I: THE TEACHINGS OF THE SERPENTS OF WISDOM

THE CREATION, PRESERVATION, AND DESTRUCTION OF THE UNIVERSE

Text in bold
with
Commentary in normal type

THE PRALAYA: BEFORE THE CREATION ...

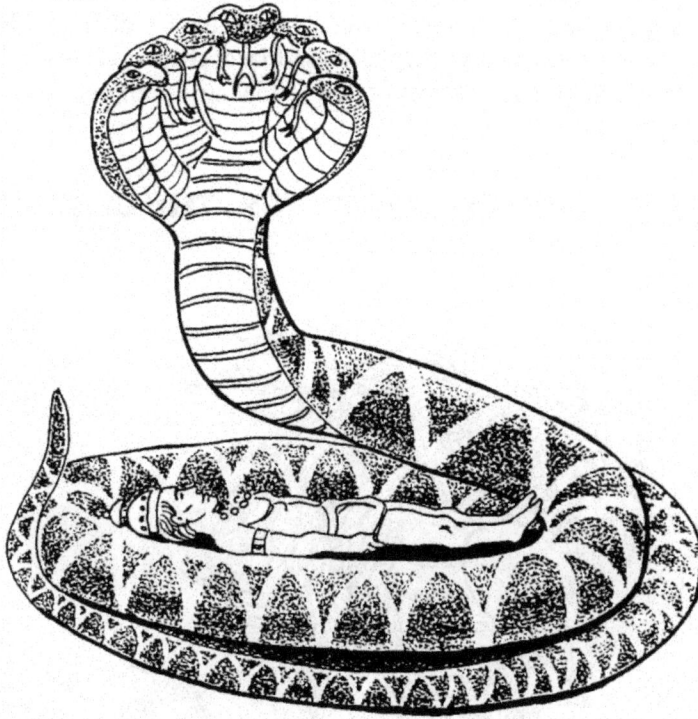

1. There was nothing but silence, a cosmic void. The sleeping God rested in a peaceful, potential state.

"... while sleeping Narayana reposed within his regal coils, Shesha (the seven headed serpent) drifted serenely upon the placid waters"- Hindu Puranas

The above passage taken from the Hindu Puranas or legends is a symbolic reference to the "void" or dormant period which preceded the creation of the universe. In India this pre-creation phase is k nown as the Pralaya. During the Pralaya Phase the universe existed in a potential state. Only infinite consciousness was present.

The Hindus symbolically portray the Pralaya Phase as a scenario in which Narayana, the sleeping God, rests peacefully upon the back of a serpent which floats upon the "waters." The sleeping Narayana represents the "sleeping" or dormant male spark latent within pure consciousness which has yet to impregnate the Goddess (the "waters") and initiate the creation of the universe. His serpent raft is representative of the crystallized shapes which will coalesce out of the Goddess's essence or cosmic sea following its impregnation and then populate the physical universe.

PART I: THE CREATION OF THE UNIVERSE

THE BIRTH OF THE PRIMAL SERPENT

1.1 In the beginning of time, the sleeping God awoke.

The God's awakening impregnated the Goddess and their co-habitation set in motion a new cycle of time.

Soon a contraction occurred upon the surface of the cosmic sea. Waves churned and the matrix of the infinite ocean began to coalesce and congeal into a distinct form.

The Primal Serpent, the beast which had existed in a potential state during the Pralaya, suddenly reared its head and rose up out of the "'deep."

"All was immobility and silence in the darkness, only the creator, the maker, the denominator, the serpent covered with feathers, they who engender, they who create, were on the waters as an ever increasing light. They were surrounded by green and *blue.*"-*Popul Vuh* (Mayan scripture)

"... and darkness was upon the face of the deep. And the Elohim Creators moved upon the face of the waters."- *Holy Bible*

The above scenario describes the birth of the Primal Serpent out of the cosmic waters during the initial creation stages of the universe, an event which could be found at the beginning of many creation myths throughout the ancient world. The early Egyptians of Thebes, for example, began their creation myth with the birth of the Primal Serpent Ammon Kematef, a reptillian creature who swam within the cosmic sea and assisted in the creation of the universe. Their neighbors at Korn Ombo venerated the Primal Serpent as the serpent/crocodile Sebek, "the first of all divinities" who came forth "out of the primordial Nu" (the cosmic ocean). According to the early Mesopotamian creation myths, at the beginning of time the Primeval Serpent Enki or Ea, the "house of water," arose out of the Apsu, a Sumerian name for the cosmic sea. Native American creation myths also commence with the birth of a Primal Serpent, usually an alligator or huge reptile, which arises out of the cosmic waters, becomes stationary, and eventually provides a solid land mass for humankind to walk and build their homes upon.

THE PRIMAL SERPENT WAS THE ANDROGYNOUS CHILD

1.2 Formed out of the union of the God and Goddess, the Primal Serpent was an androgynous offspring, both a "Daughter" and a "Son." Its timeless symbol is the androgynous cross.

315

Since it was the united product of the universal male and female principles (the God and Goddess), cultures around the world depicted the Primal Serpent as androgenous and endowed it with both male and female features. In this regard, the Mayan Primal Serpent of the Popul Vuh incorporated within its form the dual characteristics of a snake body (symbol of the female "material" principle) and avian blue-green feathers (symbol of the male "spiritual" principle).

In China the Primal Dragon was a genderless creature, the androgynous union of Yin and Yang (the oriental designations for the female and male principles). Its symbol was the "androgynous" pearl which is formed underwater (female principle) by the constant friction or heat caused by the movement of a grain of sand (male principle). In Mesopotamia the androgyny of the Primal Dragon, Enki, was denoted by the

The androgynous Dragon Enki

two animals comprising its singular body, the goat and the fish. The goat half of Enki's body represented the male fecundating spark while its fish tail denoted water and the female principle. The Egyptians, Hindus and Mesoamericans depicted their Primal Serpent's androgyny by representing it as an alligator or crocodile shape. The amphibious alligator was considered to be of a dual nature because of its tendency to spend half its time in water and half on land. It was also dual by virtue of possessing two aortas and two skeletons (the second one is formed by its outer shell). The Hindu alligator was appropriately named Maka-ra. Ma signifies the female principle, ra denotes the male principle and the syllable ka refers to their union as the Primal Serpent.

As the union of the male and female principles the Primal Serpent was

316

a Son or Daughter of the God and Goddess and its symbol was the cross, the pre-eminent symbol of polarity union. In India the Primal Serpent was worshipped as Skanda, the seven headed serpent, who was the Son of Shiva and Shakti, the universal male and female principles; one of its symbols was the cross. To represent the intimate relationship between the cross and the Primal Serpent, the Mesopotamians, Egyptians, Greeks, Hebrews, Hindus and Mesoameric ans commonly coiled images of the primeval reptile upon some version of the cross. In India, the Primal Serpent was often coiled around a Shiva Lingum, a Hindu version of the cross, and ornamented with crosses and swastikas. The Mesopotamians and Hebrews also customarily attached images of the Primal Serpent to their crosses. The most famous of such motifs was the Mesopotamian Enki perched upon a cross and the Brazen Serpent of Moses which was set upon a tau cross. The Mesoamericans ornamented their temples and the pages of their creation codices (scriptures) with Primal Serpents slithering along the axes of Tau crosses. The Tau cross was the symbol of the Quiche Maya Primal Serpent, Gucumatz, and the Prima l Serpent of the Itza Mayas, Itzamna.

THE PRIMAL SERPENT WAS ALSO THE SERPENT GODDESS, THE FIRST CONTRACTION AND FORM OF SPIRIT

1.3 **Since the androgynous Primal Serpent condensed out of the "female" cosmic ocean it was alternately a Serpent "Goddess." As the first contraction of infinite Spirit, this androgynous Serpent "Goddess" was the first form of God/ Spirit and the vehicle of the deity's wisdom and power.**

T he androgynous Primal Serpent was a Serpent "Goddess" because it precipitated out of the "female" cosmic waters. T he Primal Serpent was also referred to as the Serpent Goddess because, in some cultures, the cosmic waters were recognized to be symbolic of the infinite sea of consciousness which was not female, but pure "male" Spirit. Any emanation or contraction out of this "male" sea was judged to be material and "female."

As the first contraction out of the "sea" of Spirit the Primal Serpent Goddess was the first form of God and the vehicle of the deity's infinite wisdom and three powers of creation, preservation and destruction. T he Shavite philosophers of India referred to the Primal Serpent as the Goddess Shakti, an emanation or contraction from the infinite Spirit, the "male" God, Shiva. T hrough the vehicle of his power or Shakti, Shiva created the universe. ln parts of Mesopotamia the Primal Serpent was known as Inanna, the Great Goddess, whose special symbol was a serpent coiled upon a staff. Goddess Inanna was venerated as "the serpent deity who emanated from the heaven god Anu." In Egypt the theologians of Memphis held that the Primal Serpent was Sekhmet, meaning "the power,"while other cosmologists in the Nile Delta maintained that it was Uadjet, the Serpent Goddess which emanated from the eye (i.e., the all-seeing consciousness) of the male Solar God, Ra. Uadjet symbolized the power and wisdom of Ra and her symbol, the snake, became the classic hieroglyph for "Goddess" throughout Egypt. Among the Jews and Greek Gnostics the contraction of Spirit as the Serpent Goddess was known as Shekinah, meaning "light" and "presence," as well as Chokmah and Sophia, two names which mean the "Wisdom of God."

THE PRIMAL SERPENT WAS
THE CREATOR OF THE UNIVERSE

1.4   The androgynous Primal Serpent "Goddess" which arose from out of the cosmic sea became the Creator of the Universe.

According to the ancient theologians around the world, once the Primal Serpent arose from the cosmic sea it proceeded to become the Creator of the Universe. In Egyptian Thebes this Creator Serpent, Ammon, was worshipped both as the serpent Ammon Irta of Lux.or, he/she "who made the Earth," and the serpent Ammon Kematuf of Karnak, he/she "who has made his time." In Heliopolis the Creator Serpent was worshipped as Atum, the "nothing and the everything." The Greek Gnostics of the Hellenistic culture, heirs to the Egyptians, adopted the serpent form of Ammon as their Creator and renamed it Kneph and/or the Agathodeamon. Their close relatives, the Hermetics and Templars, ushered the Egyptian Serpent Creator into their traditions under the names of Pymander and Baphomet respectively.

The Sumerian theologians of Eridu recognized the Creator of the Universe as their beloved androgenous serpent Ea or Enki which was born from the Apsu or cosmic ocean. The Austrialian Aborigines knew it as the Rainbow Serpent which lived in a water hole, and the Mediterranean Pelasgians venerated it as the Primal Serpent Ophion, progeny of the primeval sea. The Bon Shamans of Tibet conceived the creator to be Chidag Nagpo, the Primal Dragon which hatched out of the Cosmic Egg.

Among the Itza Mayas of Yucatan Mexico, the Creator was the Dragon Itzamna, "House of the Reptile." According to their neighbors, the Nahuatls of central Mexico, it was the androgenous dragon goddess Coatlicue, "She of the

Serpent Skirt" and among the Mayan tribes of Central America it was Quetzlcoatl, the "Plumed Serpent," and Huracan, the slithering, spiralling serpent.

The coastal Indians of ancient Peru depicted the Creator of the Universe as a great sea dragon which had its home in a large sea shell. From its body issued forth the four primary gods of their sacred pantheon: the Sun, Moon and a divine couple, the mother and father of all humankind. The Yaruro people of Venezuela claim that their Creator Serpent, Puana, created the world, the trees, the flowers and Kuna, the common ancestress of all humans. Tribes all over Africa worship their beloved Creator Serpent in the form of a live Python. When a native of this continent encounters a python in his path he respectfully acknowledges the creature by stating "you are my father and my mother."

TIIE PRIMAL SERPENT WAS THE DIVINE MIND AND ARCHITECT

1.5   As the vehicle of the Divine Mind, the Primal Serpent Creator held the blueprint of creation. It was, therefore, the "Architect of the Universe."

In Egypt, the various manifestations of the Creator Serpent, i.e., Ammon, Atum, and Chnoumis were all venerated as embodiments of the Divine Mind and each was referred to as the "Architect of the Universe." From Chnoumis evolved the word Nous, a term for the Divine Mind and "Architect" within the philosophy of Neoplatonism.

In Mesopotamia the embodiment of the Divine Mind and the Architect of the Universe was the water dragon, Ea or Enki, the "god of wisdom." Ba's home, the cosmic waters, was the Apsu, meaning the "dwelling place of knowledge." The Greek Gnostics recognized the Architect of the Universe and the wisdom of God to be embodied in the Goddess Sophia, a creatress who appeared to Adam and Eve as the "Serpent on the Tree" in the Garden of Eden. The practitioners of Voodoo pay homage to their Serpent Creator Danbalah while acknowledging him to be the Divine Mind and "Grand Cosmic Architect of the Universe." Other cultures which recognize their Serpent Creators to be a divine Architect include the Chinese, the Hindus, the Greeks and the Mesoamericans.

THE VIBRATION OF THE PRIMAL SERPENT WAS THE CREATIVE WORD, AUM

1.6   As the first emanation of God, the Primal Serpent Creator was the

319

vibration, sound, or "Word' of contracted Spirit. Through his word God brought forth all the forms of Creation.

The primeval creative Word was the vibration or sound of Spirit and the frequency/name of the Primal Serpent. This divine Word was Aumor some version of it. The Christians recognized the primal Word to be Amen and St. John maintained in his Gospel that it existed at the beginning of time "with God and it was God." Among the Egyptians the primal Word was Ammon (the name of the Theban Serpent god); and it was Aum, the Shabda Brahman or "God in the form of a word," among the Hindus. The three letters of Aum can be thought of as representing the three powers of the Primal Serpent, i.e., creation, preservation and destruction.

Around the world it is claimed that through God's Word the physical universe came into existence. In a series of famous passages found at the beginning of Genesis in the Holy Bible, God speaks the Heavens and Earth into existence. Echoing this Genesis motif, Sumerian cosmology maintained that the universe came into existence through Mummu, God's word spoken by the Creator Serpent Enki. A similar scenario is depicted by Egyptian tomb reliefs which show God's vehicle, the Great Serpent, with its mouth agape and shouting forth the Creative Word. Other Egyptian tombs have motifs of the Phoenix Dragon with his mouth opened wide and the vibration of the creative "breath of life" flowing from his throat. This creative "breath" eventually solidified into the physical shapes of the universe.

According to Hindu cosmology once Aum is spoken by God it divides or shatters into the many sub-sound s. These sub-sounds, which are the sounds and letters of the Sanskrit alphabet, eventually crystallize into the physical shapes of the universe. According to Gnostic philosophy, during the creative process the primal word Aum, Ammon or Amen splits into Alpha and Omega, the first and last letters of the Greek alphabet. These two letters, as well as the letters between them, represent the sub-sounds which crystallize into the shapes of the physical universe.

THE SEVEN PARTS OF THE PRIMAL SERPENT WERE THE SEVEN CREATORS

1.7   There were seven parts or aspects of the Primal Serpent Creator. They worked together as the Seven Creators.

In the opening chapter of the *Popul Vuh,* the Quiche Mayans referred to the Primal Serpent as a group of entities: "they who engender, they who create." This group of Creators are the seven parts, divisions or aspects of the Primal

Creator Serpent which worked together to create of the universe. In a similar passage of *Genesis* in the Holy Bible, the Creator God of the Hebrews is referred to as the Elohim, a plural designation, thereby also denoting a collective of deities involved in the creation of the cosmos.

The Australian Aborigines maintain that the universe was created by a group of gods which issued out of their father/mother, Wondjina, the Rainbow Serpent. The Greek Hermetics claimed that their Creator Serpent, Pymander, fashioned "Seven Governors" out of itself while the Greek Gnostics claimed that the Seven Creators, i.e., Ildaboath and his six brothers, were created by their mother, the Serpent Goddess Sophia. The fire serpent of Memphis Egypt, Ptah, was assisted in his work of creating the universe by his seven creative progeny, the Khnemmu.

The Seven Creators or seven aspects of the singular Serpent Goddess which emanates out of the "male" Spirit are alternatively referred to in creation myths as the "Seven Creative Sons" which emanate out of the Solar Spirit. In Egypt the Seven Creative Spirits were the "Seven Wise Ones" who emanated out of the eye of the Solar Spirit Ra. Within the Christian tradition the Seven Sons were Seven Creative Archangels, progeny of the Solar Spirit YHVH. In Mesopotamian legend Seven Ancient Elders assisted the Solar Spirit, Marduck, in the creation of the universe. The Satta-Kuro-Dzusagai-ai, a group of seven creative Sons, similarly assisted the Yakut sky god of Asia as he manifested the solid farms of the physical universe.

1.8 The seven parts or aspects of the Primal Serpent Creator are found represented in serpent iconography around the world as seven heads, tails, or curves attached to the Serpent's tortuous body.

In many parts of the world the seven aspects or creative principles of the Primal Serpent are represented as seven heads attached to a serpent's body. Temples throughout India are populated with statues and portraits of the Primal Serpent, Shesha, with seven heads. The Primal Serpent Enki of Mesopotamia can be found seven-headed on seals from Akkad which date to the third millennium B. C. The Biblical dragon, the "Beast" of the *Book of Revelation,* is portrayed as possessing seven heads and ten horns.

The seven aspects of the Primal Serpent are sometimes denoted by the seven curves or coils incorporated in the body of a serpent effigy. At Serpent

Mound in Ohio the ancient Native Americans constructed an effigy with seven curves to its body. At 700 feet long (7+0=7), this serpent monument is the largest in the world. A serpent with seven curves to its body and coiled around a fiery red lion (symbolic of the Serpent emanating from the Solar Spirit) constituted the image of Zurvan, a Creator God found in the ancient religion of Mithra, and a serpent with seven coils was pictured wrapped around the Cosmic Egg of the Greek Orphites. The shadow of a serpent composed of seven triangles is worshipped by the Mayan peoples as it slithers down the steps of the Temple of Quetzlcoatl, the Plumed Serpent, at Chichen Itza, Mexico, during the spring and fall equinoxes.

An interesting association between the Serpent and the number seven can be found in the western system of numerology. There are seven letters in Serpent, numerologically all the letters in the word reduce to a seven, and the word pivots around the "p" which has its own value of seven. Interestingly, the word for seven in the French language is sept (pronounced set), which appears to be related to an Egyptian name for the Serpent, Set.

The Primal Serpent coiled 7x around the Cosmic Egg

OUR SERPENT CREATOR IS THE SEVEN SISTERS, THE PLEIADES

1.9   The seven aspects of the Primal Serpent Creator were anciently worshipped in the heavens as the seven stars of the Pleiades.

Collectively, the seven stars of the Pleiades were recognized by the ancients as a manifestation in our part of the galaxy of the Primal Serpent

Creator, and therefore venerated by them as the septenary Serpent Goddess. The Mayans paid homage to the Pleiades as a manifestation of the great Celestial Serpent; their name for the stars, Tzab, denoted both the Pleiades as well as a rattlesnake's rattles. The Greek Gnostics referred to the star group as the "Seven Pillars" of Sofia, their Serpent Creatress, which was an embodiment of the "Wisdom of God."

In the Bible the Pleiades are represented as the seven creative stars in the right hand, the creative hand, of God. In *The Keys of Enoch*, ex-NASA scientist J.J. Hurtak states that the Pleiades are the Divine Mind and Creator for our corner of the universe. He contends that they determine the physical shapes of the galaxy.

SEQUENTIAL STEPS TAKEN BY THE PRIMAL SERPENT WHEN IT CREATED THE UNIVERSE

1.10   When it began to coalesce out of the cosmic sea the body of the Primal Serpent took the form of snake-like udulating waves. These serpentine wave patterns united to form whirlpools.

The Primal Serpent was created by waves of energy, perturbations upon the cosmic sea of consciousness, which united to form a whirlpool. This cosmic whirlpool was the "progeny" of two opposing waves or "currents," manifestations of the opposing male and female principles, which united to produce the androgenous Serpent. While referring to the Primal Serpent's whirlpool form, one tribe of Mayas called their primordial Creator Serpent Huracan, the serpent with the whirlpool body. From Huracan evolved the word Hurricane. Modem physics also refers to the Primal Serpent and its whirlpool shape when it asserts that the form taken by subtle energy, the primeval form of matter, is that of a whirlpool or spiral.

1.11   The basis of the whirlpool form of the Primal Serpent was the geometric spiral.

Mathematics, particularly that branch of it known as sacred geometry, recognizes the spiral to be the primary form of the whirlpool. In mathematical language it also recognizes the spiral to be the foundational form of the Primal Serpent. The mathematical constant which determines the spiral, Phi, can be derived by dividing the esoteric value of the universal male principle, 666, into the esoteric value assigned to the universal female principle, 1078. The result, 1.61, mathematically represents the impregnation of the female principle by the male principle and the creation of the Primal Serpent. While commenting on Phi the sacred geometricist R.A. Schwaller de Libicz remarks: "it is the fire of life... the Logos (the Word and Mind of God) of the Gospel of St. John."[87]

THE SERPENT ON THE TREE OR CROSS IS A SYMBOL OF CREATION

1.12   The whirlpool/spiraling form of the Primal Serpent grew or expanded in all four directions. The symbol of this movement is the classical "Serpent on the Cross" motif.

The motif of the spiraling serpent traveling in all four directions is represented in iconography as a serp ent coiling its slinky body up on the four shafts of a cross. Such motifs are common in Asia, Europe and the Americas.

1.13   The substance comprising the expanding body of the Primal Serpent was energy, the etheric "water" of the cosmic ocean, which is called "Astral Fluid," "Fiery Water" and "Life Force."

Most all ancient cultures adop ted a name for the substance which comp rised the body of the exp anding Primal Serp ent, including "astral fluid," "life force," and "fiery water."The Hindus refer to the p rimordial substance of the Primal Serp ent as Prana, and one of their creation myths begins with "first came Prana." Aum, the name and vibration of their Primal Serp ent, is sometimes referred to as the Pranava, "made of prana." The Egyptians knew the life force as Ka (the letter or sound of K is an archetyp al sound syllable of the Primal Serpent throughout the world) and personified it as their Fire Serp ent, Ptah, the smith god who created the universe at his anvil. The Chinese refer to it as Chi (p ronounced Ki by the Jap anese) and believe it to be the form of the "First born" of the Tao or Spirit, i.e., the Primal Dragon. (Note: many names of the Primal Serp ent worldwide include Ka or Ki such as Kan or Can and Enki, thus showing they embody the life force)

The Kabbalists recognized the primal substance as Schamayin, which means "Fiery Water" (male/female). Their cousins, the Alchemists, referred to the etheric water as the Prima Materia, the "First Substance," and gave it the form of a dragon in their cryp tic manuscripts. The Hebrews called it Manna, the "Water of Life." The term Manna was also adopted by the Polynesians of the Pacific Islands to denote the life force. Medieval magicians called this serpentine material Astral Light or Astral Fluid and maintained they could materialize any object with its help. The American Indians referred to the life force as Orenda (Iroquois), Wakan (Sioux), or Manitou (Algonquins) and recognized all snakes as physical embodiments of this etheric energy.

The European pioneers Wilhelm Reich and Richenbach referred to this etheric substance as Orgone and the Odic Force respectively. Modern scientists approximate it with electro-magnetic energy, which is actually a densification of the life force but similarly travels in spirals.

1.14 To emphasize the creative potency of the life force comprising the Primal Serpent's expanding body, the "Serpent on the Cross" evolved into the "Serpent on the Tree."

In order to emphasize the life-giving essence comprising the Primal Serpent's expanding body, some cultures added foliage to the "Serpent on the Cross" and thereby created the "Serpent on the Tree." This foliage also symbolizes the solid forms the Serpent life force will eventually condense into as the physical universe is created.

Tau crosses richly embellished with vegetation and serpents illustrate the pages of the Mayan and Nahuatl Codices (scriptures) and the interior of certain Mesoamerican temples, such as the Temple of the Foliated Cross in Palenque, Mexico. Such crosses were often referred to by the Mesoamericans as simply "trees." In the scriptures of Mesopotamia the cross upon which the dragon Enki coiled was the Gish Gana, the foliated tree which united Heaven and Earth. According to the legends of the Freemasons and Kabbalists the tree of Eden was also a foliated cross. Supposedly when Adam sent his son Seth back to the Garden to obtain the Oil of Mercy which God had promised humankind, Seth found the tree of Genesis in the form of a huge cross extending from Earth to Heaven. This tree/cross was eventually cut down and later provided the wood for the crucifix of Christ.

1.15 The Garden of Eden and the Serpent on the Tree of the Knowledge of Good and Evil at its center is a representation of the expansion of the universe from a central point of creation. The apples on the tree represent the material forms which condense out of the serpentine life force.

The Tree of Good and Evil within the Garden of Eden is clearly a representation of an early phase in the creation of the cosmos when the Serpent life force crystallized into the material forms of the physical universe (represented as the tree's apples). This condensation phase was necessary so that Yod He Vau He, the Spirit of the Hebrews, could experience his own creation through his two polar halves, Adam and Eve, the archetypal male and female genders.

Other evolutionary phases of creation are also revealed by the famous Eden myth. For example, after Adam and Eve were placed in the paradisaical garden and tasted of the fruits of the Tree of Good and Evil, they

The Serpent on the Tree in the Garden of Eden

soon noticed differences between themselves and everything around them. Their sudden lack of unity consciousness represents a stage of creation when the genders were placed in the crystallizing universe, began "tasting" or enjoying the solidified "fruits," and subsequently developed an intellect in order to classify the material forms according to designations of health-giving or not health-giving, or "good and evil" (thus the meaning of the name Tree of the Knowledge of Good and Evil). The dawn of the discriminating intellect led to the couple's loss of connection to the transcendental Spirit which is beyond the intellect, and their eventual expulsion from the holy garden.

An additional consequence of enjoying the crystallized fruits of the physical universe is the development of a physical body which lives and dies. This is what is meant by the scene in Genesis in which the divine couple are cursed by God to live and die as mortals, and Eve is alloted the pains of childbirth. Giving birth in a physical form which has its limitations due to elasticity is naturally painful. And, finally, in order for there to be ample fruits to nourish the mortal, physical bodies of the divine couple and their descendants, the life force needed to completely crystallize. This is why the wily Serpent was cursed by God to crawl upon its belly and be bruised by the heel of the seed of woman while it in turn bruised their heels. In other words, the Serpent (the etheric life force) was commanded by Spirit to descend from the cosmic tree (the higher dimensions) and solidify into dense vegetation and hard ground so that Adam, Eve and their descendants could enjoy and walk upon it and potentially get their heels bruised by it-while simultaneously bruising it.

Over time the allegory of Eden has been accorded many levels of interpretation. Its archetypal symbolism, for example, has been interpreted as a representation of not only the sequential stages of densification undergone by the entire physical universe, but also of the early stages of life on planet Earth. The story could, for example, be an accurate representation of a phase of evolution upon the Motherlands when some of the earliest, etheric Lemurians or Atlanteans assumed bodies with increasing solidity, thus allowing them to enjoy the enticing, crystallized forms of nature being produced by the Devas or Nature Spirits From yet another perspective, the yogis of India have claimed that the Tree of the Knowledge of Good and Evil with its trunk and divergent branches represents the human spine and the nerves which branch from it. This inner "tree" bestows intellectual wisdom by allowing humans to interact with and learn from the phenomenal world. The serpent at the tree's base is the body's root life force which, at some point during the evolution of the dense, physical body, descended to the Root or Earth Chakra at the base of the spine and perpetually fuels the body from that distal location. Eventually, however, the serpent life force will once again ascend the spine. This event, claims the yogis, is depicted in the Eden allegory as the Tree of Life. The flaming sword-wielding cherub which guards the base of the tree, they say, is the fiery Kundalini Serpent which resides at the base of the human spine. When a person can move this transformative serpent up the Tree of Life or spine (the yogis actually refer to the human spine as the Tree of Life) and merge it in the the top of the head, he or she will achieve eternal life and potentially live forever.

THE DRAGON'S UNIVERSAL BODY
DIVIDES INTO THE ZODIAC

1.16   When the Primal Serpent finally reached the full extent of its expansio within the universe, it divided itself into 12 parts. These 12 parts became the signs of the Zodiac, the "Circle of Animals."

Cultures worldwide believed that the universal body of the Primal Dragon had 12 parts, or "animals" which were collectively called the Zodiac or "Circle of Animals." A famous creation myth of B abylonia alludes to this division. When the hero Marduck had defeated the Serpent Goddess Tiamat he divided her body into 12 parts or children and placed them in the sky as the 12 signs of the Zodiac.

1.17   As the initial vehicle of infinite Spirit, the Dragon was the synthesis of all possible material forms, including the 12 "animals" of the Zodiac.

The Primal Dragon was the composite of all animals including the twelve "animals" which comprise the Circle of Animals. The Dragon's many faceted form was expressed in the following Mesopotamian description of the Dragon Enki:

> "The head is the head of a serpent
> from his nostrils mucus trickles
> the mouth is beslaved with water
> The ears are those of a basilisk
> His horns are twisted in three curls
> He wears a veil in his head band
> The body is a sun fish full of stars
> The base of his feet are claws
> The sole of his feet has no sole ... "[86]

The Primal Dragon's composite form was also recognized in China where the Taoist philosopher Hwai Nan Tsze (2nd century B.C.) referred to the dragon as the origin of all creatures. According to the Taoist "Nine Resemblances," the composite dragon's horns resemble those of a stag, his head reflects the form of a camel's head, his neck has the slithering form of a snake, his belly is composed of a clam, his scales are those of a carp, his claws are those of an eagle, his nails are those of a tiger and his ears are those of a cow.

328

1.18   The iconographic image of the expanded body of the Primal Serpent or Zodiac is the Sphinx.

The Egyptians, Mesopotamians and Greeks venerated the Universal or Zodiacal body of the Dragon in the form of the Sphinx. There were numerous versions of the Sphinx in and around the Mediterranean and Asia Minor, each of which was a composite of two, three or four foundational "animals" of the Zodiac, i.e., the lion of Leo, the eagle of

Scorpio, the bull of Taurus and the man/woman of Aquarius. The famous archaeologist G. Elliot Smith maintained that one of the ear list forms of the dragon-sphinx in Egypt united the wings of the eagle to the body of a lion. The largest of all Sphinxes, that which existed in the front of the Great Pyramid in Egypt, may have incorporated within its structure the head of the man/woman of Aquarius and the body of Leo the

The Egyptian Sphinx with wings

lion. Some ancient historians claimed that this Sphinx may have also originally possessed the hind legs of Taurus the bull and the wings of the Scorpio eagle. The Roman historian Plutarch, for example, maintained that the great Sphinx once possessed wings of a "multicolored hue."

If the Sphinx was indeed a model of the Zodiac and represented its twelve signs and the twelve stages of human evolution they symbolized, then passing under and beyond the beast represented that the candidate had completed human evolution and was ready to return to the realm of pure Spirit (via the initiation). The Greek myth of Oedipus allegorizes the journey of the initiate; it reveals that for a seeker to reach the end of the path he or she must understand the riddle of life (by attaining the wisdom of life). The seeker can then defeat the Sphinx, the symbol of earthly wisdom gained through life (zodiacal) experience, and pass safely on his or her way.

THE MYRIAD PHYSICAL FORMS OF THE COSMOS WERE CREATED IN THE IMAGE OF THE PRIMAL DRAGON

1.19   After reaching the full extent of its expansion , the Primal Serpent's body crystallized into all the solid material forms of the universe. These myriad physical shapes were wholistic, microcosmic images of the Serpent; each one inherited the Dragon's spiraling form and one or more of its seven aspects or principles. For this reason, the Serpent is called the mother/father and "Provider of Attributes" of all material form.

> "I am the outflow of the primeval flood,
> he who emerged from the water
> I am the Provider of Attributes Serpent with its many coils." [111]
> - Egyptian Pyramid Text

1.20   The Serpent spiral and its constant, Phi, became the structural basis of all material form.

The structural basis of all material forms is the geometric spiral shape of the Serpent and/or the mathematical proportion and constant which determines the spiral, 5:8 and 1.61. The Serpent's spiralling form determines the shapes of many physical forms, from the huge Milky Way Galaxy, which was known among the ancient Mesopotamian Akkadians as the "River of the Snake," to the minutest life form. It is distinctly noticeable within the shapes of sunflowers, budding roses, pine cones, certain minerals and sea shells.

The mathematical constant determining the spiral, Phi, is also inherent in many physical forms. Phi is, for example, the basis of the Fibronacci series of numbers, a sequence which can be found determining certain growing patterns in nature, including "the arrangement of leav es on a plant, the pads on a cat's foot, and the spirals encountered in the shells of microscopic formanifera." [112] As Peter Tompkins, a well known author, eloquently asserts: "Phi is the symbol of generation, of procreation, of growth in all directions ... it is a symbol to which all of nature subscribes, from molluscs to giant redwoods, from the structure of bones to the ages of growth in man." [87]

1.21   The solidified forms of the physical universe also inherited the Serpent's

seven principles. These seven principles determine an object's color, sound and internal axis.

Many of the characteristics of physical matter are clustered in groups of seven, thus representing the Serpent's seven principles. Each object is built around one of the seven crystalline axis systems; it reflects one or more of the seven colors and it emanates one, or a combination of, the seven tones.

THE PRIMAL DRAGON CREATED MICROCOSMIC IMAGES OF ITSELF

1.22   The Earth was created as a microcosmic image of the Primal Dragon.

Chinese Taoist mystics experienced first hand how the Earth is a conscious, living and breathing embodiment of the Dragon. According to the Taoist classic *Huang-ti Chai-ching*: "the forms and configurations (of the Earth) should be looked upon as the body of the Dragon; the water and underground springs (as) the blood and veins of the Dragon; the surface of the Earth (as) the skin of the Dragon; the foliage upon it, the (Dragon's) hair; and the dwellings as clothes (of the Dragon) ... " The Chinese mystics also recognized the clouds to be the Dragon's breath, the rain to be the Dragon's blood or essence, and the high jagged peaks which descend sharply into lowland valleys to be the Dragon's back.

1.23   The human family unit is also a microcosmic image of the Dragon.

Within some cultures, the family was also a manifestation of the Dragon. The ancient Hawaiians, for example, referred to their family structures as Mo'o, the Dragon. In *Tales from the Night Rainbow*, a Hawaiian author explains the structure of a Dragon family: "The front feet of the Dragon are Na Opio-the young children of the family, always restless, always changing position, always in motion. The middle feet of the Dragon are the parents, Ka Makua-the providers of the food, the house, the ones that take care of the young. Then there are the hind feet of the Dragon, Na Kupuna-the grandparents. These stabilizers are ever prepared for anyone needing help-always full of Aloha, always strong. Behind the Kupuna is Ka iwi-the bone of the ancestors who have passed out of the body. They help the family in ways beyond the physical realm-caring, protecting and guiding from the spiritual side of the Rainbow. Each person is a small part of the whole yet each part is integral and necessary for the whole to be complete."

1.24   Humankind was similarly created in the image of the Serpent

Humans are also microcosmic images of the Primal Serpent and possess both the Serpent's spiral and its seven principles. This truth is confirmed in the *Holy Bible* wherein God or the Elohim, i.e., God's seven principles which are collectively the Primal Serpent, is recorded as proclaiming "...let us make man in our image, after our likeness." According to a Gnostic version of Eden, after Adam and Eve ate of the forbidden fruit "they saw their makers (the Elohim) and loathed them since they were beastly (reptillian) forms. They understood very much."[113]

1.25   The base proportion of the human body is 5:8 or 1.61, the numerological value which determines the spiral.

The Golden Proportion of Phi, 5:8 (Phi expressed as a proportion) and its constant, 1.61, under lie the lengths of the sequential parts or segments composing the human form. It can, for example, be found in the measurements of the hands and feet where the first, second, and third phalanges of the fingers and feet are in a proportional relationship of 5:8 to each other. The length of the upper arm is in a 5:8 proportion relative to the lower arm and hand, i.e., the distance

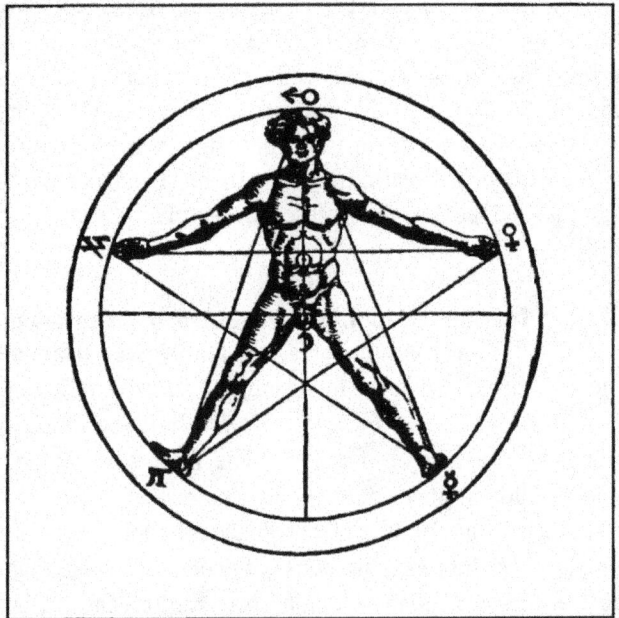

The Human aligns perfectly with the Golden Mean Pentagram

from the elbow to the tip of the middle finger. The distance from the solar plexus to the top of the head is in a 5:8 proportion relative to the distance from the heel to the solar plexus and the distance from the heel to the solar plexus is in a 5:8 proportion relative to the distance from the heel to the top of the head. Vitruvius proved that the human body is based upon the spiral by perfectly fitting it within a pentagram or five-pointed star, a geometrical form which is determined by the Golden Proportion. Interestingly, the pentagram has for countless ages been the definitive symbol of the Dragon throughout the world.

1.26   The spiral is the basis of the DNA molecule.

The spiral is the basis of the double helix configuration of the DNA molecule. Therefore, at its most minute level, the human body reflects the shape of the Primal Serpent.

1.27   As a microcosmic image of the Serpent, the human body reflects the Serpent's septenary imprint.

A ccording to the Maya, humans are the "integration of the seven powers of light traveling in the form of a serpent."[82] Humankind "integrates" these seven powers or principles of the Serpent in a variety of ways. For example, every human possess seven "bodies," six of which are etheric and surround and interpenetrate the physical. Each person possesses seven main energy centers or chakras which reflect the seven colors. These chakras are situated along the course of the human spine and divide the body into seven zones. Furthermore, each person has seven organs essential to life, seven essential functions performed by these organs (respiration, circulation etc.), seven parts of the brain, seven kinds of epithelial tissue, seven layers to the skin, etc. [114]

PART II: THE SERPENT PRESERVES THE UNIVERSE

11.1   Once the creation of the universe and its myriad   forms is complete, the   second   of   the Serpent's three powers, Preservation, becomes active. During the ensuing Preservation Phase of the Universe the Serpent sustains and preserves the physical cosmos in   the same way a mother cares for her children.

Cultures around the world acknowledged the Primal Serpent's power of preservation in their legends and cosmologies. In India the Hindus referred to this preserving power of the Serpent as Uchista, meaning "residual." The Serpent Shesha (whose name means "residual") preserves the creation with the residual life force remaining after its body has crystallized into the physical forms of the universe. In Hindu iconography this preserving residual power is graphically represented as a huge serpent which supports the entire universe upon its back. Other cultures similarly rest the entire creation upon the back of their serpent creator.

THE PRESERVING SERPENT LIFE FORCE ARRIVES ON EARTH FROM THE COSMOS

11.2   The Preserving Power of the Serpent, ie, the life force, is projected to Earth via the stars and planets of the cosmos. Of all the celestial orbs, the Sun provides Earth with its main source of preserving life force.

Much of the Serpent's preserving power was anciently recognized as arriving from the Sun. At On or Heliopolis in Egypt where the Sun was cons idered to be the main s ource of life force, the s olar orb was wors hipped as a heavenly manifestation of Spirit and its rays were recognized to be needles or serpentine shafts of light which emanated from the Solar Spirit, Ra. Thes e solar rays were artistically rendered as s lender, tapering s tone columns called obelisks or "needles " and "frozen snakes .'In Mesoamerica the Sun was similarly acknowledged to be the primary s ource of the Earth's life force and its rays were also represented as fire serpents .In this regard great fire serpents were s aid to accompany the Sun during its daily pas s age acros s the s ky, and s olar icons were produced as an orb projecting s even rays.

11.3   The Moon is a secondary source of Serpent life force coming to Earth.

The Serpent life force was also believed to emanate from the Moon, especially during the waxing and full Moon. In Egypt the Moon and its rays were associated with the gods Seth and Thoth-Hennes, both of whom were intimately associated with the Primal Dragon and the serpent/life force. In Europe, the Moon was consistently associated with the Dragon, especially within the paganistic nature cults. In India, the Moon and its rays was often associated with the Serpent Goddess Shakti and the Dragon Goddess Kali.

11.4   The preserving life force also arrives from the Pleiades, the Celestial Serpent.

The ancients also recognized the point of creation in our local galaxy, the Pleiades, to be a transmitter of preserving life force to Earth. Each spring when the Pleiades hovered above the horizon at dawn and/or reached its apex in the sky at noon, there was believed to be a fresh infusion of life force projected to Earth through the "teats of the rattlesnake." This annual infusion of cosmic energy manifested on Earth as the nourishing spring rains and the activating spark which stimulated the growth of new vegetation.

THE SERPENT LIFE FORCE CIRCULATES WITHIN EARTH'S ENERGY GRID, THE PLANET'S DRAGON BODY

11.5   After the Serpent life force has reached the Earth it enters dragons' lairs or vortex points and circumntnigates around the planet within a network of subtle channels. Collectively these vortexes and channels comprise the Earth's Grid.

It was common knowledge among most of the ancient peoples that the Serpent life force entered the Earth at certain energy conductive points called "dragons' lairs," gathering points of the Serpent life force, or "vortexes." The life force would then travel around the planet through a network of energy channels called dragon lines, dragon paths, or ley lines.

11.6   Dragon lairs are created by the intersection of two or more dragon lines. They are earthly representatives of the male and female principles that unite to produce androgynous dragons. Altogether there are   1746 major intersections or dragon lairs within the Earth's etheric grid.

A dragon's lair is formed when two dragon lines cross and produce a whirlpool or vortex. Vortex means "whirling." The spiral of a vortex or dragon's lair is the actual whirling body of the Serpent life force which moves up into the heavens and down into the Earth, thereby uniting Heaven and Earth. An energy pattern of seven concentric circles is also formed at a dragon's lair, thus reflecting the Serpent's seven principles.

The number of dragon lairs upon the planet, 1746, is a number of the Primal Dragon produced by adding together 666 and 1080, numbers associated with the male and female principles.   The 1746 grid work of vortexes and the subtle lines connecting them is thus the Earth's androgynous   "Dragon Body."

II. 7   The Earth's subtle grid of lines and vortexes, also known as it's "Dragon Body," is comprised of five interlocking sub-grids, each of which have the shape of one of the five Pythagorean solids, the geometric forms of the five elements.

The Primal Dragon is the composite of the five "elements" of matter-aether, air, fire, water and earth. The Dragon Body or subtle grid of the Earth is composed of these five elements as five interlocking sub-grids.115

The interlocking sub-grids of the five elements take the form of the five Pythagorean solids: the cube, icosohedron , tetrahedron, octahedron, and dodecahedron. The sub-grid of the earth element surrounds the Earth in the form of a huge cube; the sub-grid of the water element surrounds the Earth in the shape of a huge icosohedron; the sub-grid of the fire element covers the globe as a colossal tetrahedron; the sub-grid of the air element covers the planet as a gigantic octahedron; and the sub-grid of ether sheaths the Earth as a mammoth dodecahedron.

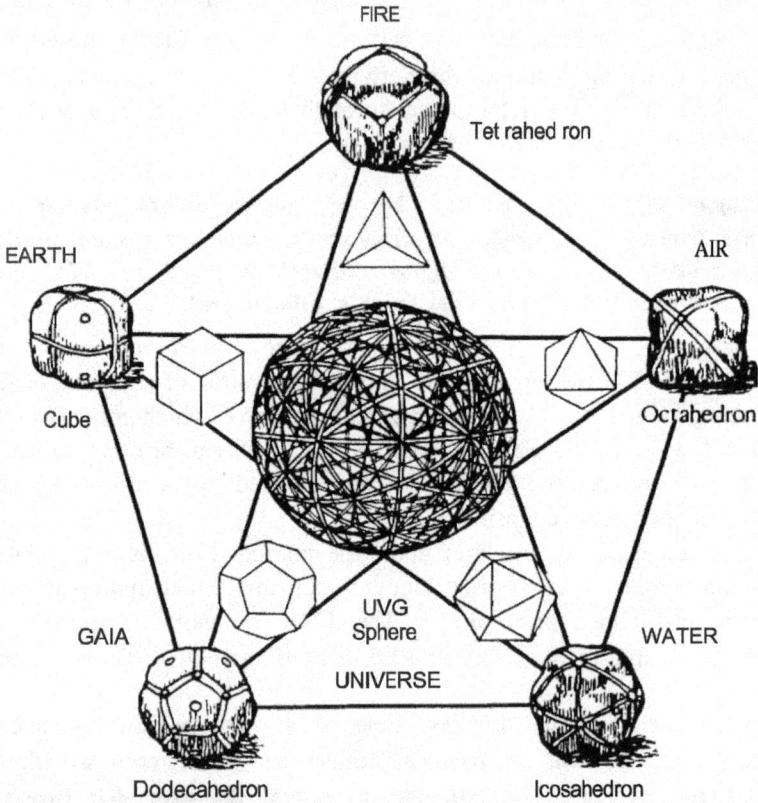

FIRE

Tet rahed ron

EARTH

AIR

Cube

Octahedron

UVG
Sphere

UNIVERSE

GAIA

WATER

Dodecahedron

Icosahedron

Pythagorean Cosmic Morphology

Becker-Hagens 1984

11.8 Throughout time stone circles, standing stones, pyramids and mounds have been set over dragon lairs to facilitate the movement of life force in and out of the Earth's Dragon Body.

To mark the planetary dragon lairs and facilitate the movement of life force in and out of the Earth, the ancient people placed different shapes of conduits and conductors around and over them. These vortex facilitators took the form of earthen mounds, standing stones, stone circles, and pyramids.

The vortex markers provided a physical matrix to support, stabilize and amplify the life force as it spiraled up or down. To assist this function many markers contained high concentrations of amplifying quartz crystal. A further function served by the vortex markers was to monitor the amount of life force circulating throughout the Earth's grid and keep it at a safe level. If necessary, such markers were able to siphon off any excess accumulations of life force within the grid, thereby preventing the rise of earthquakes and volcanoes.

11.9 The stone circles, pyramids and mounds also served as life force generators and accumulators.

The crystalline materials of the stone markers(such as quartz crystal), as well as their unique shapes, made them generators of the life force as well as accumulators of it. Pyramid shaped markers which incorporated into their forms the union of the cube (representing the female principle) and the tetrahedron (representing the male principle) to produce the life force were especially efficient generators. The word pyramid, meaning "fire in the middle," designates these structures as natural homes of the Serpent Fire or life force. The design of earthen mounds, which alternated earthen layers (female principle) with stone layers (male principle), also helped to make them effective generators and accumulators of the life force.

Because of their accumulating properties, mounds, pyramids and stone circles were specially chosen to act as temples for spiritual transformation and as tombs for the dead. The life force moving within these structures could be used either for spiritual transformation or preservation of the physical and etheric bodies of the deceased.

THE SERPENT LIFE FORCE CIRCULATES WITHIN THE HUMAN ENERGY GRID, THE HUMAN DRAGON BODY

11.10 The Preserving Power of the Serpent sustains the Human physical body by circulating through an etheric grid system similar to the Earth's.

The human body also has an etheric energy sheath composed of numerous subtle energy vessels and vortex points like the Earth's through which the life force enters and travels. In India the subtle channels comprising this network are called nadis and estimated to be 72,000 in number. In China the etheric channels are referred to as jinglou-meridians and collaterals. According to both the Indian and Chinese systems there are 14 major meridians and numerous minor ones.

11.11   The human etheric grid is synonymous with the human Dragon Body.

The human etheric grid is referred to in various traditions as the etheric body, the Pranamya Kosha (the sheath of Prana), and the human Dragon Body. As a manifestation of the Dragon this subtle body is well endowed with "serpent" symbolism. It has, for example, 14 or 2x7 major meridians, which represent the Dragon's 2 opposing principles and its 7 aspects. These 14 meridians are traditionally divided into 2 principal vessels, corresponding to the Dragon's male and female principles, and 12 major channels, which correspond to the 12 signs of the Dragon's Zodiacal body. Of the 12 major channels, 6 are yin and 6 are yang, thus reflecting the 6 feminine and 6 masculine signs of the Zodiac. The human Dragon Body also contains seven major vortexes or chakras corresponding to the seven principles of the Dragon.

11.12   The life force enters the human etheric grid through the mouth as food and water and through the nose as a component of the air. The life force also enters the human grid through the seven chakras and the innumerable vortexes which comprise the Dragon Body.

Once food, water and air is taken into the physical body, the life force is extracted from these substances via the processes of respiration and digestion and then circulated throughout the Dragon Body.

Life force is also taken directly into the Dragon Body from the atmosphere through major and minor vortexes, power points on the surface of the body which exist as intersection points of the nadis and meridians. The major vortexes are the chakras (meaning wheels), the seven main power centers situated along the spine. In sequential order the seven centers are: the Muladhara Chakra located at the base of the spine, the Svadisthana Chakra located in the area of the sexual organs, the Manipura Chakra at the solar plexus, the Anahata Chakra at the heart, the Visuddha Chakra at the throat, the Ajna Chakra between the eyes and the Sahasrara Chakra at the top of the head. Of these seven, the most important energy insertion and escape points for the life force are the three chakras located at the solar plexus (sometimes referred to as the Spleen Chakra) and at the top and bottom of the spine.

The minor vortexes are points of low electrical resistance which serve as portals for the life force to move directly in and out of the Dragon Body. Like the Earth's vortex points they also monitor the amount of life force circulating in the human grid. To facilitate this monitoring function, numerous cultures have placed "vortex markers" over or within these conductive points in the form of needles of bamboo, porcelain, stone or metal. These markers then act as conduits to either siphon off or infuse energy into the human energy system, thus preventing accumulations, stress and eventual disease. This approach to balancing the life force within the human grid is commonly known as acupuncture.

The Human Chakra System

THE THREE SPECIAL SEATS OF THE SERPENT IN THE HUMAN BODY

11.13   **Within the Human Dragon Body are three chakras of special importance as seats or lairs of the Serpent's Preserving Power. Also known as "knots," these three special dragons' lairs are located in the lower abdomen/base of the spine (area of the Muladhara Chakra), the heart (area of the Anahata Chakra), and the Third Eye (area of the Ajna Chakra).**

In its lower lair the Serpent's Preserving Power exists as the Mundane Kundalini or Source Chi.

From its seat at the base of the spine and Muladhara Chakra, an area which the Hindus also call the Brahma Knot, the Mundane Kundalini is continually entering the grid of 72,000 nadis and fueling both the etheric and physical bodies. This androgynous energy also divides into its male and female components and then travels through two major nadis, the Ida and Pingalanadis, while controlling the fire/water or hot/cold balance in the body. Similarly, the Chinese maintain that the Source Chi, which is also referred to as the "Moving Chi between the Kidneys," thereby denoting its location, fuels the entire body through the network of Meridians. It also controls the balance of yin and yang energies within the body by moving predominantly in one or the other of the two major Meridians, the Ren and Du Meridians.

In its middle seat at the heart the Serpent's Preserving Power manifests as Prana, and Ancestral Chi.

The heart is the "Seat of Spirit." From its seat in the heart, the Spirit is continually emanating Serpent power as life force to control and regulate the heart muscle and the pumping of blood throughout the body. Because it is such an important seat of the preserving serpent within the body, the heart is referred to by the Hindus as the "Seat of Prana" and by the Chinese as the "Seat of Fire" or the "Seat of Ancestral Chi." This seat of the Serpent is also referred to as the Vishnu Knot by the Hindus.

In its upper lair the Serpent's Preserving Power controls the body as the Divine Mind.

From its seat between the eye-brows and within the Ajna Chakra, the Serpent functions as the Divine Mind of God. From this area, also known as the Rudra Knot by the Hindus, this manifestation of the preserving Serpent masterminds all the functions of the human body by controlling the actions of the two master glands of the physical sheath, the Pineal and Pituitary glands. Western science has confirmed that these glands are the master glands and principal control centers of the human body.

THE PRIMAL SERPENT DIVIDES INTO THE PRESERVING TWINS

The two twin halves of Coatlicue, the Mexican Serpent Goddess

11.14 To balance and preserve its creation, the Serpent divides into Twins, its two "children."

While generating nourishing life force during the preservation phase, the Primal Dragon also preserves the universe by dividing itself in half to produce two "children" or "Twins." These dragon progeny, the male/female aspects of the androgenous Serpent, represent the dual forces of the physical universe, i.e., night and day, hot and cold, fire and water, creation and destruction, life and

341

death. Without the checks and balances they impose upon each other, the creation would soon collapse.

11.15   The Legend of the Twins' birth takes place in the later portion of many creation myths.

The legend of the Twins' birth can be found in the later portion of most creation myths or within allegories which recount the beginning of the preservation phase. The manifestations assumed by the Twins in these legends include the twin serpents, a serpent and a bull, a serpent and an eagle, a divine human couple or twin brothers.

11.16   The Twins can often be found in these legends in perhaps their oldest manifestation, that of twin serpents.

In some☐ creation myths the Twins are depicted as what they truly are, two serpents or twin divisions of the Primal Dragon. Among the Nahuatls of Central America these serpent twins are clearly evident as the serpent pair inhabiting the singular body of the creator dragon Coatlicue. Within the Hebrew tradition they were represented as the twin Cherubs guarding the Ark of the Covenant. According to the Jewish historian Josephus, the Hebrew Cherubs originally possesed dragon-like appearances. In the Mediterranean countries two popular manifestations of the serpent twins were the Kaberoi and Dioskuri twins, sons of Vulcan, the fire serpent, and Zeus in his manifestation of the Primal Serpent. An additional manifestation of the twin serpents in Greece was Agatho Daimon and Agatho Tyche the twin offspring of Agathodeamon, the Primal Serpent. The Sumerians represented the Serpent Twins as two intertwined serpents comprising the symbol of Ningishzida. Ningishzida was a manifestation of Tammuz, the "Serpent who emanated from the heaven god Anu."

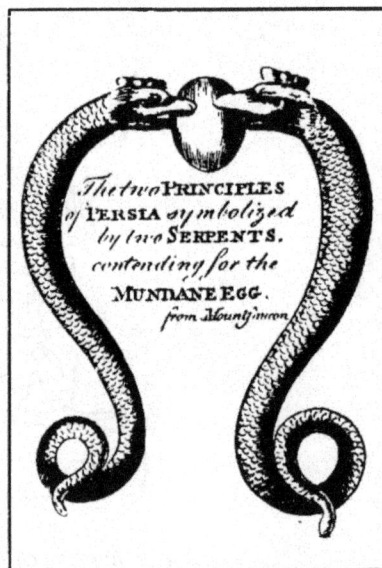

The Twin Persian Serpents

In some creation myths the Twin Serpents were depicted as dual emanations of the Solar Spirit or Sun (together they are the one Serpent

Goddess). In Persian iconography the twin serpent gods Ahriman and Orzmund were twin progeny of the Solar Spirit Ahura Mazda. In Chinese symbology the Serpent Twins were superimposed over a solar/spiritual disc as part of the famous Tao symbol. The Egyptians had a similar motif decorating the porticos of their temples which consisted of the Serpent Twins emanating out of a winged, solar/spiritual disc.

11.17   Like their parent, the Primal Serpent, the Serpent Twins are similarly found in legend coiled upon a tree/cross. They were also found coiled upon a dual cross, the Dakona.

According to some traditions, when the primal "Serpent on the Tree" divided into twin serpents, the two progeny remained attached to their parent's tree/cross perch and the motif of the "Twin Serpents on the tree/cross" was thus born. The most famous version of this motif is the caduceus or Staff of Mercury, a cross/tree with twin serpents entwining themselves around its axis. This caduceus was adopted by the Voodoo tradition and enlarged to become the tree/pillar which is today set in the center of their sacred temples. Upon this Voodoo tree/cross slithers humankind's "first ancestors" Dunbhalah, the "male," solar serpent and Aida Wedo the "female," lunar serpent. Another variation of the tree/cross is found in the Mayan *Seldon Codex* which depicts two slithering serpents dangling over the cross beam of a foliated Tau cross.

A Greek version of the dual tree/cross is the Dakona, a structure which connects two vertical "trees" or pillars by two horizontal shafts. The Dakona was a favorite perch of the Dioskuri serpents who could often be found dangling from its cross beams or spiraling up or down its pillars. The Dakona later became the basis for the glyph of the astrological sign of the twins, Gemini.

11.18   The twin serpentine aspects of the Primal Serpent can be found in nature as the twin spirals.

The Primal Serpent has left is dual imprint in nature as twin spirals winding around or within pine cones, sea shells, certain flowers, crystals and some minerals. The twin spirals can also be found at the center of all human cells as the double helix of the DNA molecule.

11.19   The twin serpentine aspects of the Primal Serpent can also be found in the Human Dragon Body as the Ida and Pinga Nadis and the Du and Ren Meridians.

Within the human body, the twin aspects of the preserving Serpent manifest as the two primary serpentine vessels, the Ida and Pingala nadis and the

Ahura Mazda was forgotten. In the end, Spenta Mainyu and Angra Mainyu as Ormuzd and Ahriman represented two absolute and eternally separate principles.

When the Persians conquered Mesopotamia they brought their dualistic religion with them. In Babylonia, the Persian faith blended with the ancient religion of the Middle East to produce the cult of Mithraism. According to the theology which then emerged from this synthesized faith, the only Son of Ahura Mazda, Mithra (a version of a classical Twin Son), was sent to Earth to rid the world of Ahriman and his army of demons. The Savior Mithra was born on December 25th, quickly matured, and set about establishing himself as a formidable beast slayer. Then when his earthly mission was near completion, Mithra gathered his devotees together for one "last supper" during which he vowed to return one day and complete his battle with Ahriman's dark forces. During his time away, however, Mithra promised to continue to assist his devotees from the heavenly realms and informed them that they could still commune with him through the sacramental meal of bread and wine.

11.25 The absolute duality of the Twins influenced the development of the Christian legend of Jesus Christ and the Devil.

The absolute duality propagated within the synthesized Persian/Babylonian cult of Mithra helped influence the development of the famous Christian legend of Christ and the Devil. Christ, like Mithra, was born on December the 25th as the only begotten Son of God. He came to Earth to battle the king of demons, the Devil, who was a Judeo/Christian version of Ahriman. Christ also departed after a last supper during which he pledged his return. His projected return in the *Book of Revelation* as a celestial knight upon radiant white stallion is a verbatim description of Ormuzd/Mithra's return to Earth during the planet's "latter days."

11.26 The legendary story of Jesus Christ and the Devil incorporates the ancient symbolism of the Lord of Light and the timeless motifs associated with the Lord of Darkness.

According to his legend, Jesus Christ was associated with the Dove, symbol of the Pleiades, and he took a virgin birth, both of which are ancient motifs associated with the Lord of Light and his power of creativity. The myth
of the Christian Devil was fabricated out of the legends of numerous Dark Lord figures which had existed in the ancient world leading up to the time of Christianity. The personality of the Devil and his underworld abode was borrowed partly fro m the Persian Dark Lord Ahriman who helped supply

the Devil with his later nickname of "Old Henry." The Devil's fiery, destructive nature, as well as his red color and his name, Satan, were influenced both by the Dark Lord Set or Sat, the red colored deity of the scorching Egyptian desert, as well as Azzazel, the red hued Dark Lord of the Palestinian desert. Eventually through the Egyptian Goat of Mendes, a manifestation of Pan and Azzazel, whose sacred anima ls were the goat, this animal became associated with the Dark Lord.

THE DEVIL EVOLVED FROM THE FIRE SERPENT VOLCAN

11.27   The myth of the Devil and his fiery, underworld kingdom began with Volcan, the androgynous Fire Serpent

The legend of the Devil who resides in the fiery, underworld kingdom of Hell began with Vol-can (can is a universal name for serpent), an ancient fire god whose name means "whirling serpent" and "fire serpent." According to information gathered by the archaeologist and anthropologist L.Taylor Hansen from Native American records, Volcan was a fire serpent of the legendary continent of Atlantis who lived within the bowels of Volcan-oes as molten lava and explosive power. The androgynous Volcan also moved under the E arth as the beneficent life force which pushed up new seedlings each spring, but could be a deadly force of destruction if congested, thereby giving rise to cataclysmic earthquakes and violent volcanic eruptions. To placate Volcan and acquire some of its immense power, the Atlantean Serpent clan occasionally worshiped the fire serpent as a red colored, trident wielding god. This ancient worship of the fire serpent can still be found observed today by descendants of the Atlantean Serpent Clan, the North American Mescalero Apaches and the Tuareg peoples of North Africa.

The volcano god of Atlantis was eventually transported to E urope and Africa by colonists of the Atlantean Serpent Clan, where it evolved into the E gyptian and Greek fire gods Ptah and Hesphestus, as well as the dark "Goat of Mendes" and the Greek underworld lord, Pluto. From Greece the subterranean fire god was adopted into the Roman pantheon as Vulcan, the smith god who was said to have been thrown down to E arth from Heaven (the fire serpent or life force arrives from the heavens) and resided within the fiery bowels of volcanoes. Vulcan assimilated the destructive nature of the fire serpent of Atlantis and became famous for producing the deadly weapons of war. Volcan or Vulcan eventually found his way into the Hebrew pantheon as Vel'cain or Cain (meaning "smith" and "possessor of fire") and as Lucifer or Azzazel, the "fallen angel" from Heaven, who taught the daughters of men the art of smithing.

349

11.28   The trident, preeminent symbol of the Devil, is a modified version of the cross. To construct a trident, the ends of the horizontal of a cross are turned upward to produce the prongs.

The trident, famous weapon of the Christian Devil, is the ancient symbol of the Atlantean fire serpent and a version of the cross. It represents the union of the male and female principles and the three powers of god (the three prongs) which the divine union of opposites engenders. The Devil's association with the trident is proof of his evolution from Volcan, the dragon/goat Pan (the symbolic animal of Atlantis), and the Serpent on the tree/cross.

PART III: THE SERPENT DESTROYS THE UNIVERSE

THE TWINS REUNITE AS THE PRIMAL SERPENT

III.1   The Destruction Phase of the universe commences when the Twin Sons reunite as the Primal Serpent.

At the end of time, the Twin Sons reunite as their father/mother, the Primal or Fire Serpent. The universe is thereby thrown out of balance and full scale destruction results.

111.2   During the Destruction   Phase, the Primal Serpent in the form of a Fire Serpent completely annihalates the universe and reverts all material form back to pure life force or cosmic fire.

When the Twins reunite, the androgynous Primal Serpent is resynthesized and its fiery power of destruction is activated. In the blink of an eye the Primal Serpent in the form of a colossal Fire Serpent consumes all life in its path and reverts all material forms back to pure life force or cosmic fire, the original form of the First Serpent. The Hindus refer to this final consumptive phase as "flames belched forth from the fangs of Shesha" which incinerate all material forms in the universe. The ancient Egyptians of Heliopolis alluded to the universal dissolution as "the end of time (when) the world will revert to the primary state of chaos and Atum (the Creator Dragon) will once again become a Serpent (pure life force)."[64]

111.3   The final destruction of the   universe culminates in the ascent of the Serpent up the cosmic tree and its re-emersion in the cosmic sea.

From the perspective of the cosmic tree motif, the dissolution of all material form and its return to pure life force is metaphorically conceived to be the reascent of the snake (matter) up the cosmic tree and its reunion with its bird twin (Spirit). The union of Spirit and matter thus creates the original Plumed Serpent, the etheric creature which is composed of cosmic fire or life force.

After its resynthesis, the winged serpent will theoretically dive back into the cosmic tree's infinite source, the cosmic sea. Then during the ensuing "in-between" or Pralaya Phase, the Serpent (now in a dormant/potential state) will drift peacefully upon or within the cosmic sea while awaiting the re-creation of the universe.

MINOR DESTRUCTIVE PHASES AWAKEN THE EARTH'S FIRE SERPENT

111.4   Between   the   creation   and   destruction   of the   universe   the   Earth goes   through   many   minor   phases   of destruction.

Many minor destruction phases occur on Earth during a major universal preservation phase and these serve to catalyze both destruction as well as evolutionary transformation upon the planet. During these minor transformative periods, the Serpent destroys matter in order to re-shape it and evolve it into a higher level of organization.

111.5   During the minor terrestrial phases of destuction the twins unite and

351

activate the Earth's inner fire serpent, Volcan.

During the minor terrestrial destructive phases the reunion of the Twins precipitates the full awakening of Volcan, the Earth's "underworld," androgynous, fire serpent. The activated serpent fire or planetary Kundalini then proceeds to reorganize and purify the Earth via earthquakes, volcanoes and other natural "disasters."

DESTRUCTIVE PHASES AWAKEN THE SPIRITUAL KUNDALINI AND PRODUCE THE SERPENTS OF WISDOM

III.6   During Earth's destructive phases the Twins also unite within the human body and awaken the androgynous fire serpent or "Spiritual Kundalini" at the base of the spine. Once awakened, the Spiritual Kundalini destroys all limitations and eventually makes a person immortal.

During a terrestrial destructive phase the male and female principles and their vehicles, the Ida and Pingala Nadis (the Serpent Twins), reunite at the base of the human spine as the "Spiritual Kundalini. The Spiritual Kundalini is a higher frequency of life force than the normally active Mundane Kundalini.

Once the Spiritual Kundalini is awakened within a person, it rises up the spine to the top of the head and eventually merges with the Crown Chakra, the seat of Spirit in the body. Along the way, this high frequency fire serpent fully activates all the chakras, destroys limitations on all levels of a person's being, and finally transforms him or her into a god or goddess.

III.7   When the snake (the Kundalini) reunites with the eagle (the brain) in the upper branches of the "yogic tree of life" (the spine) a person becomes a "Serpent of Wisdom."

The re-ascent of the Serpent up the cosmic tree occurs in the human body as the Spiritual Kundalini's ascent up the spine or "yogic tree of life." The union of the eagle and serpent as the winged or feathered serpent then occurs as the Kundalini Serpent reaches the two lobed (or two winged) brain and merges with Spirit in the crown chakra.

Those evolved Masters who complete the union of the serpent and eagle within their own bodies become Dragons, Plumed Serpents and "Serpents of Wisdom." Such accomplished Masters can elect to leave the physical world and travel within their Dragon Bodies to the upper dimensions of the universe, the "paradise realms of the immortals" or remain on Earth as teachers. Those who femain on Earth are spiritually awake and fully established in the consciousness of Unconditional Love which exists within the heart.

111.8 Even though it is commonly awakened enmasse during a planetary destruction phase, the Spiritual Kundalini can be awakened at any time within the body of a sincere seeker of wisdom.

PART IV: CYCLES OF THE SERPENT, THE CYCLES OF TIME

IV.1   Major destructive phases which culminate in the complete dissolution of the universe are part of major cycles of time, and minor destructive phases which culminate in the re-organization of matter on Earth are part of minor cycles of time.

Major and minor cycles of time are called "Cycles of the Serpent." Both contain the three successive phases of creation, preservation and destruction.

The cycles of time are essentially "Serpent Cycles," the life cycles of the serpentine life force. The Serpent life force, an emanation of Spirit, is born and condenses into physical shapes during the creation phase of a cycle; these physical shapes are preserved and grow (or evolve) to maturity during the preservation phase; and they are either transformed or completely destroyed and re-absorbed into Spirit during the destructive phase. During these three phases the three powers of the Serpent, i.e., creation, preservation and destruction, are successively ascendant.

THE OUROBOROS, SYMBOL OF All SERPENT CYCLES OF TIME

IV .2   The definitive symbol of a Serpent Cycle of time is the Ouroboros, a ring shaped snake which swallows its own tail. .

An Ouroboros snake motif swallows its own tail while forming a circle, archetypal symbol of cyclic continuity, with its body. The Ouroboros can be divided into three parts, each one of which symbolizes one of the three phases of a Serpent Cycle. The snake's head at the top of the Ouroboros represents the initial creation of the Serpent life force. The middle part of the Ouroboros represents the growth/maturation period of the Serpent life force, and the point where the snake swallows its own tail represents the destruction or transformation of the forms crystallized out of the Serpent life force.

IV.3   Some Ouroboros motifs have been found with a representation of the Earth within their core, thereby symbolizing the ongoing minor Serpent Cycles of time which occur upon the planet

Perhaps the most famous Ouroboros of this genre is the one encircling the middle of the Norse tree of Yggdrasil. As the Midgard Serpent or Jormundgard, an Ouroboros Serpent continually encircles the Earth while swimming within the "cosmic ocean," the infinite sea within which the planet floats. Besides the Norse culture, the ancient Gnostics and certain modem African tribes, such as the Dayak, have also subscribed to the belief that the Earth is surrounded by a giant Ouroboros Serpent.

354

MINOR SERPENT CYCLES OF TIME: THE DAY AND YEAR

IV.4   The perpetual cycle of day and night is a minor Serpent Cycle of time.

In a passage from the "Egyptian Book of the Dead," the daily cycle of day and night is represented as the life cycle of the Serpent Sito who proclaims:"I am Sito, dilated with years, I die and am reborn every day."₁₁₁ The natives of Fiji maintain that day begins when the Great Serpent, Ndengei, awakens from its nightly slumber, and ends when it once again closes it eyes and returns to the dream world.

IV.5   Tite annual cycle of nature is also a minor Serpent Cycle.

The annual cycle of vegetative growth in nature is another minor Serpent Cycle. During this yearly cycle the Serpent life force takes birth, grows and dies. It first crystallizes into lush vegetation during the spring, grows and matures during the summer months, and then decays and dies in the fall. The nature gods venerated by many ancient cultures, such as Zan of the Cretans and Dionysus of the Greeks, took the form of a serpent which was bom, grew to maturation and died annually.

THE ZODIACAL SERPENT CYCLES

IV.6   Among the ancient astrologers, a yearly Serpent Cycle was synonymous with the journey of the Sun through the Zodiacal body of the Dragon.

A yearly Serpent Cycle was witnessed by the ancient astrologers as the transit of the Sun through the celestial body of the Dragon, the twelve signs of the Zodiac. In spring, at the beginning of the yearly cycle of nature, the astrologers watched as the Sun entered the head of the Dragon, the sign Aries, and then continued on through the other signs until it reached the feet of the Dragon, Pisces.

IV.7   The ancient astrologers were also aware of a Zodiacal cycle during which the entire Solar System precessed (went backwards) through the Dragon's Zodiacal body. This longer Serpent Cycle is known as the Precession of the Equinoxes.

During the greater Serpent Cycle of 26,000 years, the Precession of the

Equinoxes, the ancient astrologers observed the Solar System as it slowly moved backwards through the entire body of the Zodiacal Dragon. Every 2000 years it precessed into one of the twelve parts of the Dragon, i.e., one of the twelve astrological signs; this sign determined the theme of the ensuing 2000 year age. For example, during the Age of Taurus, the Age of the Bull, 4000-2000 B.C., the theme on Earth was nature religion and the worship of the bull. During the Age of the warrior-like Ram, Aries, circa 2000-0 B.C., the theme on the planet was conquest through war, etc..

The ancient Native Americans, Egyptians, Greeks and Mesopotamians were all aware of the 26,000 year cycle. The Egyptians encoded the length of this cycle into the Great Pyramid as one of its dimensions. The Mayan□ calendar, the Tzekier, was also based upon this cycle.

CYCLES OF THE CELESTIAL AND PLANETARY SERPENTS

IV.8   Certain stars, planets and constellations are celestial or planetary Serpents and their cosmic cycles are determiners of various Serpent Cycles upon the Earth.

THE CYCLE OF THE CELESTIAL SERPENT, THE PLEIADES

IV .9   The movement of the "Celestial Serpent," the Pleiades, is an indicator of both the yearly and 52 year Serpent Cycles.

Many ancient people constructed their calendars around the annual and 52 year cycles of the Celestial Serpent, the Pleiades. Some cultures began their new year either in the spring when the Seven Sisters made an appearance on the horizon preceding dawn, or in the fall when the stars would sparkle above the horizon immediately before and after sunset. Autumn was also the time of the star cluster's midnight transit across the zenith point of the night sky, an event which marked the starting point of a calendar year. This midnight transit of the Pleiades was especially significant every 52 years when the star cluster's passage over the zenith point signalled not only the end of a year but potentially the end and final destruction of all life in the universe.

The Aztecs and Mayas recognized the sacred 52 year Serpent Cycle to be encoded in the physical manifestations of the Primal Serpent which slithered throughout their country. It is reflected in certain species of snakes called Trisera tus Anahuacus, which has 13 scales bordering each side of its upper and lower lips (13x4=52), as well as Crotalus Durissus, which has numerous diamonds embellishing its reptillian skin, each of which is composed of four sides of 13 scales apiece.

THE CYCLE OF THE CELESTIAL DRAGON, THE BIG DIPPER

IV.10   The movement of another Celestial Dragon, the Big Dipper, is influential in the rotation of the four seasons.

In ancient times the Big Dipper constellation was recognized to be a huge celestial time clock whose movement around the north pole determined the rotation of the four seasons. Its position north, south, east or west of the pole star corresponded to the appearance of spring, summer, fall, and winter. Among the Greek astrologers Ursa Major was perceived as "a mammoth whirlpool which whipped the seasons into rotation."117The Chinese referred to the constellation as the Dragon or chariot of the Cosmic Emperor (the Dragon is the vehicle or chariot of Spirit), and believed its movements controlled the cycle of seasons as well as the planetary balance of yin and yang (hot/cold, light/darkness), and the five "elements."

IV.11   Before it was set apart as the seven stars of the Big Dipper, Ursa Major was united with the constellation of Draco as a huge Celestial Dragon.

In early Mesopotamia the constellations of Draco and the Big Dipper were united to produce a gigantic Celesti al Dragon complete with outstretched wings and talons. The Egyptians recognized the Big Dipper and Draco, which they called Tua rt and Sebek, to be the male and female components of the Celestial Dragon and portrayed them as being in eternal embrace. Both Mesopotamian and Egyptian Celestial Dragons pivoted around the anc ient pole star, Thuban or Alpha Draconis (the "First Dragon"), which was regarded to be a universal "Serpent" point of creation, preservation and destruction. Alpha Draconis endowed the Celestial Dragon with the thre e powers of the Serpent.

THE CYCLES OF SATURN AND THE MOON, THE PLANETARY DRAGONS

IV.12   Saturn, a Planetary Dragon, is influential in determining the Serpent Cycles of seven, fourteen and twenty eight years.

Of all planets, Saturn has been the one most often associated with time and cycles. It has, for millennium, been recognized by peoples around the Earth as the "planet of time," as "Father Time," or as the "dragon" or "devil." In Greek mythology one of Saturn's names was Chronus, a name from which we derive the term "chronological"–meaning linear, as in time. The root of Saturn, Sat, also possesses the meaning of time, so its compound name, Sat-turn implies the "turning of time." Saturn is related to the Jewish Sat-an, meaning "adversary," and denotes the adversarial nature of time.

Saturn's 28 year cycle around the Sun determines the Earth's Serpent Cycles of seven, fourteen and twenty eight years. These cycles, and especially their completions, are particularly pivotal in the evolution and renewal of the human species. Western science allows that during the course of a seven year cycle every cell of the human body is renewed. Astrologers claim that every 28 years, during the "Saturn Return," each person establishes new goals and embarks☐upon a new cycle of responsibility, ambition and accomplishment. Midway through the 28 year cycle, or every 14 years, there is a potential crisis and restructuring of these goals.

IV.13   The Moon, a planetary representative of the female principle or Dragon, is influential in determining the Serpent Cycles of seven, fourteen and twenty eight days.

The Moon is Saturn's micro counterpart. Saturn rules over the cycles of years which are multiples of seven, and the Moon rules over the cycles of days which are multiples of seven. The cycle of the Moon determines the fourteen day fortnight and the 28 day monthly Serpent Cycle. The Lunar Serpent Cycle has three phases, the new and waxing moon (creation phase), the full Moon (preservation phase) and the waning moon (destruction phase). These three phases of the Lunar Goddess, which were represented by the ancient cultures as the three aspects of the Goddess (the virgin, the mature goddess and the crone), rule over the female fertility cycle. During the lunar cycle a woman's egg is born, grows to the maturity at ovulation and then dies at menstruation.

THE CYCLE OF THE PHOENIX

IV .14   Sirius, the star of the Serpent Goddess Isis, determined an Egyptian Cycle of the Serpent called the Sothis Cyck or Phoenix Cycle.

The celestial serpent Sirius determined the Sothis or Phoenix Cycle of 1,461 years, which commenced when Sirius or Sothis appeared on the horizon during a certain day of the Egyptian calendar year and ended when this fixed star appeared on the horizon during the same calendar day 1,461 years later.

During its cycle the Dragon/Phoenix was said to take birth, grow and die. Egyptian legend maintained that at the end of the Sothis Cycle the Phoenix

Dragon consumed itself on a burning pyre at Heliopolis and then arose resurrected from its own ashes, ready to initiate a fresh cycle.

IV.15   Other Phoenix Cycles take 10,000 or 13,000 years to complete.

According to Cicero, a larger Phoenix Cycle is 12,954 years in length. After lengthy computation based on Egyptian manuscripts, the Egyptologist R.T. Rundle Clark determined that 12,954 years was, in fact, based upon authentic astronomical data. This longer cycle, approximately 13,000 years, is one-half of a 26,000 year cycle of the Precession of the Equinoxes. Thirteen is the classical number of the Phoenix and the numerological phase of the death and resurrection.

In recent times geologists have found magnetically reversed sediment in soil samples dating back to 13,000 years ago. Because of this, some have theorized that a dramatic Earth change, such as a polar shift, might have occurred then. It was approximately 13,000 years ago that Atlantis was destroyed by a cataclysm that rocked the Earth and culminated in a new cycle of civilization.

IV.16   The Phoenix appears in the heavens as the planet Venus.

Throughout many parts of the world the resurrected Phoenix was venerated as the planet Venus. Her morning appearance above the horizon represented both the Phoenix and the resurrected sage who had overcome the darkness of the night (the darkness of material existence) and arisen victorious along with the Sun. When the sages Osiris of Egypt and Quetzlcoatl of Mesoamerica ascended into the heavens they became the planet Venus.

As the Phoenix, Venus was the androgynous Fire Serpent whose twin aspects manifested as the morning and evening stars. According to the legends of the Mediterranean and Middle East, as a flaming fire dragon (a meteor) Venus was anciently sent down to Earth by her father and consort, the infinite Spirit, and worshipped within these areas as a crystallized meteorite.

Venus's movements in the cosmos helped determine cycles of life and death such as the cycles of 8, 52, and 104 years. She also contributed to calendars based upon the "Phoenix" numbers of 5 and 13, her sacred numbers.

THE SERPENT CALENDARS

IV.17   Serpent Cycles and Serpent Calendars reflect the features and nature of a terrestrial serpent or dragon.

In Egypt a cycle of 60 days reflected the 60 teeth in the mouth of a crocodile, an indigenous form of the Dragon. The 7 day week and the 12 months in a year reflect the Serpent's seven principles and the 12 signs within the Zodiacal body of the Dragon respectively. The sacred 260 day cycle of the Mesoamericans, with its 13 months of twenty days, reflects the sacred number of the Phoenix Dragon as well as the physical features of a species of snake in Mexico. It incorporates the features and tendencies of the Crotalus Durissus which grows two new fangs every 20 days and has numerous diamonds ornamenting its colorful skin, each of which contains four sides composed of 13 scales apiece.110 The 260 day cycle is woven into a sacred calendar which has as its foundation two ribbon-like snakes. The two snakes represent the two fangs and forked penis of Durissus Crotalus, as well as the Serpent Twins, the twin aspects of the Serpent's androgynous nature.

BIBLOGRAPHY & FOOTNOTES

1. The Keys Of Enoch, J.J. Hurtak, 1982, The Academy For Future Science, Los Gatos, Ca.
2. Dimensions, A Casebook of Alien Contact, Jacques Vallee, 1988, Contemporary Books, Chicago, N.Y.
3. Children of the Rainbow, Leinani Melville, 1969, Theosophical Publishing House, Wheaton IL.
4. Babaji and the 18 Siddha Kriya Yoga Tradition, M.Govindam, 1991, Kriya Yoga Publications, Montreal
5. The Lost Continent of Mu, James Churchward,1987, B.E. Books, Albuquerque N.M.5.
6. Lost Cities of Ancient Lemuria and the Pacific, D.H.Childress, 1988, Adventures Unlimited Press, Kempton, IL.
7. In Search of the Wise ONE, Anton Pónce de León Paiva, Bluestar Communications, Woodside CA.
8. The Book of the Hopi, Frank Waters, 1976, Viking Press
9. Edgar Cayce on Atlantis, Edgar Evans Cayce, 1968, Warner Books, N.Y.C.
10. Secret Of The Andes, Brother Philip, 1976, Leaves Of Grass Press, San Rafeal CA.
11. The Ancient Atlantic, L.Taylor Hansen, 1969, Amherst Press, Amherst, Wisconsin
12. Lemuria the Incomparable, 1936, Lemurian Fellowship, Ramona, Ca.
13. Gem Elixers and Virbrational Healing, Vol. 1, Gurudas, 1985, Cassandra Press, Boulder, CO.
14. Secret Places of the Lion, George Hunt Williamson, 1983, Destiny Books, N.Y.C.
15. The Secret Doctrine, H.P. Blavatsky, 1888, The Theosophical Publishing Co., N.Y.C.
16. Lost Cities of Atlantis, Ancient Europe and the Mediterranean, Childress, 1996, A.U. Press, Kempton, IL.
17. The Stones of Atlantis, David Zink, 1978, Prentice-Hall, Englewood Cliffs, NJ.
18. Atlantis, the Eighth Continent, Charles Berlitz, 1984, G.B Putnam's Sons, NYC
19. Windows of Light, Baer, 1984, Harper and Row, San Francisco
20. Voices of our Ancestors, Dhyani Ywahoo, 1987, Shamballa Books, Boston, Mass

21. The 12th Planet, Zecharia Sitchin, 1976, Avon Books, NYC
22. The Occult Sciences on Atlantis, Lewis Spence, 1970, Samuel Weiser, NYC
23. HerBak vols 1,11- Egyptian Initiate and The Living face of Ancient Egypt, Isba Schwaller de Lubicz, 1978, Inner Traditions Int., Rochester, Vermont
24. The Secret Teachings of all Ages, Manley Palmer Hall, 1975, Philosphical Research Society Inc, L.A., Ca.
25. Themis, A Study of the Social Origins of Greek Religion, Jane Harrison, 1974, Peter Smith Pub, Glouster, Mass.
26. The Message of the Sphinx, Hancock and Bauval, 1996, Crown Publishers, NYC
27. Profiles in Wisdom, Steven Mcfadden, 1991, Bear and Co., Santa Fe
28. The Ancient Egyptians vol.III, Sir J. Gardener Wilkinson, 1879, Dodd, Mead and Co., NYC (State)
29. The White Goddess, Robert Graves, 1972, Octagon Books, NYC
30. The Cult of Pan in Ancient Greece, 1988, Phillippe Borgeaud U. of Chicago Press, Chicago
31. Mythology of All Races, Vol. 5, Semitic, 1931, Marshall Jones Co. Boston Mass.
32. The Mysteries of Britain, Lewis Spence, 1994, Senate, England
33. God Sages and Kings, David Frawley, 1991, Passage Press, Salt Lake City, Utah
34. The Sun and the Serpent, C.F.Oldham, 1905, Archibald Constable and Co. Ltd., London
35. Lost Cities of China, Central Asia, and India, D.H.Childress, 1985, Adventures Unlimited Press, Kempton, IL.
36. The Mysteries of Asia, M.P. Hall, 1935, Manly Hall Publications, L.A. Ca.
37. The Way to Shamballa, Edwin Bernbaum PHO., Jeremy P. Tarcher Inc. L.A.
38. Shamanism, Archaic Techniques of Ecstacy, Mircea Eliade, 1974, Princeton University Press, Princeton, Mass.
39. Heart of Asia, Nicholas Roerich, 1929, Roerich Museum Press, N.Y., N.Y.
40 Subterranean Worlds, Walter Kaffon-Minkel, 1989, Loomparics Unlimited, Port Towmsend, Washington
41. The Lost Realms, Z. Sitchin, 1990, Avon Books, NYC
42. General History of the things of New Spain, Bernadina Sahagun, 1974, School of American Research, Santa Fe
43. People of the Serpent, Edward Thompson, 1965, Capricorn Books, NYC
44. Mysteries of the Mexican Pyramids, Peter Tompkins, 1976, Harper and

Row, N.Y., N.Y.

45. Early Man and the Ocean, Thor Hyerdahl, 1979, Doubleday and Co. NYC.
46. The Maya, Micheal D. Coe, 1984, Thames and Hudson, N.Y., N.Y ..
47. The Orion Mystery, Bauval and Gilbert, 1994, Crown Publishers, NYC
48. The Ancient Stones Speak, David Zink, 1979, E.P. Dutton, N.Y.
49. Dionysos, Karl Kerenyi, 1976, Princeton U. Press, N.J.
50 The Realm of the Great Goddess, Sibylle von Cles-Reden, 1962, Prentice Hall Inc., Englewood Cliffs, NJ
51. The Book of Druidry, History Sites and Wisdom, 1990, Ross Nichols, The Aquarian Press, London
52. The New View Over Atlantis, John Michell, 1983, Harper and Row, San Francisco, Ca.
53. The History and Origins of Druidism, Lewis Spence, 1949, Rider, London and NY
54. The Mayan Factor, Jose Arguelles, 1987, Bear and Co., Santa Fe, N.M.
55. He Walked The Americas, L.Taylor Hanson, 1963, Amherst Press, Amherst, WI.
56. The Mysteries of Ancient South America, Harold Wilkens, 1946, Citadel Press, NYC
57. The Greatness that was Babylon, H.W.F. Saggs, 1962, Praeger Publishers N.Y.C.
58. When Time Began, Z. Sitchin, 1993, Avon Books, NYC.
59. The Lost Language of Symbolism, Harold Bayley, Citadel Press, N.Y.C.
60. The Sign of the Serpent, Marc Balfour, 1990, Avery Pub. Group, Garden City Park, NY
61. The Goddess Sekhmet, Robert Masters, 1991, Llewellyn Publications St. Paul, Minnesota
62. The Antiquities of Egypt, Edwin Murphy, 1990, Transaction Pub., New Brunswick, U.S.A.
63. Yoga: The Technology of Ecstasy, Georg Feuerstein, 1989, J.P. Tarcher, L.A.
64. History of the Tantric Religion, Narendra Bhattacharya, 1982, Manchar Pub., New Delhi, India
65. Sadhus, India's Mystic Holy Men, Dolf Hartsuker, 1993, Inner Traditions Int., Rochester, Vermont
66. Devatma Shakti, Swami Vishnu Tirtha, 1980, Yoga Shri Peeth Trust, U.P., India
67. Shaivism and the Phallic Worship, 1975, Oxford and IBH Pub. Co, New Dehli, India

68. The Cultural Heritage of India vols. 1+2, 1958, The Ramakrishna Mission, Calcutta, India
69. Biography of Sri Swami Samarth Akkalkot Maharaj, N.S. Karandikar, Akkalkot Swami Math, Bombay
70. Bhagavan Nityananda, Swami Muktananda, 1972, Gurudev Siddha Peeth, Ganeshpuri, India
71. Introduction to Tantra Shastra, Sir John Woodroffe, 1980, Ganesh and Co., Madras
72. The Gospel of Buddha, Paul Carus, 1915, Open Court Pub., Chicago, London
73. The Cult of the Serpent, Balaji Mundkur, 1983, State U. of New York Press, Albany, N.Y.
74. Taoism-The Road to Immortality, John Blofeld, 1978, Shamballa, Boulder Colorado.
75. The Roots of Chinese Chi Gung, Dr. Yang Jwing-Ming, 1992, YMAA Pub. Center, Jamaica Plains, Mass,
76. The Wisdom of the Ancient ONE, Anton Pónce de León Paiva, 1995, Bluestar Communications, Woodside CA.
77. Olmec Religion, Karl Lucken, 1976, U. of Oklahoma Press, Oklahoma
78. Beneath the Moon and under the SWl, Tony Shearer, 1975, SWl Books, Albuquerque, N.M.
79. Burning Water, Thought and Religion in Ancient Mexico, Laurette Sejoume, Grove Press, N.Y., N.Y.
80. The Aztecs, People of the Sun, Alfonso Caso, 1958, U. of Oklahoma Press, Norman, Oklahoma
81. Mexico Mystique, Frank Waters,1975, Swallow Press, Chicago
82. Secrets of Mayan Science/Religion, Hunbatz Men, 1990, Bear and Co., Santa Fe, N.M.
83. Magic, A Sociological Study, Hutton Webster, 1948, Stanford U. Press, Stanford Ca.
84. Indian Tribes of Aboriginal America, Sol Tax, 1952, U. of Chicago Press, Chicago
85. Return of the Thunderbeings, Iron Thunderhorse, 1990, Bear and Co., Santa Fe.
86. The Sumerians, Samuel Noah Kramer, 1963, University of Chicago Press
87. The Magic Of Obelisks, Peter Tompkins, 1981, Harper and Row, NYC
88. Egyptian Mysteries, Lucy Lamy, 1981, The Crossroad Publishing Co. NYC.
89. Where the Spirits Ride the Wind, Felicitas Goodman, 1990, Indianapolis U.

Press, Indianapolis In.

90. Awakening to Zero Point: The Collective Initiation, Gregg Braden, 1994, Sacred Spaces/Ancient Wisdom, Questa, NM

91. Initiation, Elisabeth Baich, 1974, The Seed Center, Palo Alto, California

92. A Search in Ancient Egypt, Brunton, 1970, Weiser, N.Y.C

93. Ancient Egyptian Magic, Bob Brier, 1980, William Morrow and Co., Inc., NYC

94. Whence the Goddess, A Source Book, Miriam Robbins Dexter, 1990, Pergamon Press, N.Y.

95. Man, Grand Symbol of the Mysteries, M.P.Hall, 1972, The Theosophical Research Society, L.A.

96. History of Mysticism, S. Abhayananda, 1987, Atma Books, Naples, Florida

97. The Cipher of Genesis, Carlos Suares, 1978, Shambala Pub. Boulder and London

98. The Women's Dictionary of Symbols and Sacred Objects, 1988, Barbara Walker, Harper, San Francisco

99. The Holy Bible, Cambridge University Press, NYC

100. Rosicrucian Questions and Answers - with complete history, H.Spencer. Lewis, 1975, AMORC Pub. San Jose, Ca.

101. The Gnostic Gospels, Elaine Pagels, 1989, Vintage Books, NYC

102. The Golden Ass, Jack Lindsay - translater, 1962, Indiana U. Press, Bloomington, IN.

103. The Sufis, Idries Shah, 1977, W.H. Allen Co. Ltd. London

104. Sufism, A.J. Arberry, 1950, Allen and Unwin, London

105. Holy Blood, Holy Grail, Baigent, Leigh, and Lincoln, 1982, Delacorte Press, NYC

106. The Rosicrucian Enlightenment, Frances Yates, 1972, Rutledge and Kegan Paul, London and Boston

107. The God's of Eden, William Bramley, 1990, Avon Books, NYC

108. America's Secret Destiny, Robert Hieronimus, 1989, Destiny Books, Rochester, Vermont,

109. We are becoming Galactic Humans, Sheldon Nindle

110. The Plieadian Agenda, Barbara Hand Clow, 1995, Bear and Co., Santa Fe, New Mexico.

111. Myth and Symbol in Ancient Egypt, R.T. Rundle Clark, 1960, Grove Press, Inc. NYC

112. Sacred Geometry, Nigel Pennick, 1980, Harper and Row, San Francisco, London and NY

113. Flying Serpents and Dragons, R.A. Boulay, 1990, Galaxy Books,

Clearwater, Florida
114. The Key to the Universe, Curtiss, 1983, Newcastle Publishing, N. Hollywood Ca
115. Anti-Gravity and the World Grid, David Hatcher Childress, 1987, Adventures Unlimited Press, Kempton IL.
116. Asvina in the Rig Veda and other Indological Essays, Prof. G.C. Jhala, Munshiram Manohari Pub. N. Dehli
117. Outer Space, Jobes, 1964, Scarecrow Press, N.Y., N.Y.

The Author

Mark Amaru Pinkham is the author of six books that together cover the mystery traditions of humanity since the dawn of the human race on Earth. Mark is an initiate of many mystery traditions around the globe and the Director/Founder of The Order and Mystery School of the Seven Rays (www.sevenrayorder.com), and the Seven Rays of Healing School (www.sevenrayorder.com/seven-ray-healing-system). During the past 30 years Mark has traveled the globe while leading spiritual tours for Sacred Sites Journeys (www.SacredSitesJourneys.com) and intensively researching the mystery traditions of many countries, including India, Tibet, China, Peru, Egypt, France, England, Ireland, Malta and Scotland. During this time Mark has also been researching the ancient past of Sedona, Arizona and found it to be built upon the ruins of a city known in Hopi legend as Palatkwapi, the "Red House," that was built and anciently lived in by the Star People or Kachinas. Recently, Mark discovered in Sedona's largest vortex the remains of the ancient court of Masau'u, the Hopis legendary King of the World. His 30 years of discoveries were recently published in his book *Sedona: City of the Star People.*

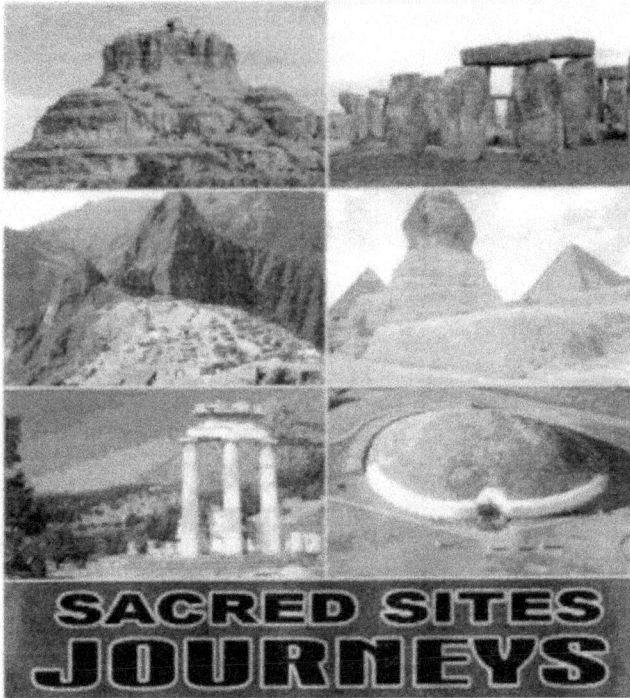

Since 1994... Spiritual Pilgrimages to the World's Sacred Sites

Easter Island, Egypt, England, France, Greece, Iceland, Ireland, Malta, Peru, Scotland, and Vortex & City of the Star People Tours in Sedona, Arizona.

www.SacredSitesJourneys.com
info@SacredSitesJourneys.com
928-284-1429

www.SevenRayOrder.com

Become a member of the World's Most Ancient Mystery School: The Order of the Seven Rays, which has also been known as the Melchizedek Priesthood and The Great White Brotherhood. This order was founded by the Pleiadian Master Sanat Kumara or Karttikeya, the "Son of the Pleiades," who first taught the Serpent Mysteries and Gnostic-Alchemical Path on Earth. Over many ages this Orders' teachings have awakened many worthy spiritual seekers to the highest Self-Knowledge & intutive revelation of I AM THE CREATOR; THE INFINITE, ETERNAL SPIRIT DWELLS WITHIN ME AS ME.

The Order and Mystery School of the Seven Rays is a complete online school of esotericism that teaches: *Alchemy *Gnosticism *Yoga and Meditation *Sacred Geometry *Martial Arts *Esoteric World History Survival Skills *Shaivism *Esoteric Astrology, Healing and much more!

The Order and Mystery School of the Seven Rays includes these branches:
*The School of Seven Ray Healing
*The School of Seven Ray Astrology
*The School of the Dragon Mysteries
*The Mysteries of the Knights Templar
*The Sisterhood of Sophia
*The Knights of the Peacock Prince
*The School of Shaivism
*Spiritual Warrior Training

The teachings of the Order and Mystery School of the Seven Rays and its branches are offered online and via Live Stream. Please visit the above website for a list of the books, DVDs, courses, spiritual tours,and upcoming seminars it is currently offering.

CPSIA information can be obtained
at www.ICGtesting.com
Printed in the USA
BVHW070837221119
564515BV00005B/198/P

9 781640 082267